Muffled Echoes

Power, Conflict, and Democracy Series

Robert Y. Shapiro, Editor

Power, Conflict, and Democracy Series

Robert Y. Shapiro, Editor

Power, Conflict, and Democracy:
American Politics Into the Twenty-first Century

This series focuses on how the will of the people and the public interest are promoted, encouraged, or thwarted. It aims to question not only the direction American politics will take as it enters the twenty-first century but also the direction American politics has already taken.

The series addresses the role of interest groups and social and political movements; openness in American politics; important developments in institutions such as the executive, legislative, and judicial branches at all levels of government as well as the bureaucracies thus created; the changing behavior of politicians and political parties; the role of public opinion; and the functioning of mass media. Because problems drive politics, the series also examines important policy issues in both domestic and foreign affairs.

The series welcomes all theoretical perspectives, methodologies, and types of evidence that answer important questions about trends in American politics.

John G. Geer, *From Tea Leaves to Opinion Polls: A Theory of Democratic Leadership*

Kim Fridkin Kahn, *The Political Consequences of Being a Woman: How Stereotypes Influence the Conduct and Consequences of Political Campaigns*

Kelly D. Patterson, *Political Parties and the Maintenance of Liberal Democracy*

Dona Cooper Hamilton and Charles V. Hamilton, *The Dual Agenda: Race and Social Welfare Policies of Civil Rights Organizations*

Hanes Walton, Jr., *African-American Politics: The Political Context Variable*

Muffled Echoes

Oliver North and the Politics of Public Opinion

Amy Fried

Columbia University Press

New York

1997

Columbia University Press
Publishers Since 1893
New York   Chichester, West Sussex
Copyright © 1997 Columbia University Press
All rights reserved

Library of Congress Cataloging-in-Publication Data
Fried, Amy.
    Muffled echoes : Oliver North and the politics of public opinion /
Amy Fried.
        p.   cm. — (Power, conflict, and democracy)
    Includes bibliographical references (p.   ) and index.
    ISBN 0–231–10820–6 (cloth). — ISBN 0–231–10821–4 (paper)
        1. Iran–Contra Affair, 1985–1990—Public opinion.   2. North,
    Oliver—Public opinion.   3. Public opinion—United States.   4. Mass
    media—United States—Influence.   I. Title.   II. Series.
    E876.F78   1997
    973.927—dc21   96–52988

Casebound editions of Columbia University Press books are printed on permanent
and durable acid-free paper.
Printed in the United States of America
c 10 9 8 7 6 5 4 3 2 1
p 10 9 8 7 6 5 4 3 2 1

Dedicated to Estelle B. Fried
and to the memory of Leonard H. Fried

Contents

Preface

This book grew out of a fascination with the political process and a concern with the role of citizens in American democracy. I became interested in how perceptions of public opinion developed and how they influenced and were influenced by active participants in American politics. These concerns are rooted in long-standing debates about the nature of democracy and in short-term developments in the practices of pollsters, public relations experts, journalists, and media-savvy politicians and political operatives.

Much has been said in recent years about the sad state of American political discourse, the role of the media, the power of interest groups, stalemate and polarization in government, and increasing political alienation. Many people have contributed to a better understanding of the political system, with each illuminating one aspect of it. In this book, however, rather than focusing on public views, the media, interest groups, or government action, I emphasize the ways in which all these interact to create politically consequential impressions of public opinion. I analyze these interactions in five cases, with an emphasis on Oliver North and the Iran–contra affair, which raised fundamental issues for the conduct of foreign policy. Some hold that the lessons of this affair were not adequately understood by the American people or assimilated by policymakers. Whether or not one agrees with this assessment, it is worth looking more closely at how the affair was handled and how legislators, the media, various interest groups, and citizens reacted. By doing so, we can find out how the *system* operated when confronted with serious problems. Although the situation was exceptional in some respects, the way in which Iran–contra was handled is not unique. Throughout American politics there have been many attempts to influence the perception of public opinion, during which the media, politicians, and citizens have been vulnerable to misinterpretations. Nonetheless, American democracy also sometimes reveals leadership and a properly critical citizenry.

Although this book makes a broad argument about the politics of public opinion, some readers may be most interested in the particular situation of Oliver North's testimony to the congressional Iran–contra committee. They should focus on chapters 3 through 6. Those most interested in the theoretical discussion of how public opinion is incorporated into the political system and its implications for democracy should concentrate on chapters 1, 2, and 7. Since these different parts of the book reinforce each other, readers are encouraged to read the work in its entirety.

In this book, I argue that the public opinion that matters is not necessarily equivalent to the privately held views of citizens; it develops instead in a strategic and competitive political environment. I am, of course, responsible for this argument and my research—for any contributions and limitations—but I also am greatly indebted to many scholars and authors. Because I have tried to make connections across disciplinary and intradisciplinary borders and to reveal something important about contemporary politics, I owe much to social and political theorists, to researchers in a number of areas, and to fine journalists, who do indeed write the first draft of history.

Several institutions provided the financial support for this work. A small portion of the book (the citizen interviews discussed in chapter 3) is based on research conducted for my dissertation, which was funded by a University of Minnesota Graduate School Dissertation Fellowship. The main research was supported by a Colgate University Picker Fellowship and several faculty discretionary grants. Support from Colgate enabled me to present papers discussing this work at meetings of the

Midwest Political Science Association, the Western Political Science Association, and the International Society of Political Psychology. I thank these institutions and the discussants and participants at these meetings, including Stanley Feldman, John Aldrich, Laura Stoker, Michael Delli Carpini, Diane Duffy, Burdett Loomis, Allan Cigler, and John McIver.

For their work at Colgate University, I thank Elizabeth Boynton and Tobi Soeldner-Prim, both extremely able research assistants. Other useful assistance was provided by Becca Ashley and Tabber Benedict. The library staff at Colgate was very helpful, and the government document librarian, Mary Jane Walsh, was exceptional. For secretarial services and her calm demeanor, I thank Cindy Terrier. During trips to Washington, D.C., Matt Welbes and Edith and Bill Levine were fine companions and hosts. I also thank the staff at the Library of Congress; Carol Keyes at the People for the American Way, who helped me use its files on interest groups and Oliver North; and Peter Kornbluh of the National Security Archive, who made some useful suggestions. For their openness and time, I thank all those who were interviewed or completed a questionnaire. During the time I was developing my interview and written questions, Susan Herbst assisted by graciously sending me a copy of the questions she used for *Numbered Voices*. Marcus Flathman provided research assistance at the University of Minnesota.

I am indebted to those who read and criticized this work and my dissertation research on political heroism. Even though I followed much of their advice, undoubtedly I should have listened to some suggestions but did not. Important readers and support people for the earlier project were John Sullivan, Larry Jacobs, Phil Shively, George Lipsitz, Ron Aminzade, Davida Alperin, Dan Rubenstein, and Linda Silber. I thank Michael Hayes and Joe Wagner of Colgate's political science department for comments on this book and for other help as well. Ulla Grapard and I have regularly swapped papers and chapters, and discussed them; I have much appreciated our intellectual and personal companionship and will miss her very much. Anne Pitcher, Elayne Zorn, Sylvie and Ray Bach, and Kathy Lighthall have been important for personal and professional support. John Michel, my editor at Columbia University Press, provided assistance and good humor. The anonymous reviewers for the press made many good recommendations. Beth Theiss-Morse went above and beyond the call of friendship and collegiality, for she listened to my evolving ideas, read the entire manuscript, and offered detailed comments.

This book is dedicated to my parents, whose help to me goes very deep. Estelle and Leonard Fried provided a stimulating home, fostered my intellectual development, taught me perseverance, and encouraged connection with the broader community. In my family, my daughter Sarah continues to distract and entertain me and so nourishes beneficial sensibilities. Caleb, the considerate baby, delayed his arrival until a major set of revisions were complete and then quickly began sleeping through the night. My husband, David Halvorson, was important to this work in many ways. One of the most crucial was that he is very interested in politics but not impressed by most political science. Because I wanted to talk to him about my ideas, I was inspired to do research that clearly said something about the political phenomena we discuss regularly. An unwelcome broken leg gave him the time to assist me with picky but necessary tasks. Dave also carefully read the manuscript, commented on it, and provided emotional sustenance.

Muffled Echoes

Introduction

How does public opinion matter in the politics of governing? People in politics certainly talk a lot about what the people want, and as policy debates unfold, members of Congress can be found standing on the House or Senate floor making claims about public opinion. Back in their offices, congressional staffers count and classify incoming calls, telegrams, postcards, and letters. The president speaks about public opinion, assisted by a cadre of pollsters and political operatives. Interest groups make substantive arguments about policies, but they also assert that the public does or does not support some government plan. And the news media report on public opinion in their stories and broadcasts.

All this talk about public opinion is not simply a good-faith effort to discern the popular will. Rather, the main participants in interpreting public opinion have policy desires and interests, and they frame interpretations of the public voice to benefit their ambitions. Each participant in politics tries to convince others that public opinion is on his or her side, because public support legitimizes policy ideas and carries political weight. At the same time, efforts to shape perceptions of public opinion have limits. Citizens are not rendered mute by others' interpretations of public opinion and may challenge prevailing interpretations. In addition, when engaging in policy battles and negotiations, elected officials assess citizens' views and consider which cultural and political frames are likely to resonate with key constituencies. Because upcoming campaigns give elected officials a powerful incentive to try to understand the people, representatives attend to "anticipated public opinion."[1] For those in the political fray, there are strategic reasons to understand and misunderstand popular opinion.

The main argument of this book is that public opinion is a political resource that is an integral part of the political system. Public opinion and perceptions of that opinion are forged in a context in which interest groups, journalists, and politicians seek to influence these opinions, describe them, and use these descriptions to try to influence policy. Even when members of the public communicate directly, their voices are always translated by the primary political actors and may be misinterpreted. This view of public opinion emphasizes struggles over the construction, interpretation, and use of public opinion. Out of this political conflict over the meaning of the public voice comes the public opinion that matters.

Although we often use the term *public opinion* to refer to citizens' privately held views, this is not the public opinion that matters. If citizens do not speak out, their point of view may very well not be heard. Citizens' motivations and willingness to articulate their views are influenced by individual factors and the climate of opinion constructed by news makers and news reporters. In making this argument, I use the theories of a number of scholars, especially V. O. Key's idea that public opinion exists in a political echo chamber and Habermas's work on the reactive nature of public opinion in contemporary politics and society.[2] Key maintains that the public hears what is spoken into the echo chamber by elected officials, interest groups, political parties, and the media. Although citizens also can speak in the chamber, their voices must compete with others. Habermas argues that public opinion now usually consists of reactions to limited and often stereotyped alternatives staged before them. In crafting their presentations, groups, the media, and politicians often rely on symbols, personae, stereotypes, and other dramatic devices. Citizens can respond, mainly by means of simple acclamations or refusals to acclaim.

The Politics of Public Opinion: Oliver North and Beyond

This book makes four contributions to our understanding of the role of public opinion in American politics. First, I conceptualize public opinion as part of the political process and so see the impact of public opinion as depending on multiple political actors and their attempts to legitimize particular interpretations of the public voice. In contrast to most scholars, I do not treat public opinion as equivalent to poll results. Rather, public opinion also entails expressions and translations of citizens' views in public discourse. Because I take this view of public opinion, I concentrate less on how citizens' perspectives are shaped and more on how interpretations of public views are used.

Second, I focus on the use of public opinion during the long season of governing. Democratic communication occurs continuously, not just during election time. Even though assessing what the public thinks is almost always part of an elected official's decision-making calculus when considering how to vote, the public's voice is not easily heard.

Third, this work raises normative questions about the health of American democracy. Politics ultimately involves choices about which values are to be pursued and whose interests are to be served. If most citizens are severely limited in what they can say and how well they can say it, popular sovereignty and civic skills will be undermined. If, in addition, interpretations of public opinion have an "upper-class accent,"[3] inequalities in political power will become further entrenched.

Fourth, to provide detailed empirical evidence of the politics of public opinion, this study analyzes the construction and use of public opinion in the Iran–contra hearings, with special attention to reactions to Oliver North's testimony. I also briefly consider the politics of public opinion during the fight over higher automobile fuel efficiency standards, a short-lived legislative effort to cap credit card interest rates, and the ongoing struggle over abortion.

Constructions of public opinion matter for a great range of policies, including the disposition of President Bill Clinton's health care proposal, and for the shape of 1995–1996 budget negotiations.[4] I invite each reader to think about how the politics of public opinion applies to issues now in the news. For the North case, my argument is that perceptions of public opinion about Oliver North were influenced by the media's tendency to emphasize demonstrations and other dramatic means of expressing opinions rather than by polls, by unevenly mobilized interest groups, by the availability and accessibility of cultural symbols and frames, by decisions made by the joint House–Senate investigating committee about how to question North, and by Congress's entrepreneurial and partisan character.

Like other political spectacles, such as the confirmation hearings of Supreme Court Associate Justice Clarence Thomas,[5] the testimony of Oliver North in July 1987 was marked by intense media scrutiny and a strong public response. When North, in his marine uniform, stood and raised his hand to be sworn for his congressional testimony, this image became the most striking and most memorable of the Iran–contra affair. In the glare of the cameras, Oliver North upheld executive supremacy in foreign affairs and vowed he would go "man to man" with Abu Nidal to protect his family. Within days of North's public appearance, letters that excoriated Congress and praised North began to arrive on Capitol Hill. Commentators suggested that North had become a new American hero, and indeed, this seemed to be borne out by the initial marketing success of ballads, dolls, and bumper stickers celebrating the colonel. Members of Congress seemed to take seriously these reports and evidence of North's popularity. Even critical questioners often prefaced their remarks to North by commenting that the marine had touched a chord with the public.

This portrait of public opinion concerning Oliver North was not accurate, however, as poll results show that most citizens did not view North as heroic. How, then, were these perceptions of public opinion generated? In large part, the disparity was created by a typical dynamic— that is, people who feel intensely are more likely to act politically, whether they are moved spontaneously or are mobilized by groups. As a result, some voices were amplified, whereas others were barely heard. In addition, members of Congress and their staffs typically interpret such action skeptically and decide whether the activists do represent the underlying public opinion. After Oliver North began to testify, unusually large numbers of citizens contacted Congress, and most of them initially supported North. The media and most legislators took this first wave of citizen messages quite seriously. By repeating the idea that North was widely esteemed, legislators reinforced this perception of public opinion, giving it greater credibility and wider circulation.

Oliver North's testimony helped activate conservatives and contra aid supporters and made the lieutenant colonel a national celebrity. Soon after he left Capitol Hill, North began to work with right-wing interest groups and candidates, helping them pursue their policy goals and establish themselves as organizations. Even as he fought his own criminal charges, North gave numerous speeches and allowed his name to be used for fund-raising purposes. In late 1989, he formed his own direct mail organization, the Freedom Alliance, and began to collect millions of dollars. When he later declared his candidacy for a Virginia Senate seat in January 1994, North already had accumulated a large list of contributors and a significant amount of money for his campaign.

Oliver North's experience in the 1994 Senate race showed that he had strong and enthusiastic backing from a core set of supporters but that most Virginians viewed him critically. His candidacy also brought both positive and negative responses from across the nation. Indeed, after North won the Republican nomination, many Republicans—including Ronald Reagan, Nancy Reagan, John Poindexter, and the senior senator from Virginia, John Warner—spoke out against him. Nonetheless, North had substantial financial resources, having raised more from outside his state than had any other Senate candidate in the nation. His mail drive raised more than $15 million, twice as much as his major rival, Senator Chuck Robb, had. Even so, in a Republican year—in which the Republicans regained a majority in the House of Representatives and the Senate, a majority of governorships became Republican, and numerous Democratic incumbents lost—Oliver North also lost. Unlike most other races across the country, the turnout in Virginia was high, and after the votes were counted, North had received 43 percent of the vote, to Robb's 46 percent and independent Republican candidate Marshall Coleman's 11 percent.

North's truthfulness became a key issue in the race. Whereas other Republicans in 1994 had been able to focus their campaigns on weaknesses in the Clinton administration, organize their supporters, and thereby mobilize electoral majorities, a central concern in North's race was his character. Although he tried to turn the voters' attention to Robb's character and to charges regarding the senator's personal behavior, exit polls found that 53 percent of the voters believed that North's behavior in Iran–contra was "morally wrong." Although North finished the Senate race undoubtedly a hero to some in Virginia and across the nation, for most Virginia voters he was not a model of excellence.

North's 1994 Senate loss showed how his charisma and persona could rally some people but also mobilize supporters of his opponents. Indeed, North was such a polarizing figure (and Robb such a weak candidate) that more than half of Robb's voters cast their ballot against North rather than for Robb.[6] North's intense appeal to one segment of the electorate—in particular, one constituency of the Republican Party—made it likely that he would continue to be a potent fund-raiser and firebrand, if not a future candidate. Following in this pattern, two years after losing to Robb, North sought to mobilize his supporters to deny Warner the 1996 senatorial Republican nomination. Yet again North was unsuccessful. In fact, North had never been the hero figure America esteemed, even though this was the story told by the mass media and heard in Congress during North's 1987 Iran–contra testimony.

The difficulty of translating the public voice raises fundamental issues for democratic governance that apply both to cases like North's and to situations in which there is much less publicity and the public has not been activated. If government officials do not readily hear what the public wants, they cannot be responsive. But voices from the media and mobilized groups become entangled with broad public opinion, and they compete for politicians' attention.

The Plan of This Book

Chapters 1 and 2 develop my core argument that public opinion is a political resource used strategically by news makers and reporters. Chapter 1 discusses the political nature of public opinion. Drawing on Key's and Habermas's arguments, I contend that the use and impact of public opinion occur in particular political and historical contexts. By providing a context for public opinion, we can better understand its strategic role and can address crucial normative questions about the promise and practice of American democracy.

Chapter 2 considers the hearing and expression of public opinion as a communication problem. I discuss the requirements for clear communication among people and then contrast this ideal dialogue to the communication of public opinion in a democratic polity. Then the chapter maps out the echo chamber of politics, describing the social psychology of citizen speech or silence and the likelihood for citizens' views to be heard clearly through the media, as translated by interest groups and political elites. Finally, the chapter outlines my research strategy.

Chapters 3 through 6 focus on the use of public opinion during Oliver North's testimony in the Iran–contra hearings. Each chapter examines public opinion from a different perspective, and so each gives a partial view of public opinion in the political process. Taken together, these chapters demonstrate the complex web of incentives and strategies used by activists, observers, and legislators in presenting, misrepresenting, and listening to the public voice. After presenting an overview of the Iran–contra affair and its aftermath, I argue in chapter 3 that citizens' views of North were influenced by culturally significant themes and symbols. Using poll data and information from qualitative studies,

I explore the cultural values that framed the public discourse and contributed to a politics of hero creation.

Chapter 4 analyzes the news media's coverage and public opinion of Oliver North. The chapter demonstrates that the narratives regarding North differed from the polling results. This discrepancy was based in the hero frame used in media reports, the media's focus on vivid but unreliable data concerning public views, and the media's enthusiasm with North's performative abilities.

Chapter 5 discusses interest-group efforts to use public opinion as a resource to influence public opinion, the perception of public opinion, and elected officials during the contra aid fight, at the time of the Iran–contra hearings and afterward. Support groups for North used his putative popularity to try to achieve policy success and to enhance organizational maintenance and growth.

Chapter 6 examines the perceptions of public opinion held by members and staff of the congressional committee investigating Iran–contra. This chapter traces the most important influences on their views of public sentiment, including phone calls, letters, telegrams, media reports, and conversations with peers. Decisions made by the committee before public testimony began also colored the climate of opinion. This chapter considers the effects of partisan and House–Senate differences concerning the legislators' perceptions of public opinion and their response to the perceived public mood.

The final chapter applies the theory of public opinion to other political issues, looking at differences in the politics of public opinion that depend on various conditions. I present a fourfold typology that distinguishes between issues that are relatively symbolic or nonsymbolic and those that pertain to evenly or unevenly mobilized interest groups. Reactions to perceived public opinion during the Iran–contra hearings were strongly symbolic and involved unevenly mobilized groups. The chapter briefly examines three contrasting case studies: (1) abortion politics since *Roe v. Wade*, a situation of symbolic politics and evenly mobilized groups; (2) the debate over increasing average auto fuel efficiency during the 1990 reauthorization of the Clean Air Act, a relatively nonsymbolic issue with interest groups mobilized on both sides; and (3) the attempt to impose a cap on credit card interest rates in 1991, which involved unevenly mobilized groups and was not symbolic.

This last chapter also considers changes in the political environment that influence the politics of public opinion, including the growing power of interest groups, the introduction of technologies to create false grassroots reactions, the rise of the visual media, and the new campaign requisites and practices. Finally, the chapter describes how the current politics of public opinion challenges democratic principles such as representation, deliberation, and civic development. Even though we do not want leaders who follow every blip in the opinion polls, it is also not appropriate for elected officials simply to go their own way. The potential for distorting public views means, however, that determining the proper role for public opinion in democracy entails more than choosing between responsiveness and leadership. Whether or not elected officials want to follow their constituents' wishes or to explain an autonomous position, they cannot take public opinion into account if they cannot easily hear what the public wants. But because the public calls out in the echo chamber of politics, its voice is easily muffled.

I

The Politics of Public Opinion

The voice of the people is but an echo.

V. O. Key, *The Responsible Electorate*

Activists, politicians, and journalists tout, decry, defend, analyze, and, above all, use public opinion. Arguments about interpretations of public opinion involve all political actors because public opinion is a political resource in the politics of governing. Both participants in and chroniclers of politics use information about the public mind to promote their missions. Groups and political figures refer to and attempt to modify public opinion because they want to employ this important political resource. Perceptions of public opinion legitimize policy stands, provide political cover for government officials, and become a matter of political struggle. The politics of public opinion affects which proposals are made and which are held back, which congressional witnesses are grilled and which are treated gingerly, which bills pass and which bills fail, and which speeches are made and which are never written. If public figures believe that citizens are not interested in an issue, they may devote little attention to it, may handle the policy outside the public eye and negotiate it with elites, or may decide to try to make the question a matter of public concern. In politics, like war or business, resources are deployed strategically. Although the development of polls has rationalized to some extent the expression of public opinion, the translation of public opinion remains a political activity, not a rational process.[1] The attention paid to public opinion is thus an attentiveness engendered by strategic interest.

The Politics of Public Opinion Today

Participants in the political scene now have tremendous amounts of data about the national public's views on policy questions and contemporary events. But polls, by themselves, do not shift politicians. One reason is that legislators rarely conduct surveys in their states or districts, and national polls cannot tell them what their constituents think. But if legislators want to return to Congress, they will be concerned with whether their constituents will reward or punish them on election day. In addition, politicians today are flooded with other kinds of information about their constituents' views. Mail, telephone calls, and telegrams flow into congressional offices; members of Congress meet their constituents during visits home; and group leaders tell them what their members want. Legislators then use their accumulated political wisdom to discern whether the sounds from citizens represent their core constituents. Finally, politicians are sometimes influenced by national reports of public opinion. Media reports and media polls can convince legislators that citizens have begun to shout louder or differently from before. If a legislator intends to seek higher office or feels vulnerable, these readings of the nation's mood are more likely to have an impact on his or her decisions.

In some ways, this is an old story. Elected officials and office seekers have always taken public opinion into account when crafting campaign appeals and taking the pulse of the public between elections. American journalists also have consistently sought to characterize the public mood. Even though the age of openly partisan newspapers, straw polls, and other nonscientific methods has given way to rigorous surveys conducted by purportedly neutral news organizations, journalists' interest in public opinion remains a constant.

The politics of public opinion today occurs within a particular political environment, and so the use of public opinion takes specific forms and poses particular problems. We live in a time of strong interest groups, expensive and negative election campaigns, and visually oriented and profit-seeking news media. The public as a whole feels alienated from politics and distrusts politicians. In addition, the federal government has become involved in nearly all spheres of life, creating specific constituencies that care a great deal about what is to be done. This environment creates an opening in the political system for pressure groups to try to shape the perception of public opinion. In order to use public opinion as a political tool, citizen groups recruit and mobilize members, and business groups hire public relations and grassroots lobbying firms. Although legislators use varied sources of information to assess public opinion, their total sum of knowledge is skewed by the activities of groups that can selectively mobilize the public and by media reports on public opinion. Yet neither the media nor interest groups are primarily interested in presenting a highly accurate picture of public views. Although canons of journalistic objectivity provide incentives for careful reporting, television news programs (and nearly all news media) are also driven by the desire for dramatic and interesting-looking stories. As a result, television news often devotes a disproportionate amount of airtime to group action and emotionally resonant symbolic messages, and the other media typically follow their story line.[2]

In addition, governing has come to look more and more like a political campaign. In our election campaigns, politics is increasingly dominated by television; its eye focuses on negativism, personality and character, strategy, insult rather than advocacy, public gatherings, and pictures of triumph or defeat. The media's coverage of campaigns spends much time on the horse race and the public's current assessments of the candidates. Furthermore, the focus on such information does not change after the votes have been counted. Instead of a relatively quiet period in which legislation can be crafted (and covered in the news), the media offer only more of the same. Politicians help create and are confronted by sound bites, hyperbole, symbolic recastings of public issues, and dramatic statements and displays of public sentiments. To a certain extent, we cannot blame legislators for their speaking styles and responses. Because of the new incentives and opportunity structures, the media do not carry the voices of the elected officials to the public unless they are shrilly pitched. Although never quiet, the politics of governing is becoming increasingly noisy, so much so that it is now more difficult to think or to hear the soft voices.

Scholarship on the Role of Public Opinion

Concerns about the impact of public opinion on politics are not new; indeed, they can be traced back to the earliest writings on politics. In recent years, a great deal of scholarship has analyzed the relationship between citizens' views and politics by examining the correlations between opinion and policy, often using times-series methods.[3] These studies assume that a strong relationship between public opinion and policies demonstrates that citizens' views have an important influence. A prominent study by Page and Shapiro concludes that "government responsiveness to public opinion is substantial but imperfect; policy tends to be out of harmony with what the public wants roughly one-third of the time, a significant proportion."[4] But even though this line of research has yielded important information about the correlation between opinion and policy, it has not explained which political forces reinforce or reduce these connections. As Page acknowledges, other approaches are needed "for getting inside the black box of policy making and sorting out the effects of particular institutions and policies" on the linkage between public opinion and governmental response.[5]

In another scholarly tradition, public opinion does matter, but only for symbolic reassurance and arousal.[6] Although citizens are talked to, their actions rarely initiate any real change. Political discourse among elites and in the news media constructs problems, creates enemies, and calms the public. According to Murray Edelman, "While most political language marks little change in how well people live, it has a great deal to do with the legitimation of regimes and the acquiescence of people in actions they had no part in initiating."[7] This approach has made an important contribution in stressing how symbols, language, and discourse frame problems, but it often assumes that citizens are controlled by discursive strategies. Citizens can and do, however, take positions different from those espoused by elites. No matter how unified the voices of political actors are—and, at times, they are more divided than harmonious—members of the general public are not wholly captured by elites' utterances.[8] Citizens' views of the political world may not agree with what political leaders see, whether or not the people speak loudly in dissent or refrain. In fact, elites may be more convinced that the public thinks a certain way than is really the case, and these political actors take into account perceptions of public opinion when they make decisions. However, it is less important politically what the public thinks than what the media and political elites believe the public thinks.

This book's argument about public opinion challenges scholars' understandings of the role of citizen psychology. Citizens are not just processors of information about politics but are also the subject of political events. They are not just talked to but are talked about. How they

are talked about helps determine whether they care to join in the tumul-
tuous conversation. What difference this makes to citizens also partly
rests on their psychological states and reactions. Citizens' psychological
processes take place in a complex political world, simultaneously filled
with messages from the media, action by interest groups, and pronouncements by elected officials. If overwhelming support for one
point of view causes many others to fall silent, as Noelle-Neumann suggests, this will have political consequences.[9]

Empirical and Normative Issues

In focusing on the political processes involved in invoking public
opinion and bringing perceptions of public opinion to bear on political decision makers, I stress the strategic use of public opinion by
interest groups, the ways that the mass media influence the climate of
opinion, and the qualities of the communication environment.[10]
Communication between citizens and legislators is shaped by existing
conduits and styles of interaction. For example, the typical biases in
interpreting public opinion today reflect the relative strength—compared with that of the political parties—of organized groups and the
media. The process of constructing politically consequential perceptions of public opinion is always inherently political, as it involves
efforts by political actors who have their own agendas.

   These arguments draw significantly on the work of V. O. Key and
Jürgen Habermas, each of whom concentrates on particular political
dynamics and value concerns. As I will show, Key contends that sub-
groups of the public express themselves in a noisy environment of political actors who operate in or on political institutions. Using Key's work,
I develop an account of the basic relationships between public opinion
and various aspects of the political system. I employ Habermas's analysis to explain the style of communication between citizens and legislators and to understand the use of symbolic messages. During our time,
information is presented to citizens through news media that emphasize
dramatic images and clamorous sounds.

   Not only do Key and Habermas illuminate public opinion's place in
the overall context of political discourse and contest, but their analyses
also direct our attention to certain questions about the health of the
American political system. In particular, the quality of citizen–legislator
communication is important to the health of American democracy. In
governing, democratic values impel representatives to carry out the pop-

ular will, or at least to take into account citizens' views when deciding to take an independent course. But it is quite difficult for elected officials to know what the public thinks. If the public voice is, in Key's metaphor, an echo in an echo chamber, legislators can hear only muffled echoes.[11] The sound of savvy political contestants muffles citizens' voices by dominating the conversation and convincing legislators that they are the public. In a time when, as Habermas suggests, politics is structured like mass entertainment, the resulting politics of public opinion challenges the promise of American democracy.

Public Opinion as a Political Phenomenon

V. O. Key and the Political Echo Chamber

Writing in the 1950s and early 1960s, when survey research was emerging as a powerful approach for studying citizens, V. O. Key was a subtle analyst and critic of this development.[12] In the posthumously published *The Responsible Electorate*, Key compared public opinion to an echo in an echo chamber, one input into a noisy field of competing voices. He held that opinion is part of a dynamic system in which activists, organized groups, and elected officials influence mass opinion. Advocates seek to draw citizens to their side in order to claim legitimacy; and strong majorities on one side threaten opponents with marginalization and electoral failure. If citizens do not always possess full information about an issue, organized interests may be partially to blame. "Incompleteness in information flow may come from deliberate misrepresentation by those who seek to mold public attitudes." Even if the information in circulation does not have any significant biases, mass opinions are structured by the frames and terms of debate presented by elites. According to Key, "Mass opinion is not self-generating; in the main, it is a response to the cues, the proposals, and the visions propagated by the political activists."[13]

Key's work points to the importance of political processes and institutions for understanding public opinion and its impact. He also criticized the approach to public opinion then current as too focused on the individual, arguing against the implicit individualism of most of this work.[14] In his 1960 review of *The American Voter*, Key addressed the limitations of pure opinion research:

> Ultimately the concern of the student of politics must center on the operation of the state apparatus in one way or another. Both the characteristics of the survey instrument and the curiosities of those with a mas-

tery of survey technique have tended to encourage a focus of attention on microscopic political phenomena more or less in isolation from the total political process.[15]

By emphasizing the opinions found by surveyors, researchers had stripped away the broader political contexts of citizen views and behavior.

Public opinion research developed in this individualistic manner partly because early survey research methods had been first introduced in the service of commercial activities, primarily as a marketing tool. Looking back, Hadley Cantril remembered that

> in the late 1930s there were practically no social scientists who gave any serious consideration to these methods. Most of my social science colleagues either were ignorant about them or tended to belittle them because none of the men doing the pioneer work in the field were members of the academic fraternity.[16]

Nonetheless, Paul Lazarsfeld used these methods to study consumers and then turned to study voting decisions in the 1940 presidential election.[17] This groundbreaking voting study, *The People's Choice*, and later work done by Lazarsfeld and his colleagues not only led scholars to adopt surveys as a research tool but also had an important influence on their subsequent theorizing.

In starting with market activity, the consumer became the model for civic behavior and political opinions. Thus the questions addressed were based on models of individual choice—why a person bought a particular product or decided to vote for a specific candidate. To answer either of these questions, the researcher was to examine the stimuli on that person and determine the impact of new messages, brand loyalties, and demographic characteristics. The early studies of both consumers and vote choice systematically examined people's beliefs, immediate social contexts, and demographic variables in order to understand how communication influenced their behavior. The messages in marketing are most numerous during advertising campaigns, and those in politics are most numerous during election campaigns; consumer brand loyalty means regularly buying a particular product, whereas brand loyalty in politics involves identification with and support for a political party.

This market model for understanding politics offered a rather narrow context for the vote choice process and the vote itself. But just as a marketer is not concerned with the impact of a consumer's choice of cola or laundry detergent on the distribution of economic resources, scholars of voting choice were not concerned with the place of voting in the larger political–institutional system. To be sure, scholars were interested in citizens' capacities and were concerned about the effects of what they saw as ignorance and irrationality on the polity. At the same time, this emphasis on the voter as an individual consumer in a political market wrongly assumed that people's voting decisions were the primary way by which citizens communicated their preferences to the political elites. Political communication and miscommunication also occur, however, outside the election season, and political institutions and practices also structure citizen–politician linkages.

These criticisms of survey research were originally leveled at the research prevalent thirty or more years ago, but they are just as compelling today. One reason is that the political world itself has changed in ways that increase the role of opinion movers and translators. In our time, public relations specialists engage in technically sophisticated efforts to influence mass opinion, to mobilize elements of the public, and to shift perceptions of public opinion. These efforts can be quite effective, given the context of media politics and political parties that must deal with interest groups' increased ability to organize issues and citizens. Key's arguments also have special import now because recent scholarship has focused much of its attention on microphenomena, such as individuals' cognitive structures, citizens' approaches to managing incoming political information, and people's decision-making procedures. Schema theory[18] and other cognitive approaches,[19] along with other research traditions,[20] have provided a useful correction to the assertion that citizens do not think coherently about politics.[21] In large part, however, these paradigms still ignore the echoes of the public's voice in the echo chamber of politics.[22] Rather than studying the political use of public opinion by groups, activated citizens, media, and elites, this line of scholarship emphasizes privately held views. But these private opinions may not even be spoken and so may not enter the echo chamber. As Paul Anderson notes, "It is clear that understanding what goes on inside people's heads is not generally sufficient to explain how those individual cognitions will combine to produce institutional action."[23]

By separating public opinion from institutional contexts, the empirical emphasis on "what goes on inside people's heads" limits the normative questions that can be asked. For example, one line of research concerns citizens' means of processing information, asking whether people examine and assess every single piece of information or instead rely on stereotypes to classify the incoming data more quickly.[24] In concentrating on whether cognitive processing is task based or on-line, piecemeal or holistic, the central democratic concern is based on citizens' modes of processing information and making decisions. Of course, the ways that citizens process political information do matter, although the questions relating to individuals do not tell us much about democracy unless they are connected to the political system. As Carmines and Kuklinski argue, the U.S. system is "elite driven" but is also concerned with representation.[25] Placing public opinion in the political echo chamber thus brings particular normative issues up front.

Normative Concerns in the Echo Chamber

Because public opinion is only one element of the polity, it is inappropriate to assume that the health or sickness of a democratic system rests solely on its citizenry. Rather, to assess how well a democracy is operating, normative concerns should reach beyond the public and examine the role of leaders and activists. Leaders must believe in the basic rules of the game, including freedom of speech, and must avoid inflammatory demagoguery. In addition, leaders need to have some commitment to represent the will of the people or to stand up for policies with which the majority does not agree. In any case, the system of regular elections usually forces politicians at least to pretend to pay attention to their constituents. Finally, precisely because elites reside in the echo chamber, they may not hear the public's voice clearly. Notwithstanding all the polls, politicians must use their own judgment to evaluate what their constituents think, as well as the strength and stability of the voters' opinions. Elected officials and those who seek to influence policies try to influence the public and perceptions of public opinion.

My approach to public opinion and Key's argument holds that democracy is not equivalent to a popular electoral mandate, since institutions, elites, the media, and organized interests all are important to mediating and translating the public will. This starting point means that instead of concentrating on citizens' knowledge and rationality, normative assessments should examine how activists, interest groups, the media, party leaders, and elected officials influence, represent, misinterpret, and misunderstand public opinion.[26] Popular sovereignty takes place in a particular system with certain institutional capacities and tendencies. Although citizens are a part of the system, their actions do not determine whether there is popular sovereignty in a republic because popular control is not plebiscitary.

Nor were citizens ever meant to wield absolute control. Both political theorists and the founders of the American republic believed that the majority's role should be limited, and so they called for the representatives to make decisions and argued for particular institutional structures to constrain popular passions and avoid tyranny. Popular sovereignty thus depends on institutions and elites as much as it does on civic activity.

Because Rousseau believed that proper public opinion and participatory democracy were essential parts of a legitimate state, his ideas provide a hard case to test my contention that a rational, informed, and active citizenry is not a sufficient condition for popular sovereignty. Rousseau saw the legitimate state as an association to serve justice and utility. For him, legitimacy rested in part on the state's basis in consent via the social contract and in the continuance of consent by future generations. The social contract is itself a great good, for it replaces natural freedom with moral and civil freedom. These new freedoms change the nature of human beings, replacing slavish appetites with reason. Citizens' characteristics are indeed important to the maintenance of the state, and the absence of their participation leads to corruption of the state. Indeed, civic attributes were so crucial that Rousseau termed "public opinion . . . manners and morals" the "real constitution of the state . . . its immovable keystone."[27]

But despite the change in human nature resulting from the development of the civil state, and an insistence that certain civic capacities are important to its maintenance, Rousseau did not expect the public to rule directly. Rather, the Legislator is to design institutions and convince the people what should be done. The Legislator may manipulate the public and is expected to develop a "civil religion" to maintain their loyalty and stability. In addition, the General Will—what is in the community's best interests—cannot be reduced to mass opinion. Even though Rousseau desired active, reasoning, and concerned citizens, he did not cede complete responsibility for the condition of the nation to its citizenry.

Rousseau and the Federalists agreed on the necessary but limited role of citizens, but the Federalists took more seriously the need for institutions to check the political elites. Citizens needed to be limited, particularly if "majority factions" threatened property rights and other permanent interests in the community. Although the Federalists wanted popular control, they also feared mob rule. Leadership was necessary for an effective and energetic republic, but elites also needed to be checked. The American Constitution provided an institutional basis for stable popular control, with features such as regular but overlapping elections, the indirect selection of some offices, checks and balances, and an extended federal republic. By these means, the country's founders hoped that the new nation would be protected from mobocracy, factions, and tyrannical leaders. Popular control and elite responsiveness—these political theorists realized—require more than involved citizens.

Examining public opinion in today's political echo chamber requires us to consider the public's ability to speak and to be heard, the influences on the clarity of expression, and the process and biases in translating the public's voice. These empirical concerns raise a series of normative questions about the connection between public views and policy needed in a healthy democracy. In part, assessments depend on what causes incomplete linkage and transmission. Efforts to obscure citizens' views that do not enable politicians to discover what the people want are very different from a poor correspondence between opinion and policy caused by leaders' independent judgments. In any case, emphasizing the political context of public opinion helps us see that political elites attempt to use public opinion for their own purposes. When the competition is robust, elites will make competing claims about public opinion, with each group using whatever data are available. But when one side is better organized, counterclaims about public opinion may not be made, even if they are viable. Although beliefs about public opinion are sometimes closely related to authentic opinion, citizens' views are situated in a system in which interpretive biases may well develop.

Habermas and Public Opinion as a Social and Historical Phenomenon

The work of German philosopher Jürgen Habermas provides additional insight into the political use of public opinion, by demonstrating that the shape of our mass culture and social and political structures results from a historical process and has implications for democratic communication. Habermas argues that the quality of communication among citizens and between leaders and citizens has become highly constrained and dominated by a simple level of discourse. That is, these arguments and views are translated in the context of a burgeoning culture industry, which delivers formulaic messages to citizens and restricts likely replies. Our current conduits of public discourse limit the expression of public opinion, encouraging its formation around the views espoused by the press, political parties, interest groups, and political elites. Habermas's ideas are closely associated with those of the Frankfurt school. His major work on this subject is *The Structural Transformation of the Public Sphere*, published in Germany in 1962 but not translated into English until 1989.[28]

The Frankfurt School's Critique of Mass Culture

Although in certain ways a break from the tradition that nurtured Habermas, the approach he uses in *The Structural Transformation of the Public Sphere* is closely related to the Frankfurt school's historical approach to mass culture. Writers linked to this school of thought— including Max Horkheimer, Theodor Adorno, Herbert Marcuse, Eric Fromm, and Walter Benjamin—combined normative and empirical theory and addressed a range of topics, including cultural and aesthetic criticism, political economy, social psychology, and political sociology.[29] Scholars associated with the Frankfurt school were influenced by disparate intellectual currents, such as the interpretive and hermeneutical theory of Dilthey, the psychoanalytic perspective of Freud, and the materialist political economy of Marx. The scholars in this tradition had a strong historical perspective, as they were interested in the ways that social structures, economic systems, political institutions, and people's understandings were combined in various ways at different times.[30] Although they were critical of modernist instrumental rationality, scholars connected with the Frankfurt school never repudiated the Enlightenment's commitment to reason. According to David Held, "Each of the critical theorists maintained that although all knowledge is historically conditioned, truth claims can be rationally adjudicated independent of immediate social (e.g. class) interests."[31]

Despite their concern with history, Frankfurt school theorists continually sought to understand the present and look toward the future. Their commitment to history, in fact, enabled them to develop the intellectual tools to analyze contemporary events against the background of macrohistorical conditions and dynamics. Working in an age of major shifts and catastrophic events, including Stalinism and Nazism, scholars of the Frankfurt school felt compelled to examine what was around them and to develop their theories in reaction to these dramatic times.

Given both their theoretical closeness to Marx and their strong allegiance to the ideal of human emancipation, the first critical theorists were deeply disturbed by the centralization of the communist parties and the rise of Stalinism. These scholars sought to preserve the historical and humanist qualities of Marx's thought and rejected attempts to impose a hegemonic and oppressive interpretation of Marxism. Frankfurt school scholars repudiated the theory and practice of Stalinism and the Soviet Union's attempt to discipline thought. Indeed, in reacting to Stalinism as political theory, these scholars rejected the reductionistic sorts of Marxism.[32] The Frankfurt school opposed the idea that historical developments were automatic, unstoppable changes that could be described and predicted without reference to individual action. They also disagreed with the base–superstructure metaphor that held that culture was the simple reflection of economic structures (i.e., with the economy as the base and culture as the superstructure). Instead, consciousness was an essential element of a historical epoch and revolutionary change. Since consciousness, social structures, and institutions varied historically, they contended that it was necessary to update empirical theory to the actual historical and social circumstances. Rather than turning away from Marxism, they argued that reformulating theory was consistent with Marx's view that basic economic and social structures differ in various places and epochs.

As theorists addressing the relationship between theory and practice and as leftist German intellectuals, these scholars were forced to attend to the events around them, upheavals that ultimately forced them to flee their country. Even before the Nazis came to power, Adorno and others studied the German working class. Rather than finding a pre-revolutionary class, however, Adorno discovered tendencies toward authoritarianism. After the war, he continued to investigate authoritarianism, in a series entitled *Studies in Prejudice*, which included the important work *The Authoritarian Personality*.[33] Although this research project studied individuals, "frequent reminders ran throughout the volumes, especially those sections written by Adorno, that prejudice had to be understood on its most basic level as a social rather than individual problem."[34]

Both before and after World War II, critical theorists spent much of their time analyzing art, music, film, and, later, television. Horkheimer and Adorno diagnosed the rise of the "culture industry" which created a mass culture, nearly overwhelming art created by individual artists and local populations.[35] In the past, elite artists usually were supported by a patron, and their work reached a small and either wealthy or bourgeois audience. Most people lived their cultures, dancing and singing folk works, usually on celebratory occasions. Mass culture assimilated unique folk cultures and was characterized by increasingly large concentrations of capital, the pooling of artistic talent by corporations, the need for budgets to publicize work, and relatively large audiences of "culture consumers." In this new culture industry, cultural works aimed toward the masses were characterized by formulaic tunes, images, or plots; relied on stereotypes; and allowed audience members to predict an entire work from only a small segment, thus requiring little effort from them. Television sitcom laugh tracks and music in film and television cued the people watching to how they should react. Culture consumers were entertained, not challenged, by art. The result of such work was to soothe their audience and allow them to adjust to their everyday lives.

In developing an analysis of public opinion as a historical phenomenon and in his later work, Habermas carried on the fundamental ideas of the Frankfurt school. He was concerned with human emancipation and judged situations in terms of how well they achieved this goal. Consistent with this tradition, Habermas's empirical work demonstrates a concern with the relationships between social arrangements and subjective understandings. Since consciousness and social structures are mutually constitutive, one cannot be fully understood without the other. In addition, Habermas's work on public opinion mirrored Horkheimer's and Adorno's ideas about the culture industry and the development of mass culture. Habermas's analysis of public opinion is rooted in the Frankfurt's school's emphasis on the broad historical sweep.

Habermas on Public Opinion

Habermas argues that public opinion has undergone a qualitative shift since the eighteenth century. For a period before then, the social, economic, and political arrangements allowed for deliberative and discursive public opinion in a public sphere. In this sense, public opinion was truly *public*. Unlike the typical social science view of public opinion as the aggregated views of isolated persons who separately respond to a survey, Habermas's understanding of public opinion encompasses "the views held by those who join in rational–critical debate on an issue."[36] Public opinion is, in this sense, active, open, and unrestricted; it is expressed through multiple, free channels of communication; and it requires and creates a political public sphere.

This political public sphere is not a particular place and does not necessitate the gathering of large numbers of people. Instead, Habermas believes that

a portion of the public sphere comes into being in every conversation in which private individuals assemble to form a public body. They then behave neither like business or professional people transacting private affairs, nor like members of a constitutional order subject to the legal constraints of a state bureaucracy. Citizens behave as a public body when they confer in an unrestricted fashion—that is, with the guarantee of freedom of assembly and association and the freedom to express and publish their opinions—about matters of general interest. In a large public body this kind of communication requires specific means for transmitting information and influencing those who receive it.[37]

The public sphere is largely autonomous from political, private, and economic structures and institutions. That is, the political public sphere is not controlled by the state (although the state is the guarantor of free speech); it is outside the family and other private associations; and it is not limited by market conditions or subsumed into the market.

The bourgeoisie of the seventeenth, eighteenth, and nineteenth centuries in France, Germany, and England constituted an emerging class that challenged the traditional institutions of the nobility and the court, sought a greater political role and greater economic power, and led public opinion and the political public sphere. The first public sphere created by this class was literary (or what Habermas called "the public sphere in the world of letters"), and it began to take shape in the seventeenth century. Later, the political public sphere emerged.

Although the specific forms differed in each country, the French salons, the English coffee houses, and the German table societies shared a number of similarities: Social status, in principle at least, had no bearing on the resolution of a discussion. Traditional rank based on the court and the nobility did not carry the argument. Instead, all persons were open to challenge, and reason and persuasive argumentation decided what view prevailed. In addition, the public convened into the public sphere addressed a wide range of topics. Whereas previously the church and court had maintained a "monopoly of interpretation" over certain questions, "discussion within such a public presupposed the problematization of areas that until then had not been questioned."[38] One of the most important topics addressed was popular political control.

A wide variety of newspapers supported the political public sphere, and papers and magazines were additional means to carry out debate. Political discussion inside and outside these written forms included reactions to articles. Because of the many communication channels, it was relatively easy to participate in a public discussion. Nonetheless, the public sphere incorporated only a limited public, as the working class was often unable to participate. But this space was based on the principle of accessibility to real discursive participation, and those who were included were not judged by their status but by their argumentative skills.

Over time, the public political sphere decayed and eventually disintegrated, and thus the space needed for *public* opinion was lost. Habermas attributes this shift in large part to the transition to monopoly capitalism. With greater concentrations of wealth, the content of the discussion and the means of carrying it out were transformed. The citizenry focused more and more on economic issues. At first this new focus segmented the public, because it brought status and economic differences into the debate and made it more difficult to discuss matters in terms of the common interest. Eventually, political consideration of economic interests led to increased state involvement in the economy and in the provision of basic welfare services. As this latter development took hold, the separate familial, economic, statist, and public spheres became blurred, and the autonomous public sphere was gradually combined with other spheres and their unique concerns.

In the twentieth century, communication channels have been limited by ever growing capital requirements. Even though the total number of access points has not decreased, it has become more difficult to create or take control of a major means of public communication. As newspapers and magazines have lost their hegemony, radio and television have become dominant channels to the public. Monetary considerations (and regulation) have made access more difficult, and the public is less able to talk back. Citizens simply cannot express their opinion in the same sense as they did before.[39]

In addition, political communication has become part of the burgeoning culture industry. In order to attract culture consumers, the creators of cultural products must make the merchandise easily understood, enjoyable, and assimilable. As one aspect of the culture industry, political news and commentary aimed toward the masses are simplified and made more exciting. Cartoons, human-interest stories, photography, moving images, layout, and design are used to attract readers without challenging them. Stock plot lines and conclusions, with alternating swings of cynicism and sentimentalism, have replaced rational criticism. With the increasing fusion of information and entertainment, contact with news "leaves no lasting trace; it affords a kind of experience which is not cumulative but regressive."[40]

Habermas believes that the changes in politics and political news emerging during the time of the mass culture industry have modified the form and content of public opinion. The public does not participate but is instead acted on. Whereas citizens were once able to influence the subject of political dialogue, members of the public are now reduced to news consumers who can either buy or not buy a particular product. That is, the public reacts to what is presented to them, and they can either approve or disapprove. Choices are structured for them and embedded in formulaic, stereotyped arguments. Public relations campaigns present alternatives to political consumers. "Public relations do not genuinely concern public opinion, but opinion in the sense of reputation. The public sphere becomes the court *before* whose public prestige can be displayed—rather than *in* which public critical debate is carried on."[41] Today the members of the public are increasingly consumers rather than participants in the political debate. Citizens are now reduced in large part to giving or refusing to give their approval to what they find before them.

With the disintegration of the public sphere, political organizations, elites, and the media compete to structure the alternatives to which the public will be asked to react. Because interest groups and political parties are "big, bureaucratized organizations," they are able to exert a dominant role, to "enjoy an oligopoly of the publicistically effective and politically relevant formation of assemblies and association." Political parties need not involve party voters or make them full members in party rule. Instead, Habermas argues that the parties concentrate on "packag[ing] and display[ing]" the party leader and other party candidates "in a way that makes them marketable."[42] In this situation, political organizations must accommodate the people, although this does not imply that the people rule. Instead, groups analyze the people so that they can figure out how best to package candidates and policy options and how best to put on displays to which the citizenry will react.

While political commentary continues, the only politically meaningful discussion takes place between the large political press and the actors carrying out political public relations. Party leaders, interest groups, and professional commentators ignore the public. Habermas holds that with our system of paid political commentators who speak to the masses, "conversation itself is administered"; commentary is itself a commodity. Rather than public opinion in the older, more active sense, groups linked through the mass media try to create a "plebiscitary follower-mentality on the part of a mediated public."[43] Calhoun summarizes these changes:

> By means of these transformations, the public sphere has become more an arena for advertising than a setting for rational–critical debate.

Legislators stage displays for constituents. Special-interest organizations use publicity work to increase the prestige of their own positions, without making the topics to which those positions refer subjects of genuine public debate. The media are used to create occasions for consumers to identify with the public positions or personas of others. . . . [T]he public responds by acclamation, or the withholding of acclamation.[44]

According to Habermas, institutions, organizations, and elites interact with the public in different ways at various times. Since the public political sphere has disintegrated, the public can respond only in limited ways and only in reaction to what is put before it.

Although I believe that this political sociology of public opinion illuminates the patterns of communication between citizens and elites, Habermas's analysis, at least in its original form, does have limitations. At times, he seems to suggest a near-absolute quiescence among the public, with citizens' consent to the political system almost engineered and individuals easily manipulated. However, Habermas's later comments suggest that the public has some power to resist dominant frames. In addition, he now views the move from a "culture debating to culture-consuming public" as less a dichotomy and more a relative shift.[45] Indeed, it would be just as incorrect to assume that public opinion is determined by other social forces as it would be to assume that public opinion can directly steer political outcomes.

Granted that this change is along a continuum, how great has the shift really been? Some scholars have questioned Habermas's historical account, charging that public political action in the nineteenth century was not limited to the bourgeoisie. Working-class organizations and women activists and reformers created and participated in a range of political actions based on their associations.[46] In addition, some scholarship maintains that the press was commercialized earlier than Habermas would have us believe[47] and that parliamentary action was less the result of an attentive, discursive public opinion and more the product of elite compromise than Habermas suggests.[48]

Even though Habermas's historical picture may not be wholly accurate, *The Structural Transformation of the Public Sphere* nonetheless remains very valuable. One reason is that Habermas's account of the past does not seem to be that far off the mark. Social historian Geoff Eley— although he is critical of some nuances of Habermas's work—maintains that "the value of Habermas's perspective has been fundamentally borne out by recent social history in a variety of fields. . . . I found it striking to see how securely and imaginatively the argument is historically grounded, given the thinness of the literature available at the time" that Habermas wrote this book.[49] Eley also writes that Habermas's basic framework can be extended without injuring its fundamentals.[50] Another response to whether inaccuracies undermine Habermas's argument is to assume that the model is essentially an ideal type. Thus, national variations are expected, and incorrect details are not fatal flaws. As Hohendahl contends, "It provides a paradigm for analyzing historical change, while also serving as a normative category for political critique."[51]

Habermas's perspective on public opinion suggests that it is essential to investigate the reduction of alternatives and definitions of issues presented to the public, the limited responses of acclamation or refusal, the minor part in political discourse allowed to citizens, the effect of mediated realities, and the role of packaging, publicity, stereotypes, simplification, and personae. As one scholar notes, Habermas points to "the indissoluble link between the institutions and practices of mass public communication and the institutions and practices of democratic politics."[52] This dynamic of political presentation and citizen response has important normative implications.

Public Opinion and Normative Political Sociology

Two fundamental normative concerns are raised by the view that public opinion is now largely a reaction to staged presentations by elites and interest groups. The first pertains to the contributions of high-quality discourse to personal development and good policy and is associated with the communicative ethics controversy. The staging of simplified alternatives in front of the public jeopardizes possibilities for unconstrained discourse, individual growth, and policy, which take all views into account. The second normative issue entails the threat to democracy from potential domination or manipulation of public opinion. By simplifying alternatives, crafting personae, employing symbols, and using other techniques of the culture industry, political elites and the media can move the public or influence the perception of public opinion.

The communicative ethics debate reflects the long-standing view— as articulated by theorists as varied as Aristotle, John Stuart Mill, and Hannah Arendt—that full human development requires active engagement in politics and political discourse. Theorists joining this controversy have disagreed about the sorts of discursive arrangements that should and can be pursued, the sort of discussion necessary to promote human potential and reach outcomes that will serve the public good, and the social conditions and institutions needed for the sort of communication they believe is proper. In addition, concern with communicative competence and involvement has been increasingly connected to ethical issues of how best to reach collective judgments and policy outcomes. These theorists start from the perhaps unremarkable contention that to the greatest possible extent, ethical polities avoid force. But a difficult question soon follows: If judgments are not to be imposed, what procedures will allow ethical outcomes? Those who find the answer in communication disagree about whether discussion is to be limited or unrestricted.[53] Habermas calls for a highly unconstrained discussion among self-reflective speakers, to take place in a sphere without coercion—the ideal speech community. He contends that communicative rationality can yield outcomes that serve the general good. Although no procedures exist that can guarantee a lasting consensus or supply the "truth" once and for all, some procedures, Habermas thinks, can generate good reasons to accept or reject competing knowledge claims: "By stipulating that the consensus arrived at must be constraint free (if one is possible on a given issue), there is a guarantee that the consensus expresses the desires of all—the common interest."[54] In Habermas's ideal speech community, all questions of justice and the good life are open to critical debate and scrutiny.[55]

Other theorists contend that politics requires some limits on public discussion.[56] For example, although Ackerman views "dialogue as the first obligation of citizenship" and believes that citizens should be prepared to justify choices in dialogue, he seeks the "path of conversational restraint."[57] To gain agreement on issues in a polity, avoid force, and reach ethical decisions, Ackerman argues that participants must limit themselves to a field of common moral principles.

To observers of the political scene, the theorists' debates about constrained versus unconstrained speech may seem somewhat naive. But these political philosophers are far from gullible, for they recognize the distance between our contemporary politics and their hoped-for ethical polities. In recognizing the gap, the theorists both demonstrate normative visions (which might be possible someday) and propose conditions that can help us better approximate communicative rationality.[58]

Certain political organizations can teach communicative competence, whereas other associations may need to be redesigned. Habermas, for example, cites new social movements as a locale for discursive development. Some scholars of social movements would agree, seeing them as "free spaces" for democratic citizenship and as environments that can use narratives to promote political leadership and group action.[59] Autonomous groups might provide a place for emancipatory speech not otherwise available. After all, as Scott notes, dominated groups often disguise their speech when they are with others, and the oppressed use speech among themselves as a form of resistance and a means of creating and maintaining identities.[60] It might be possible to transform political organizations so they might lead to communicative rationality; these could include workplaces, political parties, and even bureaucracies.[61]

Theories of communicative ethics provide a rather stringent test for today's political discourse. But even if we lower our standards to some extent, clearly there will be normative difficulties if discussions of politics and public opinion are dominated by stereotypes and oversimplification. When the public's voice is not a partner to reasoned consideration but is instead a political resource used strategically, our fundamental humanity is objectified.

The second major normative concern related to Habermas's view of public opinion is the troubling possibility of public domination and manipulation. If politics is staged by political elites, citizens cannot meaningfully participate in public dialogue, even as representations of their views are invoked by elites. As Donald Moon observes,

> It should go without saying that the judgments of many are never articulated and sometimes are not even formed in the first place. This silence is often due to the suppression of certain voices by structures of domination and oppression, although deciding what counts as domination is itself problematic. However, the possibility of domination reminds us that the alternative to agreement is imposition, whether by force or by more subtle forms of manipulation.[62]

Factors that may limit political debate include the use of technical experts and instrumental rationality, efforts to legitimate the political system, the restriction of alternatives presented in the media, and government efforts to use information about public opinion to enhance its control.

Max Weber and, later, the Frankfurt school were concerned with the rise of instrumental reason and its ability to threaten democratic control. Establishing certain problems as technical in nature restricts the discussion to relatively small cadres of experts. In most cases, however, there is no objective distinction between scientific and political matters. Drawing such a line has political consequences, for it grants control to specialists and takes it away from representatives and constituents. This shift occurs when procedures are used that imply scientific precision and objectivity but that are themselves value laden. For example, the use of cost–benefit analysis to evaluate air pollution or forest-harvest policies implies that the enjoyment of clean air, the prevention of lung cancer, the preservation of forests as recreational sites and ecosystems, pollution control technologies, and lumber industry employment can be reduced to the same metric and that only experts can translate these differences.

If the ideology of technical expertise and instrumental reason prevails, the public will be prevented from participating in policy discussions. Even attempts to question the privileged position of experts are themselves suspect. As Habermas points out in his essay "The Scientization of Politics and Public Opinion," "anyone who adheres to the notion of permanent communication between the sciences, considered in terms of their political relevance, and informed public opinion becomes suspect of wanting to put scientific discussion on a mass basis and thus to misuse it ideologically."[63] Although expertise is necessary in some cases, the commitment to instrumental reason becomes a dogma and a limit on public opinion and decision.[64]

Other scholars have pointed to the media and the government's capacity to restrict the alternatives presented to the public. They acknowledge that despite the occasional grassroots activity that can influence politics, by and large the public is reactive. Media critic Noam Chomsky goes so far as to say that the media set the "bounds of the expressible." Since the mass media are the creations of corporate oligopoly, the range of opinion is fairly narrow. Although the media create the illusion that they convey controversy and free expression, they actually serve as adjuncts of the state, particularly in the area of foreign policy.[65] Along the same lines, Bennett argues that journalism takes its cues from government officials. That is, if debate among elected representatives fades and one point of view dominates among elites, the media will not present an opposing point of view even if there is significant support for the alternative among the public. "The over-riding norm of contemporary journalism seems to involve comprising public opinion (at least law-abiding, legitimate opinion) to fit into the range of debate between decisive institutional power blocs."[66] As public opinion is ignored or marginalized, citizens become less able to play a controlling role in the political system.

Polling and surveys may open the public to manipulation. Benjamin Ginsberg, particularly in *The Captive Public*, argues that the advent of survey technologies helped create a reactive public that can express themselves in limited ways. Polling, Ginsberg holds, went through four fundamental changes. First was the shift from voluntary expression to subsidized opinion. Whereas citizens once took it upon themselves to communicate their opinions, the expense of surveys now means that the cost of opinion expression must be subsidized from the outside. Since more moderate people rarely express themselves voluntarily but are included in surveys, public opinion appears more temperate. Second, public opinion is conceptualized as attitudinal, not behavioral. Before polls, the public expressed themselves through actions such as riots, strikes, demonstrations, and boycotts. Third, public opinion is now viewed as a characteristic of individual people, not groups. Fourth, surveys change the meaning of public opinion from a spontaneous assertion to a constrained response. Polls limit the topics that can be considered and further restrict public expression by forcing citizens to respond to survey designers' carefully crafted questions.

The greater use of polls, Ginsberg argues, tames the public and allows for greater government control. Politicians use results from public opinion polls to discredit small groups. Both elected officials and bureaucrats refer to polling data when planning how to introduce or implement policy without resistance. Public opinion as an acclamation or a refusal to acclaim is a domesticated public opinion. Ginsberg writes:

> Taken together, the changes produced by polling contribute to the transformation of public opinion from an unpredictable, extreme, and often dangerous force into a more docile expression of public sentiment. . . . [P]olling can give public opinion a plebiscitary character—robbing opinion of precisely those features that might maximize its impact on government and policy.[67]

The rise of polls has other effects as well. Susan Herbst observes that polls are used for both symbolic and instrumental reasons and can be used for surveillance of the population.[68]

Normative concerns linked to the idea that public opinion is not active but, rather, is reactive to stagings and prone to domination and manipulation make it questionable that one should judge democracy simply by how well public opinion (as measured by polls) conforms to policy. Because a high degree of correlation can arise from manipulation or reactions to limited alternatives, it is important to examine the quality of political discourse. The media, for example, can be evaluated as to how well they present the complexity of citizens' views and policy alternatives. Citizens are not full participants in political dialogue if they can rarely do more than respond to material staged before them.

Even if the public is either responsive or unresponsive to elites' presentations, this does not mean that the public is ignored. Because public opinion is a political resource, these limited public expressions become part of political struggles. Competition makes this interpretive process dynamic and blocks hegemony. Responses to poll questions are taken into account when arguing over what the citizenry believes, when competing elites try to find data that support politically advantageous interpretations. Public views also influence how political appeals are framed and how events are staged, as political figures and the media seek themes with cultural and ideological appeal. Moreover, in a diverse nation with free expression and association, citizens are by no means gagged and so can raise new concerns or reframe existing issues. At the same time, real competition over authoritative interpretations of public opinion does not always exist. And if it does not, those elites who speak in the name of the public have the advantage by default, and they also have a substantial capacity to misinterpret the public's voice. In addition, given the power of elites to frame issues in public debate and for those viewpoints to influence the sorts of questions asked in polls, it is difficult for other perspectives to develop in the citizenry and to gain a hearing. The media, dominant elites, technocratic values, and polling methods and other forces frequently limit the means of public expression, alternative views, and democratic discussion. As a result, citizens' ability to form reasoned opinions and lend their voices to policy decisions may well be squelched.

Conversing in the Echo Chamber

This chapter has argued that public opinion is a political resource used strategically in the political system. Political elites try to move public opinion and shape the perception of public opinion in order to serve their ends. In explaining that the role of public opinion depends on understanding the contexts of politics, this chapter has drawn from the work of Key and Habermas. Key's primary context for the public voice is the echo chamber of politics inhabited by politicians, interest groups, political parties, active and inactive citizens, and the media. According to Habermas, the locale in which politically meaningful public opinion develops is the result of a historical process that reduced the role of active citizen deliberation and replaced it with a regime of commercialized presentations, created personae, and competing stagings of political events. Both Key and Habermas emphasize the importance of communication in politics. Democratic control, Key insists, is dependent on the quality of interactive communication among elected officials, political groups, and the public. Citizens' capacities, activities, and knowl-edge are not the primary factors for maintaining a democracy. For Habermas, good polities foster communicative rationality. In order to allow citizens to discuss freely, it is necessary to avoid coercion and the framing of issues by a small elite.

If we view our polity as a communication system—in Key's terms, an echo chamber—we must understand how public voices are heard, misheard, ignored, and interpreted. In the next chapter, I map out the echo chamber of politics and discuss the particular political locales and dynamics that influence whether and how well citizens and lead-ers can converse.

Mapping the Echo Chamber

Master, you hear the New,
trembling and droning?
Come now heralds who
praise it, intoning.
Really no hearing's still
hale in this turmoil . . .

Rainer Maria Rilke, *Sonnets to Orpheus*

When pressure-group leaders, activated citizens, elected officials, and the media champion competing interpretations of public opinion for their strategic purposes, each contributes to the noisy political environment. As a result, it is difficult for politicians to hear what the public wants. Drawing on Key and Habermas, I argue that in the echo chamber of politics, the echoes of the people's voice may be garbled and misunderstood. In our mass culture of commodified political discourse, the major participants present political alternatives to the public, and in most cases, citizens either react to the assortment arrayed before them or ignore the drama. In this chapter I examine politics as a communication system and analyze where politics as conversation can go wrong.

Politics as Conversation

In this section I ask the following questions: If we think of politics as a conversation, what enables the participants to have a dialogue? What will interfere with the conversational partners' comprehension and understanding? By extending Key's metaphor of the "voice of the peo-

ple" as an "echo" in an "echo chamber," we can recognize how the political system transmits or distorts citizens' views. I first discuss the qualities of a good conversation between individuals. To be sure, personal
conversations are different from public exchanges. However, by beginning with common conversations, we can identify the requirements for
productive discussions and the common problems faced in any communication situation. I then discuss the role of individuals' attributes and
situational characteristics and consider some problem situations that
make it difficult for conversational partners to understand each other.
Finally, I compare the conversational model to talk in politics, with an
emphasis on political communication between citizens and elites.[1]

The Practice of Conversation

Conversations are exchanges of opinions and arguments between partners. Unlike lectures, in which one person talks and others listen, in
conversations at least two people respond to each other in a continuous
and reciprocal way. And unlike arguments, conversations, however
lively, are reasoned and reasonable venues for exploring different points
of view. When conversing, the participants present evidence to support
why they think as they do, and they respond to what others have presented. They do not order each other; instead, they suggest, counsel,
and exhort. Although differences between conversational partners
may—and often do—remain after a conversation, the participants in a
good conversation gain an appreciation of each other's perspectives.

Although words are the main currency of conversation, nonverbal
messages also are often employed. For instance, participants may use
their hands to express astonishment, intensity of conviction, or humor.
Or if they wish to describe or show something, they may draw a picture,
display an image, or use hand gestures. Because symbols and metaphors
can efficiently express many ideas and emotions, they also are com-
monly used in conversation.[2] A good conversation holds the participants' interest but remains fairly focused. Often there is a need to adjust
during the conversation, to follow side lines while also avoiding significant diversions.

If you were asked what makes a good conversation, probably one of
the first things you would mention would be a good partner. Indeed, the
participants in a conversation should possess certain characteristics in
order for it to be an interesting and fruitful discussion. Challenging and
enjoyable conversationalists use rhetorical skills, an extensive base of

information, and intelligence. In addition, they are willing and eager to enter into discussions. If a conversation is to be educative and possibly even lead to one party's changing his or her mind, the participants should not be too dominant or aggressive. Active involvement must be balanced with a willingness to listen and to respond to other partners. This combination of attentiveness and reaction is a hallmark of a conversational partner who is committed to tolerant discussion.

The participants in a dialogue must also have some shared ground. Some argue that a fruitful conversation can take place only if the partners agree that they will not talk about certain matters. According to dialogic theorist Bruce Ackerman, those engaged in ethical political conversation must be willing to limit themselves to matters of shared fundamental values. For Ackerman, the necessary shared ground for dialogue is the field of "conversational restraint." Taking this approach, Ackerman maintains, is well suited to the modern liberal state, for "it calls upon us to reflect upon the pragmatic imperative to talk to strangers as well as soul-mates; and to consider whether, despite the strangers' strangeness, we might still have something reasonable to say to one another about our efforts to coexist on this puzzling planet."[3]

Ackerman argues that his solution is more pragmatic than those of other dialogic theorists, since he does not "search for some common value that will trump this disagreement; nor . . . try to translate it into some putatively neutral framework; nor . . . seek to transcend it by talking about how some unearthly creature might resolve it."[4] In reality, how practical is this solution? I agree with Ackerman's critics, including Donald Moon and Seyla Benhabib, that many recent issues in American politics (and elsewhere as well) have involved fundamental values, including the equality of the races and sexes and the acceptability of gays and lesbians as full participants in all spheres of life.[5] If we accepted Ackerman's contention that discussions should be constrained, we would not consider these issues—even though conversation can change what issues are considered and how they are discussed. For example, talking about family concerns—gender roles in child rearing and domestic violence come to mind—has made them public issues and has transformed practices and values pertaining to them. Whether an issue is considered public or private has varied throughout history, and this is influenced by political action. In addition, conversational restraint may prevent the development of a new social consensus, since "one of the most important ways by which we actually discover beliefs held in common with others is by challenging the beliefs that seem wrong and coming to see the grounds on which they are held."[6]

Although I would not ground dialogic involvement on a limited subject matter, some aspects of the discussion should be shared in order for the discussion to be productive. For people to be able to communicate, they must speak the same language and share some fundamental values. This condition should not be taken too literally, however; the actual words used may not be the same. Nonetheless, conversational participants cannot be partners in a shared endeavor if their ways of proceeding are incommensurable. Indeed, the need for some connection between partners can be found in the source of the very word *conversation*, whose root comes from the Latin *conversari*, "to associate with." *Conversation, conversant,* and *converse* also share this root, and being conversant with someone means that one is familiar with that person's circumstances and ideas. As this linguistic history implies, people engaged in conversation must share something, must have a certain familiarity. To be sure, this knowledge of another does not have to be deep or intimate. In addition, one becomes conversant, in part, by engaging in conversation, although the initial conversation requires a certain shared basis, such as a commitment to fair play and tolerance.

One of the requirements of a productive conversation, then, is that the participants have a common allegiance to the rules that make conversation possible. The reason is that dialogue is a choice, a way of discussing and possibly resolving disagreements that avoids the alternative of force and imposition. Conversational partners must believe in free speech, tolerate diverse views, and share a commitment to a rational basis for evaluating arguments. And these are some of the qualities that Habermas required for his ideal speech community.

But even for those who do have these qualities, a good conversation still may be impossible. As I pointed out in the first chapter, citizens' ability to speak depends on the political system's attributes at a particular time. Evaluating a system requires that we understand the context that people have created, find themselves in, and try to change. One of the greatest dangers to a conversation is that some potential participants will not speak. It is very likely, too, that silence or speech is related to power. That is, major class or cultural differences often make it difficult for participants to enter a dialogue as equal partners. Or typical gender differences in speaking styles can make it difficult for women to speak and be heard. In addition, institutions, informal arrangements, and social structures influence the possibility of free conversation.

Particular arrangements can be more or less permeable. If a system is relatively restrictive, certain voices will be much louder than others. As Habermas contends, the bourgeois public sphere was more accessible than structures either before or since.[7] Although this political public sphere allowed more real engagement in the formulation of political discussion, our current politics relegates many people to the sidelines, permitting them only to cheer or boo. These limitations on participation, power, and access to the system thus leave some people out of the main conversation.

Where the actual conversation takes place also matters. Full engagement in a conversation requires that one be "in the room." This space need not be an actual physical location, of course, for one could engage with others through published writings or the airwaves. In different times, the locale of the conversation that matters is in different places. But if a potential participant is not there—wherever "there" is—then it is hard for his or her voice to be heard. No wonder that a shout from the sidelines would sound like a muffled echo.

Even if certain people are not full participants in the conversation, others who are participating may nonetheless pay attention to those absent. They may do so because these spectators might decide to make trouble if their views are neglected. Or the legitimacy of decisions arising from the discussion may be dependent on acknowledging people who are not direct participants but who are influenced by what the conversational partners resolve to do. Finally, conversational participants may attend to those who are not engaged in the dialogue because the participants believe that they should do so, as a principle of public service or out of concern for the community. Thus people who are not present are not wholly absent either. It is as if they are ghostly apparitions whose existence never fully comes into focus but never completely fades away either.

If some people are acknowledged but usually are absent, what part do they play in the conversation? How do they express their points of view? Under most conditions, since they cannot speak directly to change the subject or the terms of the conversation, people outside the main conversation must express themselves through others. Someone who can speak therefore must interpret the views of the quiet outsiders. Unfortunately, even in the best of circumstances, when one person speaks for another, the original message may be garbled. Anyone who has played the game of telephone knows that words and even the basic meaning of messages often change a great deal from start to finish.

In some situations, the person who interprets the views of someone absent has a particular stake in the interpretation. If this is the case, the original words may be slanted to support the interpreter's interests. Nearly everyone has had the experience of hearing what someone has reportedly said, only to find it inaccurate or even unrecognizable. What was really said can be misunderstood because the original message was confusing, the listener did not understand what was said, the context of the message implied a different meaning, or the translator had an interest in construing the message in a particular way. Incorrect messages can also take on a life of their own. Those of us who have found ourselves in the position of trying to correct an inaccurate report of our words know how difficult that can be.

Politics and the Conversational Model

Even though contemporary American politics diverges a great deal from the model of conversation just presented, this paradigm still is useful empirically and normatively. That is, by comparing politics to a conversation, we can isolate those circumstances that can cause political communication to break down.

In the public at large, some citizens are more likely than others to be participants in the conversation of politics. Some are members of what Key called the "attentive public"—those who care about politics more than others and spend more time thinking about it. Such people regularly participate in a whole series of activities. Given their interest and knowledge and activity levels, they are more likely to be heard by policymakers than others are. As numerous studies have shown, citizens with a high socioeconomic status are much likelier to participate than are people with less wealth and status.[8] Furthermore, most citizens are less members of a conversation than portions of an audience. As such, their approval or disapproval is like the applause for or booing of the actors on the stage and the producers and directors who created the show. Other possible actions for the mass citizenry are walking out on a performance or simply not showing up at all.[9] Whether these citizens loudly communicate, remain silent, or behave in some other way, some will try to assess their reactions.

Although members of the attentive public are better able to become part of the conversation of politics, their views, along with others' opinions, are largely interpreted by others. The media, interest groups, and elected officials are both the main conversationalists and the main interpreters of the public. The interpretations that are accepted are part of a political competition in which the principal interpreters try to establish how the public is reacting to ideas and events. To determine what the public is thinking, these conversational participants rely on a range of evidence, which may give different pictures of public opinion. Although even objective analysts can come to different conclusions about the meaning of public opinion data, many of the speakers in politics are not primarily motivated by scientific objectivity. Rather, they can—often do—selectively use evidence concerning the public's views in order to buttress a political position.[10]

Competitive interpreters can often offer some evidence to support their claims. How can they make what seem to be reasonably legitimate interpretations that nonetheless contradict one another? One possibility is that some sources of information about public opinion are more accurate than others and that some interpretations depend on less representative data. Calls from activists, for instance, may demonstrate that this group feels intensely about an issue but do not indicate how the general public thinks. In another case, elected officials may speak about their constitutents, whose opinions are in fact different from those of citizens in other constituencies. Finally, even comparable groups can give dissimilar responses to varied polling questions. Those questions may frame the issue differently and thus ask about slightly different topics, thereby prompting citizens to think about different considerations or taking advantage of a certain ambivalence about the issue.[11] Although even properly designed polls have these problems, other polls are clearly designed to yield certain results. This diversity of potential interpretations makes it more difficult for the public, in effect, to speak for itself.

The public's views are thus interpreted by others, and usually by parties with a stake in the interpretation.[12] If it is wrong, a more difficult situation is created than the misunderstanding that occurs in a game of telephone, or even in the mischaracterization that results when malicious tales are told. In the first case, the incorrect message can easily be corrected. In the latter situation, the person about whom gossip is spread knows that the story is false—even if it is difficult to repair a reputation. If the interpretation of public opinion is wrong, however, members of the public do not have easy access to communication channels to make the correction. Moreover, citizens have no way of knowing if the interpretation is, in fact, correct. Each person and their associates are but small parts of the public, and so they have no reliable way to know whether an interpreter is wrong about what "the public" believes.[13]

When we consider modern political structures, it seems clear that our national politics cannot be like a personal conversation even if we wanted it to be: there are simply too many people for citizens to speak directly to one another and to political leaders. The world of the Athenian *polis* and the utopian Rousseauean community not only allowed for but also celebrated political participation through speech. Unfortunately, this way of life cannot be accommodated in a large, representative-based modern state, at least not at the national level.[14] Indeed, in order to limit the popular voice, our country's founders chose the constitutional design of an extended republic with representatives elected with overlapping terms. Although some scholars have proposed using the new electronic technologies to give the public a greater voice, others argue that these methods would not allow citizens to influence fundamentally the subject or terms of the issue under consideration.[15] According to Habermas, true public opinion can emerge only in a particular social structure, the political public sphere.

The potential for good communication depends not only on speech but also on listening. If the listeners are highly motivated, then some communication between the public and the main conversationalists is possible. And simply because there are elections, elected representatives can be motivated listeners. Politicians usually want to be reelected and often aspire to higher office, know that citizens may punish incumbents for policy choices, and fear the disclosure of unpopular votes by their opponents. Public opinion therefore can be a very real political resource to elected officials. During policy debates, officials may promote particular interpretations of public opinion, but they also will likely hear from some constituents and will hear interpretations of public opinion from competing elites, the media, and interest groups. So even though the American constitutional system limits direct participation, the electoral system requires accountability, responsiveness, and a desire to listen to the public. Nor can one listen only once, because "Discourse is not a contract where there is a privileged moment of promising which is then binding on all parties in perpetuity."[16] Citizens are thus more than ghostly apparitions barely present at political conversations. At the same time, elected officials, no matter how motivated, still have problems clearly hearing the public's voice. Politicians therefore must weigh different evidence and rely in part on their political intuition.

Democratic politics requires communication between citizens and elites. Although the voice of the people can be difficult to hear and interpret, it is crucial to a democratic system. Even if a leader decides that he will not follow the popular will, it is important that he know what the people believe so that he can later explain why he chose a different course. As I have pointed out, various conditions can cause the conversational model to fail as a paradigm for the political system. Important factors influencing how easily politicians can find out what citizens are thinking are citizens' attributes, the structure of the communication system, biases in interpretation, and a motivation to listen.

Into the Echo Chamber

Citizens, leaders, activists, and journalists can speak, remain silent, interpret, simulate, or listen. Major elements of the echo chamber of politics—in which communication or miscommunication can occur—include the social psychology of public voice or silence, as well as the media, interest groups, and elites.

The Social Psychology of Citizen Speech or Silence

If citizens are to have their voices heard by elites, they must be willing to speak up. Both political theorists and empirical research suggest that citizens' silence or speech has a social–psychological component. Although individual characteristics such as interest and education influence whether or not citizens speak up, social conditions can trigger psychological reactions. Fundamental civic attributes thus do not exist before or apart from their environment but, rather, are themselves influenced by the political context. More than 150 years ago Tocqueville observed that when there is social and political equality, "public opinion becomes more and more mistress of the world."[17] He contended that democratic citizens look to one another rather than to an authority and so mold their actions and views to fit the common wisdom. A number of scholars of American political culture still find Tocqueville's account compelling.[18]

Elisabeth Noelle-Neumann, a German scholar, has built on Tocqueville and other political theorists who considered public opinion. In short, she argues that people are social animals and therefore are concerned with the larger climate of opinion. Because people fear isolation and tend toward conformity, they monitor public opinion and make determinations about whether their views are consonant with the majority or a minority. If people believe that their views are not shared by the majority, they will be less apt to express their opinions in public. Accordingly, quiet citizens are not randomly distributed but are disproportionately found among those in the perceived minorities. Then, when their voices are not heard, the climate of opinion changes, and these small groups grow even more isolated and mute—thereby creating a spiral of silence.

In order for this process to unfold as described, citizens must have some way of determining the shape of public opinion. Noelle-Neumann contends that they use two methods. First, citizens are highly motivated social perceivers who scan their surroundings for signs of how their fellow citizens see the world. Second, they learn about the public mind from the media. If the media present relatively uniform information (consonant messages), these similar messages are stable over time (cumulative messages), and information is widely available (ubiquitous messages), the spiral of silence effect will be enhanced. Public opinion can act as a force threatening to isolate socially oriented human beings from one another. Although some members of minorities can resist, most are unable to prevent being swept into the spiral's vortex.

When describing a paradigmatic conversation in the first part of this chapter, I noted that proper conversational partners can both speak and listen. However, if some citizens fall mute when social conditions threaten their psyches, they will be kept from engaging in dialogue. If this process becomes extreme, silenced citizens may not even make sounds that could become echoes in the echo chamber or respond to stagings put on by others. Furthermore, if the wrong questions are asked in polls or if quiet citizens are intimidated by robust talkers, even professionals trained and motivated to listen may be unable to discover what these silenced citizens want.

Although Noelle-Neumann's social–psychological theory suggests that it may be difficult to prevent a spiral from spinning into a state of ever greater silence, some scholars believe that it is too pessimistic. First, some argue that her theory underestimates the role of reference groups as mediators between individual persons and society.[19] Reference groups provide essential support for those with minority perspectives and thus lessen their fear of isolation. Research based on experiments with small groups demonstrates that even minimal support from others when one is in a minority position leads to a large drop in the impact of group opinion. In addition, even when group preferences influence a single member, this drop derives from both a desire to conform and the informational content of the group opinion.[20]

Second, some researchers have suggested that the causal relationship posited in the spiral of silence theory may be reversed, largely because of perceptual biases. Although Noelle-Neumann contends that perceptions of public opinion influence individual opinions, it may be that a correlation exists because individual opinions influence the perceptions of group opinions. A number of scholars have found self-serving biases in how people perceive others' opinions. Diverse citizens may not make consistent and accurate readings of the climate of opinion but instead suffer from a "pluralistic ignorance" of public opinion. When people assess public opinion, they frequently decide that others view the world in the way that they do.[21]

Third, communication among citizens occurs in particular social networks and communities. Although Huckfeldt and Sprague's community-based study concludes that there is "informational coercion of political minorities achieved through mechanisms of social interaction," citizens are not frozen by ideological majorities.[22] They can and do choose their environments and social networks and thus can place themselves in situations in which their views are reinforced rather than challenged.

Fourth, media messages may not in fact be consonant. Even though the mainstream press may present only a limited set of ideas, alternative media offer a larger menu. Citizens expose themselves to different media and in a way that tends to reinforce their opinions.[23] A selective use of the media can thus prevent isolation and stop the spiral of silence.

Fifth, the spiral of silence theory presumes a simple process that may actually be more complex and conditional. Cultural and national variations may be quite important. For example, a homogeneous nation with a great deal of support for authority may have a stronger spiral of silence effect than does a country with a heterogeneous and critical population.

Government control of the media changes the dynamic as well. As one communications scholar points out, censorship once forced most of the Philippine media to take a unified position.[24] According to the basic spiral of silence theory, this should have led to minimal displays of disagreement. But in the Philippines, the small alternative media were quite influential in the mass activity resulting in Marcos's overthrow. In authoritarian nations, challenges to the main point of view are not suppressed by fears about social conformity but instead may be embraced because they counter the government's hegemonic control.[25]

Finally, some sorts of communications are not easily classified as either speech or silence. In an intriguing study, sociologist Nina Eliasoph stopped people in public places and asked their opinions about the Iran–contra affair.[26] Holding a microphone, Eliasoph told her subjects that their words might be used in a radio documentary. Although few people refused, their responses demonstrate that there are alternatives to reasoned, careful speech that would contribute to an ideal political dialogue. Rather than standing silent or conversing, many of Eliasoph's subjects joked, distanced themselves, responded stereotypically, and judged the Iran–contra hearings as a literary or theater critic would.

In my way of thinking, these criticisms should not lead us to abandon Noelle-Neumann's perspective, as there may well be a significant social–psychological dynamic that looks different in different circumstances. In fact, some researchers have found that variations in the public and the context influence whether and how people speak about politics. Journalism professor Dominic Lasorsa, for instance, discovered that willingness to speak out was affected by both the climate of opinion and individual differences, such as socioeconomic status, interest, and self-efficacy.[27] In another study, Charles Salmon and Kurt Neuwirth investigated whether citizens were less willing to express their views of abortion to a television reporter or a stranger when their opinions were not congruent with national or local opinion.[28] Salmon and Neuwirth found that citizens most often avoided talking to a stranger when their views differed from the national norm. In a review of the literature on the political effects of perceptions of mass opinion, Mutz concludes that the evidence shows that the climate of opinion most influences those people who are weakly committed to their initial position and who have little prior information.[29] One factor behind this contextual dynamic is that citizens who are dedicated to an opinion base their views on fewer considerations and are less ambivalent than are people whose commitments are weaker.[30]

To return to the conversational model, the characteristics of potential participants and the locale of the conversation affect whether a dialogue will take place, how useful and insightful it will be, and whether the participants can understand others whom they do not know well. Personality differences and skills also influence vulnerability to pressures that could induce silence. People may withdraw into their communities and expose themselves to only those media that support their point of view. Such segregation enables separate and separated conversations, but may prevent engagement with others outside the community.

To understand how a psychological phenomenon such as the spiral of silence affects the political conversation, we must look at how political actors and the media promote a particular climate of public opinion.[31]

The Media

The media, particularly the mass media, are a crucial part of politics as a communication system. In our large, modern nation states, it is quite difficult for citizens to learn and talk about politics directly, and—much like playing the game of telephone—indirect contact may lead to inaccurate or garbled messages. In doing their job, the media may amplify certain voices, adopt terms of debate favoring one party, give limited information, or focus on political processes over substance.

Recent research has shown that the media have a wide range of effects on the public's views of politics, including perceptions of policy importance, attributions of responsibility, political significance of personal experiences, salience of issues in assessments of political figures, and voting intentions.[32] One of the most fertile research areas is agenda setting, that is, the media's ability to influence which issues are considered most important. In a series of experiments, Iyengar and Kinder showed their subjects different compilations of news stories. What people saw on the news influenced whether they considered a problem to be important and whom they believed to be responsible for the problem. Iyengar found that by framing stories as individual situations or larger problems, the media can affect who is seen as responsible for the situation, and these attributions in turn can affect policy preferences, presidential popularity, and other assessments. Although these effects were significant, the media may not be able to shift policy priorities under all conditions. Yagade and Dozier suggest that the media's agenda-setting ability is enhanced when the issues are more concrete and less abstract.[33] They argue that concrete stories provide striking visual material with which audiences can identify. Both citizens' ability to connect an issue with their lives and the media's capacity to find and use imagery influence effective agenda setting.

But can media coverage cause shifts in public opinion? In a study of about eighty different policies, Page, Shapiro, and Dempsey investigated the effect of nearly eleven thousand news stories on public opinion.[34] They found statistically significant movements in opinion polls, with different speakers able to create different amounts of change in raw poll numbers. News commentary and expert opinion moved the largest numbers of citizens toward their position, and statements on the news by interest-group leaders led opinion away from prior positions.

This research suggests that the media influence how citizens decide what issues are important and indeed affect what they think, but certain limitations also apply. First, many citizens watch news reports in sophisticated ways and adjust for biases they expect in the media.[35] Graber studied how citizens watched news over the course of a year. She included citizens who paid much and those who paid little attention to the news, and within these two groups, some had a great deal of access to information and others had limited access. The citizens in Graber's study were not passive recipients of news but corrected for the images sent through the airwaves. For example, they were quite aware that the reports of murders they saw on the news were not representative of the percentage of murders in all crimes committed in their communities.

Studies showing that the number and tone of news stories affect public opinion may also be problematic because the amount of news coverage may well reflect real political events—such as the legislation being debated, an executive initiative introduced, a scandal breaking, or a war in progress. For example, Kinder and Krosnick argue that the intensive news coverage of the Iran–contra affair changed the criteria used for assessing the president.[36] It is hard to imagine, however, how the media could have chosen not to cover extensively this chicanery or how their disclosure could not have had an impact on how citizens evaluated Reagan. Of course, the media did not have to use the frame they chose to cover the breaking events, and this framework did influence citizens' evaluations. The precise terms used to discuss the Iran–contra affair were not a foregone conclusion; in fact, in chapter 4 I spend a considerable amount of time on this matter. My point here is that given the Reagan administration's stance on terrorism and its continuing efforts to fund the Nicaraguan contras, the media's extensive coverage of Iran–contra revelations—no matter how it was framed—reflected events of real consequence. That is, the media delivered the message of what happened, and this disclosure itself influenced how citizens assessed President Reagan.

The media do have an important impact on public opinion, one part of which comes from their place in the political process and communication system.[37] In young Habermas's terms, the media provide the stage on which political leaders and activists create personae and displays to which the public can react. Habermas's basic model may disregard citizens' capacities to resist media portraits, but his analysis helps us see the competition among interested parties about what story will be told. A particular staging is not necessarily the one that will dominate; elites compete over interpretations and try to get the media to use more of their narrative than the others.' Viewing the media as part of the political communication system means asking who is using the media to communicate, how people try to influence the media's coverage, how the media cover both events and public opinion and why, and what biases in the media influence their coverage and effects.

If we think of political communication as modeled on a conversation, we must puzzle through the media's place in connecting conversational partners. Although speakers and listeners can communicate directly, communicative relationships through the media include information about the public that is transmitted to elected officials, discussions among political elites, interest-group messages to the public, and persuasive messages from elites to the public. The media have their own biases in covering events and discourse about events. Although these biases may not be strongly ideological, news programs can adopt frames that have an important influence on the definition of issues and range of alternatives considered acceptable.

Using the conversational model, the media's biases can be understood as interpretation biases. Some voices are louder than others; some perspectives are interpreted in a positive or a negative light; and some points of view are simply ignored. One reason is that, as Entman argues, the media are part of both political and commercial markets.[38] These dual markets affect what sources are used in stories and how complex these stories will be made. Underwood charges that commercialism leads the mainstream media to drop tough investigations, neglect hard news, and focus on people and personalities rather than systems.[39] In addition, the media play an important part in creating spectacles, in which political events and actors become nearly stock characters. Edelman argues that the media adopt this sort of interpretation of events because of both marketability and the collusion between the media and other political forces. As Edelman puts it, "Those involved in making, reporting, and editing news accordingly have an incentive to shape it so as to attract audiences and, sometimes, to encourage particular interpretations through its content and form. Interest groups, public officials, and editorial staffs share an interest in making news dramatic."[40] In short, communication to the public is simplified to fit with the dramatic requisites of spectacle.

Another major bias in the news that affects the media's ability to mediate communication between the citizenry and elected officials is the media's emphasis on elites. To some extent, perhaps, this simply reflects the fact that elites are the news makers inside Washington. But this tendency can also mean that alternative views—even when they are widely found in the populace—are nearly shut out. Bennett, for example, showed that the media indexed coverage of Nicaragua to the statements made by government elites, thus keeping critics out of the news, even when much of the population was opposed to the Reagan administration's policy. Some critics have charged that media pundits define and narrow the elites' debate, thereby creating an unaccountable "punditocracy."[41] Although such an effect is difficult to assess quantitatively, one study found that news commentators influence public opinion even when many other factors are controlled for, thereby implying that media discussion and consensus do indeed color the public's view of politics.[42]

Understanding how the media communicate facts and narratives to the public is an essential element of comprehending the impact of public opinion in the political process, if only because the public's views of political events are so greatly influenced by the portraits of reality delivered through the media. In addition, the dominant frames may circumscribe the interpretations of the public mind, creating yet another translation problem: If the media and elites attempt to understand what the public wants but the public can speak only in restricted ways—within the terms of spectacle (as Edelman has it) or stagings and calls for acclamation or refusal (to use Habermas's terms)—then what the public wishes to say will become garbled. Variegated substance and content are pushed into the categories offered by the media. But the interpretation need not be as hopelessly muddled as this, and the echoes of public opinion need not be so muffled. In fact, the public has recourse to direct communication with political elites, and citizens can react spontaneously to events. Few people, however, take the initiative to contact officials to register their views.

Because the mass media translate the public voice, it is important to analyze how they both clarify and muffle the public's views as reporters convey this information to citizens and political elites. Despite the great amount of research on the media's obsession with polls, little is known about how the media cover all sources of information about public opinion and how opinion coverage is influenced by spectacles, personae, stagings, dramatic presentations, and organized activities. Nonetheless, the media's portrait of public opinion is salient information for citizens and elites alike.

An Institutional View of Public Opinion

Institutions structure politics, setting the rules by which unaffiliated citizens and organized interests can influence policy. In addition, institutions structure communication and affect actors' capacity to hear one another. As Allen pointed out, Tocqueville argued that the dynamics of public opinion are always institutionally situated.[43] In the contemporary American institutional context, political parties have declined as a means of mobilizing voters both physically and cognitively; interest groups have become more important; and elected officials are increasingly entrepreneurial. These trends have set the conditions under which public opinion can be expressed and may influence the political process and outcomes.

Pressure Groups and Public Opinion

Pressure groups—a category that includes interest groups and social movements—are major political actors in contemporary American politics. Group leaders have a place in the communication system because they listen to and generate echoes in the political echo chamber. Although both sorts of pressure groups have been effective in introducing concerns into the political system, social movements' looser organizational structures and often lesser perceived legitimacy have made it harder for them to endure and effect change over time. Although pressure groups try to influence all levels of government, I will concentrate on the federal legislature, the Congress.

Groups speak in the echo chamber of politics to a variety of actors and through different routes and various agents. For example, in speaking to public officials, groups can use insider strategies. Interest groups fund in-house political operations or hire lobbying firms to represent their desires. Lobbyists regularly visit members of Congress, attend fund-raisers, coordinate with political action committees to disburse election money, and testify to congressional committees and subcommittees. As groups supply information about the effect of a proposed or existing policy, interest-group representatives may make claims about public opinion in order to sway a member of Congress. These statements include assessments of the policy's effect on constituents as well as claims about what the public thinks or will come to think during the policy debate or after a bill is passed. Even with insider routes, with messages delivered by professional purveyors of interest group clout, representations of the public's voice are not absent.

In speaking to public officials, interest groups can choose instead to focus on outsider strategies—attempting to convince citizens and then mobilizing those convinced—to then speak to members of Congress. If the group is a membership organization, the interest group will in effect try to have its members shout, to speak louder than other citizens. Therefore, the group uses its internal communication mechanisms to influence members' opinions and induce them to contact Congress. If the group is a trade or corporate group, "grassroots lobbying" may be employed, with public relations firms or more specialized firms working to generate citizen reaction. For these efforts to be effective, practitioners must understand enough about the public's values to know how best to influence them. As trade groups have adopted more and more sophisticated technology, they are more able to avoid leaving their fingerprints, so that mobilized action appears to be spontaneous grassroots activity.[44] In addition, mobilized public opinion can become part of the elite discourse and discussion if pundits, the media, and policymakers believe they hear a genuine popular uproar. Outsider strategies can start echoes that may reverberate in the echo chamber.

As interpreters and generators of the public voice, interest groups are by no means disinterested or objective; rather, they interpret public opinion in ways that most support their own needs. If interest groups were evenly matched against one another across all or most issues, this interpretation bias would not greatly hinder officials' ability to understand what the public wanted. But as political scientists are well aware, groups are not mobilized equally, and public expressions of group sentiment thus are likely to mirror the mobilization of bias. As Mancur Olson observed, those groups seeking to provide goods from which no one can be excluded and that may be realized whether or not they contribute—public goods such as clean air—face a difficult time organizing the group and maintaining members. On the other hand, trade groups seeking private benefits that serve mostly their own group and have no one else who might organize on their behalf are formed more easily and persist. Although the burden for public goods organizations is not insurmountable, in general the uneven pattern of mobilization can create poor representation of public opinion.

Mobilization patterns for a particular issue may take shape with one side well mobilized and others less so. When the issue is not primarily economic but instead is strongly ideological or symbolic, the public goods problem may affect both sides. Thus the role of public opinion and perceptions of public opinion is likely to look different in different conditions. I address this issue at length in chapter 7. At this point, suffice it to say that differing patterns of group mobilization permit or restrict groups from shaping perceived public opinion. If groups are capable of crafting a interpretation of public opinion that is not unchallenged, their policy views will gain a better hearing through the media and in the halls of Congress.

In addition, unanswered group action might play a part in creating a spiral of silence, because groups influence the media's coverage of public opinion, thereby affecting perceptions of public opinion among the masses and diminishing the public speech for those people who believe themselves to be in the minority. The news media's tendency to dramatize and simplify news stories may leave the unorganized particularly vulnerable to the mobilization of symbols by politically savvy organized groups.[45]

Pressure groups' efforts to influence policy debate are a central element of the context shaping and defining public opinion. Whether these efforts are particularly effective in influencing policy remains an open question. Key, in fact, argues that much of what pressure groups do to mobilize and influence public opinion are rituals "on the order of the dance of the rainmakers."[46] Outsider strategies are, to be sure, just one of many tools that pressure groups can use and may well not be sufficient for the group to meet its goals. But the fact remains that no pressure-group leaders would choose to leave policy adversaries to mobilize public opinion while their group sat back quietly. If public opinion is mobilized on the other side, the ritual of organizing public voice on one's side will be more than a talisman. As Habermas points out, group leaders must compete over what policies and definitions of alternatives are presented to the public. When public opinion is reduced to accepting or rejecting one's options, it matters how those alternatives are framed. The task of defining the issue thus is as important to pressure groups as is the task of mobilizing existing supporters. In fact, the job of framing the issue is integral to rousing members and recruiting new supporters.

Pressure groups are communicators in the political echo chamber and add significantly to the cacophony of echoes. Leaders speak directly to public officials about policy and public opinion, and they seek to shape the perceived alternatives, influence the media's understanding, stimulate members to express their views, and try to persuade citizens to contact their representatives.

Elected Officials

In democracies—or so we hope—elected officials are concerned with the popular will. Although the American system was structured to prevent mass enthusiasms from causing rapid, unwise change, the principle of popular sovereignty is fundamental. When discussing the model conversation, I stated that good partners in a productive conversation must both speak and listen. Given politicians' position as representatives of the popular will, democratic ideals requires that they be good listeners. (And as James Madison and other American founders knew well, their ambition and place in the system also motivate them to be good listeners.) But politicians' democratic obligation is not just to respond but also to lead. If they are to be constructive political leaders, elected officials must frame alternatives and argue for their position. Leadership requires that public officials be good speakers, capable of communicating ideas to citizens and their fellow representatives.

In the echo chamber of politics, politicians are recipients of echoes from the public. But because they promote policies, they create what V. O. Key called inputs into the echo chamber that powerfully influence the quality of the returning and responding echoes. Like pressure groups, public officials engage in struggles over the terms of discussion, and they speak through the media. Whereas interest groups must react to public opinion in order to decide how to present their issue campaigns, politicians face different strategic requisites. Although they are partly concerned with shaping public opinion, politicians also strategize how to respond to the public voice. In this task, they sift through the evidence and develop a perception of public opinion.

The president and members of Congress face both similar and different information environments, which affect their abilities to listen and respond. I assume that all politicians are interested in having their policies enacted successfully and in being reelected. To try to understand public opinion, executive and legislative officials analyze data from national polls conducted by polling firms. These poll results are likely to be reported by the news media and to influence the opinion climate in Washington. The president has additional information and special needs. First, presidents now have a well-developed system for monitoring opinion. As Jacobs observes, "A public opinion apparatus developed during the twentieth century to perform two functions: to conduct public relations campaigns in order to manage public perceptions, and to track public sentiment, largely through the use of polls."[47] Although presidents have conducted private polls since John F. Kennedy was in the White House, the capacity to assess public reactions became especially well developed during the Reagan administration.[48] Presidents George Bush and Bill Clinton also have been interested in monitoring public reaction, and all future presidents will probably also employ private pollsters.

The president requires information about the views of the national public for policy and political reasons. The chief executive is the only official to have a national constituency. To listen to what the country wants, it is necessary to have frequent readings of polls. But the president's role is not to adjust automatically to shifts in the public mood but to consider public views and then to offer ideas and to lead. If responding to poll results means that the president must pull back from complex and difficult problems, he will not serve the nation in the long run. If the chief executive decides to pursue a fairly independent course, information about the public will be helpful when trying to change citizens' minds. The president has the only national voice and is the only political figure who can always command the media's attention. In trying to influence members of the public, the president can and often does "go public."[49] He can also mobilize his core constituents, who can contact legislators and influence their perceptions of public opinion.[50] But to be an effective leader, the president should know what the public thinks and wants. Understanding public opinion helps the president because his popularity is closely linked to the success of his legislative program. Although public approval of the president is not all that is required for bills to pass—the composition of Congress and the president's political skills with legislators also matter a lot—public opinion is nonetheless a powerful predictor of a president's legislative success.[51] Finally, if a president is unable to maintain public support and to pass legislation, his reelection chances and place in history will be jeopardized. Because the president usually wants to stay in office and accomplish more, he has a strong incentive to listen to the public, and his presidential office puts him in a central political position to try to influence citizens' views.

Like the president, members of Congress look to national polls and are affected by discussions held by the national media. Leaders of their political party also sometimes provide information from surveys and focus groups. But because legislators' constituencies are local, they also must assess local concerns and views. At the same time, members of Congress are less able to monitor opinion accurately. Polls are rarely conducted in congressional districts except during election campaigns. Data on state opinions are more readily available, particularly in the larger states, but much information is missing. Thus legislators cannot rely on surveys when gauging the public mood. In addition, their political calculations are different. Turnout rates in midterm elections are relatively low, yielding an electorate different from that faced by presidents and would-be presidents. Voters during the out years are more driven by strong feelings than are the citizenry as a whole and the presidential electorate. As a result, legislators may decide they have to listen to this group of voters. On the other hand, legislators may not respond if they have developed strong constituency ties. An efficient constituent service operation influences how voters view legislators. If their policy positions are not too far from the voters' views—and relatively small constituencies make it likely that they will not diverge much—an established relationship and service to the district will help members of Congress stay in office.

Even if some political calculations vary, the informational environment of the president and members of Congress is quite similar. Like members of Congress, the president also needs to know about local opinion, to use this information to try to persuade members of Congress to join him on key votes, and he also will need this information for upcoming elections. Like the president, members of Congress are influenced by national polls, in part because of their impact on media coverage and on discussions among pundits, consultants, and lobbyists. The combination of the national media's coverage of public opinion and conversations among legislators, staff, and political operatives helps create a policy mood in Washington. Discussions at Washington cocktail parties and other informal settings and in the halls of Congress are influenced by this policy mood and become part of elected officials' understanding of the citizenry. Public opinion is listened to in this echo chamber. But both members of Congress and the president can suffer from inaccurate translations of public opinion. Some misinterpretations can come from poor polling techniques, such as bad wording of questions, or from attention to polls examining relatively obscure issues. Other difficulties come from media biases in constructing interpretations. Politicians also may be misled by the strategic attempts to use public opinion as a resource.

Members of Congress may discount certain sorts of information as they form a picture of public opinion. However, because information is costly, valid sources may be unavailable, and even good data must be interpreted, there always are competing analyses of public opinion. As Hershey points out, interpretations of what the public thinks are often derived from election results and an analysis of the campaign.[52] Although these readings of public opinion have inherent limits on clarity, such explanations take on political importance. In the communicative task of listening, the communicants can be relatively close to or far from the politician. Sources close to the member of Congress's Washington office, however, do not necessarily provide good information about his or her constituents. If politicians were to rely on these sources, they would be as confused as the person at the end of a game of telephone.

Those people closest to the member of Congress are his or her aides and colleagues, and they also are concerned with what the people at home are saying. Political parties increasingly fund operations to gather information on public opinion, to be used in policy battles. Members of one's own political party, especially those with similar districts, might be the most reliable informants.[53] Conversely, opponents on an issue may claim public support for their view, and so other members may discount or challenge their reading of the public mind. Aides study various data on public opinion, discuss the information with other aides, and give advice to their bosses.

Lobbyists regularly make claims about public opinion to members of Congress. In addition to arguments regarding the impact of policies, such assertions are a basic element in insider pressure-group action. Groups try to generate communication from constituents to public officials, and this information about public opinion is inspected and evaluated by aides and members of Congress.

In this communication system, the media interpret and translate what they know about the public voice. In addition, news stories mediate communication among members of Congress, interest groups, and bureaucrats. Kingdon argues that the media can be important to agenda setting as "communicator[s] within a policy community," "magnifying movements that have started elsewhere," as well as having an indirect effect on Congress by coloring public opinion.[54] Members of Congress and their aides monitor the media closely, and from direct discussions with journalists, they also get information about how the media view the issue and the public's perspective. Newspapers from a member's district also are studied carefully, including editorials and letters to the editor. In fact, newspapers were once a major source of information about the public's views.[55]

In addition to these distant and mediated data concerning public opinion, elected officials communicate directly with the public. Because public officials know that many letters and phone calls are the product of group mobilization, they must distinguish spontaneous grassroots reaction from manufactured "Astroturf."[56] Politicians may hold community meetings open to all or other gatherings with constituents to assess the popular mood, and polling data also tell political leaders about their constituents' views.

The task of listening to and hearing the public voice is difficult and complex. Indeed, in interpreting the public, public officials often are in the position of translating translations. Elected officials must determine the reliability of sources of information, the intensity of the opinion, and its stability. Politicians may react quickly or slowly. In some cases, a decision to respond to what seems to be public opinion may diminish their popularity if they are viewed as violating their principles.

Noelle-Neumann's theory of the spiral of silence focuses on citizens, but we should also ask about elites' vulnerability. Elites are sometimes intentionally unresponsive to majoritarian pressures in those cases when they believe there is a higher principle to be preserved—most remarkably in the flag-burning issue. In many cases, however, elected officials seek information about their constituents' beliefs. If this information is skewed by the impact of pressures on citizens for social conformity, the media coverage of vivid information (which may be) orchestrated by mobilized groups, and direct lobbying by unrepresentative groups, political elites may also be swept into a spiral of silence.

Both democratic responsiveness and leadership require that elected officials be able to discern public opinion. However, it is not known what decision rules they use to assess public opinion and the weight they give to different sources of information. In the maelstrom of political communication, some officials, under some conditions, resist perceptions of public opinion and prefer to exert their own judgment, whereas other politicians are vulnerable to a spiral of silence. Relationships between public opinion and policy depend on a process in which elected officials make judgments of varying accuracy about constituents' views and combine this information with their principles and assessments of political risks.

In contextualizing public opinion and understanding politics as a communication system, there are a number of sites where listeners and speakers can generate messages and receive sounds. Even if one's vision of democracy insists on independence and leadership among elected officials, those political leaders need to know what the public wants. If clarity is absent and clamor prevails, leaders will not know that they must convince and educate the public about the policy issue and the representatives' political choice. And in views of representation that stress following the popular will, legislators should certainly know what their constituents think.

This chapter has detailed the locations where political communication takes place and can break down. The major speakers and interpreters of the public voice are often the parties with the greatest stake in the outcome. As a result, these participants in public dialogue try to deploy public opinion strategically, as a political resource in their struggles. Most of the public is only the audience to these fights. As Habermas explains it, the public reacts to the stagings put on by others. Key participants study and analyze the political show and spectacles as they try to predict what direction they will take and to plan further strategy. Although a spiral of silence may sometimes take hold and quiet certain citizens, others are less easily cowed. People with robust temperaments and citizens who have solid social support or who have been mobilized by political groups can break through the prevailing mood and speak their mind. Still, the communication system of politics makes it difficult for people to know what other citizens think and for elected representatives to know what the public wants. Interest groups do their best to convince the public and elites that the weight of opinion is on their side, and the media may not report opinion accurately. By plan and by inadvertent habit, the public's voice is muffled.

Methods of Study

Why Study Oliver North?

Although the Iran–contra affair and the resulting scandal were important political events, some readers may wonder why the bulk of this book concentrates on them. I have argued that public opinion should be understood as a strategic resource. But why focus on Oliver North and Iran–contra? They cannot tell us everything about the role of public opinion in the political process, for other situations differ in important ways. In a number of other cases, for example, politics takes place out of public view. When issues are restricted to elite circles, few citizens are aware of unfolding events and the issues at hand, and public opinion is not actively mobilized. Under such circumstances, the media usually pay little attention to the events and do not stage any spectacles. In chapter 7, I describe how the politics of public opinion varies, depending on the mobilization of groups and the type of issue involved. Here I make five claims about why this case is worth studying.

First, the situation of Oliver North in the Iran–contra hearings is well suited to exploring the contextual nature of public opinion. I contend that public opinion is a political resource contested by political actors in concrete historical and political circumstances. In the political echo chamber, it can be hard to hear what the people have said. Although the media often interpret the public's voice, they may not be correct. Case studies can be effective tools for analyzing perceptions and motivations and the reactions to one another of actors in different locales in the system.[57]

Iran–contra and the North hearings generated a great deal of political discussion, polls, citizen action, and media coverage—all parts of a buzzing, confusing mass of shouts, noises, arguments, and talk—that entered the echo chamber. In this book I did not conceptualize public opinion as one variable that had a unique impact on elites but, instead, followed public opinion through the political process as people responded to events through polls, the media analyzed (and perhaps influenced) the public mind, interest groups mobilized supporters to get their voice heard, and elites received information about public opinion. To see how the perception of public opinion was created, I investigated what the public thought, how the media covered public opinion, and what interest groups did to promote their preferred view of public opinion. To see if the perceived public opinion had an impact on Congress, I analyzed what elites did and how they assessed public opinion. Only by following public opinion through various political sites can we understand how it is incorporated into the political process.

Second, North and the Iran–contra hearings provide a superb opportunity to understand how spectacles and stagings are created and the role of public opinion in them. During the hearings, the media often presented the hearings as an occasion of drama, performance, and spectacle. In the following typical report, for example, North is presented as a virtual quick-change artist, able to remove and replace rapidly his different personae: "Virtually overnight, the putative villain of the piece became a freshly minted hero, even though—by his own testimony—North had lied to Congress and shredded documents in directing the Iran–contra operation."[58] North's appearance shows us how, as Habermas argues, public opinion has become a reaction to stagings put on by others. Political figures create personae that the media convey to the largely quiescent public. Much of politics, in Edelman's terms, is a spectacle, full of dramatic devices, villains, and other stock figures.

My third claim is that although in some ways the Iran–contra hearings may be an extreme case, this enables it to serve as an ideal type, which can then be compared with other situations. As one scholar of

Weberian methodology noted, ideal types help scholars "formulate general concepts of the empirical social world and at the same time to retain those elements which are historically interesting, or significant."[59] This approach contributes to social theory as a parsimonious way to understand social and political worlds and can generate theory to guide further research. The North case points to the important factors influencing a perception of public opinion, including symbols, created personae, the media's emphasis on dramatic visual images, and uneven group mobilization. This case also shows how institutional values and tendencies structured the events and the perception of the events, limiting and permitting an impact by public opinion.

My fourth claim is that the Iran–contra hearings are useful because they raise significant issues about rapid responses in democracies. Many of the studies of connections between opinion and political response are of policy areas that evolved over long periods of time. Although this issue has a history, the revelations of the scandal and the hearings themselves took a fairly short time but engendered a great deal of media coverage and political activity. Given the quickness with which the events unfolded, it may have been more difficult for politicians to evaluate what course they should take and to assess public opinion. In addition, rapid action raises the classic question of mob rule versus democratic responsiveness. Although rule by the people necessitates that elected officials be responsive to the public voice, the American constitutional system is based on the idea that political figures should be insulated from sudden shifts. In this case, we can ask how well the system performed.

Fifth, although social scientists can make a unique contribution to society by analyzing particular events, we spend very little time writing in our professional journals about the phenomena we talk about around our dinner tables. As the sociologist Kai Erickson observed, If a future historian looked at social science journals, he or she "would learn almost nothing from those pages about the pivotal events around which the flow of modern history turned; indeed, he may not even learn that they took place at all."[60] Surely, as Erickson argues, it is an important task to help us and our fellow citizens understand what we have lived through.

In the case of the Iran–contra affair, scholars and interested citizens already comprehend some of what happened. We know the basic facts and have explored constitutional issues relating to foreign policy.[61] What seemed to be a storm of public reaction during the testimony is another part of what we experienced, but we do not yet appreciate its nature and effects.

Overview of Methods

To understand the politics of public opinion in the case of Oliver North and the Iran–contra hearings and to cast light on the broader questions about the use of public opinion in politics, the book uses a combination of research methods, including an analysis of survey data, interviews of citizens and elites, a media study, and archival work. Although this mixture of studies and methodologies is not typical, all are needed to show how public opinion is interpreted and heard and how public opinion is employed as a political resource.

Surveys are the most typical source of information about public opinion and have the advantage of providing information about the distribution of opinions in the population. Data from reputable surveys can be compared, so one can examine responses to different questions during the same period or changes in opinion over time. The next chapter uses information from surveys in precisely those ways. Survey data structure what citizens can say, according to predetermined categories, but do not reveal their underlying reasoning. To escape survey-based classifications and better understand the public's views, my analysis of surveys is complemented by in-depth interviews with fifty ideologically diverse individuals. This mix of information about citizens' views, however, does not establish how public opinion is presented, generated, and heard.

Communication in the echo chamber of politics involves multiple interpretations of the public's voice, often advanced by competing groups and elites and carried by the mass media. To assess the media's position in the political communication system, I studied the ways that television news and news magazines framed North and public opinion concerning North. To understand how interest groups tried to influence policy and perceptions of public opinion, I examined group goals and strategies, interviewed group leaders, and drew on archives of organizational materials. For my analysis of how elites heard and reacted to public opinion, I explored the topic with members and staff of the congressional committee that investigated Iran–contra. The following chapters about Oliver North and Iran–contra approach public opinion from particular vantage points, and taking all of them together yields a full picture of the politics of public opinion.

3

Oliver North and the Politics of Hero Creation

The gavel has barely fallen on the last senatorial reproach to North and we already have Ollie dolls, an Ollie video, the "Ollie cut" and Ollie songs (*Hooray for Olliewood, Ollie B. Good*). . . . Turn an inquiry into a spectacle and you cannot protest that the audience is insufficiently attentive to the transcript.

Charles Krauthammer, "Ollie North and the Trajectory of Fame"

Every human being who is not in some way fundamentally cognitively damaged is at least an amateur social theorist.

John Dunn, *Rethinking Modern Political Theory*

Oliver North's testimony at the congressional Iran–contra hearings, if "amateur social theorist" Charles Krauthammer is to believed, showed us a marvelous and frightful political spectacle. Behind this spectacle and enabling its staging lay a complex interaction of culture, psychology, and politics. So far I have argued that public opinion is a strategic political resource used by activists and that citizens' views figure into this largely in response to others' presentations. At the same time, the public opinion that matters is not necessarily equivalent to the public opinion measured in polls. In this chapter, using polling data and an intensive interview study, I analyze citizens' opinions of Oliver North and conclude that there was a considerable amount of ambivalence toward North.

The Contra Aid Fight, Iran–Contra, and Oliver North

Breaking into public consciousness in the fall of 1986, the events known as the Iran–contra affair led to a sharp plunge in President Reagan's popularity, three separate inquiries, a series of trials, lingering questions about George Bush's role as vice president that were raised anew during the waning days of the 1992 presidential election, and the 1992 Christmas Eve pardons by lame duck President George Bush. Even though our picture may never be complete, the investigations and prosecutions yielded a great deal of information, with more fifty thousand pages of depositions, testimony, and documents.[1]

After all this time and information, for most Americans the dramatic high point of the Iran–contra affair was the testimony given by Lieutenant Colonel Oliver North during the summer of 1987. North's appearance before the congressional investigating committee was preceded by a great deal of speculation, and his appearance was the only one that the networks broadcast during the usual soap opera hours. Breaking with their usual custom, vast numbers of citizens paid attention to political news.

The Policies Pursued

Iran–contra encompassed two different scandals in two parts of the world, connected by a set of persons and a trail of money. Iran–contra also raised a shared set of policy and constitutional concerns. In brief, the affair involved (1) the sale of weapons to the Iranian government in order to gain freedom for the American hostages and (2) the use of these funds (and other monies raised from private individuals and other governments) to fund the contras in Nicaragua, after Congress had withheld funds from them. Iran–contra became a major scandal because of the serious issues involved. In the Iranian initiative, President Reagan adopted a course counter to his publicly stated policy against terrorism. In assisting the contras, the executive branch took steps against the explicit will of Congress. Both cases raised questions about the privatization of foreign policy, the poor management of policy when carried out by people not trained for the tasks, secrecy versus democracy, the role of Congress versus the president in foreign policy, the accountability of the president, and the role of the president's White House staff.[2] Oliver North was one of those staff, assigned to the National Security Council (NSC).

Critics of the affair were dismayed by both tracks of covert policy, and many were bothered by the operational role of the NSC's staff. The council was established under the National Security Act of 1947. According to this legislation, the NSC was to be composed of the president, the vice president, and the secretaries of state and defense. The director of the Central Intelligence Agency (CIA) and the chair of the Joint Chiefs of Staff were to serve as advisory members, and the NSC was meant to coordinate information and advise the president on all national security matters. In 1953 President Dwight D. Eisenhower reorganized the NSC. He incorporated the NSC's staff into the Executive Office of the President and transformed the head of staff for the NSC into a national security adviser who had "the task of managing the staff and, in effect, becoming the president's personal foreign-policy coordinator and adviser as well as serving as executive secretary of the NSC."[3] NSC staff members were meant to support this advisory role and were not supposed to carry on diplomatic, military, or intelligence operations. The national security advisers during the Iran–contra events were John Poindexter and Robert (Bud) McFarlane.

As an aide to the national security adviser, Marine Lieutenant Colonel North went beyond the usual NSC staff role and was involved in both phases of Iran–contra. Thus it is not surprising that the media and political actors focused a great deal on North's activities. But as Peter Kornbluh and Malcolm Byrne point out, "Iran–Contra Mythology has erroneously cast North as a veritable lone ranger within the Reagan administration; he was the central figure, but he did not run the . . . program alone."[4]

The U.S. government also had dealings with Iran, a nation that many Americans loved to hate. Following the Iranian revolution and the entry of the shah of Iran into the United States for medical treatment, the Iranian revolutionary guard seized the U.S. embassy in Tehran and held the embassy staff hostage. Scenes of Iranians chanting "Death to America" and burning American flags filled the airwaves. ABC launched a late news program (which eventually evolved into *Nightline*) that covered the hostage crisis nightly. The hostage crisis and the subsequent failed rescue attempt severely hurt President Jimmy Carter's reelection bid. Finally, as Ronald Reagan was being sworn in as the new president, the remaining fifty-two hostages were released. Later, however, additional Americans were taken hostage in Lebanon by terrorist groups with ties to fundamentalist Iran. In response, President Reagan's State Department labeled Iran a terrorist nation and launched an international arms control effort named Operation Staunch. "A steady stream of protests went out from Washington to countries known or suspected to have made such sales, including South Korea, Italy, Portugal, China, and Israel. . . . The watchwords were: No deals with terrorists, no bargaining for hostages, no compromise with blackmail."[5]

Despite this history, the hard-line position was undermined by President Reagan's desire to free the American hostages and by his administration officials' arguments that military aid to Iran could help establish better relations, lead to the freeing of the hostages, and support moderate groups in the Iranian political leadership. Over the objections of the secretaries of defense and state, President Reagan approved a policy in which arms were covertly delivered to Iran. Private individuals—not all U.S. citizens—were used to make contacts, assist in negotiations, and arrange arms transfers. These private agents received substantial profits for the arms sales and their other activities. As a result of these activities, three hostages were freed, but others were taken. No wonder that during the Iran–contra hearings, Secretary of State George Shultz testified that "our guys, . . . they got taken to the cleaners."[6] In addition, contrary to statutory requirements, the administration never informed congressional intelligence committees about this operation.

While the Iranian initiative contradicted the Reagan administration's explicit policy, support for the contras' effort to overthrow the Nicaraguan government was quite public. Indeed, the Reagan administration devoted a good deal of effort to try to convince the public and Congress to grant aid to the Nicaraguan contras. Following the Nicaraguan revolution in 1979, the Carter administration sought to help Nicaraguan moderates and maintain a trusting relationship with the Nicaraguan government. In May 1980, President Carter signed legislation to send $75 million of economic aid to Nicaragua. After his inauguration, President Reagan quickly reversed this policy. In February 1981, Reagan suspended the final $15 million of the aid, citing the relationship between the ruling Sandinista Party and the Soviet Union and Cuba, as well as the flow of arms from Nicaragua to the rebels in El Salvador. By November 1981, President Reagan decided that the Nicaraguan government should be overthrown, and in 1982 the CIA took increasing responsibility for training and coordinating an armed force.[7] While the administration was telling Congress and the American people that the United States was only trying to interdict arms, a November 1982 *Newsweek* story about CIA activities and other occasional press accounts told otherwise.

Following reports of U.S. involvement in efforts to overthrow the Sandinista government in Nicaragua, Congress acted to restrict such activities. On December 21, 1982, Congress passed an amendment to its defense appropriations, which later became known as Boland I. Sponsored by Representative Edward Boland of Massachusetts,

Boland I barred the CIA and the Defense Department from using funds to try to overthrow the Sandinista regime or to provoke a military conflict between Nicaragua and Honduras. Boland I was in effect until December 1983, when the House and Senate agreed to a $24 million cap on funding for the contras, an amount that was expected to last for less than a full year. In April 1984, press reports revealed that the CIA was involved in mining the harbors of Nicaragua. Feeling angry and misled, Congress rejected further funding for the contras in late June 1984 and passed a more restrictive Boland amendment (Boland II) in October 1984. Boland II prohibited the use of any money from the CIA, the Department of Defense, or "any other agency or entity of the United States involved in intelligence activities" for "the purpose or which would have the effect of supporting, directly or indirectly, military or paramilitary operations in Nicaragua by any nation, group, organization, movement, or individual."[8] Boland II's provisions were so clear and broad that both supporters and opponents of the amendment agreed that its passage effectively terminated U.S. support for the contras.[9]

Later Congress restored the funding, with nonmilitary aid voted in June 1985 and military aid resumed in June 1986. However, for the years that legislators refused to grant money, the Reagan administration found itself stymied. President Reagan had characterized the contras as "freedom fighters" struggling against an oppressive communist regime. Although Congress had prohibited U.S. aid, in 1984 Reagan advised National Security Adviser McFarlane to keep the contras together "body and soul."[10] Thus began the contra phase of the Iran–contra affair. Orchestrated through the NSC staff, with Marine Lieutenant Colonel Oliver North playing a crucial role, these operatives advised the contras, passed along intelligence information, used CIA assets, and raised money from American citizens and third-party nations. In addition, NSC staff worked with a "public diplomacy" campaign that wrote opinion pieces and other "white propaganda" and engaged in public relations efforts to change the climate of opinion and therefore influence Congress.[11]

To camouflage contra funds flowing from NSC staff–coordinated sources, advertisements were placed in U.S. newspapers in July 1984 calling for donations from the American people. Another aspect— which proved the most dramatic once the Iran–contra affair was revealed—was the diversion of Iranian arms sale profits to Swiss bank accounts for support of the contras.[12]

The Revelation of the Affair and the Initial Investigation

Press coverage of the arms sales to Iran and U.S. funding of the contras came to a boil in November 1986. Although North's involvement with the contras was first reported in June 1985,[13] press interest did not intensify until Eugene Hasenfus, an American citizen, was shot down during an October 5, 1986, crash of a contra resupply plane. U.S. officials, including the assistant secretary of state for Inter-American affairs, Elliott Abrams, vociferously and falsely denied any government involvement with Hasenfus.[14] The Iranian initiative was revealed in a Lebanese weekly, *Al-Shiraa*, on November 3, 1986, and was quickly picked up by Western news services. As Iran–contra began to unravel, the White House began to cover up. National Security Adviser Poindexter

> ordered the preparation of a chronological narrative soon after the appearance of the *Al-Shiraa* story. As usual, he put North in charge, telling him only to leave out all mention of the diversion of Iran funds to the Nicaraguan contras. The production of this chronology is of special interest because it confronted North and others with an awkward dilemma—if they told the truth, they risked admitting to unlawful acts, and if they told untruths, they might not be able to sustain them if they were looked into, especially by Congressional committees. . . . North, with the help of a few others, wrote and rewrote the chronology at least a dozen times between November 5 and November 20 [and] tried to hide or distort some aspects of the story.[15]

By November 13, President Reagan was forced to reply directly to the stories about arms sales to Iran. Reagan took to the airwaves and denied that the administration had been involved with an "arms-for-hostages" trade. With the questions continuing and his credibility strained, the president held a press conference on November 19 that proved contentious and settled nothing. Outside the public eye, Secretary of State Shultz quickly moved to investigate the NSC's covert activities after the first public disclosures. The State Department's legal adviser, Abraham D. Sofaer, was drawn into White House meetings intended to coordinate information for the president. Although Sofaer had no previous knowledge of the Iran initiative or other elements of the affair, he quickly grew suspicious about certain parts of the story. On November 20, Sofaer contacted Assistant Attorney General Charles J. Cooper to tell him that he saw problems with the account expressed in North's chronology and in proposed congressional testimony for CIA Chief William Casey and that a cover-up seemed to be developing. Iran–contra chronicler Draper contends that "if Sofaer had not been so determined to expose the suspected cover-up, there is no reason to believe that it might not have succeeded—at least for a time."[16]

In his November 19 press conference, President Reagan announced that he had asked Attorney General Edwin Meese to carry out an internal probe. In conducting this inquiry, Meese did not bring in investigators from the criminal division of the Justice Department, nor did he seal offices to secure records. Thus with no one to watch or stop him, Oliver North began to shred documents, conducting what he later called a "shredding party." But North did not destroy all that he had wished, and on November 22, 1986, aides to Attorney General Meese found what has been termed the *diversion memo*. This memorandum, dated April 4, 1986, detailed a link between the Iranian arms sales and aid to the contras. The amount of $12 million in "residual funds" were to "purchase critically needed supplies for the Democratic Resistance Forces" and to "bridge the period between now and when Congressionally approved lethal assistance . . . can be delivered."[17] On November 25, President Reagan and Attorney General Meese held a news conference and revealed the diversion.

Reagan and Meese also claimed that they had not known about the diversion until quite recently, and that the arrangements had been carried out and supervised by North and Poindexter. The destruction of documents made it impossible to establish whether the president had known. North later claimed he believed the president knew, but acknowledged he had destroyed potential proof. Poindexter claimed that Reagan was not informed of the diversion. Many argued that presidential ignorance, if it had occurred, was nearly as troubling a situation as presidential involvement in the diversion operation. This revelation ended North's career on the NSC staff. Poindexter privately resigned as national security adviser earlier that day.

Publicity about the Iran–contra dealings quickly led to a series of investigations. On November 26, the Reagan administration appointed the Tower Commission, composed of John Tower, Brent Scowcroft, and Edmund Muskie. Released on February 26, 1987, the Tower Commission's report concluded that the Reagan administration suffered from a poor administrative structure. The NSC had gone beyond its charge and had thereby badly performed both its original and adopted missions. Poor process had led to inadequate advice, faulty policy implementation, and insufficient review. NSC staff, such as Oliver North, were not trained in diplomacy or intelligence but had carried out tasks in those areas.

North worked with "individuals with questionable credentials and potentially large personal financial interests. . . . The result was a very unprofessional operation."[18] If only the correct process had been followed, the commission concluded, Iran–contra would have never happened. The Tower Commission insisted that law and prudent administration require oversight by and coordination with the CIA and the Departments of State and Defense, as well as consultation with Congress.

The Congressional Hearings and Investigation

Congress carried out the second major investigation. Acting quickly, the joint House–Senate Investigating Committee was named in mid-December 1986. In an attempt to wrap up its inquiry in short order, the committee chose to complete its work by a predetermined deadline. As a result, the committee was unable to pursue all leads as fully as it might have. The committee heard its first public witness, retired General Richard Secord, in early May 1987 and ended its hearings on August 6. During that time, there were plenty of fireworks, most of them supplied by the young marine NSC staffer Oliver North.

By the time North appeared before the committee, he was already a recognizable media figure. President Reagan had essentially fired North over national television at the press conference announcing the diversion. Then, only several weeks later, President Reagan told a journalist that North was a national hero. Extensive media speculation preceded North's July 1987 testimony, with much of it focused on the question of whether North was a "loose cannon" who had instigated the Iran–contra programs himself or whether he had followed orders from above. Since this latter possibility suggested that the president himself had known of or even commanded the operations, North's testimony had important political implications. Given the stakes, journalists questioned whether North would tell the truth, and pollsters asked citizens whether they believed North would lie or tell all.

In his testimony from July 7 to 14, North declared that he would indeed tell the truth—"the good, the bad, and the ugly," according to his opening statement. North also admitted that he had shredded documents and had previously lied to Congress about his activities. In an unrepentant defense, he proclaimed that his activities were for a good cause. North stated that he had always believed he was acting under the authority of the commander in chief and that the president was the supreme institutional actor in foreign policy. Furthermore, while he had been willing to be the political fall guy, he had never anticipated facing legal charges if the covert policies were revealed. In a dramatic moment, Oliver North disclosed that he and CIA Director Casey tried to create an "off-the-shelf, self-sustaining, stand-alone" foreign policy capability, run with private funds by public employees and private parties. Once developed, the executive branch would be able to use this creation—the Enterprise—and would thus avoid congressional restraints on the president's foreign policy.

Oliver North emerged from the hearings a celebrity. Dressed in full uniform and by all accounts photogenic, his appearance provoked numerous phone calls and telegrams to Congress. Although his words revealed past lies, his cracking voice and proud stance carried a different message. As political scientist James David Barber put it at the time, North "arouses the feeling of candor."[19] By the end of the hearings, the Senate committee chairman, Daniel Inouye, told North, "In the past week, I believe we have participated in creating and developing a new American hero."[20]

In a headlong dash to meet their self-imposed deadline,[21] the congressional committee released its report on November 18, 1987. The majority report was signed by all committee Democrats and three of five Senate Republicans, and a minority report was issued by all House Republicans and two Senate Republicans. Although some of their criticisms echoed the Tower Commission's concerns, the majority report's conclusions focused on constitutional issues.[22] In funding the contras through private sources, the administration had invaded the constitutional prerogatives of the legislative branch. The report read:

> Because the President's program depended upon providing financial assistance to the Contras, appropriations bills became the forum for debating what the Nation's policy should be. . . . The Constitution contemplates that the Government will conduct its affairs only with funds appropriated by Congress. . . . The Framers were determined not to combine the power of the purse and the power of the sword in the same branch of government.[23]

Maintaining that the Constitution gives the legislative branch an important role in foreign policy, the majority report castigated the administration for withholding information. Both North and former National Security Adviser Poindexter had testified that they did not want "outside interference" in their jobs, and according to them, members of Congress were outsiders. This attitude led North and Poindexter (among others) to restrict Congress's access to information about policy matters and thus limited its ability to act as a check on the executive

branch. When members of Congress directly asked administration officials if the government was involved in helping the contras when such
assistance was prohibited, the officials did not give them accurate
answers. The executive branch did not use established systems of sharing information about covert activities. Because North destroyed documents, certain facts might never be known.

The majority report acknowledged that it was a challenge to balance
the goal of democratic accountability with the necessity for secrecy in
matters of national security. Despite these difficulties, the majority
argued that it was essential to maintain a line of control between covert
activities and elected legislators. Thus North's efforts to establish an
unaccountable, privatized covert apparatus greatly disturbed the majority. The majority report concluded, "The scheme, taken as a whole, to
raise money to conduct a secret Contra-support capacity (the Enterprise) operating as an appendage to the NSC staff violated cardinal principles of the Constitution."[24]

In response, the minority report rejected some of the majority's facts
and all of its basic critique. The minority cast doubt on North's claim
that former CIA chief Casey wanted to create a privatized covert capability, calling it a possible speculation by Casey and "an uncorroborated,
disputed North statement that happens to fit [the majority's] political
purpose." Although it acknowledged that the policies pursued in the
Iran–contra affair were mistaken, these acts were "mistakes in judgment,
and nothing more."[25] Furthermore, the errors leading to the unfortu-
nate policies were not the executive branch's alone.

> A substantial number of the mistakes of the Iran–Contra Affair resulted
> directly from an ongoing state of political guerrilla warfare over foreign
> policy between the legislative and executive branches. We would include
> in this category the excessive secrecy of the Iran initiative that resulted
> from a history and legitimate fear of leaks. We also would include the
> approach both branches took toward the so-called Boland Amendments.
> Congressional Democrats tried to use vaguely worded and constantly
> changing laws to impose policies in Central America that went beyond
> the law itself. For its own part, the Administration decided to work
> within the letter of the law covertly, instead of forcing a public and prin-
> cipled confrontation that would have been healthier in the long run.[26]

Legal Aspects of Iran–Contra

The third major investigation of Iran–contra, conducted by Independent
Counsel Lawrence Walsh, started quickly but did not release its final

report until seven years after the initial revelations. President Reagan asked for an investigation by a special prosecutor on December 2, 1986, and Walsh was named to the post by a three-judge panel on December 19, 1986. On April 29, 1987, the first prosecution was secured. Carl "Spitz" Channell entered a guilty plea to conspiracy to defraud the United States with his tax-exempt foundation to raise money for the contras.

By the time Walsh had completed his work, fourteen persons had been charged with criminal acts. President Bush pardoned Secretary of Defense Casper Weinberger and CIA officer Duane Clarridge before they went to trial and after the president's defeat in the 1992 election. Twelve were convicted. Oliver North was found guilty of three felonies: altering and destroying documents (i.e., shredding documents), accepting an illegal gratuity (a security fence for his home, paid for by Secord and Hakim, who had greatly profited from the arms sales), and aiding and abetting in obstructing congressional inquiries (preparing the false chronology). The prosecutions were stymied, however, by two main factors besides the pardon. First, many defendants argued that they needed classified documents to mount a proper defense. Procedures established under the Classified Information Procedures Act of 1980 allowed for the review of classified information by the government and the court. Under this law, material could be declassified and introduced in court; it could be deemed irrelevant and not used in trial; or its disclosure could be forbidden. If this last step were taken, charges could be dismissed if the judge believed that this limitation of evidence threatened the defendant's right to a fair trial. In fact, a CIA official's case was dismissed because the documents to be used at trial were not declassified. Document problems also led the independent counsel to drop two charges[27] against North— a broad conspiracy charge focusing on planned breaches of the Boland amendments[28] and another pertaining to the diversion of funds from the Iranian arms sales to the contras.

Second, problems associated with immunized congressional testimony influenced the independent counsel's investigation procedures, the grand jury process, and the selection of the trial jury, and they ultimately led to reversals of North's and Poindexter's convictions. Legal dealings with witnesses were broadly governed by a 1972 case, *Kastigar v. United States*, which protected immunized witnesses from prosecution. North and others were to testify under immunity to Congress during the spring and summer of 1987, and Independent Counsel Walsh knew that none of these witnesses' statements could be used in their likely prosecutions. After considering indicting them before they gave their immunized congressional testimony, Walsh instead decided to lay out case summaries in memos delivered under seal to the U.S. District Court for the District of Columbia, develop the cases further, and use procedures to prevent exposing the investigators to immunized testimony. Despite these precautions, North's May 1989 guilty verdicts were set aside in a July 1990 ruling by two members of a three-judge federal appeals court. The majority ruled that the trial judge had not assessed whether the witnesses' memories of events had been influenced by North's immunized testimony. To uphold the verdicts, the trial judge needed to determine that no testimony had been affected and could do so only by conducting a "witness-by-witness," "line-by-line and item-by-item" review of the trial transcript. The dissenting opinion noted that North's counsel "cannot point to a single instance of alleged witness testimony tainted by exposure to North's immunized testimony" and that this ruling "makes a subsequent trial of any congressionally immunized witness virtually impossible." According to Walsh's final report, "Independent Counsel concluded that satisfaction of the court of appeals' requirements would be both very difficult and enormously burdensome"; thus no further steps were taken and the dismissal of North's verdicts stood.[29]

Even after the time and energy devoted to Iran–contra, many people felt that the issue had not been resolved. Draper observed that the affair left lots of "unfinished business" in constitutional matters.[30] Legal scholar Koh concluded:

> None of the investigators squarely addressed the constitutional question of who decides. The Tower commission dodged the question because it viewed its function as one of reinforcing, not challenging, executive prerogative. The House and Senate select committees raised the issue but left it buried amid their single-minded search for facts. The independent counsel considered the question but was forced by pursuit of convictions to put it to one side.[31]

Serious constitutional issues were involved in Reagan's Iranian and contra policies. But the experience of confronting the Iran–contra affair poses another, nonconstitutional challenge to our democratic politics.

In particular, the public reaction and the perceived citizen response raise questions about the construction and use of public opinion and the role of legislators in listening to constituents' voices. If various political institutions and organizations have a shared interest in creating spectacles and personae, they can help develop situations that provoke emotional and biased responses or help create the appearance of strong reactions. What happened with Oliver North at the hearings? Did his testimony move the public to embrace him as their hero?

Oliver North and the Politics of Hero Creation

President Ronald Reagan started all the talk about whether Oliver North was heroic. In a *Time* interview published on December 8, 1986, the president ventured that North was a hero, thus offering a conceptual tool put to use by diverse individuals. Pundits and reporters, members of Congress, pollsters, political leaders, and North's lawyer regularly referred to questions about North's heroism. Public discourse about North became inextricably linked with the question of whether he was in fact heroic or a hero to the American people. (See chapter 4 for an analysis of the media coverage and the hero frame and for further discussion of the Reagan administration's characterizations of North.) Since North was not a well-known figure when the Iran–contra affair broke into public consciousness, his image was malleable. Oliver North the person thus could easily become Oliver North the persona, a stereotyped figure, stripped down and simplified.

Although Reagan's application of the label *hero* could not shield North, the debate over his heroic status constituted a political resource for North and his supporters. If Americans did view North as a hero, then the media and elected officials needed to take this into account. In creating this persona, the public was given a predetermined frame to judge North and react to him. The hero frame directed citizens' attention to particular characteristics, and North's team deliberately packaged his presentation in order to take advantage of the power of this persona. As Habermas's analysis predicts, constructions of public opinion were not active but, rather, reactive to the staging presented to the public.

Culture and Conversation

My argument here is that the power of the hero frame for creating North's personae arose from two dynamics. First, discourse about North's possible heroism was an expression of understandings and symbolic meanings in American political culture. Second, evaluations of North were influenced by the difficulty in distinguishing between performance and reality in contemporary American political culture.

Hero figures are potent symbols in cultures, as they express what is most admired and esteemed. North's advantage was that he could cast himself in the mold of a powerful and available cultural symbol. As I noted when discussing the prototype conversation in chapter 2, the participants in any conversation must have some common ground. The speakers and listeners in every conversation must assume they share certain understandings, and these commonalities can be targeted by the speakers as they make their arguments. Those who share a culture have a commonsense knowledge of the lenses that others use to see the world.

The concept of culture that I use here has structural, limiting elements and individualistic, voluntaristic aspects.[32] On the one hand, cultural meaning systems make or constitute people's understandings. As Geertz put it, the human being is "an animal suspended in webs of significance he himself has spun," and culture is "those webs."[33] People create institutions, rituals, and ways of life that express meaning and provide the structures through which they live out their understandings of the world.

Even in American culture—one of the most diverse nations on the earth—there are shared celebrations that help create a political culture and civil society. The Fourth of July, for example, is still associated with parades, fireworks, and ceremonies honoring veterans. Families and communities picnic together on the Fourth, marking the nation's birthday, the summer season, and a day off from work. I do not argue that everyone who watches a parade or enjoys a barbecue on the Fourth does so with a deep sense of love for the nation. However, involvement in common activities brings people together and reminds them of their national identity. A shared identity and culture is also constituted through commemorations (e.g., for the nation's bicentennial), monuments, holidays (including new ones such as Martin Luther King Jr.'s birthday), and the education system.

Cultural institutions and rituals may be quite contentious. For instance, recent celebrations of Columbus Day have been marked by controversy, and the effort to make Martin Luther King Jr.'s birthday a state and national holiday was not without disagreement. But the very fact that people care enough to protest or to attempt to maintain or create a holiday demonstrates the power of these celebrations and commemorations.[34] In fact, the vitality of a cultural tradition can often be read by the amount of controversy that can be created by attempts to change or modify it. Cultural institutions and symbols set the parameters for agreement or disagreement. Individuals' action or inaction can be interpreted only within those institutions and structures that make up and have meaning in and for the culture.

The second view of culture that I use focuses on the choices that people make as they recreate or challenge cultural structures and institutions. Cultural structures are constituted by individual actions, and people's actions maintain or undermine those institutions. There can be, for example, no institution of marriage without two persons' deciding to marry, buying a license, and taking vows. However, in the wedding ceremony itself and in the marriage, people make many choices—about sharing or dividing work in the household, taking married names or keeping their previous names, to name a few—that determine what sort of marriage they will have. If many people choose not to get married or make novel choices within their marriage, after a while the institution of marriage will look different.

In this sense, culture is "more like a 'tool kit' or repertoire from which actors select differing pieces for constructing lines of action."[35] Within the culture, people have available certain linguistic resources. For example, in political (and other) discourse, political actors can draw on particular concepts to develop their strategies and lines of action. In abortion politics, for instance, one side wishes to define abortion as a question of choice, and the other tries to construct it as a matter of protecting innocent life. Both choice and life are powerful symbols. Decisions to emphasize one rather than the other are politically motivated, strategic choices, made with a knowledge of cultural orientations.

Besides determining which concept they will use to anchor their argument, political actors strategize which conceptual meaning they will use. Political concepts do not have a single meaning but are, in Gallie's phrase, "essentially contested."[36] Patriotism, for example, remains a vital concept, but its meanings include loyalty to government authorities and active, principled criticism and civic action. Political leaders may emphasize one meaning over others, depending on their assessment of what the concept means to citizens and on the likelihood that their opponents will be able to mount an effective conceptual challenge. For example, the Republican Party's appeal to emotional and symbolic forms of patriotism contributed to George Bush's success in the 1988 presidential election.[37]

Determining whether a cultural symbol will work in a political strategy is by no means an exact science. Schudson sees the power of cultural symbols as depending on five factors: retrievability, rhetorical force, resonance, institutional retention, and resolution. A cultural symbol is retrievable if it can be easily accessed for use, and this depends on both cognitive availability and physical accessibility. The decision to commemorate Martin Luther King Jr.'s birthday, for example, put this date on calendars and made King's work and ideas a more retrievable part of our culture. "Making a cultural object physically present and cognitively memorable may become a matter of political strategy."[38]

Rhetorical force comes from such factors such as drama, vividness, and the ability to grab an audience's attention. In part, a symbol's rhetorical force is dependent on what else is in the field. If a vivid appeal is situated with less interesting or less evocative ones, the more vivid one is likely to have more rhetorical force. Yet the more vivid object will not influence everyone in the same way. Some people might even be repulsed by certain florid or broadly drawn symbolic appeals.[39]

If an audience easily connects with a cultural symbol, then that symbol has resonance. As Schudson points out, "For producers of mass media culture, the issue of 'resonance' will be experienced as a central problem. Whether a new television show, book, or record album will be a 'hit' is notoriously difficult for the 'culture industry' to predict."[40] Political strategists face a similar problem. In election campaigns, campaign managers must draw on past experience and any other available data to figure out how to make the candidate a "hit."[41] Sometimes campaign appeals are less substantive proposals and more symbolic signals to the electorate about the candidate. Little real policy substance, for example, was ever involved in the pledge-of-allegiance issue of the 1988 presidential election. Instead, Bush's use of the issue signaled his cultural stance to the electorate.

A symbol is more powerful in a culture if institutions help promote and maintain the symbol. The educational system tries to socialize citizens and schools prioritize certain symbols and historical figures. The military systematically uses rituals and symbolic badges to express hierarchy and authority and to promote valued qualities such as bravery in combat. Given the regularity of cultural innovation, institutional retention effectively preserves symbols. Finally, a symbol can have greater effect if it directs the audience to do something. By pointing to a particular resolution, the cultural form may have greater influence than would a diffuse symbol that offers little direction.

Oliver North and Heroism as Cultural Symbols

The dual nature of cultural symbols enabled North and his supporters to use heroism as a political resource. Each culture has shared stories, narratives, and hero figures. In the American political culture, heroism remains a vital concept. Competing hero visions in the United States include pragmatic trailblazers, activists for social change, the founding fathers, private caregivers, and military figures.[42] No single vision of heroism has dominated all others, and different groups in the public endorse particular views of heroic action. Given our cultural legacy of hero figures, political actors try to construct stories that resonate with the public. Because culture and cultural symbols are both historically structured and capable of being strategically mobilized, North and his supporters were able to use preexisting notions of heroism for their benefit.

North's hero story was in part a classic one and in part one based on certain American perspectives. Joseph Campbell showed that all cultures have some version of a classic hero tale.[43] The hero or heroine sallies forth from home, confronts something dangerous, and returns transformed. Part of what North experienced and told about his life contained some of those aspects. He was involved in a serious car accident while a student at the U.S. Naval Academy but then went on to win the school's boxing championship. After North's marriage nearly collapsed, he was treated for depression, but when he recovered, he returned to his duties. Soon after, North experienced severe back pain, but with his battalion commander, he prayed to God and was healed. North therefore decided that God was telling him, "I had been taking credit for all the things I had been able to do over the years, but I didn't deserve it, any of it. The message He had been sending was *put your faith in Me.*"[44] During his work in the White House, North felt special and indispensable. He stayed with the NSC despite advice to go to the Naval War College in order to advance in the marines; he resisted attempts to be transferred to become a battalion commander; and he told false stories about his close contacts with President Reagan and top administration officials.[45] North cast the Iran–contra investigation as a dangerous voyage in which he (armed with his lawyer) ventured into Congress's den to do combat.[46] North's personality, vigorous work habits, and stalwart and confrontational demeanor helped give him and these symbols rhetorical power.

North was also able to use the powerful hero symbols of the American armed forces. Although he never worked in uniform while at the White House, he wore it every day during the hearings. Mr. North referred to his military service, held the stance of a soldier, and argued as a soldier. He called himself "this marine" and "this lieutenant colonel." North worked for the National Security Council, an entity outside the Department of Defense that was made up of appointed and elected officials. Yet instead of claiming he received authority for his actions from the head of the executive branch, North claimed that his actions were guided by the orders of the commander in chief. These strategic choices placed North in a military context and gave him access to potent cultural symbols. As I noted earlier, military symbols have an institutionalized basis. In addition, they are accessible to many and can therefore resonate with the audience. One irony of this is that many senior officers were not moved by North's summoning of military symbols.[47]

Another heroic theme heard repeatedly was that Oliver North stood squarely in the American tradition of pragmatic risk takers, whether entrepreneurs or settlers like Daniel Boone. For example, R. W. Apple Jr. wrote in the *New York Times* that Oliver North epitomized the "underdog, true believer, one man against the crowd: there was a lot of Gary Cooper in him, the lonesome cowboy, a lot of Jimmy Stewart, too, the honest man facing down the politicians, and quite a bit of Huck Finn."[48] North and his lawyer, Brendan Sullivan, worked to create this simple, dramatic figure within a narrative structure. Given the cultural materials available to them, North made strategic choices to use such symbols to promote his cause.

Oliver North's hero persona was highly gendered and archetypically masculine; he was concerned with safeguarding his country and household and was willing to engage in individual combat to do so. On the one hand, North was a "paramilitary" hero who "became known as a man who personally fought duels with the evil ones."[49] In this vein, he told congressional committee members that he would be willing to go "man to man" with terrorist Abu Nidal. But North also proclaimed that he realized that any personal soldiering would not be enough to protect his family. Therefore, to fulfill his domestic manly duty, North had accepted a $13,800 security system from Secord and Hakim, "who stood to make millions of dollars from the deals in which North engaged them."[50] North reinforced his image as protective husband and family man by sitting with his wife behind him and standing with her when acknowledging supporters.

So far this discussion has not considered whether the audience in fact was captivated by North's strategic use of the hero persona. Nor have I explored whether the message resonated with one particular segment of the population. To answer these questions, I examined data on public views on North, and these are presented later in this chapter. In a certain way, however, the question itself tells us something about the development of public opinion regarding North. People were faced with the issue of whether North was a hero, and on this basis, they were asked to acclaim or refuse to acclaim him. Even this definition—whether one agreed or disagreed—had consequences for structuring how the public saw North and how others assessed public opinion.

Performing as a Hero

I have argued that the public could react meaningfully to North and questions about him in terms of the hero frame because the form of heroism attributed to North had cultural roots and continued vitality. But the public's views of North in terms of heroism also had meaning because the public and the media could assess North as someone who *portrayed* a hero well. As Daniel Boorstin noted more than thirty years ago, people in American society have found it increasingly difficult to distinguish between matters of substance and performance. One aspect of this confusion is that heroes cannot be easily recognized as fundamentally different from celebrities. In 1961, Boorstin wrote:

> Celebrity-worship and hero-worship should not be confused. Yet we confuse them every day, and by doing so we come dangerously close to depriving ourselves of all real models. We lose sight of the men and women who do not simply seem great because they are famous but who are famous because they are great. We come closer and closer to degrading all fame into notoriety.[51]

Boorstin cautioned that pseudoevents could drive out matters of real substance, that heroes might be replaced by celebrities, and that political discourse could be reduced to performance.

In an innovative study conducted during the summer of 1987, sociologist Nina Eliasoph explored citizens' reactions to Oliver North and found many who judged him as a performer. Eliasoph stopped people in public locations, told them that she was interviewing for a radio documentary, and asked them their opinion about Colonel North. (As Eliasoph rightly noted, her method cannot be said to have produced a representative sample. She was, however, able to elicit responses that could not be accommodated by a standard survey.) Many responses strongly suggested a confusion between a reality and performance. One man, for example, told Eliasoph, "News is not my favorite show. Oliver North is not my favorite star." And another person said,

> I like the way Oliver North handled himself in front of his peers and the people judging him. He handles himself maturely and with respect—I'd like to say honestly, but who knows? I like the way he's handling himself.

When I see people like Admiral Poindexter getting up there smoking his pipe like he's sitting in his house—it's too casual for me.

As Eliasoph remarked about the second comment, "Without rancor, he might have been discussing the staging of a play."[52]

What Eliasoph heard is consistent with Habermas's view that the public has become essentially an audience and with Boorstin's analysis of the confusion between celebrity and hero. As a public figure in American political culture, North was able to benefit from two strong cultural dynamics: he could appeal to symbols with real power, and he could be judged as a capable performer.

In fact, the current political culture suited North's performance and performative competence quite well. Electoral coverage often focuses on how well candidates have projected the proper image, rather than on a substantive analysis of issues. The pseudoevents Boorstin wrote about in 1961—staged events and debates between candidates—are now taken for granted and are evaluated by the media for their persuasive potential.[53]

Public Views of North

Survey Data

Soon after the Iran–contra affair burst into the news in November 1986, survey researchers began to ask citizens what they thought about the affair and the primary participants. Pollsters first found rather negative reactions to President Reagan, the revelations, and North. As the events unfolded, however, citizens showed increasingly complex and ambivalent responses.

Ronald Reagan devoted a good deal of presidential effort to the contra cause. Yet despite strong presidential approval ratings, Reagan's consistent philosophical basis for supporting the contras (rooted in cold-war anticommunism), and a massive victory in the 1984 electoral vote, he was never able to persuade the public to support the contras. In fact, evidence from polls suggest that Central America policy issues never really engaged the public enough for anyone's arguments to penetrate their consciousness. Citizens had a fairly hazy view of issues, often finding it difficult to distinguish the El Salvador situation (in which the Reagan administration supported the government over the rebels) from events in Nicaragua (in which Reagan supported armed opponents of the government). Even though more than three-quarters of Americans stated that they had "read or heard about" the war and fighting in El Salvador and Nicaragua, at best only about half knew which side the U.S. government supported. In 1986, only 38 percent of those persons polled could identify the contras as the group the U.S. government supported in Nicaragua. Even after more than eight months of extensive news coverage of the Iran–contra affair and following Oliver North's July testimony to Congress, in August 1987 only 54 percent knew that the United States supported "the rebels trying to overthrow the government in Nicaragua."[54]

When asked what they thought about various policy options under different hypothetical conditions, Americans expressed a distaste of intervention in other nations' affairs, except when faced with serious national security threats. About half of those surveyed (55 percent in May 1984 and 48 percent in March 1986) agreed that all steps should be used to "prevent the spread of communism in Central America."[55] But usually when asked about the use of American soldiers, very few were willing to commit American forces. Even if the Soviet Union set up missile bases in Nicaragua, only 52 percent of those Americans asked in December 1986 would support sending troops.[56] Support for helping the contras moved little, usually remaining between 25 and 38 percent. Other events caused "rally" effects, with support for the contras rising after the November 1983 invasion of Grenada, the March 1986 raid on Libya, and the March 1988 deployment of troops to Honduras. North's testimony to Congress also led to a transitory increase in support for the contras, with movement to an all-time high of 43 percent. But after each of these four incidents, public support declined soon after.[57]

The public reacted to the Iran–contra affair with strong disapproval, with particular dislike of the Iranian initiative. According to a July 1987 *U.S. News & World Report* poll, 81 percent of the public were upset about "selling arms to Iran after Iranians held U.S. Embassy personnel hostage for over a year"; 80 percent were upset that North and others destroyed evidence and shredded documents; 80 percent also were upset about unelected officials' making foreign policy without the public's or Congress's knowledge; and 70 percent were upset about sending "profits from the arms sales to the Contras in violation of Congress's ban on aid to the contras."[58] A July 1987 *Time* magazine poll found two-to-one margins against selling arms to Iran for release of the hostages, diverting funds to the contras, and concealing Nicaraguan and Iranian operations from Congress.[59]

Following disclosures of the affair, President Reagan's popularity ratings quickly fell. According to one source, Reagan's approval dropped from 67 to 46 percent during the month of November 1986, the largest single drop for a president.[60] His disapproval ratings increased as well, with a sharp increase in early November after the first revelations.[61] During most of November Reagan had about 32 percent disapproval. On November 28, Attorney General Meese announced that the administration was investigating events. A further rise followed, with an average of 39 percent disapproval through January. By June 1987, Reagan's disapproval ratings stood at 48 percent. The public also grew increasingly distrustful of the president's contention that he did not know about the diversion of funds from the Iranians to the contras. Between February and May 1987, the number of Americans who believed Mr. Reagan had lied rose from 47 percent to 59 percent. When asked what should be done if it were discovered that Reagan had approved of the diversion, in July 1987 only 7 percent said the president should be congratulated; 41 percent called for a reprimand; and 26 percent wanted him to be impeached.[62]

The Iran–contra affair changed the way that citizens assessed Reagan.[63] Before the affair, other factors—such as their views toward the economy or national security—strongly influenced how people viewed President Reagan. After the affair, attitudes toward Central American intervention had much more to do with how citizens rated the president. As I have shown, few people approved of the intervention. Once those attitudes were primed by the affair, they became an important way to measure Reagan's performance, and his approval ratings dropped, although not consistently throughout the population. For highly aware citizens, Iran–contra did not have much impact on their presidential evaluation compared with those with moderate levels of political awareness. Highly aware persons were less affected, Zaller argues, because they already had a great deal of other information and considerations that influenced their views of President Reagan.[64]

Citizens did not have an impression of North before the Iran–contra affair, and public reactions were fairly complex. In this case, some survey findings suggested a positive public response, and others, a critical view.[65] Instead of finding a wave of hero worship for North, the responses demonstrated a more muted evaluation and a certain degree of ambivalence.

North did best in those polls asking about his overall favorability and whether he sincerely cared for his country. When pollsters asked whether the respondent had a favorable or unfavorable opinion of Oliver North, citizens gave Mr. North increasingly positive ratings after the hearings began (see table 3.1). Whereas a Gallup poll conducted in December 1986 found that only 23 percent of the respondents viewed North favorably and a CBS/*New York Times* poll in early July found 43 percent with a favorable impression, North's numbers jumped after the hearings began. Favorability ratings between mid-July and August 1987 ranged between 56 and 69 percent. By March 1988, CBS/*New York Times* found that only 39 percent of respondents had a favorable impression and 22 percent had an unfavorable view.

Even at the height of North's favorability, it was not clear what his strong ratings meant. That is, at the same time that North was receiving strong favorability rankings, *Time* magazine polls found only 37 percent of respondents agreeing that North was "someone we need in government" and 26 percent agreeing that North was "someone I would want to marry my daughter."[66] Given the public dislike of the Iran–contra policies, it seems unlikely that people approved of what North did as a NSC aide.

If North's favorability ratings were not based on policy or government actions, perhaps they were some sort of personal approval, based on sympathy and his sincere love of country. Since most citizens disapproved of the policy and believed that President Reagan knew of the diversion, they had a strong reason to be sympathetic to North. In fact, in a July 1987 *Newsweek* poll, 70 percent said that they believed North had authorization for his actions, and in a *Time* poll, 77 percent said that North was a scapegoat. Given North's limited power in the executive branch and his defense at the congressional hearings, many

TABLE 3.1
Favorability Ratings of Oliver North

Source	Date	Favorable	Unfavorable
Gallup	December 1986	23%	35%
CBS/*New York Times*	July 9, 1987	43%	14%
Los Angeles Times	July 10–13, 1987	67%	20%
ABC/*Washington Post*	July 11–12, 1987	60%	12%
ABC/*Washington Post*	July 15, 1987	66%	13%
CBS/*New York Times*	July 16, 1987	56%	13%
ABC/*Washington Post*	July 21, 1987	64%	12%
ABC/*Washington Post*	August 3–5, 1987	69%	28%
Los Angeles Times	August 15–19, 1987	61%	23%
Gallup	September 1–13, 1987	57%	34%
CBS/*New York Times*	March 19–22, 1988	39%	22%

Americans believed that Congress treated him poorly. In a *Newsweek* poll, 48 percent said that Congress had harassed North; 23 percent said that North was uncooperative; 4 percent said that both had occurred; and 12 percent said that neither was the case.

North did not come across as a pathetic pawn but, rather, as a strong proponent of the Iran–contra policy initiatives. And as I have noted, his testimony led to an increase in approval for aid to the contras. Furthermore, North seemed to be devoted and energetic and a person who deeply loved his country. A July 1987 *Time* magazine poll asked if North was "a true patriot": 67 percent said yes, 24 percent no, and 9 percent not sure. This high percentage tracks the strong approval ratings and goes far beyond all other positive characterizations.[67]

Although a great deal of polling data about Mr. North were collected, it is the questions about his possible heroic status that are invaluable for assessing the climate of opinion and the possibility of a spiral of silence. Following President Reagan's comments about North, there was a good deal of commentary about whether the lieutenant colonel was a hero, and the polling organizations used questions that alluded to this. What makes the items so helpful is that the questions asked either whether the respondent believed North's actions to be heroic or presumed that the nation found North to be a hero; that is, they asked whether North was a hero or a national hero. The first asks the respondents about their personal views of North, and the second, their assessments of the climate of public opinion.

Before we examine the survey results, it is important to recognize that even though the questions' different wording (hero versus national hero) suggests either personal evaluations or assessments of others' opinions, these answers are not definitive measures. That is, citizens may not have interpreted the items in the way that I think they did. In addition to subjective differences in understanding these questions, the items' contexts were different. First, some questions varied in the number of alternatives they presented to the subjects. If we accept that the items measured different things, then we can compare personal views and assessments of the national mood. If not, we still can observe ratings trends and compare survey responses with data from the intensive interviews. As I show later, many interview subjects were ambivalent toward North and distinguished between their views of North and their views of the national opinion concerning North.

During July 1987 two polls asked whether North were a hero or whether other descriptions applied (see table 3.2). An ABC news poll reported the highest percentages of members of the public who consid-ered North to be a hero; 19 percent agreed that North was a hero; 64 per-cent believed him to be a victim; 8 percent considered him a villain; and varying percentages of the sample chose other characterizations. In a *Los Angeles Times* poll, only 4 percent said North was a hero; 37 percent called him dedicated; 27 percent viewed him as a person who could get things done; 11 percent held that he could be bought; and others char-acterized him differently.

Four polls asked whether North was a national hero (see table 3.3). A Roper poll in late June 1987 found that only 9 percent believed that Reagan was right to call him a national hero; 42 percent found this to be

TABLE 3.2

Oliver North: Hero Versus Other Characterizations

Source: Los Angeles Times	Date: July 10, 1987

Question: Now I'm going to call off some words and phrases and ask you to tell me which one of them best describes Oliver North. Of course, if none of them fits, or all of them seem to describe him equally well, just say so. Would you say Oliver North is "dangerous" or "dedicated" or "a man who can get things done" or "a fanatic" or "a hero" or "a man who can be bought" or what?

Responses:

Dangerous	4%
Dedicated	37%
Can get things done	27%
Fanatic	4%
Hero	4%
Can be bought	11%
Other phrase	3%
None fits/all equal	4%
Not sure/refused	6%

Source: ABC	Date: July 11–12, 1987

Question: Which of the following words best describes your view of Oliver North? Hero, villain, victim.

Responses:

Hero	19%
Villain	8%
Victim	64%
Other	4%
None	3%
Don't know	2%

an overstatement; and 39 percent believed this label was wrong. Although only a small number agreed that North was indeed a national hero, a majority (9 plus 42 percent) saw at least some truth in this characterization. A poll by the Yankelovich organization for *Time* magazine, conducted on July 9, 1987, found that 29 percent agreed that North was a national hero. Two polls with identically worded questions found an increase over time in the number of people seeing North as a national hero. One CBS/*New York Times* poll conducted early in July found that 18 percent agreed; a later survey by the same organization in the middle of July 1987 found that 25 percent believed North to be a national hero. These surveys suggest that people were more likely to agree that North was a national hero than to grant him this status themselves. As I demonstrate in chapter 4, the media portrayed North as an American hero. Perhaps the media's account of public support for North influenced people's perceptions of the national mood but had little effect on citizens' own assessments.

As this discussion shows, North's high favorability ratings did not translate into widespread approval or admiration. The poll numbers suggest that people believed North sincerely cared for and loved his coun-

TABLE 3.3

Oliver North as National Hero

Source	Date	Responses			
		Right	Overstatement	Wrong	Don't know
Roper[a]	June 29–30, 1987	9%	42%	39%	9%
		Describes	Does not describe		Not sure
Yankelovich[b]	July 9, 1987	29%	61%		10%
		Yes	No		Don't know
CBS/*New York Times*[c]	July 9, 1987	18%	74%		8%
CBS/*New York Times*[c]	July 16, 1987	25%	68%		7%

[a]Question: Shortly after the Iran–contra affair first broke, President Reagan described Oliver North as a national hero. Do you think that he was right in that assessment or that it was something of an overstatment or that he was wrong about North's being a national hero?

[b]Question: Which of these descriptions do you feel describes Colonel Oliver North and which do not describe him . . . A national hero?

[c]Question: Do you think Oliver North is a national hero?

try but nevertheless did not act properly. The respondents maintained that North was not treated well by elected officials, from the president to the Congress and that because North likely took the fall for the president, he did not deserve to be treated harshly by Congress. Although some agreed that the previously unknown NSC staffer was a hero, most members of the public were not enthralled by him.

The Intensive Interview Study

Surveys have their limits. As instruments for measuring public opinion, they require their subjects to answer in restricted ways. For Habermas, the introduction of mass surveys is a symptom of the decay of the public political sphere. Citizens cannot set the agenda of the discussion or change the terms of the debate but can only respond or refuse to respond. To better understand how the public viewed North, I conducted open-ended interviews with a set of diverse subjects.

My study is based on interviews with fifty persons from the Twin Cities area of Minnesota during the spring and summer of 1989. The interviews included structured and open-ended questions and followed a Q-sort on various ideas of heroism as well as questions about twenty-five public figures.[68] In choosing the people to be interviewed, I sought a group with diversity in ideology, partisanship, life experience, and type and amount of political involvement. Therefore, I drew the subjects from liberal and conservative churches, political parties, organizations concerned with military matters and economic issues, as well as a set of college students.[69]

Surveys cannot do everything, and this procedure had its limits as well. First, because I did not randomly choose my subjects, I cannot generalize about the proportion of the population that holds different views. That is, I cannot make any claims about how many people in the general population believed certain things about Oliver North. Second, all the subjects in this study lived in Minnesota, a state that is more liberal than the nation as a whole. Third, I also may not have interviewed many uninformed citizens. Given what we know about the nature of public opinion, people without high levels of information are those whose views are most fluid.[70] Accordingly, their perspectives probably contributed the most to the sudden shifts in public opinion, as occurred with North at time of the hearings. Fourth, this study was conducted in 1989, two years after the hearings, and so the subjects may have reconsidered their opinions. Given the instability in favorability ratings, these findings may not represent what public thought at the time.

Now that I have raised these criticisms, let me answer them. Although it is true that only scientific surveys can yield valid population estimates, as Hochschild notes, interviews "can generate findings that survey research does not," including information regarding reasoning processes.[71] I was able to follow up during these interviews, to ask the subjects to explain further, and to detect nuances not possible with survey questions. Since I cannot determine how well the proportion of people answering a particular way in this study represents parts of the overall population, I cannot state what percentage of my respondents thought about any one issue. Second, although the level of liberalism in Minnesota influenced the distribution of views in the subject pool, it probably did not affect individual persons' reasoning about why they liked or disapproved of North. Third, although the citizens I interviewed were more politically aware and sophisticated than the general population, I also included people who were not involved in politics, such as students who were not in political groups, politically uninvolved union members, and members of liberal and conservative churches. Fourth, although I interviewed the subjects after the hearings, their responses are still useful if they provide a convincing explanation for complex and sometimes seemingly contradictory poll results. While there is no purposively diverse set of open-ended interviews from the time of the hearings, my interviews provide direct evidence of how citizens thought, and they help us answer questions left by the survey data, in order to construct a better picture of citizen opinion.[72]

The findings from my interviews were consistent with seemingly contradictory poll results. I asked the fifty subjects if they thought Oliver North was heroic or far from heroic (on a five-point scale) and then what the reasons were for their answer. Across the board, citizens believed that North was sincere in his actions and loved his country. Yet this single attribute—sincerity—was viewed in different value contexts, and these other beliefs influenced the subjects' overall assessments of North. To everyone, North had come across as a strong, sincere advocate of his position. The respondents' different ideological views and divergent perspectives on the proper operation of democracy and the requisites of good citizenship most influenced their personal assessments of North. No matter what they personally thought of him, nearly everyone believed that he was very popular in the nation and that he had become a national hero during the Iran–contra hearings. Indeed, the subjects referred to media reports to support their perceptions of the national climate of opinion.

Those who were steadfast admirers of North all agreed with his foreign policy goals, and they all were conservative Republicans. However,
it would be a mistake to assume that policy agreement, ideology, or partisanship is all we need to know to understand people's assessments of
North. The lieutenant colonel drew critical judgments from all elements
of the political spectrum. In fact, a number of conservative Republicans
found fault with Oliver North and argued that he should be held
accountable for any illegal actions. On the other hand, conservatives
often felt more ambivalent than did the moderates or liberals I interviewed. These subjects contended that North was not altogether responsible for what happened and that he was sincerely committed to valid
policy goals. Opponents of the Reagan administration—often liberal
Democrats—had no reservoir of sympathy and were quite critical.
Although the size and nature of my study do not allow valid generalizations, it is still nonetheless striking that so many subjects that one might
have expected to support North usually were ambivalent at best, answering with both positive and negative comments. See table 3.4 for demographic information on the ambivalent subjects discussed here. All
names are pseudonyms.

Many respondents questioned North's basic judgment, believing that
the National Security Council aide misunderstood the proper relationship between means and ends. Even people who were sympathetic to
North's foreign policy and national security goals were often uneasy
about his methods and judgment. For instance, Harry, a twenty-one-
year-old conservative Republican, stated, "He's committed to democra-
tization in Central America and having a strong America. But he did

TABLE 3.4

Demographic Characteristics of Quoted Ambivalent Subjects

Subject	Age	Group	Party Identification	Ideology
Andrea	36	Women Against Military Madness	Independent	Liberal
Carl	33	Union (carpenter)	Republican	Conservative
Cathy	35	Union (nurse)	Republican	Conservative
David	71	Rotary Club	Republican	Conservative
Frank	24	Evangelical Free Church	Independent	Moderate
Fred	36	Evangelical Free Church	Democractic	Moderate
Harriet	21	Independent—Republican Party	Republican	Conservative
Harry	21	Independent—Republican Party	Republican	Conservative
Irene	24	Student	Republican	Moderate
Ivan	25	Student	Independent	Conservative

things in ways that are illegal and immoral. I agree with his goals, but the ends don't justify the means." Frank, a twenty-four-year-old moderate independent who regularly attended an Evangelical Free Church, also had mixed feelings about North. Even though the marine's military activities drew a positive response, North's inability to discriminate—to make judgments—led to criticisms. "He didn't do anything terribly heroic, excluding what he might have done in battle. He wasn't sufficiently discriminating to be heroic. He too much blindly followed the lead. He was high enough up to be beyond the battlefield blind allegiance response." Thus, even though some subjects admired North in some ways, they were troubled by what they saw as his inability to make ethical political distinctions and use good judgment.

A number of respondents discussed North's care for and commitment to his country. Nearly all contended that the National Security Council aide was sincere—that North truly believed he was helping his country and the cause of freedom. But they disagreed about the extent to which sincerity and pure motivations could mitigate North's faults. Carl, a thirty-three-year-old conservative Republican carpenter, stated that North's stalwart demeanor before Congress could not justify the errors he committed: "He stood up for what he believed, but it was wrong." Two respondents volunteered that if belief in one's own principles were all that mattered, then even the Nazis would be immune from criticism. Fred, a thirty-six-year-old moderate Democrat, stated, "North was sincere, but that's how Nazism got going. People have to be accountable for what they do." Andrea, a thirty-six-year-old liberal, also was concerned about the need to take responsibility. Of North, she said:

> He is sincere, but so were the Nazis. You can't just follow orders and be sincere, Or see one choice and do it, and don't see options they have. North knew, he was told that he was breaking the law. It's OK to break the law sometimes, but you need a good reason. He did it because he knew the president would back him up. But most people don't want to fund the contras. He was going against public opinion. I'm nervous about people who know they are right.

Others saw North as sincere and felt that his position in the government organization and the expectations placed on him by his superiors mitigated his responsibility to some extent. David, a seventy-one-year-old conservative former executive who was active in the Rotary Club, drew on his management experience when evaluating North's actions.

He thought he was being a patriotic American. I resent the higher-ups who let him take the rap. This is more of a sympathy vote for him than an endorsement of what he did. I'd include Reagan in that—if he didn't know, he should have known about the whole convoluted, bizarre deal. I have sympathy for the position North was left in. You shouldn't put subordinates in that position. But I'm also someone for whom motivation counts a lot. He was trying to do the best for his country.

Although David did not think much of the project in which North was entangled, he attributed responsibility to North's overseers, including President Reagan. Since the marine lieutenant colonel was not fully culpable for the "convoluted, bizarre" Iran–contra affair, David evaluated North in light of North's desire to serve his nation.

The issue of whether North acted legally was important to many. Like David, a number of other persons contended that personal motivation was a valid and important consideration for judging North, although nearly all of them also were quite ambivalent. These subjects were troubled by North's lawbreaking, but at the same time they were impressed by his dedication to country and policy. Cathy, a thirty-five-year-old conservative Republican registered nurse, was rather sympathetic to North but believed that he must take legal responsibility. She stated,

> He had no intention to do wrong. I'm not condoning it if he did do wrong. He really was trying to act in the best interests of the country. This is a complex issue and the trial was tough. Poor guy . . . although he should have to account for his actions.

Others could not sanction North's actions because they were against the law, but they were not willing to condemn him either. Harriet, a twenty-one-year-old conservative, observed, "I'm not sure about North. I have a deep respect for the rule of law and the integrity of our political process. Yet he did, with deep conviction, uphold his own moral ideals." For these citizens, sincerity could not outweigh the fact that North broke the law.

Yet there was more going on with these subjects than the belief that following the law was more important than caring sincerely. Such a view could have been a simple endorsement of the need for law and order. On the other hand, for some subjects the law itself had a deeper meaning—as a reflection of the social contract between citizen and the state. To them, North's lawbreaking demonstrated a bad-faith relationship to this fundamental idea. They argued that citizens' rights were protected by the state and that therefore they were obligated to support the community's decisions, as exemplified in policies and laws. Although this idea can be found in a number of the earlier quotations, it was stated most directly by Ivan, a twenty-five-year-old conservative Republican. Ivan was convinced of North's sincerity and endorsed his policy goals, but he also was sure that North had not acted properly:

> Fighting against Communism and totalitarianism, that is an admirable thing. North in his own paradigm did support democracy. But there wasn't a national consensus about fighting Communism in Nicaragua. He took on more than he should have. I can't agree that he shouldn't have been prosecuted. He is part of the rules and contract. There is no reason that he should be exempt.

Like some of the people discussed earlier, Ivan was concerned about North's actions in light of the weight of public opinion regarding Nicaragua. Ivan's analysis, however, tied notions of popular sovereignty to an underlying philosophy on obeying the law. Because laws express the public will, inattention to legislation violates the social contract between citizen and polity. Oliver North was not immune from its strictures and was therefore subject to all legal procedures and remedies.

Although for nearly all the respondents discussed so far, North's sincerity and commitment to goals did not outweigh other values, these characteristics did play a central role for some people. Often they gave great weight to sincerity because they viewed the lieutenant colonel as neither narrowly ambitious nor self-serving. In fact, if anyone seemed self-serving, they believed it was the Congress. To Hank, a thirty-four-year-old conservative Republican activist, the Iran–contra affair sounded like a brouhaha created for political reasons: criticisms of North "sound like a liberal Democrat trying to get North. North wasn't acting to feather his own bed." Hank implied that partisanship was at the root of the critical reactions and that because he was a man who acted out of care for his country, North did not deserve condemnation.

Those people who admired North wholeheartedly based their evaluation of him on a combination of qualities usually associated with soldiers—a willingness to sacrifice and an ability to follow orders. Brian, a former marine, conservative Republican, and member of the Veterans of Foreign Wars, emphasized North's physical courage, threats to his life, and sacrifice.

> When I tell you what I think of him, I mean the North that I know about from talking to people who served under him in Vietnam and on covert actions, not the way he was portrayed in the press. There's something about the marines that never leaves you—the brotherhood. Real leader-

ship, the type that is most lasting, is by example. This is what he provided. Carrying so much steel in his body that he sets off airport metal detectors—he demonstrated great sacrifice for country. All the media and people against him didn't come close.

Brian found North admirable because he put his body on the line and was prepared to make sacrifices for his country.

Barry, a sixty-eight-year-old conservative Republican veteran, also viewed North as a great man. He focused on North's goals, particularly his support for the Nicaraguan contras. In addition, Barry did not see any problem with disobeying Congress. Rather, North took his orders from the president, as head of the armed forces, and this was how it should be. "North fought Communism and served his commander in chief well. Someone had to hold the line in Central America. Congress was too weak willed to get the job done." Barry's view of North was based on the view that citizens should give unswerving service to country, along the lines of soldierly loyalty to officials' orders. In addition, this subject believed that congressional involvement in foreign affairs was suspect. Barry argued that the situation faced by the Reagan administration called for a strong executive to ensure the policy's success. Thus, because of his role in carrying out those policy goals, North deserved admiration.

My respondents' assessments of North were often framed by their views of fundamental aspects of democratic institutions. Some of them were bothered by the inadequate information that North provided to Congress. Amanda, a sixty-six-year-old liberal Democrat, put it most simply: "You shouldn't lie to people in some of the highest offices in the country." Eric, a sixty-six-year-old moderate Republican, was disturbed that North provided incomplete and inadequate information, for he saw this as an indication that the lieutenant colonel misunderstood the Constitution. Eric explained, "He doesn't understand our government and he earns lecture fees for defying Congress." Consistent with the emphasis on North's misinformation, some subjects were quite concerned with democratic accountability, arguing that because members of Congress were chosen by the people, misrepresenting facts to legislators interfered with popular control, a primary principle of democracy. Alice, a seventy-year-old liberal, stated, "North is a traitor. He lied to Congress. I elect people to offices and they represent me. It's like he lied to me, since he lied to them."

In addition, some respondents believed that North was hypocritical. Although North boldly claimed that he was motivated by love for freedom and democracy, his actions were profoundly antidemocratic.

His supporters claim he's a hero, but he bypassed the democratic process in our country. What he believes in—freedom for people in Nicaragua—is a noble thing. But he shouldn't attack people in the United States for disagreeing with him. He bypassed constitutional ways of doing things, is a hypocrite. [Ian, twenty-one years old, liberal, Democratic, student]

He is a hypocrite. He states he is after democracy and defends democracy and is so against communism. But when he was faced with the situation where the majority didn't want to send arms to Nicaragua, he ignores this. He can't say that he was for democracy. [Gail, twenty-eight years old, Democratic–Farmer Labor Party]

According to these subjects, North's purported love for democracy was belied by his covert approach, the falsehoods he told to legally elected representatives, and his lack of respect for the opinions of the majority of the population.

A number of respondents were disturbed by North's emphasis on secrecy and military and executive power because, they held, national security concerns must be balanced with accountable and democratic processes. Ira, a twenty-one-year-old moderate independent, argued that North's actions threatened the principle of civilian control of the military: "In our society, we don't want military leaders to make decisions. It's a bad precedent for the future if we say that North is OK."

Critics of North's methods included Republicans and supporters of covert international action. For example, Irene, a twenty-four-year-old student who called herself a moderate Republican, stated,

He did have a vision, but was not really true to it. If you believe in democracy, you don't undercut the system. It shows that personal ego, a sense of one's own power can get in the way. At first I thought he was just doing his job and was taking the fall. He believed he was helping democracy, but you just can't. . . . If we are to further an ideal, you must be true to it. Even little things like installing protection for his house are just not right. I believe politics is dirty sometimes, the CIA is necessary, but dirty business isn't admirable. You need to ask if the ends justify the means.

In weighing national security needs against democratic principles, Irene argued that "dirty business" and the CIA are sometimes needed but that such activities cannot be carried out at the expense of basic democratic procedures. Attempts to preserve democracy, she maintained, cannot proceed in a way that threatens democracy.

The policy process used by the executive branch and carried out by Oliver North raised grave doubts in many subjects. They argued that except for some special circumstances, proper political action must be open and direct. In addition, they held that policy should not be made by a small cadre but, rather, collectively. Bill, a forty-one-year-old Vietnam War veteran involved with the Veterans of Foreign Wars and a moderate Democrat, was nearly incredulous at the thought that North's resistance to congressional will might be considered exemplary or even appropriate.

> I don't understand what he stands for. I don't want heroism to be a reward for wearing blinders, being a dope, for stupidity. How can any literate person in this country do what he did—supply money to the contras against the will of the Congress and the people—without knowing that it's wrong? His place was before policy was made. Society picked a path, he should go along with it.

Although Bill contended that North should have followed established public policy, others thought that this injunction was not absolute. Although the usual responsibility of a citizen is to follow or actively attempt to modify policies, they believed that it was correct to defy legal edicts if a polity were truly immoral. George stated,

> Sometimes you have to break rules, in a totally bankrupt regime—like people trying to save the Jews under Nazism. North was trying to get around a system that was not morally questionable. The laws he went against were decided democratically. He was a part of that system, and he knew that it hadn't transgressed morality in the same way.

George, like several others, believed that when a political system was run democratically, covert activities that disregarded laws and government officials were not acceptable.

Concluding Comments

These findings from surveys and intensive interviews show that most ordinary people were not swept into a hero worship of Oliver North. Majorities of citizens polled at the time of the hearings believed North to be sincere and deeply committed to his work and his country, but most did not agree that North was a hero. Nonetheless, the hero frame was important, as it influenced the characterizations people considered in evaluating their own and others' opinions. The survey data suggest a certain complexity in people's assessments of North, a conclusion supported by the intensive interviews. Some conservatives in the interview study voiced their wholehearted admiration for North. However, although most interview subjects respected North's sincerity, dedication, and love of country, these were not enough for him to be considered heroic, even for the many who agreed with North's policy goals and admired the president.

The making of the hero persona started with President Reagan's remarks, but this was by no means the only factor that influenced its prevalence in public constructions of public opinion. The ways in which citizens saw North were linked to basic features of the American political culture, including the strength and resonance of the soldier figure and the proud rebel against powerful interests. Not only did these accessible and powerful cultural symbols affect how North presented himself and how survey researchers investigated and reported on public opinion, but these heroic traits also were central elements in how North's supporters in the interview study saw him. The hero frame engaged certain groups in the public who probably held these views fervently. North's seeming popularity also fit with the cultural tendency to praise charismatic celebrities.

Views of North and perceptions of citizens' opinions were not only influenced by his presentation and linked to the culture but were also filtered through the media. Significant cultural tendencies partially framed readings of the popular mood, provided a basis for North's appeal among some, helped mobilize his supporters, and caught the eye of the media. As the next chapter demonstrates, the media saw fit to emphasize the dramatic and visually interesting moments and to emphasize certain ways of framing Iran–contra and Oliver North. In doing so, they helped create a perception of public opinion that members of Congress could not ignore.

4

Telling the Public What It Thinks

It is not an accident that we refer to "news stories" as the basic ingredient of the news. Reporters are essentially storytellers, heirs to a narrative tradition as old as mankind. Stories have settings and characters and plot lines. Whether we acknowledge it or not, we are constantly devising the scripts we think appropriate for the events we are covering.

David Broder, *Behind the Front Page*

In 1986 and 1987, when the media told the tale of Iran–contra and Oliver North, the public became another protagonist. Part of the story included citizens' reactions to the unraveling of a covert web, as well as their ongoing assessments of the Reagan presidency and the upcoming Republican and Democratic prospects. In talking about the public, the media acted as the main switchboard in a massive game of telephone. Messages from the public were filtered through the media and then sent back out to the public, the politicians, and the pressure groups. But even though this was no ordinary game of telephone, the end product was similar. Public opinion, as reported by the major media, was different from the mixed views expressed in the polls. Rather than the overall ambivalence toward Oliver North that the surveys (and the depth interviews) found, as described in chapter 3, the media told the public that North was widely admired and esteemed.

This skewed representation of the public voice arose from particular translation biases, including the amplification of organized publics, and the emphasis on visual and dramatic means of opinion expression. Instead of showing either an ideological bias or a proclivity toward independent investigatory journalism, the media were influenced by exciting story elements and information presented in public forums. As usual, politicians and pressure groups used the media as conduits for debates about policy and the public. The media do not constitute the only territory for public discourse and discussion, of course. However, debate often takes place outside the halls of Congress, over the airwaves, and on the written page. The media collectively have become the arena in which political spectacles are cast and staged. Political participants stage events for the audience of citizens, and they also seek to include the public by mobilizing some and employing perceptions of public opinion for strategic purposes.

The presentation of public opinion through the media develops from a strategic competition over whose views of public opinion will prevail. Interested parties try to use the media, but the media also operate according to their own tendencies and biases. Competent politicians are aware of the media's proclivities and therefore try to cast their messages so that the media will be more likely to cover their arguments in the most flattering manner.[1] Media-savvy campaign consultants encourage candidates to try to frame their opponents in negative terms and to frame themselves in positive terms. Even after the candidates are in office, this competition continues. When strategizing, politicians and group leaders take account of the press's power and points of least resistance—a good story and a good character.

What is meant by a good story depends, of course, on the audience and the teller. The style of the mass media tends toward simple characterizations rather than nuanced and complex characters. "Although fraught with ambiguity and uncertainty, the contested issues in politics are quickly simplified and cast in mutually exclusive ideological terms. . . . [N]arratives create a particular kind of social world, with specified heroes and villains."[2] In most cases, political protagonists—ranging from high-level officials to the public itself—become stock characters in media narratives.

Framing the News and Covering the Public

Journalists and editors make decisions every day about what events they will cover and what story they will tell about them. To do so, the news media frame the events and thereby construct social and political realities.[3] Although each occurrence could be discussed from various vantage points, specific newspapers, news magazines, and television news stories must tell the story in their own way, must decide how it is to be told. Modern journalistic norms require the media to try to do their work objectively and without a partisan slant.[4] But even when reporters strive for objectivity, they always cover the news from some perspective.

Despite diverse possibilities for framing the news, the American mass media's vantage point rarely varies to any great extent.[5] Rather, the media tend to tell the same story because they are influenced by the most prestigious press, by journalists' emphasis on official sources, by the development of a peer interpretive community, and by similar pressures to provide an interesting and entertaining story.[6] Commercial considerations encourage the news media to make a story compelling, dramatic, and visually interesting. As a result, frames are chosen that will appeal to the cultural values that audiences already hold and thus reinforce those propensities. Because the frame used can influence citizens' assessments of events and political figures, politically savvy newsmakers try to present their news in ways that the media cannot resist.[7] If the news is covered in the way that one group wants, that party will be advantaged and the others disadvantaged.

The strategic framing of events takes place in a communication and political system that has become increasingly concerned with image and presentation. Our political news is much like our campaign politics of attack ads and sound bites, dominated by critiques of political acts as performances. The mass media examine politicians in terms of how well they present themselves, what impression they leave, and what image they have created.[8] Political news is often framed strategically, not substantively. Although this tendency is most noticeable during electoral campaigns, the media now often continue to use an image and a strategic frame to analyze the politics of governing.[9]

Despite their power to frame issues, the media are neither all-powerful nor ineffectual. In speaking to and about the public, the frames used by the mass media do not stun and limit the public. According to a study that systematically compared the frames used by the media and by citizens, nonmedia people frame issues differently than the media do: "they actively filter, sort, and reorganize information in personally meaningful ways in the process of constructing an understanding of public issues."[10] Neither the news frames nor the symbols used by activists and politicians are hegemonic. Citizens can, and sometimes do, break through the amplified wall of sound created by those who can command the media's attention.[11]

Given the possibility of resisting media frames, can we conclude that frames do not lead to significant problems for democracy, such as elite manipulation and domination or the creation of a spiral of silence? I believe that we cannot. First, as the evidence discussed in chapter 2 demonstrates, some people are more susceptible to the pressures of perceived opinion than others are. Vulnerability is not only affected by personality and interest in politics, but also by situational factors. Depending on the particular conditions of a political contest and the citizenry, news frames can have a significant influence on how citizens view politics and on their willingness to speak up.

In addition, although citizens might resist news frames, this resistance does not matter politically if the political elites come to believe that most people view the world through the media's frames. The politically consequential news frames are those that the elites use and that they presume are used by everyday folk. This matter—implicit understandings regarding the ways that citizens approach political events—is a variant of *perceived* public opinion. (In fact, there may be no discrepancy between elites' frames and citizens' frames if citizens simply respond to the political stagings put on by elites.) The media can also influence the perception of public opinion by reporting citizens' views. In this way, the media create impressions of public opinion that become part of the evidence weighed by people in the business of politics. The media have an important role in creating these perceptions and also in creating possible false soundings in the echo chamber of politics.

Even though journalists are influenced by the norm of objectivity, other tendencies of the modern media encourage reporting public opinion in ways that emphasize a simple, compelling, dramatic, and visually interesting story. These characteristics create powerful tales that influence both citizens' and elites' understandings of public opinion. The media's interest in simplicity leads to stories that avoid ambivalent or multiple points of view. Hershey, for example, found that within several weeks of the election, the media's coverage of the 1984 election results contained fewer and fewer explanations of Ronald Reagan's success and Walter Mondale's loss. That is, over time the tale that the press told emphasized citizens' reactions to Mondale's statement about raising taxes and the Democratic Party's connection to particular interests, which resulted in many core Democratic voters' endorsing the Republican candidate. This explanation, Hershey argued, became a politically consequential lesson for elites and was most influenced by the elites' own prognostications. In interpreting elections, the learning comes out of a dialogue mainly among political activists and media people. The dialogue is often *about* the views of the larger public, but it is a dialogue in which the larger public is not a direct participant. This is a process, then, that speaks with an activist accent.[12]

In constructing impressions of public opinion, the media often emphasize the dramatic and the means of expression that present compelling pictures. For example, a classic study by Lang and Lang compared the perspectives of people who attended a Chicago parade in honor of General Douglas MacArthur with the view of public reaction presented on television. Observers who sampled the spectators' opinions found that less than 10 percent came to see the recently dismissed general because they believed he was a hero and they wanted to show their support. In addition, most of the people at the parade found it disappointing, because they spent most of their time waiting, developed sore feet, and then caught only a glimpse of MacArthur. In contrast, the television coverage portrayed the crowd as ardently supporting MacArthur: "the video viewer could fasten his eyes on the General and on what could be interpreted as the interplay between a heroic figure and the enthusiastic crowd. The cheering of the crowds seemed not to die down at all."[13] Specific events that appeared to be especially intense on television were not perceived in that way by the people watched by the camera. Even so, the views of people attending the parade had no special standing. Furthermore, relatively few people went to the parade, compared with the number of those who watched the event, and the memories of the people who were there might have been reinterpreted in light of discussions with others who knew about the parade from the broadcast reports. It was the dramatic pictures showing fervent supporters that had political meaning.

The media's portraits of public opinion matter politically when they influence the decisions of elites. As Lang and Lang argued thirty years after their MacArthur study, "The political effects of the mass media have to be considered within the context of the bargaining through which political coalitions are built and held together."[14] In reporting the news, the media create bystanders and a group of political actors and activists. When the media move one group of citizens from being bystanders to being speakers, the balance of expressed ideas changes, and political elites recalculate which policies and statements are politically viable. Perceived public opinion is a significant political resource.

The media can cover public opinion in different ways, offering information that is more or less reliable and more or less memorable. Surveys are not the only source of information used, even if they are the most generalizable source. Although a great deal of research has focused on the impact of media polls, scholars do not know what proportion of opinion reporting depends on poll data, compared with other methods, if different measurements portray different pictures of the public mood, or the effect of those portrayals.

When covering public opinion, the media use a variety of indicators, including polls, person-on-the-street interviews, demonstrations, marketing, cultural indicators, phone-in polls, and letters to public officials.[15] Of these, only surveys can be systematically assessed for how well they measure the distribution of public views. None of the others are reliable measures of general public opinion, mostly because people who call, write, demonstrate, or buy certain products are self-selected, not randomly chosen. These people come from particular populations and likely feel more intensely than others do. For example, one study compared the views of the general public with those of callers to talk radio shows and with other citizens who speak out politically, and it found that the "vocal minority" was more conservative than was the nation as a whole.[16] Moreover, when someone buys a product, it is not clear what view that person is expressing. Therefore, unless the product clearly states admiration for a person or policy, consumption behavior could just as easily reflect an awareness of someone's celebrity status.

Not only do these varied sources have differing levels of validity, they also have different informational characteristics. For example, person-on-the-street interviews and stories about sales of T-shirts and other political merchandise are more vivid and emotion laden than is coverage of large-sample, randomly derived polls. Although the information from polls is more valid and reliable, social psychological theories suggest that the informational qualities of the other sources make them more likely to be stored in memory and retrieved for later use.[17] Because remembered information is more likely to become part of an impression about public opinion, vivid but unreliable information could have a significant influence on developing a spiral of silence or on elites' political calculations. Since both the public and political elites listen to the media, it is important to the integrity of the democratic process whether the media transmit or distort the public voice.

The media do not just listen to the people so that they can tell them what they think. Perceived public opinion also may influence how the media cover the news. Although the media in democratic nations are not restricted by the government, commercial pressures may drive them to cast their stories in ways that they believe the public will accept or embrace. Hertsgaard characterizes the media in the early years of the Reagan administration as sycophants, "on bended knee" to the president because they feared that criticism would lead to their audience's withdrawal. For example, CBS's White House correspondent Lesley Stahl was asked by network officials to tone down her critiques of President Reagan.[18] In another case, after hostilities began, the Persian Gulf War became quite popular. Mueller reports that the public "did not want to hear anything critical about the military. The media complied."[19] When the media's coverage is colored by perceptions of public opinion, it may reinforce public views. On the other hand, the media's response to perceived public opinion may be based on misperceptions of what citizens think. In either case, elites and citizens who might have challenged the purported majority views may be quieted.

Public Opinion in the Media's Coverage of Iran–Contra and Oliver North

When Iran–contra became a public issue, the Reagan administration faced a very difficult political task. President Reagan had the most savvy White House communication office ever, yet it struggled to frame and contain the scandal. As the polling data presented in chapter 3 demonstrate, the White House's public relations efforts did not succeed in preventing President Reagan's approval ratings from sliding. However, talk about impeachment was kept to a minimum and never seriously considered. In addition, President Reagan's popularity rebounded (although not fully) by the time he left office in January 1989.

The relationship that had been established between the media and the administration created a context for reporting on Iran–contra. Before the scandal broke, the press treated President Reagan quite well. As Michael Deaver, the architect of the communications strategy, wrote, "Ronald Reagan enjoyed the most generous treatment by the press of any President in the postwar era."[20] The media's coverage of Reagan was influenced by his popularity, the persona of warmth he cultivated, the contrast with the media's previous poor dealings with the Carter administration, and, perhaps most important, the White House Communication Office's careful strategy. Under the stewardship of David Gergen and Michael Deaver, the Reagan White House limited access to the president, focused administration officials on a specific message each day, used the president to appeal directly to voters, created visuals to reinforce the administration's message, and coordinated its publicity efforts with legislative action.[21] Executive branch officials could find out the line-of-the-day by consulting a computer terminal; President Reagan cooperated by standing on the chalk marks designed for the proper lighting and camera angles; and communications staff regularly called the television networks before the nightly news to deliver the daily message. In promoting Reagan's legislative agenda, public relations people worked with the congressional liaison team, local media, the White House Speakers' Bureau, the Senate television studio, and the Office of Public Liaison (which networked with interest groups). As a result of this and the press's willingness to live under this public relations regime, the White House presented a unified front and limited the news media's questions, access, and ability to frame the news independently.

With the operatives of the White House communications team, President Reagan created the persona of the Teflon president, the Great Communicator.[22] Although often stymied, the media admired Reagan's performative competence, his ability to project himself as genial, tough, and energetic.[23] This impression was created with Boorstinian pseudo-events—photo opportunities at which the president posed at a home building site or a working-class bar, for instance—which, the communications staff believed, would deliver visual messages that voters would receive and remember. Visuals helped create the message of a unified, reborn country in the 1984 election, and these were distributed by paid media and news organizations. As Stephen Skowronek notes:

> Reagan had effectively cast himself as the leading symbol of hope for sal-
> vation from a bankrupt past, and, even in contemporary America's "pol-
> itics of high exposure," no one cared to take that on. He was held to a
> different standard by virtue of the politics he had made; he survived
> because in the political world he had constructed, he was a leader with
> impeccable intentions who occasionally made mistakes.[24]

Despite Reagan's persona and effective communications strategy, he was not successful in all his policy undertakings, among which was his inability to obtain aid for the contras consistently, a failure that led to the executive branch's frustration and ultimately to Iran–contra.

President Reagan did manage, however, to influence the political culture, which itself influenced how the press did its job. During the early years of the Reagan administration, many commentators proclaimed that there was a "new patriotism," a time when citizens forged and reproduced their national identities by cheering for the state and materialistic and militarist values. "By the mid-1980s orthodox Americanism was very much in vogue again, prompted by President Reagan's rhetoric, catastrophic setbacks for the U.S. Marines in Beirut, splendid little wars in places like Grenada, and assorted other episodes foreign and domestic."[25] Given this cultural environment and Reagan's role as protector-father of the nation, the media were generally not in a position to be critical. In fact, the press most often allowed itself to be used as a stage for the spectacles designed by the Reagan White House.

In using the media to promote his contra policy, the president portrayed the Sandinistas as communist threats on the United States' doorstep and the contras as freedom fighters, the equivalent of the American founding fathers. A public relations operation for the contras was launched in the White House (and is discussed in more detail in chapter 5). But despite his communication advantages, Ronald Reagan's appeals for the contras did not move public opinion to any great extent. He also spoke out against terrorism and focused much of his attention on the governments of Iran and Libya.[26] In fact, Reagan's strong public stance against terrorists and his portrayal of them as cruel and lawless made the revelations about the administration's arms sales to Iran quite shocking.

The media reacted to the disclosures quickly, making the affair the leading news of the day. Between November 1986 and September 1987, Iyengar reports, the three major networks aired more than twelve hundred reports, occupying more than sixty hours of airtime.[27] In covering Iran–contra, the media framed the issue as akin to Watergate, responded to the Reagan administration's attempts to limit political damage, and examined its previous poor coverage of the events. Before November 1986, although some papers had covered the contra resupply efforts, the prestige papers and the networks had not followed up. "From January to July 1986, attention was repeatedly drawn to [Oliver North] in the press, mainly in *The Miami Herald*, which far outdid the larger newspapers in New York and Washington in covering the contra-support operation."[28] The Iranian side of the scandal received less press attention but was reported by Dale Van Atta, a columnist, and John Wallach, foreign editor for the Hearst newspapers in 1985 and 1986. These reports were denied by White House sources and were rarely examined in the major news outlets. Some media critics argued that the strong public support for Reagan and the cozy relationships between reporters and news sources accounted for the limited investigations and press interest before November 1986.[29]

Once the Iran–contra scandal was out in the open, the White House Communication Office moved to respond. Patrick Buchanan had been its head since February 1985, and his instincts were to stand and fight. He advised the White House chief of staff in November 1986 that the administration needed to make clear why it had sold arms to Iran.[30] In a December 1986 op–ed piece in the *Washington Post*, Buchanan came to Oliver North's defense and lambasted those Republicans who had criticized the Reagan administration on Iran–contra.[31] But White House Chief of Staff Don Regan believed that Buchanan was too adversarial, and in February 1987, Buchanan left his post. The White House's communication director for most of the months before and during the congressional investigation was Thomas Griscom, the former Senate press secretary for Howard Baker, Regan's replacement as chief of staff. Griscom took a less pugnacious stance than Buchanan's and tried to limit the administration's association with Iran–contra. Under Griscom, the president said little about the investigations and findings and instead spoke out on domestic issues, as part of a diversionary strategy. Griscom later told an interviewer that the White House was concerned "about who was going to be seen on TV around this country every night talking about Iran–Contra."[32] The White House preferred that the media report from Capitol Hill and therefore rarely spoke about Iran–contra on camera. As a result, background visuals in television news reports nearly always showed the Capitol Building.

Watergate provided the most prominent frame in the media's coverage of this event, despite the differences between Iran–contra and Watergate.[33] Unlike Watergate, Iran–contra involved issues relating to Congress's role in setting foreign policy. However, for the press during the height of Iran–contra coverage, Watergate provided the frame of presidential scandal and directed the media's attention to the issue of credibility and cover-up. When Watergate had unraveled, President Richard M. Nixon was shown to have known about efforts to sabotage and spy on his political opponents and about plans to keep the people involved quiet. He had resisted investigations and claimed that executive privilege shielded review of the president's actions. After revelations made future impeachment certain, Nixon resigned. Because the Reagan administration was aware of this sequence, it revealed the diversion and other information,[34] removed North and Poindexter from their positions, and initiated the Tower Commission investigation. That is, the Reagan administration "staged effective shows of disclosure" to which the media responded.[35]

In fact, one media critic argues that the release of the Tower Commission's report marked a turn in the press's coverage of Iran–contra. Before the report was released, journalists had engaged in some aggressive independent investigations. But according to Scott Armstrong,

> As members of Congress readied themselves for the joint House and Senate hearings on the Iran–contra affair, the press began posing an Iran–contra version of the famous Watergate question: What did the president know and when did he know it? . . . What had been an informed and effective corps of journalists, independently pursuing the story in the preceding months, mysteriously gravitated toward this one question. Reporters who covered other aspects of the scandal were forced off the front page.[36]

The fairly narrow Watergatesque question of previous presidential information took precedence over other issues.

The media's emphasis on Reagan's knowledge and his credibility among the public derived from the Watergate frame but also encouraged them to cover public and elite impressions of how credible the administration officials appeared. Communications scholars Cornfield and Yalof maintain that the credibility topic was convenient for the media and also provided drama. "Anyone, at any time, could provide explanatory grist by responding to the question, 'Is the president acting like a man who is guilty?' " One early poll found that citizens were more bothered by the fact that they had not been told what happened than by either the arms sales or the funding of the contras. "Then *Time* highlighted the results, and called credibility the 'key issue.' The circle of readers and journalists excluded political actors except in the limited, second sense of the word 'acting,' i.e., communicative performances before them."[37] In emphasizing credibility, the media slighted consideration of the broader constitutional issues at stake in the Iran–contra affair.

Framing Oliver North as Hero, Loose Cannon, Scapegoat, and Performer

Oliver North, a hardworking staffer barely known to outsiders, soon became a key public figure and symbol of the Iran–contra affair. Because he had previously been unknown, citizens did not have a clear image of him. But rather quickly, several public portraits of North began to emerge. Media discussions of Oliver North in the first weeks emphasized two images, those of hero and loose cannon. What is rather curious is that both portrayals of North came from Ronald Reagan and his administration. Yet this contradiction might not be too surprising, since both impressions served the Reagan administration's public purposes. During the November 25, 1986, press conference in which they revealed the diversion, President Reagan and Attorney General Edwin Meese cast North as a man on his own. Reagan told reporters that North had been "relieved of his duties," and then Meese informed them that North was "the only person in the United States government that knew precisely about this" and that the administration would explore whether "there's any criminality involved." After this, President Reagan usually maintained that he had not known the full extent of North's activities.[38] President Reagan and his associates also insisted that Oliver North often exaggerated and made up stories about his close relationship and contacts with the president.[39] By arguing that North had acted alone, Reagan insulated himself from responsibility for the commission of the policy, although he could not block criticisms of his poor management and oversight.

Early on, President Reagan also described North as a hero and, by so doing, initiated the discussion about North framed around this characterization. By using this label, Reagan employed a powerful cultural frame, a concept linked to individual excellence. This, too, served Ronald Reagan politically, as it reinforced his commitment to his conservative base. Even though Reagan's depiction of Oliver North as heroic was contested by others, it set the frame for much debate and thus was successful in influencing public discourse. At the same time, Reagan's remarks about North's heroism remained problematic because it was not clear what made North heroic. Did the president mean that North had acted heroically in the Iran–contra affair? This interpretation was undermined by Reagan's statements about North's acting independently and his later explanation of what he meant by calling North a hero.

President Reagan first called North a hero in a private telephone conversation to him a few hours after the November 25 press conference in which Reagan had revealed the diversion and fired North. The president later wrote that he called North because "when it first began to appear that North and Poindexter had done things that they hadn't advised me of, my initial reaction was, well, perhaps they thought they were doing the right thing and trying to protect me, and I felt compassion for both of them."[40] Several weeks later and just before leaving the White House to go to his ranch for Thanksgiving, Reagan also told Hugh Sidey of *Time* that "I do not feel betrayed. Lieutenant Colonel North was involved in all our operations: the *Achille Lauro*, Libya. He has a fine record. He is a national hero. My only criticism is that I wasn't told everything."[41] Later the White House claimed that Reagan had not intended these remarks to Sidey to be made public, but it never denied that he had made them.[42]

What did Ronald Reagan mean when he called North a hero and a national hero? Reagan claimed in his autobiography that when he made these statements, he did not realize the magnitude of the affair, North's shredding of documents, or the diversion and that his later knowledge of those things changed his view of North. In addition, Reagan stated that "I was thinking about his service in Vietnam."[43] In other words, Reagan maintained that he had not been thinking about North's Iran–contra activities when he called North and labeled him a hero. In any case, North reported a very different interpretation, a view that guided him and his followers during his testimony, his trial, and all his public appearances. North later wrote that

> I knew what he meant by those words, and I was grateful for his appreciation. President Reagan was well aware that in addition to my work on the Iran initiative and on behalf of the contras, I had also been involved in a variety of antiterrorist activities. . . . [When Reagan later said that he had been thinking of North's Vietnam service], I found it very hard to believe. For one thing, during my tenure at the NSC I don't believe that anyone at the White House was even aware of my Vietnam war effort.[44]

North also contended that he had been "prepared to be the victim. Offering me up as a *political* scapegoat was part of the plan," but he never expected to face criminal charges.[45]

White House spokespeople offered different explanations of Reagan's remarks, and their comments and responses helped keep alive the hero frame in the early weeks of press coverage. The conservative White House communications chief Patrick Buchanan criticized Republicans who had found fault with the president and Oliver North. In an op-ed piece in the *Washington Post* Buchanan wrote,

> Well, the day the United States ceases to produce soldiers of the kidney and spleen and heart and soul of Oliver North is the day this country enters on its irreversible decline. The President was right. Ollie North is an American hero, and I am proud to know him as a friend.[46]

But Reagan's press secretary, Larry Speakes, took a rather different tone, later noting that "as North's shenanigans became known, I had to develop a response to the question, 'Does the President still think Ollie North is a national hero?' And I would say, 'I haven't heard him call him that lately. Period.' "[47]

Reagan's contradictions regarding North's heroism and the different statements made by administration staff made no logical sense, but they might have made political sense. As Draper maintains, "Reagan was able to have it both ways by permitting North to be made a potential criminal in public and hailing him as an American hero in private."[48] In claiming that North was a hero for activities other than Iran–contra, Reagan was projecting the image of someone who was committed to reveal the truth and clean house. On the other hand, in creating the impression that North's heroism derived from his work on the Iranian and contra initiatives, Reagan was appealing to political conservatives, a fundamental part of his political coalition. As Reagan biographer Lou Cannon observes about Reagan's comments about the diversion, "Reagan would have a difficult time keeping his story straight. This was partly because of his mental confusion and partly because he seems to have wanted to claim credit for helping the contras even while distancing himself from the diversion."[49] Consistent with the media's overall coverage of the Reagan administration, journalists proved unable or unwilling to describe contradictions consistently and instead reported isolated comments as they were made. In any case, Reagan used the hero frame and made it a part of the media's lexicon, and in doing so, he put into play a powerful and resonant cultural symbol, implying high character and good motivations. With its linkages to drama and narratives about independent seekers who face danger, the hero frame was irresistible to the media, especially after North took center stage.

The hero label enabled the media to discuss North in a dramatic fashion and to play up an individualistic and personal framing of Iran–contra. Rather than emphasizing constitutional concerns, the affair could be reduced to claims about various people's motives, character, and knowledge. When the media adopted heroism as a central frame, they were inadvertently stuck with a fundamentally ambiguous concept, one that unwittingly precluded certain issues. If linked to activities other than Iran–contra, North's heroism could be derived from his military service. But when based on Iran–contra, the media's presentation of North's heroism revolved around his sincerity, hard work, and willingness to place himself in dangerous situations. As I showed in chapter 3, most citizens believed that North was sincere and truly loved his country. North's critics, however, argued that Oliver North's sincerity was joined to a zealotry, a belief that the ends justified the means, and a proclivity to lie and break the law whenever he felt it was necessary. But even this negative assessment of North had much in common with the

independent, hard-driving hero of American culture, which could be
seen in cowboy and Rambo movies alike. In its more genteel version, the
independent folk hero looked more like Mr. Smith of Capra's film *Mr.
Smith Goes to Washington*.[50] When North was portrayed as the courageous man who stood alone, he could easily be tied to a vital and pro-
tective hero characterization. The media could portray North as heroic
but not stop to ask whether his sincerity and independence were
admired, even as his goals and acts were questioned.

Reagan's early statements about North's heroism thus initiated the
hero frame, which fit so well with the media's propensity for the dramatic. The hero characterization influenced how public opinion was
measured and covered, although North was also framed as a cowboy or
loose cannon. North and his lawyers used cultural predispositions, the
media's weakness for a good character, and North's own forceful personality in deciding how he would testify. When not presenting himself
as a hero worthy of acclamation, North portrayed himself as a loyal soldier who deserved sympathy. In covering the public's assessments, the
media focused on these characterizations and North's performative
competence. Like President Reagan, the media by and large decided
that North had put on an convincing performance, creating good theater for mass consumption and applause.

The Study of Public Opinion Coverage

To investigate how the media presented public opinion of North during
the hearings, I used an interpretive approach, focusing on the narratives
and symbolic frames used in *Time, Newsweek*, and television news programs during this period. To assess the television news coverage, I used
the Abstracts and Index of Vanderbilt University's Television News
Archives to identify segments in evening news programs that specifically
concerned public opinion. News segments are discrete parts of news-
casts having a brief opening and closing statement by a broadcaster; they
also are summarized and identifiable as sections in the Abstracts. Most
of these segments were broadcast during July 1987, with several aired
later that year. These news segments are described in table 4.1. Although
this table lists the complete length of the segments, it should be kept in
mind that not all material in the segment concerned public opinion. I
viewed and analyzed this footage as well as an additional ten hours of
July 1987 Iran–contra news coverage. My analysis of these network news
segments concentrated on the indicators of public opinion used, the

sorts of statements made about public views, and the narrative frames employed by journalists. Because visuals are an essential element of news coverage and social cognition studies suggest that vivid information is better remembered, I noted the visual characteristics as well.[51]

Creating Conventional Wisdom in Covering the Public's Views

News coverage of the public's views of North relied heavily on the hero frame and presented a largely positive view of public opinion. Over time, a conventional wisdom developed that North had become an American hero. Stories in *Time* and *Newsweek* were characterized by clear disjunctures between their texts and their reports of poll data. Although the narratives implied that North was widely and deeply admired by the nation, the magazines' poll data did not support this analysis. In the July 29, 1987, issue, *Time* reported that "the Boy Scout and the patriot had the nation rooting for him" and argued that his lawlessness appealed to American values because "Americans have a visceral attraction to cowboy morality."[52] But the magazine's poll data showed that 61 percent held that "national hero" did not describe North.

Newsweek's cover story of July 20, 1987, "Ollie Takes the Hill," subtitled "The Fall Guy Becomes a Folk Hero," stated,

> Lt. Colonel Oliver L. North charged up Capitol Hill last week as the Rambo of diplomacy. . . . But he captured the Hill as Ollie: a new national folk hero who somehow embodied Jimmy Stewart, Gary Cooper and John Wayne in one bemedaled uniform. He touched off a tidal wave of telegrams, flowers and letters; "Give 'em hell, Ollie" bumper stickers, T-shirts and banners blossomed across the country.[53]

According to *Newsweek*'s polls, 45 percent of the respondents believed he was a patriot and a hero, and 48 percent did not. Although 45 percent is a rather high percentage, it is not even a bare majority. In addition, it is worth noting that the question mixed patriotism with heroism and that no question focusing on heroism alone yielded anywhere close to that level of support.

In addition, both news magazines used colorful but unreliable means of gauging public opinion and then gave these sources greater impact by combining them with pictures. Both *Time* and *Newsweek* showed demonstrators with signs supporting North.[54] The July 13, 1987, edition of *Newsweek* reported on Oliver North dolls, cakes, sandwiches, buttons, bumper stickers, and "Ollie for President" T-shirts.[55] *Time* carried a story entitled "Olliemania Breaks out All Over" on July 20, 1987,

TABLE 4.1
Television News Coverage Relating to Oliver North and Public Opinion

Date	Network	Length of Segment	Source of Information on Public Opinion	View of Public Opinion on North
July 4, 1987	ABC	:40	Polls	Negative
July 4, 1987	NBC	:20	Poll	Negative
July 6, 1987	ABC	5:00	Comments by public and friends, wife, people from hometown	Mixed, mostly positive
July 6, 1987	CBS	6:50	Comments by friends, teachers, people from hometown	Positive
July 7, 1987	ABC	2:10	Comments by public, including radio talk show callers	Mixed
July 7, 1987	CBS	2:50	Comments by public, members of Congress, polls, radio talk show callers	Mixed
July 7, 1987	NBC	2:40	Comments by public, people in hometown, radio talk show callers	Mixed
July 8, 1987	NBC	:50	TV audience reactions, phone calls, donations and expressions of support (telegrams, letters) for North	Positive
July 9, 1987	CBS	3:10	Demonstrations, phone-in polls, telegrams, public comments, North compared with movie characters	Mixed, mostly positive
July 10, 1987	ABC	5:00	Comments by North's lawyer on public expressions of support (letters, telegrams, phone calls) for North	Positive
July 10, 1987	CBS	10:10	Public expressions of support (telegrams, phone calls) and polls	Mixed, mostly positive
July 10, 1987	NBC	2:40	Comments from citizens in Denver, including radio talk show callers	Mixed, mostly positive
July 11, 1987	ABC	2:30	Young Republicans convention, marketing, polls, supportive phone calls	Positive
July 11, 1987	NBC	5:40	Supportive telegrams and phone calls, polls mentioned	Positive
July 13, 1987	ABC	7:50	Comments to North by members of Congress on his actions and public reactions, polls	Positive, except for polls
July 13, 1987	NBC	7:40	Supportive telegrams,	Positive

TABLE 4.1

(continued)

Date	Network	Length of Segment	Source of Information on Public Opinion	View of Public Opinion on North
			comments by members of Congress, poll on contras	
July 13, 1987	NBC	:40	Polls	Positive
July 13, 1987	NBC	3:10	Polls, comments by members of Congress	Mixed
July 14, 1987	NBC	1:50	Commentary by John Chancellor, reviews contradictions in polls and other evidence	Mixed, mostly positive
July 17, 1987	CBS	9:40	Polls on Reagan administration, policy, Oliver North	Mixed
July 18, 1987	NBC	:40	Sales of book containing North's testimony	Positive
July 20, 1987	CBS	:30	Hollywood sign changed to "Ollywood," comment by person who made change	Positive
July 20, 1987	NBC	:30	Hollywood sign changed to "Ollywood," comment by person who made change	Positive
July 21, 1987	ABC	2:00	Sales of book, video, other products, Ollieburger	Positive
July 22, 1987	ABC	:50	Polls	Mixed
July 30, 1987	NBC	:10	Sales of book of North's testimony	High public interest
August 8, 1987	NBC	2:50	Comedians on Oliver North and President Reagan	Mixed
August 11, 1987	NBC	2:40	Polls on contra aid in wake of North's testimony, remarks by conservative groups on North's popularity	Positive
August 15, 1987	ABC	:30	Parade in honor of North in his hometown	Positive
September 9, 1987	NBC	2:10	Product marketing failures, use of name by conservative fundraisers, with images of past demonstrations of support during time of testimony	Mixed, positive during time of testimony
November 18, 1987	CBS	1:50	Retrospective, notes supportive telegrams, phone calls, and marketing at time of testimony, later waning of Olliemania	Mixed, positive during time of testimony

Note: Table includes segments indentified as including information about public opinion using the Abstracts and Index of the Vanderbilt University Television News Archive.

which described a "Fawn Hall Shredding Party" held in a Southern California bar, a vigil of one hundred at the Utah state capitol, the sale of buttons at a Young Republican convention in Washington State, a rock and roll song called "Ollie B. Goode," and the twenty-to-one ratio of supportive letters and telegrams received by members of Congress. Both news magazines promoted the picture that North was seen as heroic, although the objective evidence did not support this picture.[56]

In fact, *Time* noted that public expressions of support were not necessarily representative indicators of mass opinion, although this information was placed outside the main text. At the top of the box containing the survey data, one could read, "Although the capital was awash with expressions of support for Oliver North, reactions to the Marine lieutenant colonel among the public at large was more qualified." Thus if readers just looked at the pictures and read the narrative provided, they would not be aware that the public was critical of and ambivalent toward Oliver North. In fact, the perception of public opinion conveyed by the news story was instead positive and even adulatory.

In the network coverage of public opinion of Oliver North, neutral-to-positive coverage before North's testimony gave way to discussions of nearly unqualified strong public support, and then the coverage returned to mixed but mostly positive views of public opinion. News stories relied quite strongly on nonpoll data, which usually suggested popular support for North.

Immediately before the lieutenant colonel's July 1987 appearance, the networks ran stories featuring poll data, person-on-the-street interviews, and interviews with people who had known North over the years. Poll data were presented in simple ways, often including only a "talking head" and quick flashes of poll results. In these brief stories—from twenty to forty seconds long—reporters announced that most people believed that North would lie to Congress. The background stories, however, were much more positive in tone and featured interviews, still photographs from North's childhood, and information on Annapolis, Vietnam, and North's early National Security Council days. These more vivid stories ranged from three minutes and twenty seconds to five minutes long. Although one ABC story began, "On the eve of Colonel North's testimony, we were thinking how very strong the reaction to him can be" and then went on to talk about three former marines who told North what a disgrace it was that he had worn his uniform while defending himself, nearly all the following material in this five-minute segment relied on positive "character witnesses" from North's past. North's high school track coach told viewers that North always tried hard; his childhood friend declared that North's family was strict; and a man that North commanded in Vietnam proclaimed, "He's a compassionate man, a loyal man, he's patriotic, he's a Marine." Approximately fifty seconds of this five-minute story featured people who insisted that North was wrong or were ambivalent about him.

After North began to testify in July, the initial stories were fairly balanced but then rapidly turned to readings of public opinion that were strongly positive. A two-minute, ten-second ABC segment on July 7, 1987—following the first day of North's testimony—included ten interviews with ordinary Americans, five of whom were critical of North, four who were more positive, and one who had no interest in the events. On the same night, CBS held that Americans were more ambivalent about North than they earlier had been. North was "not simple red, white and blue . . . like most of us, he comes in shades of gray." NBC presented a mixed sampling of statements from citizens.

After these mixed views from the public, however, the coverage increasingly implied that North was wildly popular. Small demonstrations, phone calls and written expressions of support for North, donations to North's defense fund, phone-in polls, radio talk shows, and interviews were used as informational sources, which had quite a positive view of how the public saw North.

Perhaps the most extreme of these news stories was a July 9, 1987, piece on CBS. Dan Rather began by asking, "What impression is North making in the living rooms of Americans who are listening and watching?" The story then featured a candlelight vigil in Salt Lake City and positive comments from Miami's Little Havana, a remark by a reporter that Oliver North had become a hero, and then examples of strongly positive phone-in polls. In introducing one survey based on a self-selected group of respondents, the announcer proclaimed that "96 percent of you back North up, saying you approve of his actions." Another nonrandom survey claimed that about 41,000 respondents thought that North was a hero, and only about 5,000 called him a villain. This story then went on to explain why North had become a hero, contending that he was so popular because he embodied the frontier mythology, Rambo, and Dirty Harry. The segment ended with several interviews—only one of which was critical—and a discussion and picture of supportive telegrams. In this three-minute story, no reliable poll data at all were included, and generalizations about North's popularity were drawn from poor sources of information. Nonetheless, the idea that North had become a hero became a fact to be reported, and highly vivid images supported this point of view.

The television coverage of North demonstrates the making of conventional wisdom. In stories on public opinion for the next month and in comments by political figures, reporters simply assumed that North was popular and viewed as heroic. This is not to say that other, challenging information was not offered. In fact, the networks did sometimes offer information that did not fit the general mold. But discussions of poll data contradicting this picture were given very little time and attention and did not influence the general tenor of coverage. Again and again, reporters, anchors, and political figures announced that North had won the admiration of the American people, that he was a new folk hero. Once the poll data were released, the nearly unconditional positive tone shifted a bit, but still the news stories assumed that North was highly popular and esteemed.

One story did attempt to grapple with contradictory and ambivalent poll results. Given its good-faith attempt to escape the typical frame of coverage, it is worth examining closely, if only to show how it, too, was limited by the basic interpretation. NBC aired a story on July 14, 1987, toward the end of its broadcast. This was the only segment on public opinion that was clearly labeled as a commentary, and it was delivered by John Chancellor. The entire story was visually uninteresting, as it included only talking heads. Chancellor started by noting the contradictions in how the public saw North. "He broke laws, but he shouldn't be prosecuted. Not a national hero, but a true patriot. . . . When *Time* magazine asked if you'd want him to marry your daughter, only 26 percent said yes." But then Chancellor went on to ask, "Why did he become so popular?" and to declare that North was admired because he challenged the bureaucracy and Congress and could get things done. "What was important was the image of this go-getting, rule-breaking, full-speed-ahead marine." Even in this story, the simplistic and positive picture of public opinion prevailed.

After North's testimony ended, the stories included positive portrayals of public opinion, based on sales of merchandise, the changing of the "Hollywood" sign to "Ollywood," a support demonstration in North's hometown, and references to "Olliemania." Then about a month after the testimony ended, the news coverage became less unequivocally positive. A NBC story about comedians on August 8, 1987, included fairly negative statements about North and Reagan. And an NBC story in early September, aired at the very end of the broadcast on Labor Day, asked, "Whatever happened to Olliemania?" and reported that the sales of North books, videos, dolls, and other merchandise had fallen short and that Ollieburgers had been discontinued. The story concluded that "like pet rocks and mood rings, Oliver North is yesterday's craze." A final story in 1987, aired by CBS on November 11, stated that "Olliemania" had cooled as more information about the scandal was revealed. Even in these two stories, however, the spoken message was joined with very positive images, such as signs proclaiming North a hero, and the narratives implied that North had once been quite popular.

Throughout this news coverage, information about public opinion that relied on scientific polling received very little airtime. Table 4.2 gives the amount of time devoted to different sources of information concerning public opinion. I constructed this table by timing portions from news segments that focused on public reactions; these segments are listed in table 4.1. As table 4.2 shows, discussions of polls took only four minutes, thirty-five seconds of airtime, whereas other sorts of information

TABLE 4.2

Time Spent on Different Sources of Information on
Public Opinion in Television News Coverage

1. Polling	4:35	
2. Person-on-the-street interviews	11:30	
3. Demonstrations and conventions	1:30	
4. Cultural manifestations	3:50	Includes comparisons with movies, comedy on North
5. Merchandise	5:20	
6. Signs	1:30	
7. Support calls, mail, telegrams	2:50	
8. Radio call-in programs	:30	
9. Phone-in polls	:10	
10. Comments by North, lawyer, and public officials on North's popularity	3:50	
11. News commentary	6:00	

Polling Versus All Else

Polls	Other Sources
4 minutes, 35 seconds	36 minutes, 40 seconds

Notes: Figures were compiled by timing presentations of opinion information in segments identified as focusing on public opinion information and citizen reactions. These segments are listed in table 4.1.

received thirty-six minutes, forty seconds of airtime. Thus reliable data were used in only about 10 percent of the coverage of public opinion. In fact, these figures for the time spent on each sort of information are conservative in estimating the amount and bias of nonpoll data because the totals are derived from only those news segments focusing on public reactions. As the conventional wisdom developed that North was highly popular, this "fact" was regularly restated by reporters, anchors, North, his lawyer, and government officials. Most news segments reporting on the hearings included this conventional wisdom. In addition, nonpoll data implied that North was much more popular than the poll data indicated. Finally, the presentations of poll data typically were visually uninteresting, featuring only simple tables (usually flashed on the screen very quickly) and talking heads. Other sorts of information about public opinion were much more interesting and vivid, were frequently dramatized and used symbols. Cognitive psychologists would expect that this sort of information would be more easily stored and retrieved. All in all, the media interpreted the public mind to the public in ways that probably left the impression that most Americans admired North.

The Media as Theater Critic and Audience Assessor

When the media discussed the public's reactions to North, commentators and reporters often characterized him as a performer. For example, North was given glowing reviews for his performance, that is, for his ability to present himself well. In characterizing North as a fine performer, the media assumed that the public was attracted to his persona and that citizens found him convincing. The media's concern with performance was therefore part of their conventional wisdom about the public's opinion of Oliver North. Although journalists usually agreed that North had put on a good performance, some were troubled by this and by the media's emphasis on North's performative competence. One problem was that this emphasis precluded discussions of constitutional issues and took time that could have been spent explaining the context and historical chronology of Iran–contra. In addition, critics argued that this sort of coverage marked a disturbing turn in the American political culture. No matter how they were evaluated, the media's discussions of performances helped create false impressions of the public's views of North, in that they assumed more positive reactions than the opinion data found. The media thus wrongly informed elites about citizens' perspectives.

By 1986 and 1987, the media had become quite comfortable with using criteria from theater and entertainment television to cover public figures. President Reagan, the Great Communicator, was admired for his ability to perform well. Later, in the 1988 and 1992 presidential election campaigns, the media often assumed the position of a drama critic or campaign consultant and assessed the candidates' communications strategies. Strategic and performance news stories drove out substantive issue analyses. "The performance criteria ask not what you are but how you seem or appear."[57] This tendency had progressed so far in 1992 that the *New York Times* found it reasonable to have its theater critic, Frank Rich, cover the presidential campaign.[58] During North's 1987 congressional testimony, the performance criterion was used extensively, with the emphasis on North's ability to seem credible, sympathetic, courageous, and independent.

In the early days of the congressional hearings, commentators had already begun to assess the possible entertainment values. *Newsweek* printed "A TV Viewer's Guide" in early May that compared Iran–contra with the previous "show" of Watergate. Jonathan Alter and Eleanor Clift wrote, "If it all works out, the show will be a hit spinoff: Watergate with a new cast and fresh plot. . . . So who's starring in the Iran-contra pilot anyway? . . . Unfortunately for the committee, this year's show could be quickly canceled." The article went on to evaluate the appeal and personae of committee members and staff lawyers and to state, "That may seem like a lot of characters to keep track of, and there are 11 more besides. Too many to make it a hit series? Size never seems to hurt 'General Hospital.' If the plot works, the fans will follow."[59]

Other early commentators assumed that performance was important to the media and the public but nonetheless found this disturbing. For example, an article in the *Chicago Tribune* observed,

> The testimony of witnesses such as retired Air Force Maj. Gen. Richard Secord and former National Security Adviser Robert McFarlane is being reviewed as intently as it is being reported. . . . We know Richard Secord is "stolid." We don't know if he's a profiteer in the misery of hostage-taking and hostage-keeping. We know McFarlane is "tense" and "tight-lipped." But will we ever know what he has to be tense and tight-lipped about? . . . The operative verb in the postmortems on the network news shows focuses on how the witnesses "handled themselves" or "handled the committee." Content is for the nitpickers, for the folks who insist on reading all the way to the bottom of the page.[60]

Once North appeared, his testimony was regularly characterized on the network news and in the print press as a remarkable performance. Television reporters often noted the lieutenant colonel's ability to use the medium well. Sometimes journalists devoted themselves to one aspect of North's performance or to one part of his body. For example, a *Time* piece by Lance Morrow meticulously analyzed North's use of facial expressions:

> North is a natural actor and a conjurer of illusion. His face is an instrument that he plays with an almost unconscious genius. His countenance is dominated by his eyes. Now they are the eyes of a vulnerable child: innocence at risk in a dark forest. Now an indignation rises in them, dark weathers of injured virtue. And an instant later, there comes across the landscape of North's face something chilling, a glimpse perhaps of the capacity to kill, and the eyes constrict their apertures a little, taking aim. The altar boy who might charm the nuns could take on ferocities. His voice was low and passionate. It cracked in the affecting way that Jimmy Stewart's does, although sometimes with a force of anger behind it, the voice sounded like Kirk Douglas in a manic moment.[61]

Not only did Morrow's writing seem like a drama review, but he also wrote as if this performance frame defined others' views of North's testimony: "The Iran–contra hearings last week may have had more to do with theater and symbolism than with great constitutional questions."

For these journalists, there was no question that North's bravura performance was effective. In addition to his general ability to perform well, they held that North's testimony worked for him because it was consistent with cultural traditions. North admitted that he had previously lied to Congress, which was consistent with "the cult of celebrity confession."[62] He argued for the contras and so came across as a dramatic, independent protagonist.

> Ollie North took care of the anchorman. . . . Television, no less than television's audience, wants to see public figures displaying the courage of their convictions, especially conservatives who make large claims to intellectual principle. By standing up to the committee, Ollie North stood up to the medium. He sent the anchormen into neutral corners.[63]

After North testified, his immediate boss, John Poindexter, took the stand, and his milder performance was contrasted with North's. In a preview to Poindexter's appearance, *Newsweek* wrote, "Balding and bespectacled, Poindexter may lack the telegenic charisma that made Oliver North an instant TV celebrity. But despite the vast attention focused on the swashbuckling Marine, committee members expect Poindexter to be nothing less than the most important witness of the Iran–Contra investigation."[64] When Poindexter spoke quietly and lit his pipe, a *New York Times* article concluded, "It didn't matter if Admiral Poindexter was saying something important or even dropping bombshells. Television said something else."[65]

As journalists assessed the testimony in terms of performance, some argued that this approach was bad for the political system. For example, after analyzing North's presentation, *Newsweek*'s Jonathan Alter observed,

> The problem with all of this, of course, is that when the house lights come up, the audience must put the performance in the context of the plot. Especially when the drama is not, at bottom, a piece of entertainment but the conduct of the government of the United States.[66]

Others contended that the concentration on performance demonstrated the corruption of values in the American political culture. A film critic writing in the *New Republic* lamented,

> It's a measure of how thoroughly values in this country have become subsumed to media considerations that "sincerity"—i.e., how well someone plays himself—becomes an issue in the Iran–contra hearings. . . . There's no center, no core, just endless media images that are believed or not believed, and anyone who tries to see something for what it is risks sounding priggish, dull, and out of it.[67]

Clearly the media's emphasis on North as a performer was a sign of the problems with their approach to Mr. North and their coverage of public views. In addition, the overall coverage prevented the media from concentrating on other, more fundamental issues. For one, the media could have done a better job in telling the story of Iran–contra during the hearings. They had covered the affair extensively before the testimony began and therefore may not have found it necessary to go over that information again. However, as Scott Armstrong pointed out,

> The committee, for its part, ignored the natural chronology of the tale, starting in the middle with the most contentious of all witnesses, Richard Secord. This made a coherent exposition of the events impossible. If the storyline of the Iran–contra affair was going to be laid out intelligibly it would be up to the press to do so. Instead, reporters concentrated on who was scoring more public relations points on any given day—the witnesses or the committee members and their counsel.[68]

In addition, the media's perception that the public was moved by Oliver North's performance limited their policy analysis and criticism. David Denby wrote,

> North's performance may have marked the first time that appearances ever hustled the Constitution off the stage. Faced with a star turn like

North's, reporters and media personalities with a reputation for critical acumen either kept their mouths shut—as if, suddenly, their own opinions had become worthless—or jumped on the bandwagon, connoisseurs of the image-maker's success. The man was a hit, and that was all that mattered.[69]

But even if media observers were right in noting that the media concentrated on performance, why were they so sure that the performance convinced the public? Stories about North's presentation, about "Oliver North's face[, which] possessed the power and guile of an actor's instrument," nearly always concluded that he had moved the public, that "most people reacted as if they were still looking at a myth."[70] Certainly this assessment is understandable if commentators and journalists decided they knew what the public thought by looking at the media coverage, since the news coverage and analysis of public opinion presented a very positive reading of public responses to Oliver North. Even critics of the media were caught by the media's skewed translation of the voice of the people.

Explaining Biases and Skews

Television news' interpretive attempts demonstrated a number of the ways that analyses of public opinion may have led to misperceptions of the public mind. First, many interpretations of the public's mood were not explicit but were woven into the news coverage on a regular basis. Even though the amount of time taken in a story for these short bits was relatively small, its impact may have been much greater, since it formed the background of facts and became part of the conventional wisdom. Second, the dramatizing, symbolic, and visual orientations of television news contributed to an emphasis on unreliable data. The media's interest in creating a powerful dramatic narrative also encouraged them to focus on North as a performer. He was framed as an actor in a spectacle, and the public's responses were framed as reactions by an enthusiastic audience. Third, when poll data were presented, they were not closely interpreted. Data that did not fit and alternative explanations could have been carefully explained but instead were often ignored or slighted.[71]

In the case of Oliver North and the Iran–contra hearings, the media told the public what it thought. Since the history of opinion measurement shows that news reports have always included both coverage of events and public views, it should not be surprising that the major television networks, newspapers, and news magazines reported on public opinion extensively and used multiple sources of information.[72] What is more surprising is the extent to which unreliable but vivid data were used to interpret North's impact on the public. These sources favored a positive view of public opinion on the young marine lieutenant colonel. Even when polling data were available and presented, they took a decidedly back seat in news stories.

One source of information about public opinion came from activities that were often coordinated by political groups, such as rallies and communications with Congress. Those groups mobilized to support North gained a fair amount of coverage and contributed to the impression that he was popular and admired. Often mobilization is biased so that one side of an issue is better represented. In this case, critical and ambivalent members of the public were not mobilized, and this "mobilization of bias" had a disproportionate impact on the news coverage of public opinion.[73] Activities in support of Oliver North are discussed in detail in chapter 5.

Did a spiral of silence result from the media's presentation of public opinion? If so, whom did it affect? Poll data suggest that people's assessments of their fellows citizens' views of North were somewhat more positive than their own evaluation of him. Although this perspective was not hegemonic, people were given an unrepresentative view of the public mind. At the same time, findings from public opinion surveys show the real limits to the effect of a spiral of silence. Reference groups, selective media exposure, and perceptual biases all probably helped limit the impact on citizens of the media's coverage of public opinion.

It is important to remember that the spiral of silence involves more than citizens' opinions. Noelle-Neumann's theory is explicitly concerned with public expressions of opinion, and in this respect, it is clear that the support mobilized for North was not met by a significant countermobilization by critical or ambivalent citizens. I found only one report of a demonstration against North (which was held outside a Young Republicans convention) and no reports of sales of bumper stickers, signs, or T-shirts by North's critics. In addition, these uneven patterns of public expressions of opinion may have had political effects.

Oliver North became very well known as a result of his congressional testimony and was viewed sympathetically by many. Polling data suggest that large numbers of Americans believed North's contentions that he had assumed that the president approved his actions and that he was the designated scapegoat. But there was no overwhelming admiration for North. His support base was strongly committed, intense in their preferences, and quick to act. The media created the impression that the public as a whole had made North into a folk hero, by covering him as a performer and focusing on the segment of the population that rallied to his side. But the media's repeated claims that North's performance captivated the public and their repeated pictures of support and statements about North's popularity could go only so far. Surveys showed that most people had serious reservations about North's actions, and interviews with citizens demonstrated that a wide variety of people found him to be sincere and well intentioned, but wrong.

Despite the gap between the public's views and the media's presentation of mass opinion, the media's portrait could still have a political effect. Politically consequential public opinion is opinion as perceived by public officials, which is not necessarily the same as opinions held by citizens. When the media tell the public what it thinks, they also tell this to those who pay the most attention to political affairs—the politicians and political activists. The media's coverage of public opinion therefore influences politicians' impressions of public opinion. In the political communication system as echo chamber, the media speak about the public when speaking to citizens and to elites. But this communication process is colored by the media's own tendencies to stress drama, performance, and culturally resonant symbols and by the intense efforts of some members of the public to shout on the political stage. In telling the public what they thought about Oliver North, the media's emphasis on North's ability to perform well assumed that the public reacted positively and reinforced the emerging conventional wisdom about North's effect on the public.

5

Taking an Interest in the Public

For he's a spirit of persuasion, only
Professes to persuade.

Shakespeare, *The Tempest*

Although Oliver North's testimony and media coverage of Iran–contra reached millions of Americans who previously had little interest in foreign policy, the congressional testimony also mobilized groups and individuals who had already cared a great deal about the fate of the contras. Conservative interest groups and long-standing friends of North organized support actions, ranging from letter drives to candlelight marches. When covering public opinion, the media treated these activities as manifestations of North's new popularity and performative competence. Because they provided good visuals and drama, the media amplified these voices of support and admiration, which reverberated in the political echo chamber. To be sure, much of the public reaction was not organized by any interest group. However, conservative groups were primed to be there, to try to speak and shape the perception of public opinion. In the spectacle of Iran–contra, these groups tried to serve as an enthusiastic audience.

As chapters 3 and 4 demonstrated, public opinion regarding North was complex and ambivalent, yet the media presented a very positive view of it. The media's coverage of public opinion devoted very little time—

only 10 percent of the total coverage of public opinion—to analyses of reliable polling data. As the conventional wisdom had it, "Olliemania" was rampant, and Oliver North was an American hero.

Even before the Iran–contra affair became a public issue, interest groups were deeply involved in the contra aid issue. To try to sway members of Congress, pressure groups tried to mobilize group members and influence both public opinion and media coverage. Both pro-contra and anticontra aid coalitions emphasized outsider strategies, the usual approach of citizen groups. Moreover, the members of these groups were motivated by ideological concerns, not material or self-interested incentives.

Once the hearings were over, the conservative groups that had supported the contras tried to use public opinion to gain new support for the Nicaraguan rebels. In addition, groups used support for Oliver North as a resource for organizational development and maintenance. North's name helped them target potential members and develop large, productive mailing lists. Eventually Oliver North turned to these groups to help him build his own political organization, which later served as one of the foundations of his Senate campaign. Public opinion and the perception that the public strongly supported North were important group resources.

Public Opinion as a Strategic Interest-Group Resource

In responding to North's testimony and in the contra aid controversy, interest groups tried to use public opinion and perceptions of public opinion as a strategic group resource. Although the particulars of this case differentiate it from other political disputes, interest groups often show the same concern for public opinion. As communicators between citizens and government, interest groups take an interest in the public. Interest groups and group leaders try to persuade the public to adopt their position, work to recruit and mobilize members and other citizens, and attempt to create the impression that the public supports their position. When arguing that their view should be adopted, group leaders assert that the people are on their side. Claims about public opinion are a regular feature of political advertising and public declarations. As Herbst notes, "Today, poll data are collected and publicized by survey or news organizations, but are used by a variety of parties for their own rhetorical purposes."[1]

Many interest groups take an interest in the public because they cannot do otherwise. Group leaders know that mobilized publics and public opinion are potent political resources.[2] If one side of an issue is not well mobilized or has not made credible claims that it represents public opinion, groups on the other side will win the advantage by default. Because nothing prevents the opposing group from arguing that the public is on their side, groups need to organize (or at least to monitor soundings of public opinion) in order to be prepared to counter groups on the other side of the issue.

Not all groups focus on the public to the same extent, of course. Some prefer insider strategies, such as lobbying, and do not appeal to the public much at all. Gais and Walker contend that "the choice of whether to adopt an inside or outside strategy depends on organizational resources under a group's control, the character of its membership, and its principal sources of financial support."[3] Other resources are important as well, including money, a professional staff, a Washington office, reputation, coalition partners, and expertise.[4] In some cases, groups' policy efforts mostly entail direct negotiations with elites. In an age of intense media scrutiny and increasingly independent members of Congress, however, nearly all interest organizations must pay some attention to the public. In some cases, considering public opinion means mobilizing members who feel intensely, in order to project an image of public concern. In other situations, politicians may be aware that a group does not reflect the public opinion found in polls but, rather, is composed of highly concerned listeners and speakers (e.g., the National Rifle Association).

Groups speak for and to the public. In describing public opinion, groups are by no means disinterested interpreters of public opinion. Instead, struggles among groups are like competitive teams of biased translators. Each group represents public opinion in the best light for its own purposes. Thus when interest groups try to use public opinion as a resource, opinion is something other than private responses to poll questions or individualized cognitive maps. That is, private and idiosyncratic views of politics are raw materials that groups may either use or ignore, depending on how well they serve the groups' needs.

When groups attempt to influence public opinion and the perception of public opinion, they become part of what Habermas calls *stagings* and Edelman terms *spectacles*. Political elites and groups create displays to which citizens can react. Those groups that can influence the frames used in political spectacles are more powerful than those that cannot. The media deliver to the public these presentations of problems, alternative solutions, and political personae such as heroes, villains, and leaders. In addition, audiences (i.e., citizens) play a dual role in such spectacles. Groups can influence the audience by framing predicaments, possibilities, and arguments. In addition, groups have an impact on the public by helping construct the audience that is incorporated into the spectacle. For this latter case, groups may use selective mobilization and dramatic action to influence how the media report on public opinion. Mobilized action—particularly if it is dramatic and reported by the media—can influence the perception of group strength. "Mass media, particularly television, magnify individual actions by entering them into the collective consciousness. When demonstrators perform on cue for the TV camera, they know they can produce an impression that they represent a much larger constituency, that their views are much more universally held than they actually are."[5] The framing of the audience— as supporting or opposed to some political situation—becomes part of the spectacle that can influence citizens and elites. In today's political environment, the media rely on symbolic frames to report the news; politicians are more independent of political parties than ever before; and interest groups find it expedient to mobilize the public and try to influence the perception of public opinion.

Public Opinion and Interest-Group Tasks and Goals

Interest groups using outside strategies have two tasks involving public opinion. Groups seek to convince citizens to support the group's position on a policy. Convincing citizens may mean changing their opinions, bolstering their existing views, or exhorting them to join the group or, independently, to contact policymakers. In addition, interest groups also seek to create the impression that public opinion is on its side or that momentum is shifting toward the group's position. Attempts to shape the perception of public opinion can color media coverage and affect citizens and political leaders. Citizens who believe that they are part of the majority might become more vocal, in a bandwagon effect. Those who believe that they are in the minority might also become less active, helping create a spiral of silence. If mobilized groups are successful, political elites may be moved by what they see as a wave of intense views or mass opinion.

Interest groups engage in these two tasks in order to further their two fundamental goals: to influence policy and to maintain themselves as organizations.[6] Pressure groups use public opinion as a political resource for the pursuit of their policy goals. If they can move the public and convince policymakers that they have done so, this will help them with their policy goals. But even if they do not cause a shift in public views, changing the perception of public opinion can influence politicians as well. Groups use mobilizing tactics, such as contacting Congress and staging public demonstrations, to help define majority opinion. The media, in turn, can magnify the effect of political action on the perception of public opinion.[7] News programs may use phone calls to Congress and the like as indicators of what the public thinks.

In addition, groups attempt to shape public opinion and the perception of public opinion in order to maintain themselves and prosper. Public opinion is a fundamental part of the political environment and so must be reckoned with by group founders and leaders. Groups develop themselves in relation to both real and perceived public opinion. When recruiting members, groups can refer to public opinion to explain why their support is required. Groups may argue that the public supports the policies preferred by the group but that entrenched interests or an out-of-touch government has stymied their adoption. Therefore, potential members should join and contribute to the group so that the people's will can be realized. Claims that the group represents the majority may be based on sketchy data or biased poll questions, of course. Whether or not the assertion is accurate, groups make these claims because they believe they add rhetorical force.

In some cases, group leaders acknowledge that their views are not shared by the majority and argue that citizens should support their groups in order to move the public and influence policymakers. Groups may claim that the media have not given their position a fair shake. For example, groups may contend that because the media have been biased, the public has not been given the full story. Thus, the argument continues, citizens need to join or continue to support the pressure group in order to counteract media biases. In addition, groups may argue that although they are not yet in the majority, they are a growing force. And in order to continue growing and to affect policy, citizens need to lend a hand.

Contra Aid, Iran–Contra, and Oliver North

Group Activity and Nicaragua Policy Before Iran–Contra

More than two hundred groups joined the debate over contra aid, a foreign policy issue remarkable in the "scale, duration and intensity" of interest-group activity.[8] Before President Ronald Reagan called the opponents of the Nicaraguan Sandinistas *freedom fighters*, interest groups were already concerned and mobilized. On the right, groups such as the Conservative Caucus began to urge their members to work for aid for the contras. But despite these efforts, even these committed conservative citizens did not act until the president began to highlight the issue.[9] Once Reagan spoke out, conservative group members became excited about and active in the contra cause.[10]

By 1983 and 1984, the contra cause was in full gear, and conservative groups were fully activated. Right-wing groups used a full array of lobbying tools and public relations methods, seeking to influence public opinion with advertising, appearances on television and radio talk shows, and op–ed articles. Right-wing groups also targeted selected members of Congress, flooding offices with petitions and postcards. When important votes were imminent, the Conservative Caucus set up phone banks and used a system in which citizens could call a free 800 number and have a mailgram sent in their name to particular members of Congress. For the 1985 contra aid vote, it was reported that "conservative groups are relying largely on mass mailings and appearances by anti-Sandinista Central Americans to generate pressure on swing-vote members of Congress."[11]

Support for the Nicaraguan rebels was a high-priority issue for the right. In a time of a fervently anticommunist administration, the president's supporters argued that Nicaragua represented a threat in the United States' own backyard. Major public relations efforts were launched in Florida and Texas, two relatively conservative states that were closer to Latin America than most others. Throughout the nation, groups argued that the Sandinista government was a serious security threat and that the Monroe Doctrine must be upheld. Groups sponsored tours of contra leaders. Group leaders traveled to contra encampments and later told of the primitive living conditions they faced.

In his public pronouncements President Reagan had declared that it was necessary to quarantine the Sandinistas, to prevent the spread of revolution. (In fact, a series of revelations established that President Reagan's goal was to overthrow the Nicaraguan government.) During the fight for contra aid, right-wing groups sought to go beyond the president's publicly stated aim and oust the leftist government.[12] In part, these groups took these positions for tactical reasons, accounting for the distribution of opinions in Congress and in opinion polls. Group leaders were aware that taking a hard-line position made Reagan's views look like a moderate and reasonable compromise and so could help the administration obtain funds for the contras.

During the legislative battles for contra aid, right-wing groups worked in concert with the White House. In his capacity as a member of the "public diplomacy" outreach group, Oliver North spoke to a number of groups about the cause, including organizations not focusing on foreign policy or national security affairs. Concerned Women for America (CWA), an antifeminist group claiming a membership of 600,000, invited North to be the keynote speaker for their 1985 and 1986 national conventions. CWA leader Beverly La Haye wrote, "Both times he examined the great need for America to be helping the Nicaraguan Freedom Fighters. He revealed, with the aid of photographs, Soviet bombers and cargo planes landing on huge airstrips in Nicaragua—pictures that had never before been released to the public."[13]

Despite the usual effectiveness of the Reagan administration's public relations operations, its open efforts to operate with interest groups did not work particularly well. One former White House official maintained that its arguments were too extreme and that the outreach group "largely brought together lobbyists who were already supporting the Administration's program. 'That evidences a complete lack of understanding of the way public support is built,' said the former official."[14] By concentrating on its right-wing base for this issue, the Reagan administration was unable to build the necessary political coalition for success.

Feeling that the media had not given the administration position its due, the White House established a covert public relations group to deliver what it called *public diplomacy* and *white propaganda*.[15] Called S/LPD (for State Department Group on Latin American Public Diplomacy), the group operated out of the White House, with staff support from, among others, Oliver North. Headed by a former CIA expert in psychological operations, Walter Raymond Jr., the S/LPD coordinated efforts to influence the public that would not appear to come from the administration but would support the administration's policies.[16] S/LPD contracted out to International Business Communications (IBC), which produced letters to the editor, op-ed pieces, and advertising. According to an internal memo, one goal was to "review and restate themes in view of results of public opinion poll."[17]

S/LPD worked with Carl ("Spitz") Channell's group, the National Endowment for the Preservation of Liberty (NEPL), which launched a major campaign to persuade the public to support the contras[18] and became a conduit for funds to the contras.[19] Channell had shown impressive fund-raising abilities in his earlier work as the national finance chairman of the National Conservative Political Action Committee, "where he was known for arranging Washington briefings for large contributors. This would become his specialty on the Contra beat as well."[20] Wealthy donors were given briefings by Oliver North, and some met the president to receive his thanks. The NEPL was an important element of the contra aid operation because it provided a cover story for White House claims about how the contras had survived despite Congress's unwillingness to give them money. Channell also allowed North to launder contra aid money from the Iranian diversion.

The NEPL proved to be a big money maker for Channell. Of the nearly $10.4 million raised for the contras in 1985–86, only 20 percent went to the contras.[21] After the Iran–contra affair became public and this information was revealed, the General Accounting Office (GAO) ruled that S/LPD had engaged in illegal propaganda and lobbying activities, and Channell pleaded guilty to tax irregularities in the way he conducted a registered nonprofit organization. A report by the House Foreign Affairs Committee concluded that the S/LPD was a "domestic covert operation designed to lobby the Congress, manipulate the media and influence domestic public opinion."[22]

Despite these efforts, right-wing interest groups and the administration were unable to move the public very much. As I showed in chapter 3, the public had little interest in and awareness of the issue. Public opinion concerning the contras continued to be against them and thus was not much of a political resource for them. The only bright spot in public opinion for those who wished to help the contras was President Reagan's continuing popularity. Particularly after his decisive win in 1984, groups claimed that the public had given Mr. Reagan a mandate. Unfortunately for them, this was too broad and vague a claim about the public to have an impact on legislators or the general public.[23]

On the other side, the left was able to make more specific claims about public opinion when they argued against contra aid. Numerous polls showed that the majority of the public was opposed to sending funds to the contras. But anticontra groups did not allow poll data to speak alone for their position. A number of groups mobilized their members and members of the public to contact Congress. Left-wing groups organized at the local level, sponsoring presentations at churches, union halls, and campuses and urging people to contact members of Congress. These groups prepared briefing books for activists to rebut common arguments for contra aid, made a movie for congressional briefings, obtained signatures of support from a majority of living U.S. Nobel Prize winners, targeted legislative districts, and built coalitions.

Peace groups such as SANE, Witness for Peace, and the Center for National Security Studies coordinated their efforts with mainstream religious groups. The religious groups' involvement legitimized the anti-contra position, helping insulate it from charges that they were communist sympathizers. The American Catholic bishops spoke out against covert aid to the contras in 1983, and the president of the Catholic Bishops Conference, Archbishop John R. Roach, claimed that U.S. policy toward Nicaragua "has the effect of deepening internal crises in the country and escalating the dangers of war in the region." He also condemned "a string of U.S. actions reaching from unrelentingly hostile policy rhetoric, through U.S. actions to prevent Nicaragua from obtaining credit and loans in international institutions to funding of covert activities on the Nicaraguan border."[24] One leader of a group seeking aid to the contras observed that "the main lobby against this aid is the Protestant mainline churches, no question, in alliance with some of the Catholic orders."[25]

Groups opposed to contra aid used all the tools in the public relations tool kit to rouse the public and influence legislative decisions. A coalition of groups engaged the services of Fenton Communications, a firm that works for leftist political groups.[26] Fenton created television ads that it showed in swing congressional districts, organized celebrity fund-raisers for the anticontra cause, and coordinated the Central America Media Education Project. The media project focused on contra human rights abuses and sought to counter negative reports about the Sandinista government. In addition, Fenton coordinated contacts between the media and the coalition of groups that supported the Media Education Project. Witness for Peace, a member of this coalition, sponsored citizens' trips to Nicaragua. On their return, these travelers spoke to the media and members of Congress about what they had seen.[27]

Throughout this period, group activities related to the public focused on specific legislative enactments and reasons for possible political decisions. Groups argued their cases for and against contra aid to the general public and tried to mobilize sympathizers and group members. Yet it does not appear that their work was able to shift public views. From the time the contra issue became a prominent national issue until the Iran–contra affair was revealed in November 1986, public opinion remained quite stable. In Congress, neither position dominated absolutely. Although Congress restricted funds to the contras for four years, these limits and the eventual restoration of funds for military support in 1986 probably had more to do with other factors. For example, the news in April 1984 about the CIA involvement in mining the harbor in Managua hurt advocates of contra aid, while a visit by Sandinista leader Daniel Ortega to the Soviet Union prompted Congress to vote for funds.[28]

With a near stalemate in the contra aid fight, groups found it essential to target and mobilize members of the public. Given the reality of active opposition, neither side could afford to refrain. In addition, because most citizens knew little about Central America policy, groups needed to continue their efforts to woo the public. People with a moderate amount of information are easier to move than those with a great deal of information and awareness, and both sides feared that the better-informed group might be able to influence the less-informed one.[29] This extended period of activity influenced the groups' coalitional and organizational strength. As Arnson and Brenner note, both sides became involved in internal disputes, and conflicts arose between compromisers and those who took more extreme positions. Despite these disagreements, however, interest groups were able to exert influence on particular votes.[30]

Procontra groups saw their efforts to influence the public as an educative process. Although they had a popular president on their side, conservative groups had not been able to legitimize their interpretation of events, and they believed that the biased media had created an American public that simply did not understand what was at stake in Central America. Looking back on the fight for contra aid, one conservative leader bitterly proclaimed that the media had a leftist bias that protected contra aid opponents: "They had the power to package it. Without the air cover the media gave, these left wing groups couldn't go anywhere. These left wing groups are like cockroaches, shine a light on them and see what happens. The truth comes out."[31] This level of vitriol demonstrates the intense concern such organizations had for their cause, as well as their frustration that the conservative groups' concerted efforts did not generate stable funding for the contras. Given the low levels of public support for the president's policy, Congress did not have enough reason to consistently support the contras.

With little support in polls and a noncompliant media, the right believed they simply had to mobilize and appeal to the public. Conservative groups had been committed to the contras from the very start, and with the president's support, they had been able to convince their supporters that this was an important issue requiring them to act. Even when a member was probably going to vote for contra aid because of a principled commitment, they kept the pressure on. As Charles Orndorff of the Conservative Caucus explained, "You can be sure he's hearing from the other side and so you don't just let it go by default. No matter how strong they may be on our side of the issue, if all they get is the pressure from the other side that can ruin it." With this dynamic in mind, congressional supporters of the contras sometimes called on conservative groups to generate mail so that they could say that appeals from their constituents led them to vote for contra aid.[32] Regional political dynamics also helped the procontra side. Although the anticontra groups had the advantage in the public opinion polls and in their more extensive grassroots capacity, they were not well organized among the swing congressional districts.[33]

It was the pursuit of political goals rather than organizational goals that provoked groups to appeal to the public during this period. In large measure, such groups viewed public opinion as a political resource. Organizational needs, as always, could not be ignored. However, for the right at least, the contra issue was not a sure win either politically or organizationally. The Conservative Caucus adopted the issue quite early and could not generate much membership enthusiasm at that time. Low membership response meant that direct mail efforts did not yield much money for the group. Later on, however, the situation changed, and the issue did help the Conservative Caucus prosper. After the Iran–contra hearings, appeals to the public following the testimony of Oliver North did a great deal for conservative organizations but accomplished very little for their policy goals.

Groups and the Political Spectacle of Iran–Contra

After the Iran–contra affair became a public sensation, the contra cause lost its most precious resource. Procontra groups no longer had the support of the executive branch and the leadership of a popular president. With the public dismayed at the sales of arms to Iran, Ronald Reagan's formidable ability to persuade was diminished. His claim that he did not know about the policies conducted by his staff led some citizens to distrust his assertions and others to question his competence.

Yet even before the scandal broke, right-wing groups were dismayed with the White House. Donations to conservative causes fell as the momentum of the Reagan revolution seemed to lose steam. The second Reagan administration became the reign of pragmatists, with moderate Republicans replacing those more committed to the conservative cause. After the scandal emerged, conservative groups supported the president's covert efforts to aid the contras, but they also took an increasingly independent stance. With several members of Congress as plaintiffs, the Conservative Caucus filed a lawsuit to declare the Boland amendment unconstitutional. (Some conservative activists had earlier urged the president to take such a step, but the administration had refused.) Groups continued to urge their members to support the contras, and a direct mail campaign was launched to raise funds for the legal challenge.

In short, as far as the right was concerned, the battle for policy change and public approval was by no means over. With the start of the congressional hearings in May 1987, there was a new opportunity to organize their members and the general public. At this time, the conservatives were both better mobilized and more aggressive than the left. Conservatives planned to support White House warriors for the contra cause, those who had followed the president's wishes to keep the Nicaraguan freedom fighters alive "body and soul."[34] Oliver North was, of course, one of those, and he was the man that Reagan had declared to be a national hero. Conservative groups were ready to show their support for North.

These groups played a role in influencing the perception of public opinion about Oliver North during the Iran–contra hearings. Conservative groups engaged in efforts that affected how the media, members of the public, and legislators gauged public opinion. These groups mobilized their members and organized events that structured political involvement and attracted media attention. In addition, an active right encouraged the public and the left to believe that the public was more enamored of North than the polls indicated. These activities may have muted countermobilization by the left. Unlike the long struggle over contra aid policy, the rapid responses by the right were able to dominate early public expressions of opinion. Conservative groups contributed to the noise of the political echo chamber. As they shouted into it, they created echoes that carried biased translations of public opinion.

At the same time, the loud clap of public support noted by the media was not a false sound wholly manufactured by conservative groups. Although they may have been wrong, members of Congress and their staff believed that the numbers of contacts were too large for the activity to have been mostly mobilized. In addition, opinion polls indicated that many citizens reacted spontaneously to North's persona, were bothered by his treatment by Congress, and were moved by his arguments for the contras. Very strong support for North was expressed during the early days of the hearings, although later phone calls and telegrams were balanced fairly equally. These uncoordinated public activities were reactions to the open spectacle brought into people's homes and workplaces. In this spectacle, as in any drama, highly compressed symbolic messages were delivered. Groups played a part in creating this spectacle, for coverage of mobilized action was part of the news. But North and the committee were most responsible for its staging.

If citizens looked to the network news and mass-circulation magazines, they would get the impression that North was a great hero and that Olliemania was rampant. Yet the media's reports of the public mood were off the mark. In fact, the public was critical of North's actions in the Iran–contra affair, while admiring of his sincerity, and sympathetic to how he was treated by Congress and the administration. In addition, the media got the story wrong in another significant way. Their stories ignored the fact that conservative groups mobilized to express their support. Even though some group efforts were planned before North took the stand, the media portrayed them as spontaneous expressions of public opinion.

Take, for example, the demonstrations held around the nation during the first few days of North's testimony. Two of the three networks reported on these in the context of stories about "what America thinks" about North. The major media outlets did not say who organized these events and when they were planned, leaving the impression that they were part of a popular groundswell. In Washington, D.C., the demonstrations were organized by the Legal Affairs Council, the Young Americans for Freedom, and the Unification Church of Reverend Sun Myung Moon.[35] Before North began to testify, plans were made to hold demonstrations throughout the nation, and many of them were crafted to be visually interesting in order to attract national attention. According to a report in the *Washington Times* the day before North was slated to appear before the committee, a member of North's 1968 Naval Academy graduating class planned displays of public support. According to this news story, "If all goes as planned, thousands of men, women and children will gather on the steps of public courthouses and state capitol buildings from Hawaii to the East Coast Wednesday night to show support for a favorite Marine—Lt. Colonel Oliver North." H. Keith Haines II, a classmate of North at the Naval Academy, explained that these demonstrations would help the colonel's morale and send Congress the message that the people believed in North. Haines added, "I hope Ollie will see the amount of support he has on a grass-roots basis, and more specifically I hope Congress sees the amount of public support out there and maybe then they will change their game and tactics."[36]

Haines's tactics seemed to be quite effective. A Salt Lake City candlelight vigil—one of 150 to 200 that Haines planned—made the national news immediately after it occurred. But this was not the end of this visually compelling footage. Later news stories included pictures of the demonstrations. As we know, repetition usually increases cognitive accessibility. The common wisdom that the American public were rallying to North's defense was influenced by events designed to change Congress's approach to North before he had even taken his place before Congress and the nation.

Organizations also had a role in generating and delivering letters and other communications to the committee. During North's testimony, he and his attorney displayed and spoke about telegrams of support that had been sent to Congress. Given the very large numbers of supportive messages, it is probable that the bulk were from citizens acting independently and spontaneously. At the same time, particular groups had planned telegram campaigns before North went to Capitol Hill. This first set received a good deal of publicity and was seen as evidence that the public was behind the lieutenant colonel. Conservative groups were well aware that North would receive much media attention and hoped that they could turn the tables on the committee. As a direct mail item from the Conservative Caucus, dated July 1, 1987, announced,

> Our Mailgrams are timed for the North–Poindexter testimony when the media spotlight is at its height. . . . Perhaps you've watched Senator Inouye on TV or read about his committee in your newspaper . . . and you've observed how this liberal-led committee is ruthlessly trying to lynch those patriots, military leaders and Reagan advisors who tried to aid the anti-Communist freedom fighters in Nicaragua. Well, our Mailgram asks Senator Inouye to stop.[37]

Even when groups did not directly urge members to contact Congress, they sometimes served as a conduit for letters. Groups received and forwarded mail from members who knew of North or at least supported the contra cause. A June 1988 mail solicitation from Concerned Women of America bragged that "last July when Col. North appeared before the Iran–Contra Committee, our mailbox was flooded with hundreds of letters addressed to him . . . we delivered them all."[38] It is difficult to discover how many letters of support arrived in this way. Groups have reasons both to overestimate and underestimate their participation. After North testified, conservative groups may have wanted to exaggerate their relationship with him. On the other hand, they also wished to promote the idea that North had broad popular appeal and so might have underestimated their efforts.

In their involvement with North during the hearings, groups engaged in much the same activities that any political group ordinarily does, with the additional spin that North was popular and the American public had turned to support the contras. Leaders appeared on radio and television talk shows, wrote opinion pieces for newspapers, and paid for some advertisements. People who knew North contacted the media to sing his praises. His classmate Haines, who had organized demonstrations on the lieutenant colonel's behalf, gave interviews about North's qualities as a Naval Academy cadet. Both personal testimonials and political appeals on the basis of North's character were parts of such groups' public relations tool kits.

What did these groups accomplish during and soon after North's testimony? More specifically, did they influence public opinion and the perception of public opinion? Did these groups influence U.S. policy toward Nicaragua? Did they benefit as organizations?

Although it is impossible to determine the precise effect that these groups had on public mobilization, I believe they played an important role in influencing the perception of public opinion. A number of dynamics were at work during the hearings. First, organized efforts, planned before North appeared, gave North's supporters a head start and contributed to how the public mood was perceived.

Second, both organized and unorganized conservatives had found themselves increasingly frustrated by the time North was scheduled to appear. Although right-wing groups were available to act as a conduit for some of their reactions, not all frustration flowed through or was organized by groups. In fact, the leaders of some conservative groups reported that they believed the firestorm of reaction was a reflexive, cathartic response. Brent Bozell, then president of the National Conservative Political Action Committee (NCPAC), noted:

> I think that what was going on to a great degree was a venting of frustration. Because there were people out there who were supporting the contras that were increasingly dismayed by the lack of enthusiasm by the Administration. And along comes this guy who was a hundred percent in favor of them, and that's what triggered a lot of support.[39]

Third, the intense reaction from the right was not matched by one from the left. Individual citizens critical of North did contact committee members, with their numbers eventually matching pro-North sentiments.[40] But organizations that had devoted good deal of time to block-

ing aid to the contras largely sat on the sidelines and let the investigation proceed. Although there were some counterdemonstrations after
the hearings ended, liberal groups were mostly inactive during this time.
While they had been quite involved in attacking the Reagan administration's Nicaragua policy, liberal groups stood back when the president's loyal foot soldier took center stage. As a result, during the hearings, leftist groups were unevenly mobilized, which amplified the voices
of the right entering the echo chamber.

Fourth, conservative groups were heartened by the public reaction.
Group leaders believed that public action and poll results marked a
shift in the debate over contra aid because public reaction was more
intense than they expected and because poll results showed an increase
in support for contra aid. Right-wing groups were listening to the
echoes, too. And what they heard was the sound of cheers for the contras as North educated the public about them. As one leader remarked,
North "showed them that there was something really at stake in
Nicaragua."[41]

Fifth, groups and the media helped create a spectacle outside the
hearing room. With the demonstrations and mobilization of early,
intense activity, conservative groups influenced the climate of opinion.
In helping shape how the media reported on public opinion, these
groups also partially constructed the perceived audience to the spectacle. In addition, the group activity may have contributed to limited
public action of the perceived minority, perhaps creating a spiral of
silence. Group action did amplify a rally cry for North, but what effect
did it have on policy?

Despite the conservative groups' exhilaration about North's performance and what they saw as widespread popular support, they quickly
became frustrated with a muted and limited policy response. Although
they believed Congress was influenced by the public's support of North
and the public's increased approval of contra aid, they saw this effect
quickly diminish. Conservative groups did not really blame Congress,
however, an institution for which they had low expectations.

Instead, conservatives blamed the White House. Some high-level
Reagan administration officials proclaimed that North had been able to
educate the people about the contra cause. One stated, "He has turned
the whole country around. He has done more for the contra policy in a
few days than years of speeches and testimony by White House and
State Department officials."[42] Still, the president took no new steps on
behalf of the contras.

Conservative groups believed that because the president did not act immediately, he lost his best opening to help the contra cause. Brent Bozell argued for presidential action during the first days of North's testimony:

> I had a meeting with the political director in the White House while Ollie was testifying. The testimony was supposed to end Friday. And I suggested that once it was over—all America watching Ollie, all America loving what he was saying—that Ronald Reagan have Ollie come to the Rose Garden and in a very fatherly way put his arm around Ollie. And look at the cameras and say, "I told you he was a hero. Now this is what I want for the contras." He would have gotten whatever he wanted.[43]

Conservative groups contended that the public's admiration for North should be exploited. North had brought forceful arguments for contra aid to the public's attention. Public opinion of North, group leaders believed, was a political resource that the White House was not using properly.

We will never know whether or not Bozell was correct that President Reagan could have used an appearance with Oliver North to help the contras. But we do know that in the summer of 1987 the president moved away from the conservatives' preferred Nicaraguan policy and toward a diplomatic solution. Conservatives feared this move because they did not trust the Nicaraguan government and wanted to ensure the contras' success, so group leaders met with White House officials to express their dismay. In August, conservative groups launched a television advertising campaign aimed at the White House. The TV ad said that "some in the administration want President Reagan to abandon the freedom fighters" and asked people to write the president and "insist he honor his moral commitment."[44]

North's testimony and the accompanying mobilized response, independent public reaction, and media coverage did not generate a policy triumph for conservative groups. Instead, the aftermath of the Iran–contra hearings marked increasingly bitter relations between the organized right and the presidential Republicans. Conservative groups had been the charter members of the Reagan coalition, but their disappointment with Reagan's policy achievements grew more acute. When the White House did not hear the voice of the people in the same way conservative group leaders did, conservative organizers targeted the president.

In addition, right-wing groups began to reconsider whether their political strategy had taken a wrong turn. Rather than focusing on holding the presidency and working with the executive branch to pressure Congress, group leaders considered a shift to organizing in state legislatures, local government entities, and regional movements.[45] But whether conservative groups moved toward local mobilization or continued to try to influence the national political scene, these groups needed at least to maintain themselves as organizations. With a particular public enamored of Oliver North, conservative groups had a focal point for organization building.

After the Hearings: Oliver North as an Organizational Resource

By the time he had finished testifying at the Iran–contra hearings, Oliver North had become a celebrity and the darling of the right. North's popularity with this faction and their perception that America loved Ollie North gave conservative organizations a new resource. Groups used this intense support for North for organization building and maintenance. Organizations took advantage of the strong feelings for North when they argued that he was a persecuted hero who needed their support. In making their appeals, the groups promoted a view of heroism based on military service, physical courage, and concern for national security and national service.

Groups used North's name to raise money, gain publicity, and pursue policy goals. Fund-raising efforts began on the heels of North's testimony, as direct mail contractors began to send out millions of letters soliciting support. Richard Vigurie sent out five million letters and Ann Stone sent out one million letters for four organizations. These efforts were often quite successful. Pledges to the National Conservative Political Action Committee (NCPAC) doubled, and the "sharp, months-long slump in contributions" that conservative groups had suffered was reversed.[46] In many cases, both Oliver North and conservative organizations benefited from these appeals. Groups continued to use North to raise funds and attract attention, and North received money for his legal fees and personal expenses. In addition, conservative organizations helped keep North in the public eye. The religious right had provided strong support to North early on, and North's ties to these groups solidified and further developed.[47] Rev. Jerry Falwell of the Moral Majority and Liberty University brought North to the Lynchburg, Virginia, campus to address the 1988 commencement class.[48] "In his introductory remarks, Falwell compared North to Jesus Christ, saying the soldier was not the first to be falsely accused: 'We serve a savior who was indicted and convicted and crucified.' "[49] Other religious right organizations also developed and maintained relationships with Colonel North.[50]

North began to tour the country to raise money for himself and selected candidates and groups. Traveling to events under tight security, North received $25,000 per speech, and at times, a political candidate paid North to appear at a fund-raising event or campaign stop.[51] North also occasionally appeared for free on behalf of a cause dear to his heart. For example, he helped raise $300,000 for the Media Research Center, a strongly right-wing group that monitors news organizations for any liberal bias.[52] Although North's relationships with conservative groups had continued since the hearings, one period of especially intense activity followed his indictment.

After North was indicted on March 16, 1988, conservative groups quickly went into action, launching a new wave of fund-raising and beginning the circulation of petitions for a presidential pardon. Twenty minutes after the indictment was announced, the Conservative Victory Committee put its phone bank into action.[53] Jerry Falwell aired commercials on CNN and local stations asking viewers to call an 800 number to add their names to a petition for North.[54] Falwell argued that North was a courageous hero and patriot who had been made a scapegoat. North, Falwell pleaded, had a "$20,000 salary as a retired marine" and therefore needed financial help to pay his legal fees.[55]

Although group efforts to support North never led to a pardon, they did help groups provide financial help for themselves and for Colonel North. In turn, North helped the groups raise money and attract supporters during a time when no other issues seemed to work well for them. As Richard Vigurie explained in September 1988, "There haven't been many issues on which to galvanize the religious right in the past year or so. Ollie is a certified five-star hero in a movement that is particularly short on heroes at this time."[56] Conservative group leaders understood that North's heroic status in a particular segment of the public was a potential resource.

But North and some of his supporters raised doubts about the propriety of fund-raising on his behalf. A letter from the North Defense Trust stated, "Many are using Ollie North's name to raise funds, but little if any of those monies ever reach Ollie for help in this battle."[57] And a friend and political ally of North, F. Andy Messing Jr., remarked, "There's a lot of people out there who took advantage of Ollie North. It goes from T-shirt vendors to whoever."[58] To what extent North believed he had been used is not clear, however. He may have lent his name to these activities in part because he and his strategists believed they would help him raise money. In fact, North often maintained relationships with fund-raising organizations and appeared publicly with groups who were working on his behalf.

On the other hand, many groups clearly did benefit from North's popularity and were able to use public opinion of North as an organizational resource. The typical approach was a petition drive, fund-raising for North, and gifts as "selective incentives."[59] Concerned Women for America brought in more than a million dollars after offering photographs of North and copies of his testimony. The Legal Affairs Council collected petitions and spent $20,000 to create nine albums with family pictures of supporters. These albums were presented to North as a token of support, along with $15,000.[60]

Even though many groups benefited from their work for North, the American Freedom Coalition (AFC) probably gained more than any other. At the time of its founding, the AFC determined that working for a North pardon would be a good marketing device to launch its organization. The president of AFC, Rev. Robert Grant, had earlier headed a lobbying group called Christian Voice. Grant and his associates planned to launch the AFC to carry out semi-independent projects within the states. After obtaining a bank loan and support from the Unification Church to establish the organization, the AFC initiated a petition drive for Oliver North. By focusing on North, its leaders believed that the organization would be able to attract people who would wish to become members.[61] According to Grant:

> It offered to us a number of ingredients, looking at it from both an ideological and a utilitarian point of view. We saw North as a heroic figure, if you will, standing up to the establishment and taking it on the chin and defending what political conservatives have felt was a good cause, namely, the downfall of the Sandinistas and the defense of the contras, who we would describe as a freedom-loving people and the Miskito Indians and others of Nicaragua who were being savaged by a Marxist regime. So it happened that that was an issue we were interested in, and when we came together as an organizational entity, we seized upon it as a launching issue.[62]

To be sure, the AFC was sympathetic to North's plight. But its main interest in North was as a vehicle for establishing its organization.

The American Freedom Coalition solicited potential members through a large-scale appeal for Oliver North. Ten to fifteen million pieces of direct mail were sent out with a request to send funds and sign a petition to be forwarded to President Reagan. In addition, the AFC commissioned a one-hour television documentary entitled "Oliver

North: Fight for Freedom." This program was shown on more than one hundred local affiliates and on Rev. Pat Robertson's cable outlet, the Christian Broadcasting Network. Viewers of the show were asked to call an 800 number to add their name to the pardon petition and, for $25, to obtain a photograph of North being sworn in to testify and a copy of the video. The North video was also shown in various halls and meeting places in order to recruit people locally. Another selective incentive offered by the AFC was a medallion with a picture of North on one side and the AFC logo on the other.

The high cost of buying television time prevented the AFC from making much money from this venture, but it gained something it considered more important at its stage of development—a mailing list. In Grant's words:

> How we benefited from that was not so much initial income, because it was mostly an in-and-out proposition, but the creation of a mailing list. We ended up with a half-million people on our mailing list that were sympathetic, obviously identified with North and the issue of the defeat of the Marxist regime in Nicaragua, and you could conclude from that they would be interested in other anticommunist type of issues and then that became part of the money machine to keep this organization going.[63]

Throughout this time, even though the AFC had a fairly minimal relationship with North, he received some benefits from its campaign.

The television and direct mail efforts used to launch the American Freedom Coalition gave North positive publicity, enabling him to keep his name alive and emotionally resonant among a conservative core. In addition, the AFC paid North a fee for speaking and telemarketing. Finally, the AFC gave North's legal defense fund the opportunity to use its mailing list to solicit support. The defense fund raised more than $500,000 and, in addition, was given the foundation of its own mailing list.[64] Indeed, as Grant said of the petition drive, "We've made it work very much for us."[65]

The use of Oliver North as a tool for creating good mailing lists and raising money was not a point of pride for all conservatives. In fact, some considered this tack a wrong turn, a lost opportunity as profound as President Reagan's failure to pursue contra aid immediately after North's testimony. As the head of one conservative think tank noted with some disgust:

> Oliver North's instant popularity with the American people was a dramatization of the conservative movement's potential appeal to millions of

currently unrecruited conservatives. Yet, during the height of "Ollie-mania," conservatives in casual conversation speculated not on this significant fact but on something of greater personal interest: how one might obtain access to the list of donors to Oliver North's legal defense fund, a potentially significant source of direct mail revenue.[66]

To these interest groups, the public and its support for North were a means to build organizations. Although one might argue that those groups would presumably be in a better position to influence policy after they had fattened their coffers, there is little to suggest that preexisting organizations embarked on any additional lobbying or grassroots efforts.

Perhaps it was predictable that Oliver North would found his own organization through direct mail. As Howard Phillips, head of the Conservative Caucus, remarked, "Ollie North is the most marketable political commodity" for American conservatives.[67] In late 1989, North sent out letters announcing the formation of the Freedom Alliance. North wrote that unlike General Douglas MacArthur, "I've decided I don't want to just fade away." The organization, North explained, would "promote a strong national defense, support freedom fighters around the world, counter left-wing-dominated national media, maintain traditional American values at home, strengthen families, and encourage grass roots political activism."[68]

After its founding, the Freedom Alliance took political positions on a whole host of issues, engaged in service work for Persian Gulf War soldiers and their families, and became the basis for North's planned Senate campaign.[69] In 1992, North founded another organization, V-PAC, and by the end of that year, he had raised nearly $21 million through the North Legal Defense Trust, the Freedom Alliance, and V-PAC. Between 1989 and 1991, the Freedom Alliance brought in nearly $7 million, and in 1992, V-PAC raised more than $543,000. As Thomas Mann remarked ten months before Oliver North announced his candidacy for the 1994 Virginia Senate race, "It is a stunning amount of money. This operation appears to be in a class that's matched only by Jesse Helms. It tells you that someone like Ollie North can mount a very serious campaign for the Senate."[70] North's popularity among some became, at last, a resource for his own organizations and ambitions.

As I have shown, after the Iran–contra hearings gave Oliver North name recognition, conservative groups made appeals involving North to help themselves as organizations. Across the political landscape, liberal groups did not concern themselves much with North. Some protestors appeared when North spoke, and some group leaders spoke out against a pardon for him, but in general, liberal groups seem to have decided that it was not worthwhile to speak about North to the public. Their constituents had been opposed to contra aid before the Iran–contra scandal and so likely considered Reagan responsible. Furthermore, in the public at large, North maintained a certain reservoir of sympathy, as many believed he had been treated poorly by both Congress and the Reagan administration. North's role as a fall guy was likely why the public was usually split about his getting a pardon.

In a time when they had less and less influence on policy, conservative groups concentrated on obtaining a pardon for North and raising money. These pardon campaigns lasted for years, starting before the trial and continuing after George Bush became president. They stopped only when North's convictions were set aside by a federal court in November 1990. Conservative group leaders felt frustrated by their limited policy accomplishments during the Reagan years, and they certainly were not friends with the more moderate Bush administration. In this political context, conservative groups launched campaigns for North in order to maintain their commitments to their hero and to keep themselves in the public eye, and in these organization-enhancing efforts, these groups also offered selective incentives to contributors. Oliver North was used to build several of his own organizations and one other, the American Freedom Coalition. The publicity given to North by other groups helped him plan a political career of his own. Once an angry and defiant critic of Congress, North made plans to enter it as a member. Although North lost his 1994 bid, without the organizations that had taken an interest in the public, North could never have been in a position even to consider running.

Concluding Comments

Although patterns of group activity changed from the time of the contra aid battles until the rise of Oliver North as organizational leader, throughout this period pressure groups took an interest in the public. During the legislative fight over Nicaragua policy, these groups took their case to the general public and mobilized their members to contact members of Congress. Both sides used a variety of strategies, including media appearances and advertising. Groups opposed to contra aid also worked with grassroots institutions, such as churches and unions. Conservative groups emphasized phone banks and direct mail to encourage their supporters to contact Congress but were unable to move the stable, anticontra public. The equilibrium between organized groups on both sides of the issue and a largely disengaged citizenry limited the intensity of pressure on legislators, giving them time to study policy options and citizens' views.

After the Iran–contra hearings, the pattern of even mobilization shifted to uneven degrees of organization. Right-wing groups were better organized and better able to react rapidly. When Oliver North appeared to testify, they were prepared and their work helped create the perception of an early wave of support for North. Demonstrations and telegrams fascinated the media, which used the highly symbolic and emotionally resonant hero frame to report the news. Spontaneous political activity on behalf of North followed and accompanied supportive group action. Several days after the media reported on public opinion, calls and letters to Congress were evenly divided, with many citizens expressing strong support for congressional critics of Mr. North. Nonetheless, the impression that Americans loved Oliver North remained entrenched in news accounts.

After the hearings, liberal groups did little with respect to North. In contrast, conservative groups focused on Oliver North as a cause and a means to help themselves as organizations. Groups began waves of petition drives and raised money, often with selective incentives to encourage potential participants. North was their celebrity, their hero, and their symbol. By building on the intense opinion in their publics, conservative groups proved they were on the right side, gained publicity, and generated funds. Although their policy star was no longer rising, the promotion of Oliver North kept them alive to rise again another day. Group activity on behalf of North kept him politically vital as well, and he was able to build a healthy institutional and financial foundation for his political ambitions.

At all stages, groups on both sides were concerned with their public bases and the public as a whole. Groups took an interest in the public, trying to convince citizens; mobilize supporters; promote favorable and effectual versions of public opinion to the media, the citizenry, and Congress; influence policy; and maintain and build their organizations. They were best able to affect perceptions of public opinion during the time of uneven mobilization, intense public attention, and symbolically oriented media coverage. Groups contributed to the political echo chamber, and even though the majority of the public was not convinced that North was a hero, the media reported otherwise, and members of Congress took note.

6

Trying to Hear the Echoes

Good politicians have always been better at reading the public and figuring out what the public thinks—or actually, what the different subsets of the public collectively think—and will react to than any number of pollsters and consultants. One of the fatal flaws is that polls are only a snapshot, they only tell you what is happening today. For a politician, what the public thinks today isn't relevant. For a politician what the public thinks on the day he runs for election is relevant.

Member of the congressional staff, Iran–contra committee, interview

A real politician, somebody who runs for office, doesn't just look at numbers. You have to measure the intensity of the feeling. You have to measure whether it's a cutting-edge issue. Very seldom will you find a foreign policy issue that's going to make the difference.

Representative Mickey Edwards (Republican, Oklahoma),
"Public Opinion and Contra Aid: Congressional Commentaries"

During the Iran–contra hearings, as in other situations, elected officials developed decision rules for assessing public opinion. Using a method more art than science and more intuition than design, congressional committee members came to determinations about what the public thought. They relied on a number of indicators of public opinion but were particularly dependent on incoming mail, phone calls, and telegrams, as well as media reports of public opinion. These sources of information about the public mind overrepresented support for Oliver North. Before the Iran–contra scandal was revealed, conservative activists and the Reagan administration had found themselves stalemated on the contra issue. Public opinion was largely disengaged and did not support their position, a situation that gave some legislators considerable autonomy. During the hearings, all committee members were forced to respond to the perceived public opinion, but their reactions took different forms. Although some began to pay tribute to North, others were quiet, and still others challenged the star witness. Those who resisted accommodating their views to the felt public tide believed that members of Congress needed to act as educators and leaders. In speaking critically to North, they believed that they were also speaking to the public at large and were teaching them about constitutional principles. Citizen action encouraged some members to vocalize their support of North, and these members used this rally to solidify their support among core constituents, uphold President Reagan's agenda, and argue for the contra aid policy.

The committee's early decisions affected how North and Iran–contra were seen by the public, conservative activists, and the media. The committee's choices thus ultimately influenced the perception of public opinion to which the committee members had to respond. Because the committee granted immunity to North for his testimony, he was able to proclaim boldly that he had lied to Congress and to defend the necessity of doing so. If he had not been given immunity, North would probably have invoked his Fifth Amendment right to not testify against himself. Taking the Fifth probably would have led to a certain degree of citizen suspicion. In addition, the very large size of the committee and its seating arrangement helped create a picture of a beleaguered Oliver North. The twenty-six members of the Joint House–Senate Committee sat in a series of risers facing the witness at his table, with his lawyer at his side and his wife behind him. In preparing for the complex and far-reaching investigation and hearings, elected officials unwittingly ceded the photogenic North the politically consequential territory of television image. His ability to perform well on this stage figured significantly in the media's assessment of his testimony, and this influenced elites' views of the public mood.

Elected Officials' Interest in Public Opinion

Elected officials hold a unique and central position in the echo chamber. Members of Congress and the president generate the major inputs into the political communication system, speaking to one another and to the public, and their words are mediated by commentators and news sources. Representatives have a strong influence on how issues are framed, and if the media adopt the frame they use, this can benefit their position. Politicians try to frame issues to change public opinion, influence administration policy, and affect other countries' governments.[1]

Elected officials also listen to the public, as they must form a picture of public opinion in general and of their core constituents' views in particular. This information is difficult to obtain and depends on weighing a number of sources, including mail and other constituent communication, polls, input from interest-group members and lobbyists, media reports, impressions from leaders in the district, other representatives, and staff. As I pointed out in chapter 2, public opinion cannot be ignored because it is a resource for reelection and policy. As listeners and leaders, elected officials attend to both fellow elites and the public. Although they are sometimes quite concerned with what the public thinks, other times they may not listen to the public particularly closely. Ambitious politicians and those with impending elections are especially attentive to public views.

A very basic view of democracy suggests that elected officials should try to hear what the public thinks and respond to its wishes, but there are two problems with this view. First, elected officials face the difficult task of determining what the public thinks. Like others, they are in the echo chamber and may hear distorted or unclear messages. As has been shown, during and after the Iran–contra hearings, the media presented a more positive picture of public opinion concerning North than is suggested by a close reading of polling and interview data. Interest-group activities during the hearings and the media's fascination with drama, symbols, performance, and personae helped create this impression of public opinion. Second is the normative question of whether politicians should strain to hear the echoes from the public. Members of Congress are elected in part because of their judgment, a quality that encourages a certain degree of autonomy from their constituents. In fact, advocates of the trustee view of representation and supporters of democratic elitism do not find responsiveness between elections necessary or even wise. Instead, they argue that democratic control depends on citizens' ability to hold politicians accountable at election time.[2]

Although hearing the public is a difficult task, both members of Congress and the president pay attention to the public in order to be reelected and achieve policy successes. The fact that elected officials must face the voters periodically if they wish to stay in office forces them to take account of their constituents' desires. Even though some votes may have little importance, the existence of opposition parties and candidates gives elected officials a strong incentive to assess public opinion. They know that in the midst of an election campaign, one's opponent will sift through roll-call votes to find ones that can harm the sitting member's reelection chances.[3] As Mayhew points out, this desire for reelection encourages legislators to engage in activities that are electorally useful, such as advertising, claiming credit for various achievements, and taking a particular position.[4] The third of these, taking a particular position, concerns public policy efforts the most and allows for a link between the public and legislative action. While legislators' interest in policy and public opinion is conditioned by their aspirations for reelection, this is not their only concern. As Kingdon explains, legislators are part of a world of ideas, and so they use ideas "to make sense of their behavior for others, to persuade others of the rightness of their actions, or persuade others to join their cause."[5] Legislators' views guide choices and act as constraints.[6] Other politicians want to stay in power as well, and they are needed to pass or block policies. Claims about "what the people want" add legitimacy to their policy stand and, if credible, may help build policy coalitions or prevent defections. Perceived public opinion also influences policy by putting issues on or off the political agenda.[7] In order to stay in power and make a difference in the political struggle, legislators must listen to the echoes of the public voice.

Legislators can respond to citizens in ways that have little real policy import. Elected officials listen to many complaints about problems with Social Security checks and the like, and they often have staffs that can respond quickly.[8] Sometimes legislators respond in symbolic ways, by holding press conferences or sending out press releases.[9] Legislators attend to the public when visiting their districts and their constituents. Activities back home, such as town meetings, office hours in district offices, or local public appearances give them the opportunity to listen to citizens and to explain their positions and votes. Communicating with citizens also enables legislators to build relationships and trust, if only by appearing to listen to their views. Their constituents' trust gives legislators a certain degree of leeway in the positions they take, but such trust can never be taken for granted. As Bianco argues, trust depends on a representative's reputation and the salience of the issue.[10]

In seeking to stay in office, politicians attend to some groups of citizens more than others. Legislators show concern for mobilized publics, as these citizens are likely to be standing watch between elections and to become more aware of their record during the campaign season. Arnold suggests that members of Congress are most concerned with how attentive citizens will judge them at election time. Constituents who care about politics in general or about one particular issue are likely to remember how their legislator voted and will reward or punish him or her with their vote. Members of Congress also must secure their base in the electorate. As a result, legislators are likely to be responsive to constituents who identify with their political party and who have supported them in the past.[11] Some legislators have constituencies with enough heterogeneity to be able to build electoral coalitions in different ways. This flexibility gives elected officials room to maneuver politically and enables them to pursue the policies they want.[12] What makes this so complex is that these political calculations do not operate in the same way all the time.

One thing legislators cannot do, however, is to ignore public opinion. They assess and anticipate what the public thinks because perceived, actual, and potential public opinion are important political resources.

> Legislators work hard to identify issues that could be used against them and to discover the safest position on each issue. At times these calculations impel legislators to follow the intense preferences of a small minority, at times they encourage legislators to anticipate the potential preferences of a larger group, at times they make legislators attentive to the special needs of their core supporters, and at times they encourage legislators to reach out to their regular opponents.[13]

Politicians' political skills and judgment in determining what their core or overall constituency wants are really put to the test because constituency preferences are so difficult to discover.[14] Few polls are conducted on a state or legislative district level, and in any case, politicians are concerned with more than raw numbers. They want to know how many people will care at election time, what votes they would have had that will be lost, and how many votes they can win that are not certain. All these matters are colored by their perceptions of the opinion climate, which is a matter of political engagement and struggle. Assessments of public opinion are constantly adjusted in reaction to contacts from constituents and interest groups, media reports, opinion pieces in the major local and national press outlets, and statements by other elected officials.

Changes in American politics and Congress as an institution have affected legislators' capacity to hear the public and have helped create a new incentive structure. Electoral risk is enhanced by the current environment of campaigns. Campaigns are primarily organized by candidates and their consultants and have become increasingly expensive, media oriented, and negative. Members of Congress are thus forced to be attentive to matters in their districts, as voters are less attached to political parties and so vote according to their candidate's personal characteristics and policy stands.[15] As a result, elected officials in competitive districts know they must persuade independent voters to support them. Politicians also must keep the support of those less than fully loyal voters in their political party. Any obvious departure from their constituents' opinions may prove electorally costly.

Within Congress, legislators can be entrepreneurial and are increasingly sophisticated about using the media on a regular basis.[16] Members of Congress vote more along party lines than they did in the 1970s, but legislators will act independently if they believe that their constituents will reward such action.[17] Party leaders strive for unity and, in doing so, try to develop a common public relations strategy. The widespread use of national polls, the increase in constituent mail, and the establishment of companies to create "spontaneous" grassroots activity all encourage legislators to pay attention to what the public wants. As Russett argues, "Public opinion may be more effective as elections draw near. In an era of 'permanent plebiscite' conducted by polls and electronic media, however, the interaction of public opinion and exercises of political drama by governmental leaders is a continuing phenomenon."[18]

Although both this incentive structure and the motivations of legislators encourage listening to the public, they do not mean that what the legislators hear is accurate. Although legislators frequently travel home, much of their information comes from mobilized groups and the media. Successful politicians realize that citizen contacts and media coverage may not reflect actual public concern, and so they try to correct for it, discounting it to some extent. The president and members of Congress try to portray public opinion and frame political issues in ways that help their positions. In short, elected officials are part of the echo chamber, not sequestered listeners in an isolation booth. The cacophony rages all around them and rarely ceases, making it hard to hear clearly.

Given these difficulties, how well does policy relate to public opinion? Figuring out how well legislators represent citizens' views has proved to be a very difficult task.[19] Measuring representation is not easy, for congruence between district opinion and votes does not necessarily mean that constituent opinion influenced legislators' votes. Voters may be represented simply because they chose a legislator whose views agree with theirs. "When a legislator's views coincide with those of the constituents, voting on the basis of private preferences is indistinguishable from voting on the basis of constituent opinion."[20] Research that has pooled a number of votes or tracked policy movements suggests that citizens do have an impact, although the problems of measuring representation and determining causal direction make these conclusions only tentative. In addition, these studies do not consider the particular politics of situations, thus making it impossible to analyze the processes that give rise to connections or disparities between citizen opinion and legislative action. Research on legislative decision making for specific issues, however, suggests that legislators' perceptions of the opinion climate influence their involvement in issues, votes to put off consideration of a bill, and the overall set of alternatives to be considered.[21]

In the area of foreign policy, scholarly views of public opinion and political responsiveness have changed. During the 1950s and early 1960s, it was believed that the public had incoherent and volatile beliefs about foreign policy and that policymakers generally paid little attention to the public's views.[22] Perhaps because of greater attention to foreign policy during and after the Vietnam War, it now appears that citizens have stable belief systems regarding foreign policy that allow them to organize their thinking.[23] Citizens' views of ethnocentrism and the morality of warfare are central to three basic approaches ("global postures") to foreign policy.[24] People draw on their views of foreign policy when making political choices. In presidential elections, they pay attention to foreign policy, and their views influence vote decisions.[25] Furthermore, research suggests that public opinion has affected foreign policy. Although public opinion did influence shifts in military spending, its effect was less than the influence of both Soviet military spending and the gap between U.S. and Soviet spending. Also, to some extent, constituency opinion constrained legislators' votes on strategic weapon systems.[26] An analysis of cross-national data by Risse-Kappen concludes that the link between public opinion and foreign policy is mediated by domestic structures and coalition-building processes. In none of the four countries that Risse-Kappen studied was public opinion simply dictated or manipulated by the elites, and in none did policy simply reflect the public will. Institutional structures and political processes also affect how public opinion is translated into policy.[27]

If legislators are somewhat responsive to public opinion, this implies that they will take public views into consideration when they make decisions. In foreign policy, "a major instrument of popular influence in the United States may often operate through congressional readings of public opinion and then through legislators' influence on the executive."[28] Elected officials assess public opinion in a political context, in which the media, interest groups, and other politicians try to make their cases about the merits of policy choices and about public views. Both Kingdon's study of agenda setting and Mayhew's analysis of policy adoption suggest that the impressions of opinion are often more influential than the actual public views.[29] "Policy moods" sometimes overtake Congress and influence what policies are adopted. Although members of Congress may refer to public opinion to legitimate their votes, policy moods do not directly mirror the public's views in poll results. Public officials influence one another in creating policy moods that matter.

Assessing Public Opinion

The Fight over Contra Aid

The Iran–contra scandal emerged in a political atmosphere of congressional partisanship and dispute. Members of Congress had fought hard over the issue of aid to the contras. Although the Iran–contra hearings focused principally on the executive branch's autonomous actions in Iran and Nicaragua and on the monetary gains of private arms traders, in part the hearings were also a continuation of the contra aid fight. But even though the acrimony and policy debate remained, the role that public opinion played was different. Most of the public had little interest in the contra aid fight, so public opinion played a limited role. As I stated in chapter 3, during the early and mid-1980s, the public as a whole was quite uninformed about the basics of the contra fight. Many people did not know which side the United States government supported in Nicaragua and El Salvador. In contrast, during the Iran–contra hearings, the public was highly attentive, so members of Congress were sensitive to their views.

Because Congress and the executive branch viewed public opinion as a political resource and both political parties saw the contra aid issue as crucial, public opinion was by no means overlooked during the contra aid debates. Politicians did listen to the public to some extent, especially when designing policy and trying to sell it. Congressional votes were, however, largely guided by party and ideology. Democrats were more opposed to contra aid, and Republicans usually voted to support President Reagan's requests. Northern Democrats were highly unified against the contras, voting together 94 percent of the time. Republicans were also highly unified for the contras, with 92 percent unity. Southern Democrats changed positions and often provided the margin on the close votes—and they all were quite close—voting together 59 percent of the time.[30] Due to the splits among Democrats, the legislators' ideology was a better predictor of the vote than party affiliation was.[31]

Even though the polls were quite consistent in showing the public's opposition to funding for the contras, Congress sometimes voted for aid. After Congress banned any U.S. assistance to the contras—the Boland bans ignored by Oliver North and others—they restored aid, starting in 1985. In June 1985 Congress appropriated $27 million for humanitarian purposes, and in June 1986 they restored military support. The 1986 bill approved $100 million in aid, with 70 percent for military aid and 30 percent for humanitarian assistance.

Although Congress did sometimes vote for contra aid even when the public remained opposed to it, administration officials and legislators nonetheless did take public opinion into account. The Reagan administration certainly took public views quite seriously. As I explained in chapter 5, the administration used its public relations machinery to try to influence public opinion. Inside the White House, convincing the public and the Congress that the administration had moved the public were seen as important instruments for policy success. According to Elliott Abrams, a major spokesman and the assistant secretary of state for Inter-American Affairs from 1985 to 1989,

> The polls were tools, the polls were weapons which would occasionally be used against us and occasionally be used by us. . . . The administration would show polls that would say, "The people don't want a communist Central America." The polls were purely instrumental, neither side was changing its views. It was picking the poll result that might persuade the relevant person that day.[32]

While using polls as a political resource, the Reagan administration did not waver in its commitment to the contras. However, they tailored its arguments to move publics and members of Congress in swing districts, and shaped its policy to meet the limits imposed by public opinion. Because the Reagan administration recognized that public opinion "defines the political terrain on which one must operate," it did not introduce some policies that the White House had considered. These included air strikes against resupply bases in Cuba and more funding for the contras. Any possibility of using American troops was also clearly excluded. In addition, President Reagan did not take as public a role as he might have because his political advisers realized that most citizens opposed aid to the contras. Public views "constrained the administration because they could not use it to sway Congress."[33]

Public opinion affected Congress in still other ways. First, public opinion mattered in determining the very composition of Congress. As

Sobel points out, "Ideological and party preferences are themselves reflections of constituency attitudes which reflect dominant modes of thinking and thus of public opinion within congressional districts."[34]

Second, legislators regularly assessed public opinion on contra aid. They monitored opinion and its intensity using a variety of measures, including newspaper editorials, constituent mail, discussions with citizens in their district, activities by organized groups, and, to a lesser extent, polls. In general, it appears that they came to believe that only a small percentage of their constituents cared much about contra aid. Although the poll numbers showed little support for the contras, members of Congress were not convinced that fervent opposition to contra aid was widespread. Because they believed that most voters were not interested in the issue, legislators decided that their own judgment and consciences should determine their vote.[35]

Third, support or party constituencies influenced some members of Congress.[36] Democratic legislators, particularly ambitious ones, were particularly affected by public opinion in their primary electorates and by the leadership's reading of public opinion. For example, Representative Bill Richardson (Democrat, New Mexico) usually voted against support for the contras. But when he voted for humanitarian aid in 1985, he found a 20 percent erosion in his primary vote. Richardson also felt that a leadership position would be more difficult to obtain if a Democratic member of Congress opposed the House Democratic leadership.[37]

Fourth, activities by interest groups could not be ignored. Legislators often faced citizens from mobilized groups in their Washington offices and their districts. As a result, they were forced to explain and defend their positions on contra aid.

> Active lobbying by church and human rights groups and constituent letter-writing campaigns provided administration critics and skeptics a sense that they had a cushion of support to oppose the president. These domestic pressures reinforced members' willingness to oppose policy, often serving as a justification for such opposition. Conversely, domestic campaigns in favor of administration policy, particularly when they carried the charge that a member was "soft on communism," raised the costs of opposing the president.[38]

Fifth, some legislators had concerns about what could develop. In interviews with members of Congress conducted in 1987 and 1988, William Schneider found that legislators saw the issue as quite symbolic. For Republicans, Nicaragua was another Cuba, a communist beachhead close to the U.S. border. For Democrats, Nicaragua promised to be another Vietnam, a country with its own internal upheavals and the potential to become a quagmire.[39] These represented potential national security imbroglios that would demand attention and provoke voter reaction. In addition, southern Democrats worried that "a crisis in the region would allow Reagan to act decisively, that the public would 'rally 'round the flag,' and the Democrats would be politically vulnerable."[40] Following the invasion of Grenada, legislators were reminded that American military intervention could be quite popular once begun. Anticipated scenarios motivated certain members of Congress to keep the contras afloat.

In general, however, over the course of this issue, most legislators' interpretations of public opinion gave them freedom to make their decisions. Legislators and the administration judged the public's intensity of concern to be low, a shared assessment of public opinion that affected how they acted. The low levels of salience—what was heard as the quiet voice of the people—usually allowed members of Congress judge for themselves.

The Iran–Contra Scandal

In contrast, the public's responses to Oliver North's Iran–contra testimony proved to be much noisier. The scandal and North's appearance engendered a good deal of attention from the press and the public. Large numbers of citizens watched some of the hearings on television, and many more than usual contacted members of Congress to express their views. To determine how public reactions were perceived in the halls of Congress, I interviewed and questioned committee members and high-level committee staff. During the summer of 1993, I began trying to locate these people by consulting a number of directories published in the previous five years, including the *Congressional Staff Directory, Federal Staff Directory, Washington Representatives*, and the *Congressional Directory*. The Iran–contra committee was composed of eleven senators and fifteen representatives, with thirty-eight staff people directly associated with them, who were identified as such in the final committee report.[41] I tracked down nearly all the committee members, and four agreed to be interviewed. A number of factors, however, made it difficult for me to meet with many committee members. Some now had assumed leadership positions or had left Congress and were working in politically sensitive positions in and out of government. Others, still in office, were too busy with legislative business. Fortunately, I could supplement the information from my congressional interviews with published comments and interviews. Of the thirty-eight key staff members, I found twenty-two. Four declined requests for information, ten were interviewed, and eight completed a written questionnaire.

Early Reactions to the Iran–Contra Scandal

When the Iran–contra scandal was first revealed, congressional reaction was swift and overwhelmingly critical. Even members of Congress who had supported aid to the contras were disturbed by parts of the affair, and the Iranian side of it was particularly bothersome. U.S. relations with Iran had not healed after the January 1981 release of American hostages. Since then, the government of Iran had been implicated in the taking of hostages in Lebanon, and its anti-American rhetoric had not cooled. Legislators were simply appalled that the executive branch had chosen—on its own, without concern for the Arms Export Control Act and against a highly publicized international policy to thwart terrorism—to send arms to Iran in an attempt to gain the hostages' release.

Given the history of acrimony surrounding the contra aid issue, many legislators also were dismayed to learn about the executive branch's intensive involvement in funneling money to the contras and especially with what they saw as a pattern of lies and misinformation.[42] In an earlier situation in 1984, it was learned that the CIA had been involved in mining Nicaraguan harbors. Conservative Republican Senator Barry Goldwater then wrote CIA Director William Casey that he was "pissed off" and that "this is an act violating international law." As chair of the Senate Intelligence Committee, Goldwater was angered that he had not been told and that he was unable to keep his committee members informed. "The President has asked us to back his foreign policy. . . . How can we back his foreign policy when we don't know what the hell he is doing?"[43] After the mining incident, Congress passed strong restrictions on U.S. activities in Nicaragua (Boland II). As rumors of U.S. involvement continued to make news during the next several years, members of Congress asked questions that the administration answered with carefully crafted evasions or lies.[44]

Legislators believed that the transfer of funds to the contras raised serious constitutional issues, since it was clearly an attempt to get around the restrictions voted by the Congress and to circumvent Congress's "power of the purse." At the same time, many members wished to resolve the issue as quickly as possible, in order to avoid a situation like the investigation into Watergate. At that time, the entire government had been effectively stalled when the Congress investigated the scandal and officials from the executive branch prepared to testify. If there was any possibility of impeachment, they believed this should be determined promptly. One reason was that President Reagan's second term was to end in about a year.[45] Impeachment possibilities were also considered partly in political terms. According to Senator Warren Rudman (Republican, New Hampshire), "We were on pins and needles, Democrats and Republicans. Nobody wanted it—not even the Democrats. Democrats didn't want to impeach a popular president."[46] The Watergate frame that so entranced the media also influenced congressional responses. As Schudson points out, Watergate also had a number of practical ramifications, because it had led to the position of independent counsel and prompted legislation requiring intelligence findings. There was also some continuity in the personnel of the Watergate and the Iran–contra investigations, and Watergate focused attention on the issues of both the president's knowledge and a cover-up.[47]

Many legislators were also concerned that the investigation and the administration's defense would seem politically motivated, and this prompted them to complete the investigation with dispatch. In particular, they did not want accusations of a politicized investigation to become prominent in the 1988 presidential election. Members of Congress who were critical of the Reagan administration did not want others to claim that their investigation was designed to hurt the Republicans. Supporters of the president also did not want the issue to drag on, because they feared the issue could be turned against them with voters. In this case, these legislators anticipated effects on public opinion that could arise in the coming election season.

Some legislators were less concerned about whether the investigation was seen as political. But Robert Byrd, the Democratic leader in the Senate, "knew that the line between political calamity is a thin one that can turn on a headline or a perception. Ronald Reagan, whatever his personal or political weaknesses, remained a popular leader."[48] In fact, Reagan's popularity did decline with the Iran–contra revelations. But it had been rather strong throughout his presidency and remained a political resource for the executive branch and its defenders. In choosing Democratic senators to serve on the committee, Byrd took into account public opinion about President Reagan and the potential for future shifts in opinion.

There was little resistance to the decision to hold congressional hearings. It was difficult to construe the situation as simply an attempt to get President Reagan because he had insisted that he had not been fully informed about the diversion of funds and other matters. In addition, the day after the White House revealed the diversion, President Reagan appointed the Tower Commission to study the behavior of the National Security Council staff. Plans for a congressional investigation and the appointment of an independent counsel quickly followed.[49] In general, the political climate demanded congressional action.

Some Republican House members resisted a congressional inquiry and charged that it was unnecessary and essentially political. Many House Republicans were quite bitter about their long-standing minority status and felt trampled on by their Democratic colleagues. They also were quick to attack the Democrats and loath to work with them. But the highly ideological House Republicans did not have enough support from the House as a whole, from their own ranks, or from Senate Republicans. Senator Warren Rudman, for example, rejected the idea that an Iran–contra investigation was to be used to injure the president's standing. Instead, Rudman argued that the Constitution required that the Congress investigate.[50]

Although the partisan and ideological House Republicans did not prevail early on, they emerged as a strong voice later. In part, this was influenced by the organization of the congressional committee. The committee was created as a joint House–Senate committee, and on the Senate committee, Democratic and Republican staff and members collaborated as a team. However, on the House committee, Democrats and Republicans did not work together, and the House committee maintained separate minority and majority staffs.

Although the Congress was quick to begin its investigation, members were not convinced that the public was particularly interested. The staff and members that I interviewed reported receiving little mail on Iran–contra in the early months. The media's attention, in contrast, was quite high. In general, legislators and their staff believed that citizens were more upset about the Iranian part of the scandal than about the contra aid diversion. In part, this assessment of public opinion was based on the political context established during the fight over contra aid. They realized that their constituents were relatively unaware of the situation in Central America, and they saw the public as fairly evenly split. Thus, legislators believed that improper funneling of aid to the contras was unlikely to upset some citizens. They remembered the strongly negative reaction to Iran following the extended hostage situation, recalled the range of terrorist activities associated with Muslim fundamentalists, and concluded that the public would not approve of the government's dealing with Iran. As there was limited direct communications with Congress, these assessments of public opinion were based on political intuition and opinion polls. During this period, legislators acted on the basis of their own principles and ideas and responded to one another, the president, the media, and, to a lesser extent, potential public opinion.

Legislators' decisions about how to conduct the inquiry were influenced by their assessments of current and anticipated public opinion. (Staff were also quite sensitive to the role of public opinion in the coming investigation and hearings.)[51] Because members of Congress who wanted the investigation heard Reagan administration defenders charge that the inquiry would hurt the president and because they feared that the investigation would look like a political ploy, legislators made particular choices. The committee tried to do its work as quickly as it could. Although the committee was formed in early January 1987, the original date for completing the committee report was August 1, 1987. (This date was later extended, and the report was issued on November 17, 1987.)[52] On the Senate side, Committee Chair Senator Daniel Inouye (Democrat, Hawaii) wanted to develop a bipartisan sensibility and so named Republican Senator Warren Rudman as vice chairman. Rudman then helped create the bipartisan Senate staff.[53]

Because the committee members wanted to investigate and air their findings as quickly as possible, they made decisions about how to handle North that expedited matters that later came back to haunt them. North's lawyer, Brendan Sullivan, made a series of demands, including "use immunity" for North. If granted, nothing that North said to Congress could be used in any future prosecution probes or trials. Over Independent Counsel Lawrence Walsh's objections, the committee granted use immunity to North.[54] In addition, Sullivan asked to limit the amount of time North would testify; the number of days and hours per day to be restricted; and, once North's testimony was completed, not to call him back for further questioning. Sullivan also refused to allow North to give a detailed deposition to the committee members or staff before he appeared in public, although other witnesses had or were planning to do so.

> Though this was a rebuff of Congress, the committees were faced with a choice: either accept Sullivan's terms, or institute contempt proceedings and risk a month long delay that could prevent them from keeping to their timetable of finishing the hearings in August and producing a final report by late fall.[55]

Despite disagreement within the committee, the combination of upcoming elections, the waning of Reagan's presidency, the fear of political repercussions and of appearing to be politically motivated, and the desire to air the issues and reach a resolution ultimately induced the committee to meet these demands.

In a last-minute compromise, the committee and North's attorney agreed to a plan restricting North's public and private testimony. In private, North addressed only the question of whether President Reagan knew about the diversion of funds to the contras. This deal also limited Congress's access to North's private notebooks, which were three thousand pages long and chronicled his daily activities between 1984 and late 1986. Although these documents were under congressional subpoena, the committee allowed North to deliver them to staff only three days before public testimony and to black out the parts North and his lawyer deemed irrelevant. No one from Congress oversaw the deletions, and 30 to 40 percent was blacked out. "This was a major gap in obtaining a full accounting of North's activities, and that Sullivan was able to cut such a deal was a measure of how anxious the committees were to hear from Ollie."[56]

With the goal of getting out the Iran–contra story as rapidly as feasible, the committee faced difficult choices. They wanted to avoid the appearance of a political witch-hunt, but their self-imposed deadline led to a number of problems. Not only did it push Chairman Inouye to agree to many of North's lawyer's demands, but the tight time period also made it quite difficult for the staff to review relevant documents. In many cases, staff had to fight with CIA and Justice Department lawyers to obtain relevant documents in a timely manner.[57] Many of these choices were driven by both the members' principles and their reading of public opinion.

The Congressional Hearings

Secord Begins

The public hearings began on May 6, 1987, with the testimony of Richard Secord. Secord was a graduate of West Point who rose to become an air force major general before retiring in 1983. In addition, he was a pivotal figure in both the Iranian and the contra sides of the affair. Secord and his business partner Albert Hakim had worked closely with North in negotiating with Iran and selling arms to the contras.

Secord's business, often called the Enterprise, tied together both sides when it sold arms to Iran and used some of the proceeds to fund the contras. "In effect, Secord organized a shadow CIA type of covert operation with the help of former CIA agents and retired military officers like himself."[58]

The committee chose Secord to begin the public hearings largely because of his central position in the complicated tale of Iran–contra. In addition, Secord had decided to testify without immunity, and committee members believed that their questioning of him would bring out the outline and many of the details of the long story. However, Secord's testimony did not go the way the committee hoped or planned. Rather, Secord foreshadowed much of what followed when North appeared. He was a proud and combative witness who generated public reaction on his behalf. The reverberations in the echo chamber began, as acclamations for Secord were activated, and some in Congress reacted. As happened with North later that summer, responses to Secord's testimony were linked to cultural symbols and embedded ideologies, including a promilitary and anti-Congress attitude.

Secord came to the committee chambers with his head unbowed. The title of his autobiography, released some years later—*Honored and Betrayed*—reflected his outlook and demeanor during the course of his testimony. According to Senators William Cohen (Republican, Maine) and George Mitchell (Democrat, Maine), Secord was angry because "the administration, in his view, had used him in what he believed to be legitimate covert operations, and then, upon their disclosure, left him vulnerable and alone."[59] House Majority Counsel John Nields led off and approached Secord gently. But Senate Counsel Arthur Liman took a tougher approach. Liman pushed Secord hard with questions about foreign policy run by private individuals who stood to profit. A number of committee members, including Senators David Boren (Democrat, Oklahoma), Paul Trible (Republican, Virginia), and Rudman, also took Secord to task rather strongly.

With Secord's testimony, legislators started to hear from citizens and to interpret the public voice. What did they hear? What difference did it make? For some inside Congress, what happened with Secord was relatively unimportant. According to Representative Henry Hyde (Republican, Illinois), Secord's testimony was mainly "interesting to inside the Beltway types." One staffer argued that the situation with Secord generated relatively little public reaction and had little effect, especially when compared with what happened with North. However, most people involved with the committee believed that these reactions to Secord were quite unanticipated and marked the beginning of a trend of public anger toward Congress and sympathy and praise for the witnesses.

Members of Congress based their assessments of public opinion on citizens' calls and letters to them. Although these were relatively few in number compared with those when North appeared, they were overwhelmingly pro-Secord. The authors of thousands of letters, telegrams, and phone calls viewed Secord as a patriot. Liman received anti-Semitic messages and death threats, and the motives of committee members were vigorously attacked. As the following statements show (with italics added), many on the committee perceived these communications as indicators of general public views, not as the reactions of a subset of citizens:

1. Senators Cohen and Mitchell wrote that "Secord's military bearing *had greater public appeal* than did Arthur Liman's courtroom manner."[60]
2. According to reporter Haynes Johnson, "Committee members were criticized personally and their motives impugned *as the public demanded to know* why the politicians were attacking this patriot."[61]
3. A committee staffer told me, "*What the public saw* was this lawyer for this Congressional Committee beating up on this great American hero who was a general, a retired general. Well, we got off to a rocky start there."

The mail regarding Secord's testimony from self-selected, emotionally aroused citizens helped generate a particular reading of public opinion. Legislators believed that Secord had been successful in "seizing control of the hearing and portraying himself as a righteous patriot who had been betrayed by his government" and in generating public support.[62]

Members of the committee also began to suspect that they had misunderstood how the hearings would appear on television. Taking their reading of public opinion as fact, they decided that the public's reactions were based on the visual images delivered through the media and that these made the committee look bad. According to one staffer, most people caught just parts of Secord's testimony. Without much background on Iran–contra or knowledge of Secord's activities,

> they saw Liman questioning a general in the manner that clearly shows that Liman thinks Secord is lying or maybe they don't even catch that. Maybe they just catch the fact that Secord comes out with the question-

ing before he hardly finishes his words, Liman's firing back at him in a very hostile tone with another question and that was a true court room style, confrontational style, with a hostile witness. And the people are saying, "Oh my God. How dare he?" You know, here's this nice general. They don't know what we know about him. Here's this nice general trying to tell a story, talking about his being patriotic. It can come across very very differently, and it can be even worse when you look at the perception of Congress."[63]

This initial translation of the public voice reflected the reactions of a subset of the public, but it began to create a particular set of reactions and to frame later perceptions.

Legislators reacted to Secord's testimony in varied ways. Some felt that they had failed to convey the sense and details of Secord's wrongdoing. According to Senators Cohen and Mitchell, "The Committee as a whole had been perceived as hostile, belligerent, pompous, patronizing, or unpatriotic. Because the Committee had not obtained the financial records still in the hands of Albert Hakim and Swiss banks, we were unable to elicit information that would seriously undermine Secord's credibility."[64] Despite this reading of public opinion, many committee members did not refrain from criticizing future witnesses. Republican Senators Rudman, Cohen, and Trible received a fair amount of hostile mail and other communications, yet they stood their ground and argued for their principles.

But some committee members seemed to pull back following the initial activation of the public. Off the record, several staff people told me that after Senator Boren had taken Secord to task and lectured him on the Constitution, he received some rather strong public responses.

Here was Secord, a retired air force general who was sort of citing God and country and all that, for what he did. And the reaction back in Oklahoma was very negative to Boren's questions. And I recall that evening, somebody rode by Senator Boren's house in Seminole, Oklahoma and shot out his lights, the porch lights.

These close observers believed that Boren did react to the public uproar. One staffer said, "Well, you know, it was just an indication, I think, to him: I got to be a little careful here. And he, I think, did not ever bore down like he did that first day." Another said that Boren's response influenced other legislators. Senator Boren "tempered his reaction after that. Everyone on the committee saw this as an early watershed."

Another effect of the committee's reading of public opinion on Secord was an increase in partisan acrimony. "On the House side the veneer of bipartisanship was quickly sundered. House Republicans began employing their time before the cameras to launch a spirited defense of Secord and, through him, a strong attack on the president's critics."[65] Representative Henry Hyde and others moved to support and defend the administration's policies and the motivations behind Iran–contra while also contending that the activities of Iran–contra were unwise.

Although North did not appear before the committee until about three months later, Secord's testimony set up reverberations in the echo chamber that would be heard later. During this period, more than twenty witnesses appeared, including three wealthy contributors to the contras, several assistant secretaries of state, persons involved in contra supply logistics, persons who funneled money to North or North's wife for personal costs, and contra leaders. Albert Hakim, Secord's business partner, and Fawn Hall, North's secretary, attracted the most media interest. Bits and pieces of the overall story began to be filled in as the committee prepared to question major administration officials. Committee members and staff viewed North's testimony as crucial. North had been deeply enmeshed in the hostage negotiations and arms transfers with the Iranians, and he had done a lot to raise funds for the contras from private sources and the arms sales. In addition, other than National Security Adviser Robert McFarlane (who was recalled after North's testimony), North would be the highest-ranking member of the administration questioned thus far. Both the committee and the media were interested in the question made famous during Watergate: "What did the president know, and when did he know it?" They hoped that North would be able to help them discover the extent of President Reagan's involvement and knowledge.

North Comes to the Hill

On July 7, 1987, Oliver North arrived on the Hill, ready to engage legislators and public opinion. Because of the aggressive negotiations conducted by his lawyer, Brendan Sullivan, North appeared on terms quite favorable to him—only limited private testimony was given, diaries were turned over late and with extensive editing, and documents were exchanged between the committee and North only a short time before his testimony began. Much of North's self-presentation was carefully designed to elicit a particular reaction from the public. North wore his marine uniform, complete with medals, even though he usually wore a business suit when working in the White House. The committee had a rule that opening statements had to be delivered to the staff forty-eight hours in advance so that the facts could be checked and the prosecution would not be stymied by statements made under use immunity.[66] But North's lawyer Brendan Sullivan did not request until the night before he was to appear that North be able to make a statement. A copy of the statement was delivered only forty-five minutes before his testimony was to begin. Still, Sullivan complained that North's inability to give an opening statement was evidence that his rights were threatened. Sullivan produced a striking image—a picture of North standing next to a pile of documents delivered by the committee a week before North was to testify. The documents loomed above North's head, a visual designed to create the impression that he was being treated unfairly. In fact, the committee had tried to exchange documents earlier, but Sullivan had insisted on a date close to the public testimony. But no words could easily overcome the message of this image.

From the first day on, North played with cultural themes like a violin virtuoso. Facing a divided committee strongly influenced by Watergate as a frame of reference, North sought to reframe Iran–contra. As I stated in chapter 3, the power of cultural symbols is enhanced by retrievability, rhetorical force, resonance, institutional retention, and resolution.[67] Although even powerful symbols do not affect everyone in the same way or to the same extent, they do have a considerable impact on part of the population. North effectively used retrievable, forceful, and resonant symbols that are institutionally biased and powerful in our culture. He played out the themes and personae of the dauntless little guy facing down the heartless, corrupt government. Frank Tomasulo suggested that North (with help from the mass media) presented himself in much the same way as the protagonist did in the Capra film *Mr. Smith Goes to Washington*. (Or as one staff member characterized it to me, "Mr. Smith tells Congress to go to hell.") North drew on "dominant symbolic forms" and enabled interpretations to be constructed that were "dependent on prior fictional representations."[68]

North also used his military background as a shield and proof of his sincerity, patriotism, and courage. As an institution replete with rituals and symbols, the military is able to create and maintain cultural force. North's proud stance, his uniform and medals, and his blazing eyes and catch in the throat all spoke in a vocabulary well known in our culture.[69] As Habermas and the Frankfurt school theorists argue, the consumers of modern culture are acquainted, soothed, and provoked by the stock plots of the culture industry. Modern politics, Habermas contends, is more and more dominated by the creation of symbols and stereotypes by organized groups and elites. In his first public appearance at the Iran–contra hearings, Oliver North created himself in the image of a particular persona, and he presented himself for acclamation.

Legislators on the committee were more than interested in public reactions; they were fascinated, appalled, and starstruck. Calls and telegrams flooded Capitol Hill on the morning of North's first day of testimony, and committee members took note. One staffer reported,

> They took their first break at about 10:30 or 11 that morning and there was a little anteroom off of the Caucus Room where there were banks of telephones set up. And the senators would go back and have a cup of coffee and they would call back their offices, and their offices reported with almost uniformity—the phones ringing off the hook, critical of the committee, critical of the questioning. And it was like when they came back from that recess there was an entirely different dynamic which had taken over.[70]

Legislators' offices kept tally sheets to keep track of the public's responses, and in those first few days, they strongly supported North. Overall, there was an extremely large number of citizen contacts. "The half-million letters, telegrams, and phone calls that Americans sent to the committeemen over the summer of 1987 together represented perhaps the largest spontaneous popular response to a congressional activity in American legislative history."[71]

How did those phone calls influence Congress's assessment of public opinion? What did committee members and staff believe about public opinion? On what evidence did they rely in constructing their pictures of public opinion? In the early days and hours, the committee members became convinced that the public viewed North with great sympathy. They and their staff believed that the public saw North as patriotic and sincere, a man who loved his country being treated as a scapegoat. On these questions the committee members and staff that I studied were unanimous in their feeling that North was viewed as a patriot and a fall guy. Although a consensus developed among elites that the public saw North sympathetically at first, they disagreed about a number of matters. Committee members and staff were divided regarding the public's other views in the early days and how public opinion developed later.

Most people associated with the committee were convinced that North was popular in the early days. Of the twelve members and staff who discussed the initial public reaction with me, eight believed that the public admired North and viewed him as heroic. Four disagreed, saying that the public did not approve of North's actions and that he was not a hero. Senator Rudman drew a distinction between support for the Iran–contra policies and admiration for North.

> What you can't confuse here is this is kind of a play within a play. I mean, you've got the general public opinion—which never agreed with what happened. Oliver North didn't convince me of that. There was confusion in many journalists' minds who wrote about it, that because some people admired North, they approved of what he did. They thought it was the little guy against the big guy.[72]

For Rudman and others I interviewed, the news portraits of a public enthralled with North missed the elementary fact that the public—even the active public—was made up of different groups. They believed that conservative, procontra citizens supported North and viewed him sympathetically and that many of them saw North as heroic. This group of ardent supporters were likely to remember how North was treated and would take this into account at election time. The elites also argued that there was another set of North sympathizers. (Only three out of eighteen believed that North's supporters were also in favor of contra aid.) The other North supporters were variously described as people who were moderate, had paid little attention to the affair, were not advocates of contra aid, and were moved by North's military service and demeanor. For this latter group, North was not necessarily a hero—although he was a patriot who had been badly mistreated by his superiors. Among the congressional staffers and members I studied, both opponents and supporters of aid to the contras believed that many citizens saw North as a scapegoat.

Contrary to the media's reports, many elites believed that most of North's sympathizers did not consider him to be a champion. Congress as a whole, however, felt under siege early on. In one staff member's words, "We were hammered hard in those first few days." But after a few days, many in Congress perceived a shift in public opinion. The public's views, they believed, became more mixed. The citizenry turned cool toward North. Staff and members of the committee who were themselves critical of North told me that people came to realize that North had acted illegally and without adequate oversight. Elites who supported the president and contra aid policy also found a shift in public opinion over time, although they were less likely to see much change. But how did members and staff reach these conclusions about the public?

Elites formed their impressions of public opinion from a mixture of informational sources, most of which had inherent biases. When listening in the political echo chamber, committee members and staff heard certain voices most clearly. In large part, these were the voices amplified by the media. As I showed in chapter 4, the news media focused on unrepresentative sources of information about the public's views and presented North as a hero and as a highly competent performer. Within Congress, vivid information and expressions of emotions from activated citizens also played an important role in interpreting public opinion. But it is important to keep in mind that first, not all committee members and staff were convinced that the public voice they were hearing was accurate; in fact, some were quite skeptical. Second, although certain elements of the interpretation of public opinion concerning North were widely held, reactions to perceived public opinion were far from uniform.

The flood of mail, phone calls, and telegrams was crucial to creating an impression of public opinion. As table 6.1 shows, the people I interviewed judged incoming messages to be the most important source of information about the public mood, registering as a bit more important than media reports, national polls, and discussions among staff and members of Congress. In addition, these messages became part of the hearings as North piled the yellow telegrams before him, his lawyer Brendan Sullivan commented on them, and the media reported on

TABLE 6.1

Question: How important were these sources for assessing what the public thought about Oliver North during the hearings?

Source	Very important (4)	Somewhat important (3)	Slightly important (2)	Not important (1)	Average
Mail, telegrams, phone calls	7	7	2	0	3.3 ($n = 16$)
Media reports about public opinion	4	5	3	0	3.1 ($n = 12$)
National polls	3	6	3	0	3.0 ($n = 12$)
Talks with congressional staff and members	1	9	0	1	2.9 ($n = 11$)
Demonstrations	0	3	2	4	1.9 ($n = 9$)
State or local polls	1	0	4	4	1.8 ($n = 9$)

Note: Don't know responses are excluded.

them. As time went on, newspapers and TV reported how the flow and sentiments of mail, calls, and telegrams changed, but this did not change the basic interpretation of public opinion.

Mail and other communications not only were assessed directly but also had a secondary impact through the media's coverage of them. Committee members and staff looked to media reports about public opinion in gauging the public mood. In the halls of Congress, staff and members talked to one another about the way that events were developing, including changes in the public's views. Most of these sources of information reinforced one another and overrepresented the public's support for North. As one staff member told me, "It was a chicken-and-egg situation. The calls and the media influenced each other, and we talked about it all." Elites had access to other data as well. National polls were released several days after the hearings began, and they were closely scrutinized. Committee members could not easily discern what their constituents thought, though, since state and local polls were often not taken. For a sense of how North was received in a particular state or district, members were forced to rely on local media reports featuring person-on-the-street interviews, phone-in polls, and reports of radio talk shows.

Elites relied heavily on mail, telegrams, and phone calls because they were sources of information with which they felt comfortable. Staff and members had rules of thumb to evaluate incoming messages. They considered mail and calls to be important because they were unmediated, and they looked to mail "because of the immediate, direct reaction from constituents." "The more a source is primary, the better." In addition, although staff and members recognized that people who take the time to write are not necessarily representative of their constituents, they believed that strongly held views deserved attention. According to one member of Congress, "Mail is often generated, but people do send in mail for a reason. You have to take it seriously because people care about it with intensity."[73] Calls and mail must be attended to if one cares about the next election. In one staffer's words:

> We'll keep count with all the calls we get. Also count the mail because you have to remember one thing. If you have constituents who either call or write, particularly if they write—in an era of instant communications—that means they feel deeply and seriously about the issue. When you have normal mail that comes through, the eventual result is a draw/lose situation. Someone writes you, they feel very, very strongly, have convictions about a certain issue. Or they have a problem with the

government—Social Security check, welfare check, military pension, something they want. Or they are pissed off at you. Now, if they are pissed off at you, there's not much you can say in a letter that's going to make them feel better. If they want something, you'd better deliver. If they feel strongly about the issue, you have to pay attention to that issue and if you pay attention to it in a prompt and forthright manner, you may not lose their vote. You certainly won't win their vote, especially if you disagree with them. That's why I say congressional mail is the first line of contact with most constituents. It's a draw/lose. The best you can do is keep their vote.[74]

Given their accumulated experience with dealing with constituent communication, committee members and staff took the flood of mail, telegrams, and phone calls quite seriously in putting together their picture of what the public thought about Oliver North.[75] However, the initial support for North colored legislators' impressions. When citizen input turned toward criticism of North, some prominent committee members continued to give the impression that North was widely admired.[76]

Vivid events influenced the general impression of the public mood. In quantitative terms, elites ranked public demonstrations as only very slightly important indicators. However, members and staff spontaneously told me stories about events of this sort, revealing that such incidents had a hold on their cognitions and memories. Representative Hyde recalled that people sent flowers for Mrs. North to his office, which he delivered.[77] In another story, North received adulation from the crowd.

> During the intermissions, North and his wife would go out and stand on the balcony in the Russell Senate building like the pope. There'd be these crowds down there and he'd wave and they'd cheer, and telegrams and calls were pouring into the offices about what a hero North was.[78]

T-shirt sales were an indicator to one aide of North's grip on the public. One staffer left the Hill after the first day of testimony, and then

> the next day I remember coming into work and there were vendors out on the corners selling Ollie T-shirts and Ollie memorabilia and all of this stuff. I remember one—it had a picture of Buckwheat on it—and it said "Buckwheat says Ollie is OK." I'll never forget that one, but I thought— We are in big trouble here.[79]

Others were sure that people liked North because North buttons were sold on the Mall and people had their picture taken with large cardboard representations of North.

Clearly, something unusual was going on. Many millions of Americans tuned in to watch "The Ollie North Show," and many thousands were prompted to write, call, or telegraph.[80] Members of Congress and congressional staff have much experience in dealing with public responses, and they used their cognitive and procedural rules when the reaction to North began. Members and staff began to keep track of it, "not for any specific reason other than just to get a gauge, since it was like, there's a wave coming in, why don't we measure it."[81] Besides taking tallies, the elites' intuition was engaged. Just as whenever the public response is great, the elites tried to determine whether reactions to North were spontaneous and mobilized. This was important because members of Congress usually do not ignore mobilized reactions but usually do discount them to some extent.

Using their experience as a guide, most committee members believed that public reactions to North were largely spontaneous, since they believed it was not possible to mobilize so large a response. Some argued, however, that much of the first reaction was mobilized and that it had an impact on later responses. One staff member observed, "This group influenced others. Before the hearing there was no opinion of Oliver North." Another person contended that the first wave of response "primed the pump" by generating the reaction first reported by the media, thus encouraging more reaction. Senator Rudman told me that in his and others' experience, the public response to North was far more mixed than the media suggested. By focusing on action that was clearly mobilized—such as demonstrations—the media become caught up in their own production.

> If the press would have done a good job, they would have found out that North had as many detractors across this country as he had friends. In fact, I'd say maybe more. But the Young Republicans gather around the Russell building with their signs and their American flags and have a demonstration of three hundred people, and the press will go and cover them. I mean, I could get on the phone right now, I could arrange a demonstration right down here tomorrow morning. I could have five hundred people. Does that mean that's the way everybody feels? Hell no![82]

Thus mobilized action, though only a fraction of the public response, may have had an important influence on the creation and perception of the public mood. Certain people may have been spontaneously moved to call or write when they saw media reports of demonstrations and other mobilized action. As chapter 4 showed, demonstrations and other visually interesting—but unreliable—sources of information of public opinion dominated the news coverage of public opinion.

Whether or not public communications were spontaneous or mobilized, many members and staff believed that only segments of the public had acted. They realized that the constituency that had become active was not necessarily representative of the public as a whole. People in very conservative districts, such as those represented by Representatives Henry Hyde and Bill McCollum (Republican, Florida), strongly supported North. But this was not true of all districts, and some representatives began to anticipate upcoming public opinion. One staff member prepared a memo comparing North with General Douglas MacArthur: "There was this enormous outpouring for MacArthur after Truman fired him, but then when people thought about it a bit, they reflected that what MacArthur did was a threat to democracy."[83] As all politicians must, the elites tried to assess what public opinion would be in the future.

In listening to the public voice, members and staff were caught in a maelstrom. Weary from the effort of preparing to question witnesses, elites were faced with the sounds of ringing phones, the confusion of telegrams and letters flowing into offices, the sight of media-delivered pictures of activated citizens, and the omnipresent television shots of the smiling and grim-faced lieutenant colonel. All this vivid information had a strong impact on Congress's view of public opinion. Staff and committee members spent much time talking to one another and formed their own conventional wisdom about what was happening, including explanations for North's seeming popularity in the early days and the perceived shift in the latter part of the hearings.

Reactions and Resistance

Once this impression of public opinion was created, did it influence the congressional hearings and investigation? News stories often implied that committee members were cowed by North's seeming popularity. One television report (CBS, July 10, 1987) cited an anonymous Senate staffer who said that her boss "thinks North is out of line, but won't say anything critical, since he fears the reaction of constituents supporting North." A *Congressional Quarterly Weekly Report* headline proclaimed, "Public Sympathy Proves Effective Shield for North Against Committee Critics."[84] The *New York Times* reported that owing to the public response, some members of the committee "frantically tried to jump on [North's] bandwagon, singing his praises more loudly or taking back the negative words they had uttered before he came to testify."[85] An evaluation of the committee published after the congressional report was issued found that some tough questions drafted by staff were not asked because members were frightened away by North's seeming popularity.[86] Indeed, a number of members of Congress told North himself that Americans had grown to admire him. But North did not escape some rather pointed lectures and criticisms. Responses to public opinion were by no means uniform, and they reflected varied motivations.

Congressional interpretations of the public voice forced committee members to respond to North differently than they had initially planned. Everyone I talked to said that public opinion did influence North's treatment. As table 6.2 shows, eleven of nineteen interviewees said it influenced Congress very much, six said it did somewhat, and two said it had a little effect. Reactions came in one of three forms: backing down, championing North, and planning counterresponses. Republican Representative Bill McCollum, for example, shifted from a critical stance to praise for North. On June 25, he remarked that North's shredding of documents and misleading of the attorney general was "a crime" or at least "one of the highest acts of insubordination and one of the most treacherous things that has occurred to a President." Yet on July 13, McCollum announced that North was "patriotic" and that he and the country were "grateful" to him.[87] Some saw a shift in other members, including Senator David Boren. Earlier, Boren had been targeted by supporters of General Secord and so did not take as critical a position toward North.[88] Some conservative Republicans, who had

TABLE 6.2

Questions:

Do you think public opinion played a role in how Congress treated Oliver North?

Do you think public opinion played a role in how Congress handled its investigation?

Public opinion effect on	*Yes, very much* (4)	*Yes, somewhat* (3)	*Only a little* (2)	*Not at all* (1)	*Average*
How Congress treated North?	11	6	2	0	3.5, *n* = 19
How Congress handled investigation?	4	4	5	6	2.3, *n* = 19

been consistent defenders of Reagan and Iran–contra, emerged as advocates for North. Earlier in the hearings, Representative Henry Hyde told Secord that the channeling of funds to the contras should not be called a "diversion." Instead, it was "an allocation by the Enterprise of funds over which it had dominion and control."[89] Hyde was not wholly uncritical of North but labeled him a stalwart supporter of freedom and freedom fighters.

Still other committee members responded in a very different way, by countering North's vision of constitutional government. These elites reacted to perceived public opinion by challenging North and thus educating the public about broader issues involved in Iran–contra. These legislators and their staff believed that they helped shift public views. Representative Ed Jenkins, a Democratic contra aid supporter from Georgia, was the first member to take North to task. Jenkins proceeded slowly and carefully, using what some commentators called a courtly, country lawyer approach. In a series of questions, Representative Jenkins asked North if the vice president, president, Senate, Senate Intelligence Committee, House of Representatives, or House Intelligence Committee had known about the sale of arms to Iran. After North replied no to all these, Jenkins asked if it thus was true that "there is not a single official elected by the people of this great nation that had any knowledge of that." North said it was. In response to Jenkins's line of questioning, editorials and commentators took up the congressman's points. Representative Jenkins also found that "the people who had been just wanting to tear the members apart—at least this member—suddenly quit calling."[90]

Some members of Congress responded to public opinion in other ways. Because North had a tendency to give speeches when asked questions, these members delivered their own discourses. One staff member remarked,

> We decided that we were going to get our view across. We got this national television audience. Would we have done it the same way if we hadn't had thousands and thousands and thousands of letters and phone calls coming in? Probably not, because we might not have felt the need to counter the interpretation that was getting out there.

To try to turn the public's understanding of North and Iran–contra, Senators Mitchell and Rudman, among others, made impassioned statements about the meaning of patriotism and democracy. Mitchell reported an "immediate and overwhelming" response, with thousands of supportive telegrams flowing into his office.[91]

North's perceived popularity encouraged committee members to address the lieutenant colonel in various ways.[92] Did Congress's interpretation of public opinion influence the hearings or the investigation in other ways? Many committee staff and members asserted that it had some effect, but as a group they saw less influence on the investigation and hearings than on the committee's approach to North. As table 6.2 shows, six of nineteen of those asked saw no effect, five only little, four some, and four a lot. Although committee members did not admit there was any impact, staff members believed that public opinion led to some shifts. Most of all, "the momentum grew to conclude the investigation quickly."[93] As a result, fewer people were interviewed publicly.

> After the North testimony and the Poindexter testimony, the committee began to shut down the operation. They took the necessary testimony from the cabinet members, but there had been a number of others who, the initial expectation had been, they would expected to testify at some point. At that point, the committee was no longer interested in doing all that. Basically, the lights had gone out. . . . A lot of the steam had gone out of the desire, at least to continue with public hearings.[94]

Most staff believed that the perceived wave of public support had affected the way that the committee members behaved. "Some members of the committee lost some of their interest in spending a lot of time on this themselves. The investigative staffs continued to follow things out logically and pursue interviews and depositions, but it had some impact on members."[95] Certain elected officials backed away from taking a leadership position.

> Some committee members lost their taste for wanting to be on stage with the bright lights. Instead of a career enhancer, it was beginning to look like a liability. So I think, they knew they had to take testimony from cabinet members. . . . They left it to the Intelligence Committee to follow up, but the Intelligence Committee never did.[96]

Partisan and Institutional Differences

Committee members' party affiliations colored how they saw Iran–contra and how they reacted to public opinion, but this was mediated by institutional factors. Republicans were predictably more supportive of North and the Iran–contra policies than were Democrats. After all, Republicans had strongly endorsed most of President Reagan's initiatives, including his call to aid the contras. However, Republican senators and representatives were organized into the investigating committee differently than House Republicans, and they took rather different postures. Greater partisanship in the House and more bipartisanship in the Senate were one of the main reasons for the different committee structures, but these organizational patterns also served to reinforce the bitter partisan feeling among House Republicans. As Haynes Johnson pointed out:

> In the Senate the tradition of comity and civility was long established and long observed. In the House a far more contentious spirit prevailed. The House was polarized politically. Partisanship reigned, and a partisanship especially acute during the Reagan years. Republicans chafed with frustration and fury at their inability to crack the lock the Democrats held on control of the House while their own party dominated presidential elections.[97]

The House's partisan atmosphere was reinforced by the Iran–contra committee design, with House Republicans working closely with others who were angered about their status.

Starting with Secord's testimony and then increasing sharply with North's appearance, many House Republicans began to attack the committee majority and to defend the witnesses. From the point of view of House Democrats and many Senate Republicans, the partisan House Republicans were simply trying to shield their president and avoid political damage from highly questionable policies. But from the point of view of many House Republicans, the entire Iran–contra inquiry was blatantly political.[98] Although many admitted that not all was right, they saw the hearings as driven by the worst motives. It was a "political show trial," like "Joan of Arc." As such, the House Republicans needed to fight. As one aide said, "If you're pure, do you go smile and go to the cross burning? Or do you fight it every inch of the way?"[99] Reactions to North's testimony cheered and emboldened many House Republicans. In contrast, Republican Senators Rudman and Cohen challenged North and others and did not flinch from public or party pressures. In part, the Senate Republicans differed from the House Republicans because they were different sorts of people with different institutional experiences. All the senators on the committee had just spent the last six years as part of a Republican majority, and so they had less ingrained anger and bitterness. However, the Senate Republicans' less partisan approach also reflected fundamental differences in the institutions. The senators' larger constituencies moderated ideologies. In addition, their six-year terms insulated them from sudden public pressures. Since there are only one hundred senators, the Senate was often said to have a clublike atmosphere. (The critics of bipartisanship in Iran–contra I spoke with often sarcastically commented on the clubbiness of the Senate.) The Senate's small size ensures that senators know one another, and frequently they have worked together on a committee or project. If a minority in the Senate wishes, they can use the filibuster to disrupt business. Thus, the minority never feels that they have no power. Still, the Senate's institutional realities did not mean that senators felt invulnerable to political pressures. Some backed away from Iran–contra when they felt the public breath on their neck. Of all the committee members, Senator Trible suffered the most. He lost the Republican primary in Virginia, largely owing to conservative anger over Iran–contra and other issues.[100] In choosing whether or how to react to the perceived public mood, senators and representatives were influenced by party and institution, but they also had to make individual choices and assessments.

Explaining Congressional Responsiveness

Faced with what seemed like a wave of public support for North and disdain for Congress, committee members reacted in different ways. The senators and representatives on the committee responded in the ways they did because of political calculations and policy commitments. Although they were concerned with principle, this does not imply that they ever disregarded public opinion. The shouting of the public voice, as amplified by organized groups and the media, was much too loud for that. As many staff members told me, representatives regularly monitored public and media reaction. In one staffer's words, "Members would rush to the back room to see how the media critiqued their questioning of witnesses and then they adjusted accordingly." It would be a mistake, I argue, to separate committee members into two camps, with one group characterized as electoral calculators and the other as politically courageous. Although some were moved more by one factor than the other, no members were exclusively motivated by either political pressure or personal conviction.

All members were influenced by electoral incentives, which motivated them to react to constituency pressures. Some members quickly changed their tone and moved to cheer on Mr. North. Others were fairly consistent defenders of President Reagan throughout the scandal. In general, these members were strong supporters of contra aid, and they appreciated the visibility and vigor of North's defense of that policy. They used his seeming popularity to buttress their political positions and uphold President Reagan's foreign policy approach. The constructed public opinion was a political resource that could be used to accomplish policy goals.

Not all members reacted to the conspicuous public by restraining their criticism of North when phone calls and telegrams poured in. Does this imply that those members who resisted the forceful public voice were simply unresponsive to or uninterested in what their constituents thought? Or were these members influenced only by their own judgments? I believe that neither explanation applies. These members did indeed take public opinion quite seriously; they never ignored it. In fact, some of the severest critics of North began their statements to him by acknowledging his ostensible hold on the public. These members carefully planned how they would respond to North, given his strategy and the public mood. Perceived public opinion and constituency pressures changed how critical members approached North. But in this case, responsiveness did not mean modifying their basic stance toward North's deeds. Critics of North on the committee included supporters and opponents of contra aid. However, the congressional critics disapproved of how the Iranian and contra policies were carried out. They were disturbed by the secrets kept from Congress, by the use of unappropriated funds, by the tasks performed by government staff who were not trained for diplomatic and intelligence work, and by the privatization of foreign policy. Guided by their assessment of the Iran–contra events, critical members drew on their best judgment to address North and, beyond him, to speak to the American people.

Committee members had to decide how to act under very trying and exhausting circumstances. In gauging public opinion and deciding what to do, they relied on their nearly reflexive understanding of how to comprehend and respond to public opinion. In talking to members, I found that committee members linked together the two basic elements of representation. They argued that they should sometimes act as delegates and so do what their constituents wanted. But as trustees, they believed that they needed to use their knowledge and discernment to serve the common good. Members believed that these dual roles constantly had to be balanced.

On the one hand, members argued that they sometimes needed to act as leaders. As such, they took positions on issues their constituents did not care about or acted against what they perceived as their constituents' desires. Representative Henry Hyde, for example, maintained that although his constituents were not interested in foreign affairs and generally opposed sending money to other nations, he strongly supported aid to the former Soviet Union because he believed it was in the best interest of the people. All the members of Congress that I interviewed stated that they should be prepared to lose their seat over a tough, principled vote. Leadership—acting as a trustee—was at least an affirmed value.

At the same time, legislators were quite clear that they could take a strong position in opposition only occasionally. If they voted against their state or district, they needed to explain their vote to their constituents. But in Representative Jenkins's words, "You can only go to that well so many times."[101] In the case of Iran–contra, members who resisted political pressures explained that they simply had to lead. Constitutional powers were involved, since the executive branch took steps without congressional knowledge and used funds that Congress had not appropriated. If, as North claimed, no elected official knew of the diversion of funds to the contras, democratic accountability was imperiled.

In addition to resistance based on strong policy commitments, other factors enabled members to be critical of North. Most of all, mail and other constituent input did not speak for itself but needed interpretation. Some legislators were not convinced that it reflected anything more than a temporary blip. Although citizens' views were strongly held, this did not mean that the level of intensity would remain strong and would be remembered on election day. In addition, some found that their mail was more mixed than the news media reported. Members of the committee also were wary of trusting mail as a broad indicator of constituent views and were unwilling to use such unreliable data to guide their actions on such an important matter. As Senator Rudman pointed out,

> If you can tell me how my constituents feel on a particular issue, I would be *delighted* to consider—unless I had *violent* objections to their decision—casting a vote on behalf of their view. I never knew what they thought! Does anybody? That's one of the problems you political scientists don't understand. I would vote thirty-one times some days in the United States Senate. . . . How do I find out how people in New Hampshire thought about my key votes. . . . On 99.9 percent of the issues you don't know what your constituency thinks. You know what some people who wrote to you think of you, but those are people who generally feel strongly about the issue.

Finally, the minimal constraints and rewards available to U.S. political parties allowed Republican critics of North to be largely free to stake out their own positions.[102]

Although some people might be inclined to find that legislators who spoke out against North were bound only by principles and others were slaves to electoral calculation, let me state again that this is too broad a distinction. The supporters of North also were adherents of the contra aid policy he defended, and they based both positions on their principles. In addition, the challengers of North judged the political risks and benefits. North's critics and their staff sometimes maintained that the public would respect or would eventually come to respect their position. Legislators believed that their constituents admired their integrity and independence as long as they explained their positions and did not go against the state or district too often. In making choices about responding to North, legislators anticipated future public opinion, and they also were aware that other members of Congress were watching and judging them. None of them wanted to get the reputation of being a political hack, too timid to take a position, as this label could hurt their effectiveness and standing. North's critics also faced differing political facts of life. As the former Speaker of the House Thomas (Tip) O'Neill once observed, "All politics is local." Conditions in the districts clearly had an impact. It is no accident, for example, that two of the three Republican senators who signed on to the majority report were from New England. Cohen hailed from Maine and Rudman from New Hampshire, states with traditions of independence and a less admiring attitude toward the national security state. The other Republican senator to sign on with the majority was Trible of Virginia, who did alienate conservative Republicans and suffered the consequences with a loss in the primary.

The combination of assessments of current and anticipated opinion, gains from a reputation for integrity, and local conditions both tightened and loosened the constraints of perceived public opinion on legislators. Congressional responsiveness occurred in particular contexts and thus took different shapes, ranging from a newly expressed admiration for Oliver North, arguments on behalf of the contra cause and North's motivations to help the contras, and explanations of the constitutional problems with North's activities.

After the Hearings

Did the perception of the public mood lead Congress to rush to judgment? Were the investigation and final report changed by the North spectacle? Some committee members and staff believed that the report was not affected, but others disagreed.[103] The majority of the committee—

including all the Democrats and three of five Senate Republicans—issued its own report. All House Republicans and two Senate Republicans signed on to a minority report. In addition, a number of committee members included supplementary or dissenting remarks in the documents. Both the majority and minority reports were products of compromise. Indeed, the negotiations over the majority report became so involved that, as Senators Cohen and Mitchell put it, "a separate book would be required to relate the tug of war that took place in the preparation of these two reports."[104] The fact that negotiations were needed is not hard to understand. After all, the committee reports stand as basic historical documents that any reader with a serious interest in Iran–contra would consult. Each member of the committee wanted to influence the substance and tone of the conclusions. Congress's findings also would have political implications for the future, for they would stand as statements about the proper conduct of foreign policy and covert action, as well as judgments of President Reagan's activities.

Although the negotiations surrounding the majority report entailed some substantive disagreements, the committee staff and members that I interviewed were more concerned with the impact of public opinion on the report's thoroughness.[105] Some staff and members held that the final report was not complete and attributed the gaps to the pressure of public opinion. One staff member maintained that public opinion greatly affected how Congress treated North but also that "the upsurge of public support for the persona of Oliver North" was a "sideshow that did not influence the fundamental conclusions of the Iran–contra report."[106] Senator Rudman believed that the report accomplished its goals of informing the public and gathering enough evidence to decide whether Reagan warranted impeachment. It was "a superb job of that. Mr. Walsh spent $45 million and didn't come out with anything new, except an allegation against Cap Weinberger which we frankly didn't think was very important."[107] For one aide, public opinion had less to do with the investigation than "uncontrollable factors, such as [CIA Director William] Casey's death and the need for secrecy. . . . Nothing of real consequence came out of Walsh's investigation that wasn't in the committee report."[108]

Another staff member disagreed, arguing instead that the pressure to wrap up the inquiry limited the findings and the picture of Iran–contra.[109]

> The committee probably got out 80 to 85 percent of the facts, but hidden in that 15 to 20 percent may have been the smoking gun, one or more

smoking guns. There were just lots and lots of things that had you had the chance to follow up on, you would have tried to follow up on. And who knows what among those missing facts would have changed the way people saw this whole thing.[110]

If public opinion did have an impact on the report, it appears to have worked by affecting the decision to issue a report quickly. Although many of those decisions were made before the hearings started, the pressure to conclude the investigation was increased by the perceived public mood in the early days and following North's testimony.

After the hearings, committee staffers continued to interview witnesses and began to draft the report. Staffers and members found themselves exhausted by the process. Because the process of writing the reports was less public, any felt pressures from the public had less direct impact. The staffers who drafted the reports were influenced by professional standards and members' ideologies and commitments to constitutional principles. One contentious area of disagreement pertained to discussions in the majority report about the propaganda and public relations efforts conducted by the White House. Some staffers tried to make this a prominent issue in the report, but others considered it less crucial; eventually it received only limited attention. The minority report was signed only by Republicans and was able to take a more unified position, one casting doubt on the majority's view of executive and legislative power and its factual conclusions.

Despite perceptions that North had become an American hero and survey data showing an increase in support for contra aid, the Congress did not move to appropriate new funds. At the other end of Pennsylvania Avenue, President Reagan began to embrace diplomatic solutions. In August, House Speaker Jim Wright and President Reagan "called for a ceasefire in the Nicaraguan war, an end to outside military aid to both sides in the conflict, and a process of national reconciliation and dialogue within Nicaragua." Days after this, Costa Rican President Oscar Arias introduced his own peace proposal. In October 1987 Reagan spoke to the Organization of American States and pledged that he would continue to try to aid the contras. But the new political environment created by the peace efforts and by Reagan's decreased popularity since the Iran–contra scandal surfaced made Reagan loath to act. Although the president did not seek new monies in the fall of 1987, Congress did vote for a small amount of nonlethal aid. The administration then asked for contra aid in late January 1988, but this request was voted down by the House in February. "The unstable majority in favor of contra aid, built less on consensus than on a rare confluence of domestic circumstances, proved unsustainable once Ronald Reagan had lost his magic and the region presented a viable-looking plan for dealing with the Sandinistas."[111]

Oliver North's testimony influenced his own future in both the courts and politics. North's grant of immunity came back to haunt Independent Counsel Lawrence Walsh. In his final report, Walsh charged that public pressures made it impossible for prosecutors to sustain North's convictions.

> Congress's perceived need to quickly and publicly resolve the grave political questions posed by Iran/contra nearly derailed OIC's [the Office of the Independent Counsel's] efforts to bring high officials to justice. No adverse factor shaped or constricted Independent Counsel's criminal investigation more than the congressional immunity grants made to North, Poindexter, and Hakim. The trial convictions of North and Poindexter were ultimately reversed on appeal because they prevailed in arguing that the testimony of witnesses in their trials was not proved to be unaffected by their highly publicized immunized congressional testimony.[112]

In addition, the congressional testimony of Oliver North, the response of the activated public, the media reports of public opinion, and the committee members' remarks about how the public viewed North all helped create the public persona that North later used. As chapter 5 demonstrated, this perception of public opinion was used by right-wing interest groups as a political and organizational resource and was eventually used by North himself in his own political endeavors. Congress needed Oliver North to help tell the story of Iran–contra, but it also inadvertently gave him the stage on which he made his national reputation.

Stagings: The Effect of Congressional Decisions

How did the congressional committee set the stage for its dramatic confrontation with citizen North? In what ways were its decisions important to the public reactions they received? Initial choices—based on strategic judgments and political pressures—had a major impact. The differing structures for the House and Senate committees led to certain consequences.[113] As I have shown, clashes between the bodies and their typical modes of conducting business erupted. In particular, the more partisan House members were quick to use public opinion as a political resource, which further amplified the voices of supporters of Reagan, Secord, and North.

The mixed structure also proved unwieldy because it was so large, and this affected the dialogue between elected officials and the public. Most questioning of witnesses was done by House and Senate counsels; committee members had little time to express their own opinions. As a result, the conversation about Iran–contra, particularly during North's testimony, did not include most members of Congress. Citizens had little opportunity, in effect, to get to know many committee members in the way that they did during the extensive Watergate hearings. With the North hearings, all members (except for Senate Committee Chairman Daniel Inouye) stayed in the background for the first four days.

Concessions to North, including use immunity, nearly no prior private questioning, and limited time for staff to examine North's notebooks also colored the tone of the hearings. According to Senators Cohen and Mitchell, "To get North to testify, we had let him set the time and terms of his testimony. This was the single most important decision made by the Committee."[114] Immunity enabled North to sound off and defiantly admit he had lied to Congress, all the while explaining that misleading Congress was necessary for national security reasons. If he had not been granted immunity, North would have left himself vulnerable to prosecution if he had admitted lying to Congress. Some involved with the committee believed that without immunity, North would probably have invoked his Fifth Amendment right to not incriminate himself, and as a result, his demeanor and reception would probably have been quite different. Because North had received immunity, the committee delayed taking testimony from him in order to give Independent Counsel Walsh more time to gather evidence.

> All in all, the negotiations with Congress were a clear victory for North. Not knowing what the witness' testimony was going to be, John Nields, Liman and other questioners would be at a decided disadvantage. North would come on stage without a formal dress-rehearsal, but criminal-law experts familiar with Brendan Sullivan knew that North would hardly be unrehearsed. Down at Williams & Connolly, they were drilling him with every imaginable question, and they had taken the time to study the tendencies of Liman, Nields, and each member of the committee.[115]

The committee opted to hear witnesses in a particular order, a choice based on the desire for short hearings that would not become part of the next presidential election. In criminal cases, prosecutors typically start with very low level witnesses and then build up to the more important ones. The earlier persons questioned help generate a web of facts that enable lawyers to construct a narrative and a coherent explanation of events. In this case, though, it was thought that the usual procedure would be too time-consuming. Thus, unlike the courtroom model, the committee instead started with retired General Secord, a man at the center of both the Iranian and contra imbroglios. Committee members hoped that because of his position in the schemes, Secord would present all the essential details of the story. But his tale was quite different from the one that the committee wanted him to tell; it attracted an admiring audience; and it engendered a supportive public reaction from his fans.[116] This response to Secord influenced members and staff and presaged the later situation with North. In designing the hearings' structure, committee members did not develop the informational context needed for understanding later witnesses.

In a sense, what the committee did was akin to holding a discussion among people who have a lot of background on an issue and then inviting others who know little or nothing to watch. Then when these observers saw strong criticism, they focused more on the censurious tone than on what was being censured. Although the committee was probably mistaken in having Secord start the hearings, it is unclear how they could have provided sufficient background for citizens who tuned in from time to time. Many people in the public were not well acquainted with the facts, and they watched the hearings only intermittently, usually choosing those times when the level of contention and dramatic tension was high. As one staff member put it, "The public paid close attention when the theater was good. Television sparked the interest, and this drama had it all: A hero, villains, money, drama, danger, secrecy." For an audience of this sort, a spectacle born of personal confrontation seemed to carry the day.

At least in its initial decisions, the congressional committee did not consider how the hearing would appear on television. One staffer remarked that the Iran–contra hearings were the "least media-driven operation in Congress [he had] been involved in." Committee members and staff lost track of basic elements of production in their quest to get out the basic story. The setting for the hearing was designed so that all the committee members could see and question North. But as Senators Cohen and Mitchell later concluded, "What none of us noticed was that we had transformed the hearing room into a minicoliseum and that we appeared as the equivalent of Roman potentates turning thumbs up or down."[117] In such circumstances, the energetic and aggressive North and his lawyer Brendan Sullivan were able to dominate images and story line.

North's orchestration of his appearance was helped by certain characteristics of television. As one staff member noticed,

> The sense in the room, at least on day one, was entirely different. You didn't get this dramatic sense. I remember at some point in the day, going back into the anteroom where the TV sets were on, and watching the testimony for a little while on TV and it was like, "Oh my God, this is entirely different. . . ." You know, misty-eyed Oliver North filling the screen, and the whole dynamic looked different than it did in the huge committee room with a lot of people. And here's little Oliver North sitting at the table. And with the whole background that we all had, knowing full well he was dissembling, avoiding the questions, in essence filibustering. And that wasn't coming across on TV at all.[118]

In general, television favors the personal and the emotional, with sentiment tying watchers and performers together, whereas the same incident could look false in person. North was able to use television in the way he did because of the conditions under which he testified. North was not apologetic or evasive. Instead, he was an aggressive attacker of Congress, a self-conscious booster of his own courage and patriotism and a seeming victim of his own bravado, competence, and loyalty. He exuded sincerity and confidence while playing the part of the underdog. North reframed the hearings away from the unpopular Iranian arms sale and toward a tale of boldness in defense of freedom and safety. As a narrative, it was well attuned to the vocabulary and stock plots of television.

In a sense, the committee's decisions allowed North to use cultural symbols as his defense and shield, a task for which North was temperamentally suited and well prepared. Although his personality and the committee setting were important, so was North's readiness. For example, many committee members believed that he had improperly accepted a security fence from some Iran–contra participants, yet the well-prepared North prevented the committee from damaging his persona when he was questioned about it. The security system was paid for by Secord and Hakim, arms dealers who profited from the activities that North coordinated, and North falsified documents pertaining to it. (Later North was convicted for "accepting an illegal gratuity"—this fence.) In a meeting before the public testimony commenced, North's lawyer, Brendan Sullivan, asked that the public questioning begin with this issue, suggesting to some committee members that he had a ready response. When North was questioned on this matter on the second day of testimony, he boldly claimed that the fence was necessary to protect his family from the terrorist Abu Nidal. Although he was ready to take on the terrorist "man to man," his family needed the safety provided by the security system. According to Senators Cohen and Mitchell,

> It was now clear why Sullivan had tried to get the public questioning to begin with the subject of the fence. North's response sealed his triumph. . . . Soon telegrams started to come, first in the hundreds, then in the thousands, then the tens of thousands. . . . Committee members began to worry about how many constituents would remember their feelings of antagonism toward their representative on the next election day.[119]

Even though North had never asked any government official for special security, he was able to portray himself as the courageous protector of his brood. Resonant and easily retrievable images of masculine heroism became North's defense as "he sat ramrodstiff, Clint Eastwood, Audie Murphy, Alan Ladd, and John Wayne, all buttoned up in one charismatic person."[120] The stock plots and personae of the mass culture helped construct the atmosphere of political spectacle and made the acclamations part of the drama carried by the media.

The waves of support for North that members of Congress and their staffs felt in the early days of North's testimony were not, of course, valid indicators of public opinion. But the combination of activated citizens with intense views (in part mobilized by groups) and media reports of public adulation of North created a perception that the committee members had to heed. Some members found public opinion to be more complex than the view expressed by journalists, but all strained to hear the public and all took into account what they heard when it was their chance to speak.

7

Public Opinion in Political Context

At the start of this book, I argued that public opinion is used strategically in the politics of governing. Advocates try to influence the perception of public opinion so that they can use these constructions for their political purposes. Although interpretations of public desires rely in part on public opinion polls, the polls themselves are influenced by the frames used by political elites. Given these dynamics, it can be very difficult for elected officials to know what the public wants. As this book has shown, perceived public opinion mattered in the Iran–contra hearings. Loud and activated voices dominated public communication and provided the raw material for news stories filled with dramatic narratives and images of public response. Legislators responded to the public tumult in various ways. Some members of Congress were quieted; others heralded North's sincerity and heroism; and still others criticized North's defense of secrecy and executive supremacy.

This chapter discusses what the Iran–contra hearings reveal about public opinion in politics more generally and, using a four-fold typology, compares this situation with other sorts of political circumstances. In this chapter I also examine how this dynamic relates to broader changes in

American politics and its implications for democratic representation and civic development. My analysis in this chapter does not and is not meant to explain all variations in the policy process.[1] For example, I do not consider how different sorts of policies are associated with stable or unstable coalition partnerships. Furthermore, not all policy fights fit cleanly in one cell but possess attributes that make them mixtures of several ideal types.

Politicians nearly always take into account some version of public opinion as they make decisions, whether public views are easily understood, obscured, or anticipated. At the same time, the way in which public opinion is incorporated into politics varies, and perceptions of public opinion are not so powerful that they fully constrain citizens and legislators.

Reactions to North's testimony show how difficult it is for the public to make its voice clearly heard. Even in a time of great public concern, the public opinion found in polls was not equivalent to the public opinion portrayed by the media and interest groups or as heard by Congress. Responses to North's Iran–contra testimony also demonstrate the importance of symbolic messages and group mobilization for the politics of public opinion. North's ability to dominate the translation of public opinion was, in part, a tribute to his competence with symbolic vocabularies. North drew on culturally significant images of the lone man against a powerful crowd and used his uniform and stance to embody emotionally resonant symbols of military service. President Reagan's characterization of North as a hero framed much of the coverage of both North and public opinion of him. One prevalent counter-symbol used by the media and by legislators—Watergate—applied to Iran–contra only in part, yet it nearly precluded the media's interest in unique issues in the affair. In addition, North's supporters organized before he testified and planned events too visually interesting for the news media to pass up. Those citizens who were spontaneously drawn to North's message and persona acted quickly, whereas ambivalent and critical citizens reacted less swiftly. This combination of potent symbols and uneven mobilization generated powerful, nearly uncontested images that colored the media's coverage and congressional assessments of public opinion.

Variations in the Politics of Public Opinion

During policy fights, citizens are concerned or apathetic, mobilized or quiescent, driven by emotion and symbolic predispositions or influenced by their core beliefs. If an issue becomes an object of open political struggle, interest groups, habitual activists, and committed politicians will claim that public opinion is on their side. Although public opinion is a fundamental political resource, this does not mean that it will always be used effectively or that interpretations of public opinion will reflect accurately the range of general opinion. In short, public opinion and translations of the public voice are incorporated into politics in different ways, but they always are potential or active political resources.

The politics of public opinion—the ways that partisans and opponents in political disputes use public opinion—can be associated with four basic forms. Reactions to public opinion during the Iran–contra hearings were strongly symbolic and involved unevenly mobilized groups. In other situations, groups can be fairly evenly matched, and the issues may be less symbolic.

Patterns of group mobilization influence which citizens are more easily heard by members of Congress. As I argued in chapter 5, if only one side is well mobilized, this group will have the advantage in defining the public will. Although interest groups never are precisely matched, contending groups can be fairly equal or decidedly unequal. If one group consistently dominates, the media and legislators may assume that the mobilized group represents the interested public or the public as a whole. In some cases, membership groups with intense views and well-institutionalized means of reminding members of legislators' stands have a louder voice than their numbers warrant, and politicians may recognize that their views are not representative of the citizenry, yet the groups still have a significant role in policy deliberations. In both of these situations, elected officials may be concerned about electoral retribution. Another set of highly mobilized groups—organizations that represent business interests—tend to have structural advantages in the political system.

As many studies have long shown, business groups have a decided advantage in funding and organization. Despite the rise in consumer and environmental groups in the past twenty-five years, groups representing trade associations and corporations still overshadow the interest-group universe. Business groups dominate in lobbying and television news coverage of interest groups.[2] In large part, the dominance of business is due to biases in organizing groups. The "free rider problem" hurts groups that seek benefits for most of the community because people realize that any policy success achieved by the group cannot be withheld from them and they also know that their single contribution is not enough to make the ultimate difference.[3] Citizens in these situations can simply try to get a free ride, and so refrain from contributing to public interest groups. In contrast, business groups can benefit a relatively small set of interested parties, and they know that no one else will act on their behalf. As a result, businesses are likely to use their available resources to organize politically. As highly organized groups, their lobbyists can be a constant and familiar presence at committee hearings and in less formal settings.

The better-organized business groups have other advantages as well. They represent practitioners of capitalism, a highly legitimate system in the United States.[4] In addition, they are well positioned to argue about how policy proposals may affect the overall economy. Business groups often maintain that certain courses of action will have dire consequences—such as inflation, disinvestment, or unemployment—and these claims can influence government officials. In Lindblom's terms, the market acts as a "prison," a constraint to policy action.[5]

Business groups' strength in representing the public's views further amplifies the class bias in all political participation. Educated, upper-income citizens participate more than other citizens do, have different policy concerns, and are more likely to believe that their voice will be heard.[6] Given their greater propensity to vote and to contact their representatives, and the interest group bias toward business, this perception is probably accurate.

Although historical patterns of group strength are important, they are not determinative.[7] New groups can organize and work to redefine community interests. Public-interest groups have been born and survived. They constitute a clear voice in the policy process and can be an effective counterweight to business interest groups. In addition, symbolic messages can sweep through the polity, changing the politics of public opinion.

Issues range from highly symbolic to nonsymbolic.[8] According to Edelman,

Condensation symbols evoke the emotion associated with the situation. They condense into one symbolic event, sign, or act patriotic pride, anxieties, remembrances of past glories or humiliations, promises of future greatness. . . . Practically every political act that is controversial or regarded as really important is bound to serve in part as a condensation symbol.[9]

Symbolic issues are treated gingerly by politicians and become symbolic when group leaders, activists, political parties, and politicians imbue them with meaning and emotional content. Making an issue symbolic serves to mobilize citizens selectively. Issues and people presented in strongly symbolic terms act as cognitive shortcuts and as a cue to certain members of the public.[10] As a result, symbolic issues can prompt citizens to take political action spontaneously or can help groups organize certain citizens. Realizing this, interest groups try to shift their issues onto a symbolic terrain that will benefit them. In addition, the news media are drawn to strongly symbolic messages and further magnify voices speaking in those terms, making them a louder part of the political echo chamber.

Although politicians and interested groups can make an issue symbolic through political struggle, they are not altogether free to create symbolic meanings. Partisans must be able to draw on an existing reservoir of cultural meanings as they try to frame the issue, and these cultural traditions set parameters for potential symbolic constructions. In addition, their opponents may get involved in defining the issue. Tools such as focus groups and polling enable interest groups, candidates, and political parties to field-test various definitions of issues and to discover how different terminology influences public perceptions of a policy proposal. In struggling over symbolic messages, groups try to find the best way to appeal to the public and the media.

A Typology for the Politics of Public Opinion

The degree of symbolic politics and the pattern of group mobilization combine in various ways, yielding four ideal–typical patterns. (For a summary, see table 7.1.) In *authoritative-group politics*, one side dominates the presentation of the public voice and authoritatively wields powerful symbolic messages. Symbolic appeals are highly dramatic and so capture the attention of the news media. Since no group has mobilized to represent an alternative view, the media's presentation of public opinion disproportionately emphasizes the views of the one side. In fact, this is what happened with Oliver North during the Iran–contra hearings. North served as a symbol for military heroism and executive power in the service of national security. He also cast himself as the model of a little guy under siege by powerful political interests. In the early days of his testimony, North's supporters quickly mobilized and dominated perceived public opinion. Even though many members of Congress and citizens believed that most citizens admired North, a spiral of silence did not fully grip citizens and leaders. Despite the perception that North was popular, citizens who were critical of North eventually responded, and some members of Congress took North to task despite the perceived climate of opinion.

TABLE 7.1

A Typology of the Politics of Public Opinion

Symbolic Issue	*Relatively Nonsymbolic Issue*
Uneven Group Mobilization	
Authoritative Group Politics: One group dominates activated public, employs strong emotional symbols, and influences media's construction of issue. Perception that group represents public opinion may create a spiral of silence and influence citizen action and legislators. Example: North's testimony during Iran–contra.	Elite-Driven Politics: Public may be absent. If so, iron triangles, elite bargaining, compromise, and business concerns dominate. Material groups may mobilize select publics, with grassroots lobbying firms. Example: Credit card interest rate cap.
Even Group Mobilization	
Symbolic Politics: Groups debate definition of issue and the key symbols associated with the policy, and try to construct a public that agrees with its symbolic construction of the problem. Example: Abortion.	Interest-Group Politics: Overt struggle over portrayal of public opinion. Media portrays both sides. Politics also includes bargaining and compromise among elites, during and after battles over the construction and influence of public opinion. Example: Corporate average fuel economy (CAFE) standards.

If an issue is symbolic but groups are evenly mobilized, a spiral of silence is unlikely to develop. In *symbolic politics*, each group tries to define the issue at hand, and no voice can dominate public debate. Both sides of the issue present the matter so that it will gain public support, and each claims that the public supports its position. Because the issue is symbolic, it is connected to deeply held values and strongly felt emotions, and partisans in the debate will be reluctant to compromise. Although some citizens may not view the issue symbolically, since they are less closely tied to the issue, they will be less involved. As a result, presentations of public opinion are the object of struggle by core partisans. The abortion issue is a case of this sort.

When an issue is not highly symbolic and groups are not evenly mobilized, public opinion can be involved in politics in two ways, both of which I term *elite-driven politics*. In one form, the issue is a fairly obscure or narrow policy, perhaps a tax provision that pertains to very few businesses. Lobbyists for the interested party express their view to legislators, and the issue is resolved through elite bargaining. In this situation, public opinion is notable by its absence; there is little if any publicity or media coverage of the issue, and concerned interest groups have no reason to involve the public. Politicians, however, may anticipate how their constituents would react if the deal and the policy were revealed. Given today's combative and cynical media and the presence of public-interest groups as watchdogs, it has become increasingly difficult to contain elite-driven politics. A second possibility is that one group selectively mobilizes citizens. In this case, the issue becomes public and is discussed by the news media. To try to move legislators and serve their own interests, organized groups try to influence the perception of public opinion. When no group effectively counterorganizes, the mobilized group is able to use public opinion as a political resource on its behalf. This latter situation developed when Congress took up the idea of capping credit card interest rates.

If an issue is not highly symbolic and groups are evenly mobilized, then both sides are likely to go public. In *interest-group politics*, each side appeals to the public in order to change citizens' views and to mobilize them on their behalf. Partisans use public relations methods, quote information from opinion polls, and do their best to get their supporters to contact politicians. Public opinion becomes an important element of this political process. In controversial and tightly fought situations of this sort, several things may happen. First, an inside game often complements the outside strategy. Lobbyists suggest alternatives; groups provide expert witnesses; coalitions may form and work together; and organizations may seek to generate elite bargaining and compromise. No side can wholly dominate in the halls of Congress or in the mobilization of citizens. As a result, the news media are unlikely to overrepresent one side. Second, the issue may become increasingly symbolic. As Edelman points out, controversial issues are nearly always symbolic, at least in part. The policy debate over increasing average automobile fuel economy standards is a case of this sort.

In the real and messy world of politics, some situations may not fit neatly into one of these ideal-typical categories, or a policy dispute may change in character and thus migrate from one cell into another. How public opinion itself is incorporated into decisions and public activities— what I call the *politics of public opinion*—depends on political calculations and activities. Group mobilization is influenced by the persistent bias toward business groups, but policy entrepreneurs can bring new groups into existence. The definition of issues as symbolic and the particular symbolic meanings attached to issues result from strategies and choices.

Symbolic Politics: Abortion

Sometimes violent and always contentious, abortion politics in the United States has proved nearly impervious to compromise or settlement. Participants in the abortion debate have long disagreed about the meaning of abortion and about interpretations of public opinion. Like other activists, prolife and prochoice adherents have tried to construct majorities and to create the impression that the public is on their side. Each side is highly mobilized, and each is driven by a set of moral and value concerns, which are captured in the strongly symbolic issue.

Arguments about the meaning of abortion extend to debates about the meaning of abortion in the past. John Noonan, for example, developed what Celeste Condit calls a "pro-life heritage tale," which argues that opposition to abortion was "an almost absolute value in history."[11] In contrast, legal briefs and the *Roe v. Wade* decision presented evidence that abortion had long been considered acceptable before "quickening," the time when a mother can first feel the fetus move. Why do debates about the past persist? In large part, advocates argue about past publics' views of abortion in order to legitimize their positions. If we were to believe that abortion was considered an inexcusable evil throughout time, our ancestors' views might weigh on us still. On the other hand, if people in the past did accept abortion in part, allowing legal abortion would not be a significant transgression of established moral codes.

In fact, the record shows that abortion was understood differently in the past. Kristin Luker demonstrates that during the nineteenth century, the states' successful efforts to restrict abortion were undertaken by doctors, not religious or moral authorities. Limits on abortion helped create a professionalized class of medical doctors. Before that time, abortion was fairly common and was performed using herbs and other abortifacients. "Regular doctors" had no greater powers than the folk healers, midwives, herbalists, and homeopaths with whom they competed. Then the newly established American Medical Association adopted abortion as an issue, contending that it was medically dangerous. In addition, doctors argued that ignorance of fetal development led women to interrupt the life-developing process of pregnancy. Only doctors, they maintained, had the necessary medical knowledge to understand abortion. In response, the states passed laws that restricted, but did not prohibit, abortion. "With respect to physicians, once this first anti-abortion movement was successful, statute laws prohibited all abortions except those performed by (or on the advice of) physicians."[12] As a result of the doctors' campaign, women could not legally choose abortion. At the same time, however, the life of the fetus did not have absolute precedence over the woman's health and life.

The symbolic meaning of abortion then shifted dramatically in the mid-twentieth century. Although these changes began in the 1960s, they did not crystallize until after the U.S. Supreme Court issued its *Roe v. Wade* decision in 1973. The Court ruled that women had a constitutional right to have an abortion, particularly early in their pregnancy. After *Roe*, the small prochoice and prolife organizations grew quickly. In developing as movements and pressing their cases, abortion activists used visual symbols, addressed abortion as a symbolic issue, and argued that the public agreed with their understanding of abortion.

In the fight over abortion, activists have framed abortion in fundamentally different ways. The prolife side prefers to discuss abortion as a question of protecting innocent fetal life, and the prochoice camp casts the issue as a woman's right to choose to control her reproductive life. In every political debate, advocates try to shift the underlying ground so that the issue is described in terms that favor their position. But the different language used in the abortion debate is more than a politically motivated rhetorical dispute. Abortion partisans do not just disagree about whether the U.S. Constitution protects a woman's right to choose abortion or diverge on the question of when life begins; they also disagree about what the dispute about abortion is about. The prolife and prochoice sides in the abortion debate talk about abortion differently because they understand the issue in divergent ways.

As Luker and Ginsberg demonstrate, advocates' various definitions of abortion have their roots in diverse values and ways of life. Prochoice advocates see abortion as necessary for and consistent with a life in which women are not bound by their reproductive potential. Because they tend to hold (or plan to hold) jobs that require significant education and that they consider careers, the right to have an abortion is necessary for them in order to plan when (or if) they will have children. Prolife advocates believe that abortion devalues women who have focused on caring for their children, by "undermining an informal code that links sex with reproduction and male support of families."[13] For female prolifers, these values support their ways of life, which include much time spent taking care of their families, lower levels of education than for prochoice activists, and infrequent forays into the paid labor force. Abortion gains its symbolic power from its association with values concerning motherhood, sexuality, and reproduction and from its connection to life choices.

The prochoice and prolife movements each have adopted visual symbols that compress their views of abortion and are intended to appeal to the broader public. On the prolife side, pictures of fetuses are used to press the argument that a human life is destroyed by abortion. "Without these pictures, pro-Life advocates would have only an abstract argument about the importance of chromosomes in determining human life or a religious argument about the 'soul,' and neither of those options could sustain the righteous fire of the public movement." Captions typically refer to the fetus's already-formed toes or fingernails or to the presence of a heartbeat and brain waves. To demonstrate the dangers they faced before abortion was safe and legal, prochoice advocates have often used illustrations of coat hangers as the means to perform illegal abortions and, occasionally, pictures of women who have died from an illegal abortion. The prochoice literature has also included images of the Statue of Liberty. "The statue—as a woman, a symbol of the downtrodden, and a symbol of Freedom, Liberty, and home—embodied the ideal American representation of Choice or Reproductive Freedom."[14]

Visual images and rhetoric are used not just to frame the issue of abortion but also to define public opinion. Each side wants public opinion on abortion to be defined in terms of their understanding of it, so that each can truthfully claim that the majority agrees with their position. As Elizabeth Cook, Ted Jelen, and Clyde Wilcox explain, "Pro-choice activists point out (correctly) that the public does not want a ban on abortion. Pro-life activists note (also correctly) that the public disapproves of abortion on demand."[15]

Most of the public rejects both the prolife and prochoice positions and instead accepts legal abortion with conditions and under some circumstances.[16] That is, most people accept abortion when a woman becomes pregnant from rape or incest or when her life or health is in danger. But most people do not believe that women should be able to get a legal abortion if she is unmarried and does not wish to marry the baby's father, if she is married and does not want any more children, or if the family has very little money and cannot afford more children. In addition, a majority believes that minors should obtain their parents' consent before having an abortion and also accept a short waiting period.

As these polls show, the general population does not agree with the policy prescriptions of either prochoice or prolife activists. Then what does the public at large think about abortion? Most people reject the prolife characterization of abortion as intolerable killing and the prochoice characterization of abortion as a protected right. Instead, they appear to accept part of the reasoning of both sides. "Some polls have produced the rather staggering finding that a majority can support abortion, even as a majority *of the same group* considers abortion to be the equivalent of murder."[17] Prolife and prochoice activists understand abortion in symbolic terms, whereas the people in the middle are "pragmatists who do not see abortion as involving broad social values."[18] These people view abortion with great ambivalence and regretfully accept its legality because they fear the public health consequences of banning it.

Because people in the middle try to balance a number of considerations, polling results are quite sensitive to different phrasings of questions and to the order in which they are asked.[19] "People are more likely to say they favor abortion rights when the question is framed in terms of a 'woman's right to choose' than when the question talks about 'protecting an unborn child.' "[20] Without being wholly dishonest, prolife and prochoice activists can thus strategically use different polling data to demonstrate that the public agrees with their point of view. As one commentator argues, "If ever there were an issue in which ambivalence is understandable, it is abortion. The challenge to our politics is to find ways of promoting public policy that speaks to that ambivalence."[21]

Abortion politics exemplifies the situation in which activists struggle over the meaning and symbolism of an issue. Public opinion is part of the politics of an issue, so each side tries to translate it in a way that helps its own case. Because so many citizens are ambivalent, activists on both sides can construct seeming majorities. The mobilization of polarized, emotional groups has resulted in political stalemate, as neither camp can fully define the issue or authoritatively claim public support. Arguments about abortion politics are not made quietly by elites, over the head of the public, but include grassroots activists and leaders. Advocates, unlike the mass of citizens in the middle, are motivated by symbolic concerns. These symbolic concerns do not have broad political appeal, since the emotionality and polarizing effect of the symbolic debate offends the middle. Activists are unwilling, however, to accept compromise positions, and they remain ready to try to win the standoff.

Elite-Driven Politics: The Credit Card Interest Rate Cap

In November 1991, a brief furor erupted over the idea of imposing a cap on credit card interest rates. At first it seemed as if a bill supporting a cap would pass, but it did not, because bankers and other business concerns quickly determined that a cap on credit card rates would not be in their interest. Because the citizenry as a whole remained silent, public action was organized by the American Bankers Association, and the stock market swiftly reacted. The failure of this proposal—one that legislators initially believed would be popular among their constituents—demonstrates what can happen when business groups dominate mobilized action for a nonsymbolic issue. In this case of nonsymbolic politics and uneven group mobilization, business interests were the only interest groups to define public opinion and the national interest. Unlike some cases of elite-driven politics, the issue was handled publicly, and as a result, it could not be resolved by elite bargaining alone. Once public, citizen views became a force in how policy developed, and bankers subsidized the mobilization of public opinion as a tool to kill the cap.

Without apparent design, President George Bush began the debate over a credit card interest rate cap. He faced a persistent recession and was looking for ways to increase economic growth. Although the prime rate was low by historical standards, the rates paid by many consumers for credit card debt remained high—18 to 20 percent. In a fund-raising speech to Republican contributors on November 12, 1991, Bush remarked, "I was talking to some businessmen earlier, and I'd frankly like to see the credit card rates down. I believe that would help stimulate the consumer and get the consumer confidence moving again."[22] Although President Bush did not propose legislation to achieve this end, a legislative response quickly followed. On November 13, Senator Al D'Amato of New York introduced a provision on the Senate floor. D'Amato, a Republican who faced a difficult reelection bid, advanced a bill that would cap credit card rates at four percentage points above the interest charged by the Internal Revenue Service (IRS) to late taxpayers.[23] "With no public hearings and only thirty minutes of floor discussion," the senators voted seventy-four to nineteen to adopt the cap. With this vote, the issue then went to the House.[24]

Why did the Senate act so quickly? What role did public opinion play? Although public opinion was not mobilized, legislators' assessments of the public mind influenced the Senate's action. Senator D'Amato pushed the policy proposal because it was consistent with his electoral strategy of portraying himself as an advocate of the forgotten middle class.[25] According to numerous newspaper accounts, senators believed that most voters would support a limit on credit card rates. When the cap was brought to the Senate floor, "Pro-consumer sentiment overwhelmed the chamber, and only Jake Garn of Utah, ranking Republican on the

Banking Committee, spoke against it."[26] Senators anticipated future public response, particularly if a political opponent someday reminded constituents of their vote. Senator John Chafee, a Republican from Rhode Island who voted for the D'Amato-sponsored cap, admitted that many senators "aren't anxious to see this become law. It was looked at as more a shot across the bow than becoming a permanent feature. It was one of those items in this world of TV spots that's very hard to explain voting against."[27]

But unmobilized, anticipated public opinion was not enough to move the House and pass a credit card interest rate cap. The day after the Senate passed the cap, the stock market dropped 120 points, and the provision was blamed for the loss. In addition, bankers said that a cap could lead to cancellation of half the nation's 120 million credit cards. Rather than leading to lower rates for all, bankers predicted that only the most creditworthy customers would continue to hold credit cards.[28] Over the weekend, Bush administration officials and lawmakers appeared on the television news discussion shows and backed away from the cap. By Monday, the House Banking Committee was planning a weak alternative plan calling for an eighteen-month waiting and study period.[29] Democratic House Speaker Tom Foley soon endorsed this go-slow approach.[30]

Why did the cap die in the House? We would ordinarily expect that anticipated public opinion would influence representatives more than senators, particularly because they come up for election more frequently. Anticipated public reaction, however, must be weighed against actual public reaction—and there was some citizen reaction at the time. Interest groups against the cap took public opinion into account when they designed their strategies. In addition to providing spokespeople for their position, business groups opposed to the cap mounted a citizen activization and public relations campaign. The American Bankers Association contracted out this political job and hired a grassroots lobbying firm, Bonner & Associates, to mobilize citizens on its behalf.

Bonner & Associates is "a Washington firm that specializes in orchestrating telephone and mail lobbying blitzes from the hinterlands to Capitol Hill."[31] Jack Bonner, a former aide to Republican Senator John Heinz of Pennsylvania, founded his company in 1984 to give an additional voice to corporate America. Bonner discovered that although businesses could advocate their own interests, they had not been effective in organizing the public. According to Bonner, Senator Heinz and Bonner would meet with "mine workers or we'd meet with environmentalists or other people and they would have rooms packed with people who were pounding on the desks." Bonner noticed that

> grassroots contact would stick to [Heinz's] ribs. He sat on the Senate Finance Committee, the Senate Banking Committee, two very important committees to corporate America, and he'd repeat what these people said to him, and he related to it much more than an issue paper or some lone document from a CEO. I saw that certain groups did this extraordinarily well and corporate America did this extraordinarily poorly. And it hit me that there was a niche to do business in, of organizing, helping corporate America organize groups on their behalf, which is what we do.[32]

To serve corporate interests, Bonner & Associates contacts citizens in selected constituencies and presents a political issue to them. Using Bonner's telephone switching system, citizens who agree with its clients can be transferred to the office of their member of Congress. In the House or Senate, a congressional aide answers the phone and hears the constituents' statements regarding the proposed policy. Bonner & Associates staff also discuss issues with leaders of local organizations and then encourage them to meet with members of Congress or to write a letter on the organization's letterhead. The grassroots lobbying firm is paid for each letter, phone call, or meeting that it generates on behalf of its client.[33]

Working for the bankers against the credit card cap, Bonner & Associates was alone in mobilizing the public. "During a four-day period, he generated about ten thousand calls from voters, including community leaders, in ten districts represented by members of the House Banking, Finance, and Urban Affairs Committee . . . the ABA [American Bankers Association] paid Bonner an estimated $400,000."[34] The American Bankers Association wrote to Bonner in gratitude, "We could not have won without you. . . . It was hard in several days time to gain support for an issue that at first blush looked like a good idea to most people. After all, paying less interest on your credit cards sounds great. Nevertheless, Bonner & Associates achieved all of our goals."[35]

Indeed, the bankers were politically successful. When the House and Senate conference committee completed a banking bill in the early dawn hours of November 27, the credit card interest rate cap was gone. Although Senator D'Amato proclaimed at the start of the conference session that "this senator is not going to settle for a study," the cap did not survive even in its weakened form.[36] And President Bush, who had started the political ruckus, continued to face persistent questions about his economic stewardship.[37]

Public opinion, as understood and translated by political actors, played a number of roles in the credit card cap issue. At first, anticipated public opinion prompted President Bush to suggest the idea, induced Senator D'Amato to introduce a bill, and encouraged the Senate to pass it. The credit card cap was not, however, successfully converted into a symbolic issue and remained an issue largely defined in narrow, economic terms. As such, groups with a material stake in the outcome quickly responded. Not all reactions involved public opinion: the drop in the stock market indicated business' dislike of the proposed cap. As Lindblom would have predicted, the market constrained political action. But a public voice, selectively mobilized, also helped kill the cap. In this case of elite-driven politics, a group with a direct material interest quickly took action to organize citizens. Using the relatively new mechanism of corporate grassroots lobbying, the American Bankers Association invested nearly half a million dollars and considered it money well spent.

Interest-Group Politics: Automobile Fuel Efficiency Standards

Twenty years after the first Earth Day, Congress overhauled environmental legislation, passing a series of amendments to the Clean Air Act.[38] By the time the bill came to the House and Senate floors in October 1990, compromises and negotiations had cleared the way for easy passage. The Senate vote was 89 to 10 and the House tally was 401 to 25. On November 15, 1990, President Bush signed the bill into law. In crafting this legislation, the White House and legislators took account of the public—as did lobbyists and organized groups. Fairly evenly matched associations mobilized members of the public and took positions consistent with their readings of public opinion. Industry-backed groups argued against strong environmental provisions but were constrained in the arguments they could make. Legislators who had previously blocked consideration of new laws took notice of the strong public support for action on the environment.

Although the 1990 Clean Air Act amendments took many significant steps—including provisions concerning auto emissions, urban smog, toxic air pollutants, acid rain, and chlorofluorocarbons—environmentalists and their legislative supporters were unsuccessful in obtaining higher car fuel efficiency standards, and mobilized public opinion played a part in this failure.

Environmental concerns were popular by the end of the 1980s, as politicians knew well. Although the Reagan administration had been conspicuously hostile toward environmental concerns, Republican strategists sensed that the public mood had changed. "Already an important issue in outdoors-conscious California, pollution fears were also generating big polling numbers on the East Coast."[39] And so in the 1988 presidential election George Bush, Reagan's vice president, used the lingering pollution in Boston Harbor to attack the Democratic candidate Michael Dukakis. Bush declared himself a longtime environmentalist who would be the "environmental president."

Public support for environmental concerns remained strong after Bush's election. In poll after poll, citizens declared that taking care of the environment was a priority.[40] A 1990 CBS poll found that 74 percent agreed that "protecting the environment is so important that requirements and standards cannot be too high and continuing environmental improvements must be made regardless of cost," compared with only 21 percent who disagreed. This 74-to-21 percent split was a clear break from the 1983 results of 58 to 34 percent and the 1981 findings of 45 to 42 percent. Gallup asked citizens in 1990 to make a trade-off between economic growth and the environment; 71 percent said the environment was more important, and 19 percent picked economic growth. An NBC/*Wall Street Journal* poll told respondents, "Sometimes the laws that are designed to protect the environment causes industries to spend more money and raise their prices" and asked them which was more important, "protecting the environment or keeping prices down?" In 1990, 80 percent chose the environment over price restraint, with only 13 percent selecting lower prices. In contrast, when the same organization asked citizens this question in 1981, 51 percent chose the environment, and 38 percent picked low costs.

Public opinion as measured in polls is not enough to move an issue onto Congress's agenda, of course, but the strong general support for environmental concerns did play a part in bringing the issue to the fore. Bush's strategists' discovery and use of this issue in 1988 had enabled Bush to carve out a political identity apart from Reagan's and helped him attack his Democratic opponent. Although many commentators believed Bush's declarations were hollow at the core, and Bush's chief of staff John Sununu was usually antagonistic toward environmental regulation, Bush nonetheless acted once he became president. He faced the continuing political fact that environmental issues were popular, particularly in electoral vote–rich California, and he confronted organized supporters of environmental action both inside and outside Congress. By 1989, environmental organizations were more powerful than ever before. President Reagan's hostility toward environmental regulation had only helped them gain members and funds. Mainstream environmental groups were a regular presence on Capitol Hill and were skilled at lobbying and other pressure techniques. Within the legislature, a group of committed and knowledgeable environmental advocates – Senators Al Gore (Democrat, Tennessee) and Tim Wirth (Democrat, Colorado), Representative Henry Waxman (Democrat, California), and others—had emerged as a force. These members of Congress could have acted independently and would have embarrassed Bush had he not acted. In June 1989, President Bush introduced his proposal for rewriting the Clean Air Act.

Despite the shift in public opinion and the political mood, revisions of environmental legislation faced serious obstacles. One was that some powerful members of Congress were strong advocates of particular industries and were opposed to certain environmental provisions. Democratic Representative John Dingell of Michigan was chair of the Energy and Commerce Committee and so could control the membership of the Subcommittee on Health and Environment, the main starting place for the House's environmental legislation. Dingell's constituency made him quite sensitive to auto industry concerns.[41] Democratic Senator Robert Byrd of West Virginia, the former majority leader, remained fairly powerful in the Senate and continued to oppose acid-rain provisions that could restrict the burning of coal. In addition, the White House had introduced amendments to the Clean Air Act that were weaker than many wanted. Indeed, the Bush administration was no fan of the environmental groups' wish list, and this tension could have thwarted the passage of a bill the president would be willing to sign.

Into the political fray strode groups and coalitions on both sides.

> As members of Congress began drifting back to the capital for the 1990 session—which got under way on January 23—they found that the new year's debate over proposed amendments to the 1979 Clean Air Act had started without them. Industry executives and health and environmental groups were busy unveiling rival studies that attempted to quantify the economic costs and health benefits of proposals to rewrite the act.[42]

Environmentalists banded together and formed the National Clean Air Coalition to coordinate letter-writing and phone call campaigns with their lobbying efforts.[43] Environmentalists also organized locally and informed members of Congress which votes would become part of future "Environmental Scorecards." On the other side, industry groups worked together under the rubric of the Clean Air Working Group

(CAWG). The CAWG had been established in 1980 and encompassed 160 corporate and trade groups by 1987. In 1990, the CAWG grew rapidly: it had 72,000 members and a budget of about $1 million.[44] Although the CAWG tried to keep businesses united, it was not always successful. Auto and oil interests disagreed with each other over clean fuel proposals, and they maintained independent political operations. Industry concerns worked inside Congress as lobbyists and purveyors of information and provided campaign contributions. In addition, they organized citizens within their industries, often relying on the employees, managers, and owners of local firms. Both environmentalists and industrial interests were prepared to use an array of political tools, including the mobilization of public opinion.

Although business concerns certainly did not get all that they wanted, the auto industry won a significant battle during the long fight over the Clean Air Act. CAFE (corporate average fuel economy) standards had first been adopted in 1975. In this initial incarnation, auto companies had to manufacture cars getting an average minimum of 14 miles per gallon (mpg), rising to an average of 27.5 mpg by 1985. The figure of 27.5 mpg remained the minimum legal average in 1990, and concerns over air pollution and dependence on foreign oil prompted some senators to propose higher standards. Under Senator Richard Bryan's (Democrat, Nevada), bill, CAFE levels would have been increased by 20 percent by 1995 and by 40 percent by 2001. However, the auto companies opposed the new standards—as they had the earlier CAFE law—and defeated it. The measure was stripped from the Senate's Clean Air bill in March 1990. When considered by itself on September 15, the Senate (in a vote of fifty-seven to forty-two) could not muster the sixty votes needed to overcome a filibuster. In the House, the proposal never even got out of the Subcommittee on Energy and Power.[45]

The defeat of the proposed CAFE standards demonstrates the power and limits of public opinion. Given the many changes that Congress made in the Clean Air Act, its failure seems hard to understand. After all, this was no obscure provision pertaining to complex chemical reactions, but a proposal that every American with a car could understand. The few polls that were taken in regard to CAFE standards showed strong public support. A 1990 poll, for example, found that 84 percent favored and 13 percent opposed standards that would lead to an average of 40 mpg by the year 2000. Citizens who supported a change were asked if they "would still feel this way if you knew that a new car would cost the buyer $500 more," and 89 percent still favored the change.[46] In addition, the auto industry faced credibility problems. When the 1975 CAFE standards were first proposed, the automakers claimed that they would be impossible to reach, and yet they were. In 1990, they made the same claim. (As a Ford Motor Company executive admitted, "Some things we said in the mid-1970s we would have preferred that we didn't say.")[47] Finally, the August 2, 1990, invasion of Kuwait by Iraq created new public and congressional concern about the United States' reliance on foreign oil. Despite these currents in the public mood, the auto industry was successful.

In addition to using lobbying and political action committee (PAC) money, the auto companies killed the CAFE standards by mobilizing a public on their behalf. During a time of loud, competing voices about the many aspects of the Clean Air Act, the auto industry reached out to mobilize a shout for its position. To do so, the automakers needed to shift the ground of debate and organize a public on that basis, so they changed the subject of the CAFE conversation from air pollution and oil dependence to large and small vehicles. According to an article in *Fortune* magazine, "The automakers knew that pushing even a mildly sophisticated cost–benefit analysis would sound like an argument for dirty air. They aimed instead to sell a simpler message: The extreme environmental position would endanger big cars."[48]

But the automakers did more than argue this view in public; they also reached out to activate the public, using the tool of grassroots lobbying. Bonner & Associates was hired to organize leaders of groups that would suffer if large vehicles were not available. As a result, the criticisms of the CAFE standards made to Congress did not come just from the auto companies—the group that had a direct financial stake in the policy. After mounting a campaign that cost the auto industry between $500,000 and $1 million,

> the Big Brothers and Big Sisters of the Mahoning Valley wrote to Senator John Glenn of Ohio. Sam Nunn heard from the Georgia Baptist Convention and its 1.2 million members. The Easter Seal Society of South Dakota lobbied Senator Thomas A. Daschle. The Delaware Paralyzed Veterans Association contacted Senator William V. Roth, Jr. . . . These citizen organizations were persuaded to take a stand by Bonner & Associates, which informed them, consistent with the auto industry's political propaganda, that tougher fuel standards would make it impossible to manufacture any vehicles larger than a Ford Escort or Honda Civic. Vans and station wagons, small trucks and high-speed police cruisers, they were told, would cease to exist.[49]

The auto industry was thus able to use public opinion as a resource in its fight. In getting the public involved, auto company hirelings targeted undecided and wavering members of Congress and members who supported their position but needed "to be able to say they've heard from people back home."[50]

Where were the environmental groups when this happened? Although they wanted higher CAFE standards, they were not closely focused on this issue. Instead, environmentalists concentrated on global warming and toxic air pollutants, and they were able to make policy gains in these areas, in part relying on mobilized and anticipated public opinion. In contrast, the automobile manufacturers focused their attention on fewer concerns. They worked with the CAWG and acted independently with their own lobbyists. In addition, they used their financial resources to hire Bonner & Associates to drum up popular support. Advocates for higher CAFE standards devoted less time activating members of the public than did their opposition. In the cacophony of public voices calling out about the Clean Air Act, the opponents of higher CAFE standards were able to be heard and to give the appearance of citizen command.

Mobilized public opinion was not, of course, the only thing to kill the new CAFE standards. Certainly the opposition of Representative Dingell was important, as it helped block the bill's consideration in the House. The new Senate majority leader, George Mitchell (Democrat, Maine), wanted to show that he could shepherd the bill through a complex legislative process, and once it was defined as a potential deal buster, Mitchell crafted the agreement to consider it separately.[51] Interest-group activity on the Clean Air bill was fairly evenly matched, and groups used the entire range of tools available to them. Although environmental groups were successful in that they were able to force progress on long-stalled matters, neither environmental nor industry groups were able to dominate all policy questions.

Each side used anticipated and mobilized public opinion in their efforts. Strong public support for environmental causes helped push the Clean Air Act onto the political agenda, enlisted Bush into the cause of environmentalism, and impelled House and Senate leaders to do what was necessary to get the bill passed. Both the leaders' desire for a bipartisan bill that could pass easily and the environmental groups' full plate left the door open. Into it poured citizens opposed to the CAFE standards—with a voice raised by means of auto industry payments—and they helped kill the proposed CAFE standard.

The Practice of the Politics of Public Opinion in the American Political Environment

The ways that public opinion are used in the United States today are dependent on the structure and tendencies of the American political system. Although the Constitution has not changed much in the last fifty years, some developments during this time have been powerful enough to influence the way that public opinion is incorporated in the political process. The numerous changes discussed here—the decreased role of political parties, the dominance of visual media, the importance of money and negative messages in political campaigns, the fracturing of congressional power, and the growth of the interest-group community—are well known. In addition to the many effects described by others, each has profound consequences for how public opinion can be and has been used in American politics.

Political parties were once the main organizers of American politics. Parties mobilized citizens, brought together activists, and, through their leaders, dominated legislators. Indeed, the political parties performed so many activities that numerous political scientists have argued that they are necessary for democracy.[52] But political parties are by no means as powerful as they once were. Suburbanization, the decline of urban political machines, and decreased levels of party identification all have weakened the link between citizens and political parties. During and between electoral campaigns, parties no longer hold a dominant role in organizing citizens, and local party leaders are not as important to informing elected officials about their constituents' feelings and thoughts.[53]

As local political parties have done less and less to activate citizens and interpret the public voice for national leaders, interest groups have become more important. The problem with this is that interest groups usually focus on relatively narrow concerns. Due to the biases of the interest-group community, many of their activities have always been more likely to reflect a business perspective. With the development of grassroots lobbying firms, opinion mobilization is no longer the provenance of public-interest groups. Instead, public reaction is now subsidized by corporate interests. As William Greider observed,

> Many of the citizens are no doubt flattered to be asked, since ordinary Americans are seldom invited to participate in a personal way in the larger debates, even by the national civic organizations that presumably represented them. In a twisted sense, Jack Bonner does what political parties used to do for citizens—he educates and agitates and mobilizes.[54]

With the rise of these new methods, public opinion that matters—the voice that can pierce through the noise of the political echo chamber—has been increasingly turned to support a corporate policy agenda.

In addition to the impact of interest groups, members of Congress are influenced by the atmosphere of a "permanent campaign."[55] There is no longer a clear break between campaigning and governing, no respite from the need to raise funds for their campaign organization, and a fear that their vote will be used by opponents in a negative campaign. Campaign consultants use focus groups and opinion polls to assess public opinion and determine which appeal will move voters. Often consultants design negative campaigns, and these contribute to citizen alienation and diminished participation. As a result, legislators find it necessary to respond to a certain genre of anticipated public opinion. The style of public opinion that elected officials must anticipate is not the questions that citizens thoughtfully ask about their overall record. Instead, legislators must think about future public reactions to distorted portraits of votes, which they fear will arise in a no-holds–barred advertising campaign. Legislators admit as much themselves, as did Senator George Mitchell in a 1990 *New York Times* interview:

> It is not unusual, said the Senate majority leader, George J. Mitchell of Maine, to hear Senators discussing what kind of campaign commercial could be made from a particular vote as they stand in the well of the Senate and prepare to cast their yeas and nays. "The remark is frequently made: Watch out for this one, guys: this could really be made into an effective 30-second spot," the majority leader said.[56]

How issues and public opinion are framed between elections becomes part of the environment that candidates face during the election season. Once a policy question or position has been defined by partisans and the media, candidates find it extremely difficult to redefine the issue or have their alternative interpretation of public opinion gain legitimacy. And during the governing season,[57] legislators' perceptions of public opinion are not constructed by "rationalized" expressions, such as public opinion polls.[58] All the efforts that groups employ to shift the public, the perceptions of public opinion, and the frame through which policies are understood thus serve political purposes during legislative debates and campaigns. Money spent for public relations campaigns and grassroots lobbying firms can be expected to move legislators in the short term and to yield future political benefits.

The mass media's approach to news coverage also influences the portrayal and political use of public opinion. As I showed in chapter 4, television news and the major news magazines emphasized dramatic and personal sources of information in reporting public reactions to Oliver North's testimony. In general, good pictures and exciting, controversial stories drive the dominant news frames. Ronald Reagan's Communication Office generated compelling and irresistible visual and personal portraits and thereby lured television news into covering events in the way the White House preferred. Ultimately, the Reagan administration's communications apparatus influenced the framing of North as a possible hero. These media biases are consistent with the current cultural conditions. In the Frankfurt school's terms, culture has become increasingly commodified and thus driven by stock plots and simple dramatic devices. As Habermas contends, because they are staged by political activists and leaders, political disputes are defined along stereotyped, polarized, and visually compelling lines. Portraits of public opinion are influenced by the same cultural dynamics when groups consciously use the media's interest in good pictures to stage their own portrayals of the public voice. The contemporary media cannot resist using the images provided to them and thus do not serve as disinterested interpreters of public opinion.

Muffled Echoes? Implications for Democracy

In using public opinion in the political process, American politicians, journalists, and group leaders create and promulgate contesting interpretations of the public voice. Contemporary institutional dynamics and practices structure the development of contending translations of public opinion. But what sort of threat does this pose for the health of American democracy? Although by definition, democracy means rule by the people, no democratic theorists argue for unrestrained popular command. Certainly the authors of the Constitution neither expected nor wanted public desires to be translated instantly into public action. Citizens, they believed, would be too easily moved by emotion and individual interests. Therefore the founders wanted to create a space for deliberation that was to be set away from popular passions. In addition, it would be unreasonable to expect that opinion and policy could ever completely match. My findings regarding the use of public opinion in politics are consistent with the well-established fact that people with intense preferences are more motivated to act and thus can have a stronger impact. Nonetheless, I believe that the use of public opinion today poses serious problems for democratic citizenship, leadership, and the political process. At the same time, the political use of public opinion is not all-powerful but, rather, provides a limited tool for manipulating citizens, political leaders, and the political system.

Citizens

The citizenry today is sometimes a spectator to discussions about public opinion and political affairs and is at other times an audience that responds to others' stagings. Occasionally some citizens are an active element in political discourse, typically organized by some group. Public opinion can also exist as a quiescent presence whose views are gauged and anticipated. As an essential component of a democratic polity and communication system, citizens' involvement is desirable in order to develop civic virtue and skills and to maintain a healthy degree of representation. Both goals are in jeopardy, however, when public opinion serves as a resource to be deployed.

Dialogue between citizens and between citizens and political leaders is an essential aspect of a robust communication system and public sphere and helps citizens develop a commitment to public activity and the public good. Subsidized, mobilized presentations of public opinion threaten civic action because they can disempower citizens. This is especially true in the current political culture of distrust and political alienation. Because American citizens have felt more and more remote from government, they also have been less likely to participate in politics. In generating false soundings of the public voice, interest groups may create a psychological climate that drives citizens even further into private spheres. If Tocqueville is correct, democratic citizens in conditions of relative social equality hold public opinion as the highest authority. Spirals of silence, Noelle-Neumann warns, can develop as people perceive themselves to be in the minority. If interest groups are unevenly mobilized and can design their appeals to be attractive to the media, these organizations will be able to manipulate the appearance of public opinion. Citizens who perceive themselves to be in the minority—even if the public's views are actually evenly divided or supportive of the unvocalized position—may not speak up themselves. To be sure, it is unlikely that any point of view will ever completely dominate expressed opinion, at least in an open society. But even if there is no ideological hegemony, the general psychological dynamic can restrict to some extent popular expression and democratic command.

Highly stylized representations of political issues and public opinion can short-circuit democratic discussion, posing another problem for democracy. Issues and candidates are packaged and then marketed to political consumers. Citizens face limited choices in responding to these displays and can rarely change the terms of discussion. One result is that the views of one's fellow citizens may not be well understood. After all, individual citizens do not know whether many others accept or reject the bases of political debate. Unable to counter the presentations effectively, people respond largely to the stereotypes and frames staged before them. Even if they dislike how political issues are presented—and, according to journalist E. J. Dionne, most Americans do—they are limited in their ability to reframe policy questions.[59] Public opinion becomes another part of the political contest of contending stereotypes. In effect, citizens cannot participate as full partners in the conversation of politics. Control over the content and direction of political discourse is highly restricted. Under the standards of dialogic theorists, including Habermas, they cannot fully develop as human beings or act as full citizens.

When citizens do participate—within whatever restricted conduits—the political use of public opinion helps reinforce class biases in political action. Participation rates are highly correlated with socioeconomic status, partly because of different social resources and partly because these citizens are the focus of organizing efforts.[60] As Rosenstone and Hansen found,

> Intent on creating the greatest effect with the least effort, politicians, parties, interest groups, and activists mobilize people who are well known to them, who are well placed in social networks, whose actions are effective, and who are likely to act. Their efforts to move the organized, the employed, the elite, and the advantaged into politics exacerbate rather than reduce the class biases in political participation in America.[61]

Political elites provoke public reactions—the public opinion that matters—by framing issues in particular ways and activating individuals. And as E. E. Schattschneider pointed out, who gets involved is politically consequential: "Every change in the scope of the conflict has a bias. By definition, the intervening bystanders are not neutral."[62] The activated group is likely to have more wealth and social status than the average American does, and its involvement is likely to influence how political issues are resolved. Even when an issue is not primarily material and involves two well-mobilized sides, as with the abortion issue, neither bloc represents the mass of the public very well, and the bulk of citizens may, in disgust, disengage from the policy debate.

Granted, public opinion as mobilized and perceived is not the only influence on policy. However, interest groups and other elites get involved in the interpretation of public opinion because they know it can be important. In the cacophony of the echo chamber, these efforts can cow some citizens, limit what is discussed, and give the upper class a louder voice.

Despite these effects, some evidence suggests that members of the public are not mere straws in the prevailing political breeze. When one looks carefully at the spiral of silence studies presented by Noelle-Neumann, for example, one finds that even widespread willingness to assess the public mood does not translate into pervasive unwillingness to express unpopular points of view. In addition, as I stated in chapter 2, spirals of silence can be limited by reference groups, social location, personality differences, and distancing conversational strategies. Furthermore, the media's construction of public opinion during the initial period of North's Iran–contra testimony was strongly positive, yet citizen critics of North did speak up after a few days. Although this shift was not stressed in the news coverage, positions taken in telegrams and phone calls to Congress became evenly divided. Despite the media's portrait of an adulatory climate of opinion, most citizens remained critical of North's actions and did not find him heroic. Public input, to be sure, rarely meets the standards of dialogic theorists and participatory democrats. At least in some situations, however, citizens are more resilient than many fear.[63] But the existence of robust citizens may not really matter politically if they are not well mobilized and their views are systematically misreported and misheard.

The Media

As the central nexus in the modern political communication system, the media bear a great burden in translating and interpreting citizens' views. Members of the public can only directly know what their neighbors and close associates believe, and so it is up to the media to inform citizens about the nation's prevailing views. Although public officials and interest groups have some independent data concerning the public mind, accurate and relevant information is not always available. Representative information is usually just part of what news stories report as the media develop perceptions of public opinion. As legislators and presidents respond to journalists' portrayals of policy debates and public opinion (even if this is with criticism), these political actors legitimize the media's role in generating the public opinion that matters.

Unfortunately, structural tendencies of the news media make them poorly equipped to act as coherent translators. Even though the media are disparate, there is one set of competing, commercially oriented journalistic outlets that most influence political debate. This group of mainstream news media is driven by a set of biases, including a concern for new information, vividness, drama, conflict, and simplification, that help reporters tell a compelling and resonant story. Although these biases help the mainstream media attract viewers, they also lead to distortions in how public views are interpreted. As chapter 4 demonstrated, for example, the media gave inordinate coverage to unrepresentative indicators of public opinion about Oliver North. The information used provided interesting images and was consistent with compelling cultural symbols, but it relied on unreliable data, including demonstrations organized by North's supporters before he first appeared before Congress. Journalists were rendered vulnerable to misinterpretation by their biases, and they spread this garbled message far and wide.

Media tendencies also help create an incentive structure for political actors' communications to the public. Candidates, elected officials, and interest groups craft their presentations and messages so that they will gain media attention, preferably on the best possible terms. As a result, public dialogue and deliberation suffer from the effects of simplification and other sorts of presentations implicitly rewarded by the mass media. Whether reporting on public opinion or political actors, the media allow intense and emotional messages to have greater access, thus making arguments and public views seem less complex and subtle than they actually are.

By acting as gatekeepers of public opinion interpretations in the political communication system, the media pose a very real problem for modern democracy. The media serve as a representative in the political echo chamber, mediating communication between citizens and leaders. Pundits interpret public communication, and all forms of news media are integrated into representatives' assessments of the opinion climate. However, unlike elected representatives, the media have no accountability as representatives or any real checks.

Although this quasi-representative position gives the media very real power, their direct and indirect effects are not absolute. First, the media's emphasis on objectivity forces reporters and editors to give time to competing elite interpretations, thus muting any single message. This is especially important with issues that are considered over a long period of time and involve fairly evenly mobilized groups. In addition, differences among citizens, whether these are variations in personality or political awareness, restrict the impact of even consonant media reports. Finally, elites vary in their receptiveness to news reports of public opinion. Still, the media's capacity to translate the public voice remains troubling, if only because it has not been widely recognized or researched. If more sustained attention were paid to this state of affairs, the media's interpretations of the public voice would be less susceptible to manipulations by some, including groups with an axe to grind.

Interest Groups

In directly communicating with elected officials and in stating views through the media, interest groups affect communication between citizens and leaders and influence media portraits of public opinion. Although such groups may be limited in directly affecting citizens' views, even their indirect effect can move political debates and outcomes, leading to results that do not represent public views.[64] I have suggested that in the short term and in quickly developing circumstances, groups with intense, well-mobilized views have the greatest effect on perceptions of public opinion. This was the case with North's testimony. Uneven mobilization can also have a significant impact on legislators' decisions in other circumstances, such as when material interests are involved or a policy is considered over a relatively long period of time.

In speaking for one segment of the public, interest groups stray far from the ideals of dialogic theorists, including the ideal speech community described by Habermas. These groups have no charge to create open, unconstrained communication or to go beyond their own narrow interests. At the same time, political theorist Mark Warren suggests that pressure groups can be consistent with a modified sort of deliberative democracy, one in which widespread participation is invited, some decisions are delegated, and the oversight of authorities allows all citizens to challenge those elites. Warren argues, "One important function of public pressure groups in a democratic setting is that they constitute a critical and attentive public." But he also warns that this critical context "is all too easily damaged by hierarchies of status and inequalities of resource distribution."[65] Of course, organizations that focus on material issues—and, often, groups that are driven by other concerns—have different resources, including the resources to influence the perception of public opinion.

Although pressure groups have a legitimate right to try to persuade the public, the growing use of mobilizing strategies by business interests is particularly troubling. Grassroots lobbying campaigns, such as the credit card interest cap and CAFE standards operations discussed in this chapter, are effective because they feign unmobilized, individual constituent communication. Corporate interests masquerade as spontaneous citizen reaction because it is known that unorganized public communication is the sort of input that members of Congress consider most seriously. In mobilizing citizens, business groups gain a strategic advantage because they can use the same tools that true grassroots organizations were able to monopolize. At the same time, business organizations maintain their dominance of insider strategies and resources, such as lobbying and campaign contributions. One result is a potentially greater skewing of policy outcomes, as grassroots lobbying firms supply a louder voice to their clients' interests and arguments.

Interest groups' attempts to influence the perception of public opinion are not always successful, however, and so constitute only a limited threat to democratic representation. As this book has argued, the ability to shape the perception of public opinion depends on providing the media images and stories consistent with their biases, on the ability to use powerful symbols and cultural frames, and on the capacity to dominate public messages. Although much information is available about how to attract the media, interest groups cannot guarantee that the media will use the frames they provide or that these will be judged to have resonated with the public. In addition, whether group efforts are reported in the media or are instead directed solely toward elected officials, interest groups may not have a free field of action. Competing groups may present different arguments and try to construct publics with divergent views. As the cases of abortion policy and the long struggle over contra aid policy demonstrate, relatively even group mobilization limits the impact of one side. This, of course, is one reason that groups often monitor public opinion—to make sure that one's competition is not allowed to speak for the public as a whole. In addition, even if one set of groups faces little organized opposition, they do not have the power to make authoritative decisions but can only try to affect people who can.

Elected Officials

How much, then, are political elites swayed by what may seem to be emerging public moods? Elites may be quite vulnerable to developing perceptions of public opinion, whether they are delivered mostly through the media, are influenced by interest-group efforts, or are based on polls, incoming communications, or discussions with political colleagues. In fact, Diana Mutz argues that evidence from a number of studies suggests that elected officials, not citizens, are more easily affected by perceptions of citizen views.[66]

Although the politics of public opinion takes different forms, it nearly always matters to legislators. This claim does not mean that legislators always keep their ears to the ground or are responsive to public desires. But members of Congress regularly listen to the public and evaluate claims about public opinion, particularly in terms of future electoral effects. Legislators assess the policy and electoral costs and benefits to be accrued from acting independently or in concert with their constituents. In some cases, members of Congress present themselves as moved by public reactions when, in fact, they took the position they had preferred before. Seeming responsiveness can disguise legislators' preferences. One conservative interest group, for example, sent procontra letters to several members of Congress so that they could claim that they simply did what their constituents wanted. Public relations and grassroots lobbying firms typically focus their attention on legislators who are leaning toward them already and expect that the resulting citizen communication will ensure that the legislator will help their clients' causes.

If the public's voice is absent, elected officials take this fact into consideration as well. Silent publics can lead legislators to take their own counsel or may leave them to listen to lobbyists, the most constant outside presence in the halls of Congress. In addition, legislators respond to stagings not only from the outside but also from one another. Legislative allies and opponents make claims about public opinion in private and public, and these assertions are meant to carry political force.

Efforts to influence the perception of public opinion and to use this politically thus pose real challenges to democratic representation and leadership. Politicians find it hard to discover whether the activated public is, in fact, representative of their constituents. When phone calls, letters, and media reports become pressing enough, it becomes increasingly difficult for elected officials to take a contradictory position.

Some members of Congress view themselves as relatively independent leaders put in place by the voters. But not all legislators are capable of acting independently. Political timidity or courage may be due to legislators' personalities, their view of their role, the characteristics of their constituents, or the current relationship between the legislators and the voters. Whether elected officials are willing to buck public opinion or quickly to bow to incoming messages, all pay attention and respond in some way. In today's political climate, they all try to distinguish spontaneous grassroots action from Astroturf, the actions created by firms. Experience gained over time helps them make these distinctions and may lead a legislator to resist a flood of mail or communications.

Even when legislators are not sure whether public reaction reflects their constituents' actual opinion, they have strong incentives to act. If they are wrong, there will be a political price to pay. Even if legislators believe that the public uproar is not representative of the underlying opinion, the media coverage of public communications encourages a legislative response because members of Congress do not want to appear unresponsive. After all, citizens who are watching cannot independently determine what the citizenry as a whole believes and so must rely on media reports to find out. However, this has consequences for the climate of opinion. For example, legislators acknowledged the wave of incoming public support for Oliver North, and this was widely reported in the media. By remarking on the number of people who had called or written on behalf of Mr. North, legislators reinforced the misperception that the lieutenant colonel was widely admired.

The situation of North's testimony, as well as other cases, suggests that perceptions of public opinion are limited tools for moving legislators. In response to the opinion climate, members of the congressional committee modified their approach to North, but many nonetheless took the lieutenant colonel to task. Although some might interpret this critical stance toward North not as a profile in courage but instead as a way of establishing a persona as an independent politician, these actions in a very public venue certainly demonstrate that many different sorts of reactions were possible. Simply put, the prevailing political winds did not require that a legislator blow in one direction.

The autonomy available to elected officials is, in one sense, always present. No one can force a politician to take a position other than the one she desires. However, the likelihood that elected officials will act on the basis of independent judgment and therefore restrain the impact of perceived public opinion depends on the circumstances of the issue (such as even and uneven group mobilization), the official's willingness to act autonomously, and her constituency and coalitional base. Politicians seek office to influence policy and are likely to be independent when it comes to issues they care about. Some elected officials are able to develop a trusting relationship with constituents that gives them leeway to use their judgment, at least for some issues. But no representative is immune from public pressure all the time, nor should one be.

In democracies, legislators and other politicians ought to be concerned with what the public thinks. But attention to instant reactions can be damaging to the political system, especially in our time of visually oriented media, new technologies of mobilization, and negative campaigns. Not only may legislators be mistaken about what the general public wants, but great concern for public opinion also may hinder deliberation and debate within the government, a fundamental goal of American representative democracy. Often opinion can be mobilized more easily when issues are defined—by interest groups, the media, and elected officials—in simplistic ways. In trying to bring such opinion to bear and in responding to such views, legislators find it difficult to move beyond polarized rhetoric and to craft compromises that can help resolve real problems. As a 1990 *New York Times* article reported, "Politicians in both parties say government is crippled by a new superstructure of politics that makes ideas harder to discuss and exalts public opinion over leadership."[67] In a climate of anxiety over future negative campaign ads with appeals designed by clever marketers, legislators must choose to play the same game, remove themselves from public view, stick their necks out, or leave the arena.

The Political System

Given elected officials' and citizens' ability to resist constructions of public opinion, how much of a threat does the politics of public opinion pose for democratic communication, deliberation, and policymaking? When conditions rapidly change or only one portion of the public is mobilized, it is hardest for representatives to assess public opinion and to defy what it seems the public wants. Certainly most policies do not engender very quick reactions from the public or require rapid responses from political officials. However, these cases can be quite consequential, especially if they involve military or national security matters. Although it is perhaps in these instances that elected officials feel the burden of their offices most acutely, it also then that representatives fear electoral retribution from the public's rally to the cause or from their constituents' future negative judgments. Whether or not a policy debate evolves swiftly, it is clear that people in the political realm frequently attempt to represent and misrepresent the public's views. Clear communication and representation are further distorted by the media's tendencies to give extensive coverage to certain kinds of information.

In any case, the sorts of dynamics written about here are no surprise to practitioners in lobbying and public relations firms or to elected officials. In fact, considerable evidence suggests that any lessons such parties could learn from this book are already well known. With the start of the Clinton administration in January 1993, public relations and grassroots lobbying firms went into high gear, with special efforts in the first two years of the administration to defeat both a proposed BTU tax and health care reform. Paid for by business groups, these organizations used all the sophisticated tools of political campaigns and more. By August 1993, *Fortune* magazine proclaimed that public relations and grassroots lobbying were "how to get things done in Washington" for business, and the U.S. Chamber of Congress designed a telecommunications system to contact their members and automatically connect them to the office of their member of Congress.[68] Advertising by business groups caught the media's attention in the health care debate and influenced politics in Washington. According to a study by Kathleen Hall Jamieson, ads created by the Health Insurance Association of America featuring a middle-aged, middle-income couple named Harry and Louise hurt the president's plan because the media said that they moved the public and the legislators and the president acted as if this was true. This interpretation of the public's voice was a distortion, however, since "the available indicators of effectiveness suggest that the ads had a negligible impact on the public."[69] Such activities by corporations increase the problems of interest-group bias, since citizens have fewer resources and cannot afford to fund outside groups to mobilize on their behalf or they cannot obtain enough money to develop a sophisticated communications infrastructure. Certainly not all campaigns of this sort win, and their success depends on many different factors. But the selective mobilization of public opinion, efforts to shape the perception of public opinion, and the presentation of issues in simple ways to influence anticipated public opinion can be highly successful. Given the wealth of knowledge about how to wage such campaigns, when mobilization is one-sided, it becomes very difficult for less well organized citizens and groups to be heard and to prevail, even if they are in the majority. Even when the competition is fierce, the elites that translate the public's voice offer those versions that best support their positions.[70] Certainly the current state of political discourse makes it difficult for citizens to engage in the democratic deliberation that could develop their civic skills and commitment to the common good.

The political system has not been captured completely, however, nor are political leadership and courage absent. After all, during the North hearings, Congress perceived a great wave of public pressure, yet some members directly confronted the lieutenant colonel. These members saw themselves as leaders and educators of the public. In addition, diversity in constituencies leads to some variety among members of Congress and limits the effect of public relations and mobilization campaigns, especially as representatives and senators become more aware of the new tools used to distort the public voice. Furthermore, despite efforts to create false soundings, citizens are not deafened by ideological hegemony or dazzled altogether by stagings and dramatic presentations. Yet there is an ever crowded space for democratic deliberation and communication between leaders and citizens. The public voice is interpreted by various, often interested parties, who compete over what will become the accepted translation. Public opinion is almost omnipresent but is sometimes spontaneous, sometimes contrived, and sometimes merely anticipated. For citizens and their representatives, the voice of the people is often muffled and hard to hear.

Notes

Introduction

1. R. Douglas Arnold, *The Logic of Congressional Action* (New Haven, CT: Yale University Press, 1990).

2. V. O. Key, *Public Opinion and American Democracy* (New York: Knopf, 1961); V. O. Key, *The Responsible Electorate* (Cambridge, MA: Harvard University Press, 1966); and Jürgen Habermas, *The Structural Transformation of the Public Sphere* (Cambridge, MA: MIT Press, 1989).

3. Schattschneider uses the phrase *upper-class accent* to refer to the class bias of the interest-group system. See E. E. Schattschneider, *The Semisovereign People* (New York: Harcourt Brace Jovanovich, 1988), pp. 34–35.

4. On public opinion and Clinton's health care proposals, see Haynes Johnson and David S. Broder, *The System: The American Way of Politics at the Breaking Point* (Boston: Little, Brown, 1996); and Kathleen Hall Jamieson, "When Harry Met Louise," *Washington Post National Weekly Edition*, August 22–29, 1994, p. 29. For a discussion of the role of perceptions of opinions in the budget negotiations between President Clinton and the Republican Congress, see Adam Clymer, "An Impasse of Bipartisan Appeal," *New York Times Week in Review*, January 14, 1996, p. 5. Participants in the budget battle clearly realized that public opinion was an important political resource. For example, when discussing how the Republican strategy (of pre-

senting Clinton with bills that he strongly disliked, which he ultimately vetoed and thus forced partial shutdowns of the federal government) had gone wrong, Speaker of the House Newt Gingrich told his leadership, "We expected that there would be a slump in our poll numbers, but we didn't calculate that a surge in Clinton's numbers would cause him to dig in even more." This quotation is from Garry Wills, "What Happened to the Revolution?" *New York Review of Books*, June 6, 1996, pp. 11–16, 14.

5. Murray Edelman, *Constructing the Political Spectacle* (Chicago: University of Chicago Press, 1988). On efforts to shape perceptions of public opinion during the Thomas confirmation hearings, see Jane Mayer and Jill Abramson, *Strange Justice: The Selling of Clarence Thomas* (New York: Houghton Mifflin, 1994).

6. In contrast, one-third of the North vote was more anti-Robb than pro-North. See "Robb Triumphs over North, Runs Well in Some of Rival's Strongholds," *Washington Post*, November 9, 1994, p. A32.

Chapter 1, The Politics of Public Opinion

1. See Susan Herbst, *Numbered Voices: How Opinion Polling Has Shaped American Politics* (Chicago: University of Chicago Press, 1993); and Benjamin Ginsberg, *The Captive Public: How Mass Opinion Promotes State Power* (New York: Basic Books, 1986).

2. W. Lance Bennett, *News: The Politics of Illusion* (New York: Longman, 1988).

3. For a good review of this literature, see Lawrence R. Jacobs and Robert Y. Shapiro, "Studying Substantive Democracy: Public Opinion, Institutions, and Policymaking," *PS* 27 (1994): 9–16. See also chapter 6.

4. Benjamin I. Page and Robert Y. Shapiro, *The Rational Public: Fifty Years of Trends in Americans' Policy Preferences* (Chicago: University of Chicago Press, 1992), p. 393.

5. Benjamin Page, "Democratic Responsiveness? Untangling the Links Between Public Opinion and Policy," *PS* 27 (1994): 25–29, 28. In the same vein, Stimson notes, "In our texts public opinion is a chapter or two. The various branches of government are usually a chapter each. And the connection between what the public wants and what the government does is on the page fold between them. Public opinion is conceptualized as a set of measures and processes that do not speak to government. Governing institutions are studied in a manner which doesn't deny public opinion influence, but doesn't permit its active study. . . . [L]ike an ill-coached relay team, we never quite pass the baton." See James A. Stimson, "Opinion and Representation," *American Political Science Review* 89 (1995): 179–83, 181.

6. The most important scholar in this tradition is Murray Edelman; see his *The Symbolic Uses of Politics* (Urbana: University of Illinois Press, 1964); *Politics as Symbolic Action* (New York: Academic Press, 1971); and *Constructing the Political Spectacle* (Chicago: University of Chicago Press, 1988). For a collection of essays on Edelman's work, see Richard Merelman, ed., *Language, Symbolism, and Politics* (Boulder, CO: Westview Press, 1992).

7. Edelman, *Constructing the Political Spectacle*, p. 106.

8. On public resistance, see James Scott, *Weapons of the Weak: Everyday Forms of Peasant Resistance* (New Haven, CT: Yale University Press, 1985), and *Domination and the Arts of Resistance* (New Haven, CT: Yale University Press, 1990).

9. Elisabeth Noelle-Neumann, *The Spiral of Silence: Public Opinion—Our Social Skin* (Chicago: University of Chicago Press, 1984).

10. Some scholars have integrated political, institutional, and cultural factors that influence the relationships between opinion and policy. See Lawrence Jacobs, *The Health of Nations: Public Opinion and the Making of American and British Health Policy* (Ithaca, NY: Cornell University Press, 1993); and Theda Skocpol, *Protecting Soldiers and Mothers: The Political Origins of Social Policy in the United States* (Cambridge, MA: Belknap Press of Harvard University Press, 1992).

11. Key, *The Responsible Electorate*.

12. For example, Key pointed out in *Public Opinion and American Democracy* (New York: Knopf, 1961), that public opinion can be structured in many different ways, with varied patterns of opinion, levels of intensity, degrees of conflict or consensus, and connections across opinions.

13. Ibid., pp. 414, 557.

14. Two studies that examine social contexts of public opinion, although with dissimilar approaches, are those by Robert Huckfeldt and John Sprague, *Citizens, Politics, and Social Communication* (Cambridge: Cambridge University Press, 1995); and Susan Herbst, *Politics at the Margin: Historical Studies of Public Expression Outside the Mainstream* (Cambridge: Cambridge University Press, 1994).

15. V. O. Key Jr., "The Politically Relevant in Surveys," *Public Opinion Quarterly* 24 (1960): 54–61, 55. For another early criticism of the nonpolitical nature of survey approaches, see Herbert Blumer, "Public Opinion and Public Opinion Polling," *American Sociological Review* 13 (1948): 242–49.

16. See Albert H. Cantril, *The Opinion Connection: Polling, Politics, and the Press* (Washington, DC: Congressional Quarterly Press, 1991), p. 12.

17. This discussion of the early days and development of polling relies heavily on Natchez and Cantril, and also Moore. See Peter B. Natchez, *Images of Voting/Visions of Democracy* (New York: Basic Books, 1985); Cantril, *The Opinion Connection*; and David W. Moore, *The Superpollsters: How They Measure and Manipulate Public Opinion in America* (New York: Four Walls Eight Windows, 1992).

18. Schemas are cognitive maps that express organizing principles and connections between persons, ideas, or objects. Scholars in this and other cognitive research traditions attempt to understand how citizens deal with the political world, rather than comparing them with one model of organizing beliefs. Individual persons in the same society have both shared and unique experiences that shape their schemas. In addition, the schema approach explains how people with limited information and limited background in political affairs and theory are able to store and retrieve information and make judgments. Good introductions to schema theory include those by Susan T. Fiske, "Schema-Based Versus Piecemeal Politics: A Patchwork

Quilt, but Not a Blanket of Evidence," in Richard R. Lau and David O. Sears, eds., *Political Cognition*, pp. 41–54 (Hillsdale, NJ: Erlbaum, 1986); and Pamela Johnston Conover and Stanley Feldman, "How People Organize the Political World: A Schematic Model," *American Journal of Political Science* 28 (1984): 95–126. On schemas and party identification, see Milton Lodge and Ruth Hamill, "A Partisan Schema for Political Information Processing," *American Political Science Review* 82 (1986): 737–61; and Wendy M. Rahn, "The Role of Partisan Stereotypes in Information Processing About Political Candidates," *American Journal of Political Science* 37 (1993): 472–96. On schemas and candidate assessment, see Pamela Johnston Conover and Stanley Feldman, "The Role of Inference in the Perception of Political Candidates," in Lau and Sears, eds., *Political Cognition*, pp. 127–58; Arthur H. Miller, Martin P. Wattenberg, and Oksana Malanchuk, "Schematic Assessments of Presidential Candidates," *American Political Science Review* 90 (1986): 505–40; and Richard R. Lau, "Political Schemata, Candidate Evaluation, and Voting Behavior," pp. 95–126, and Wendy M. Rahn, John H. Aldrich, Eugene Borgida, and John L. Sullivan, "A Social–Cognitive Model of Candidate Appraisal," pp. 136–59, both in John A. Ferejohn and James H. Kuklinski, eds., *Information and Democratic Processes* (Urbana: University of Illinois Press, 1990). Arguments regarding the utility and omissions of schema theory include those by James H. Kuklinski, Robert C. Luskin, and John Bolland, "Where Is the Schema? Going Beyond the 'S' Word in Political Psychology," *American Political Science Review* 85 (1991): 1341–56; Robert E. Lane, "What Are People Trying to Do with Their Schemata? The Question of Purpose," in Lau and Sears, eds., *Political Cognition*, pp. 303–18; Milton Lodge and Kathleen M. McGraw, *Political Judgment: Structure and Processes* (Ann Arbor: University of Michigan Press, 1995); and Arthur Miller, "Where Is the Schema? Critiques," *American Political Science Review* 85 (1991): 1357–80.

19. Although these scholars concede that individuals do not possess extensive information or use sophisticated reasoning, they do contend that people know enough to make reasoned choices. Opinions about politics and behavioral choices are guided by cognitive shortcuts and various heuristics. See Samuel Popkin, *The Reasoning Voter* (Chicago: University of Chicago Press, 1991); Paul Sniderman, Richard A. Brody, and Philip E. Tetlock, *Reasoning and Choice: Explorations in Political Psychology* (Cambridge: Cambridge University Press, 1991); and Jeffrey J. Mondak, "Source Cues and Policy Support: The Cognitive Dynamics of Public Support for the Reagan Agenda," *American Journal of Political Science* 37 (1993): 186–212. According to Popkin, "People use shortcuts which incorporate much political information; they triangulate and validate their opinions in conversations with people they trust and according to the opinions of national figures whose judgments and positions they have come to know. With these shortcuts, they learn to 'read' politicians and their positions" (p. 7).

20. One approach has emphasized the importance of issues. Benjamin Page's work, for example, shows that politicians often try to blur the differences among them, thus denying citizens clear choices. See Benjamin I. Page, *Choices and Echoes in Presidential*

Elections (Chicago: University of Chicago Press, 1978). Others have used idiographic methods, such as intensive interviews and Q-methodology to demonstrate diverse belief systems. In addition, these scholars question the notion that constraint is best; ambivalence may reflect an understanding of trade-offs and may be more psychologically healthy. See Robert E. Lane, *Political Ideology* (New York: Free Press, 1962); Steven Brown, *Political Subjectivity* (New Haven, CT: Yale University Press, 1980); Jennifer Hochschild, *What's Fair?* (Cambridge, MA: Harvard University Press, 1981); and William A. Gamson, *Talking Politics* (Cambridge: Cambridge University Press, 1992). A third view emphasizes aggregate stability of opinions. In *The Rational Public*, their extensive analysis of fifty years of opinion data, Page and Shapiro show that mass opinion moves in reasonable ways, often in response to events and changing circumstances. These broad patterns suggest a reasoned basis to public opinion. For a good critique of Page and Shapiro's idea of aggregate rationality, see Donald R. Kinder and Don Herzog's essay "Democratic Discussion," in George E. Marcus and Russell L. Hanson, eds., *Reconsidering the Democratic Public*, pp. 347–77 (University Park, PA: Pennsylvania State University Press, 1993).

21. For the classic argument regarding belief system incoherence, see Philip E. Converse, "The Nature of Belief Systems in Mass Publics," in David E. Apter, ed., *Ideology and Discontent*, pp. 206–61 (London: Free Press of Glencoe, 1964). The debate on whether ideological constraint has increased was in large part touched off by Norman Nie, Sidney Verba, and John Petrocik, in *The Changing American Voter* (Cambridge, MA: Harvard University Press, 1976). For a review of discussions about whether new levels of constraint were due to measurement errors, see Richard Krouse and George E. Marcus, "Electoral Studies and Democratic Theory Reconsidered," *Political Behavior* 6 (1984): 23–39. For a recent discussion about the structure and stability of belief systems, see John R. Zaller, *The Nature and Origins of Mass Opinion* (Cambridge: Cambridge University Press, 1992).

22. Some scholars have taken a more contextual approach and explored the place of public opinion in the political environment, citizens' use of information-processing strategies for understanding campaigns and elections, and the state's use of public opinion. See Popkin, *The Reasoning Voter*; and Benjamin Ginsberg, *The Captive Public: How Mass Opinion Promotes State Power* (New York: Basic Books, 1986). See also David R. Mayhew, *Divided We Govern: Party Control, Lawmaking, and Investigations, 1946–1990* (New Haven, CT: Yale University Press, 1991). These scholars seem to have taken to heart Key's admonition that "despite their power as instruments for the observation of mass opinion, sampling procedures do not bring within their range elements of the political system basic for the understanding of the role of public opinion within the system" (*Public Opinion and American Democracy*, p. 536). Key's critique should not be interpreted as a critique of the specific methodology; experimental methods are open to the same basic criticism.

23. Paul A. Anderson, "The Relevance of Social Cognition for the Study of Elites in Political Institutions, or Why It Isn't Enough to Understand What Goes on in Their Heads," in Lau and Sears, eds., *Political Cognition*, p. 341.

24. See the essays in Lodge and McGraw, *Political Judgment*.

25. See Edward G. Carmines and James H. Kuklinski, "Incentives, Opportunities, and the Logic of Public Opinion in American Political Representation," in Ferejohn and Kuklinski, eds., *Information and Democratic Processes*, pp. 240–68. See also Ferejohn and Kuklinski, eds., *Information and Democratic Processes*, for Ferejohn's theoretical analysis of the place of information in the political system.

26. Pioneers of survey research explored how little citizens knew and how little they actively considered issues. Early researchers held that "classical democratic theory" expected more from citizens than was possible, and thus it needed to be revised. But as Natchez argues, "The content of what was intended by the category 'classical democratic theory' was by no means clear. Nor was it obvious which classical writers they had in mind. What is certain is the standard of evaluation against which voters were being measured. . . . This is the image of citizens as active, participant, and rational. . . . In the history of ideas, they originate first with the utilitarians and later, in a more familiar form, with the American Progressives" (*Images of Voting/Visions of Democracy*, p. 68). This view of citizens and the failure of democratic citizenship has proved enormously resilient, continuing to influence subsequent work on citizen rationality and information.

27. Jean-Jacques Rousseau, *The Social Contract* (New York: Everyman's Library, 1973), p. 228. See book 2, ch. 12, in other editions.

28. Jürgen Habermas, *The Structural Transformation of the Public Sphere* (Cambridge, MA: MIT Press, 1989). Habermas's only work in English on public opinion and the public sphere printed before 1989 that I could find is "The Public Sphere" *New German Critique* 3 (1974): 49–55. Until recently, commentators writing on Habermas treated these early ideas in a cursory way, if at all. One exception is Peter Uwe Hohendahl, "Critical Theory, Public Sphere and Culture: Jürgen Habermas and His Critics," *New German Critique* 16 (1979): 89–118. The translation of this work was accompanied by a conference at the University of North Carolina. For the conference papers, see Craig Calhoun, ed., *Habermas and the Public Sphere* (Cambridge, MA: MIT Press, 1992).

29. On the Frankfurt school and critical theory more generally, see Martin Jay, *The Dialectical Imagination* (Boston: Little, Brown, 1973); David Held, *Introduction to Critical Theory* (Berkeley and Los Angeles: University of California Press, 1980); and Stephen T. Leonard, *Critical Theory in Political Practice* (Princeton, NJ: Princeton University Press, 1990). On Habermas in particular, see also Thomas McCarthy, *The Critical Theory of Jürgen Habermas* (Cambridge, MA: MIT Press, 1988).

30. Fay argues that the three basic properties of critical theory are (1) the interpretive contention that social science should seek to understand subjects' intentions and views of the world, (2) a recognition of the role of objective conditions in influencing social conditions, and (3) a concern with tying social theory to practices promoting human emancipation. See Brian Fay, *Social Theory and Political Practice* (London: Allen & Unwin, 1975). Leonard, in *Critical Theory in Political Practice*, faults critical theory for taking too theoretical a direction and thus failing to fulfill the third goal.

31. Held, *Introduction to Critical Theory*, p. 15.

32. The Frankfurt school's criticism of both reductionistic Marxism and the Stalinist efforts to stifle free speech and intellectual thought were sometimes united. Scholars in this tradition were drawn to the work of thinkers such as Lukács, who had argued for the role of consciousness and had also been the subject of party control. They found these ideas attractive and the attempts to limit intellectual autonomy repugnant.

33. Theodor Adorno, *The Authoritarian Personality* (New York: Harper, 1950).

34. Jay, *The Dialectical Imagination*, p. 229. According to Held, *Introduction to Critical Theory*, p. 36, Adorno maintained strong scholarly commitments to theory and the need to situate results historically. In addition, Adorno and his fellows believed that "American scholars were uncritical and overenthusiastic about the benefits of empirical research."

35. This phrase was first used by Max Horkheimer and Theodor W. Adorno in their *Dialectic of Enlightenment*, trans. John Cummings (New York: Herder and Herder, 1972).

36. Calhoun, ed., *Habermas and the Public Sphere*, p. 17.

37. Habermas, "The Public Sphere," p. 49.

38. Habermas, *Structural Transformation of the Public Sphere*, p. 36.

39. Two means of communication that developed after Habermas wrote *The Structural Transformation of the Public Sphere* are the Internet and radio talk shows, both of which allow for more spontaneous, less constrained public communication. But such discussions are unlikely to represent public opinion fully. For example, callers to talk radio are more conservative than average voters: see Andrew Kohut, *The Vocal Minority in American Politics* (Washington, DC: Times Mirror Center for the People and the Press, 1993). In addition, because their main purpose is to attract and hold listeners for commercial purposes, talk show hosts typically frame issues in simplistic and emotional ways. The Internet allows for more sophisticated and less restricted discussions, but so far it has been limited to people with a relatively high level of expertise, education, and monetary resources.

40. Habermas, *The Structural Transformation of the Public Sphere*, p. 166.

41. Ibid., pp. 200–1 (italics in original).

42. Ibid., pp. 228, 218.

43. Ibid., pp. 164, 247.

44. Calhoun, ed., *Habermas and the Public Sphere*, p. 26.

45. Ibid., p. 438.

46. See Geoff Eley, "Nations, Publics, and Political Cultures: Placing Habermas in the Nineteenth Century," p. 289, and Mary P. Ryan, "Gender and Public Access: Women's Politics in Nineteenth-Century America," p. 259, both in Calhoun, ed., *Habermas and the Public Sphere*.

47. See David Zaret, "Religion, Science, and Printing in the Public Spheres in Seventeenth-Century England," in Calhoun, ed., *Habermas and the Public Sphere*, pp. 212–35.

48. This is the conclusion of Wolgang Jager, as discussed in Hohendahl, "Critical Theory."

49. Eley, "Nations, Publics, and Political Cultures," p. 294.

50. A feminist criticism may be more damaging to Habermas's basic argument, for it cannot be answered by simply considering women's political activities. Fraser argues that Habermas reifies separate public and private spheres. In order to be consistent with his historical view, Habermas should have recognized that the definitions of public and private were historically variable and were themselves the product of power arrangements and political struggle. Therefore, Fraser charges, public and private as categories should not be taken for granted but are themselves problematized. See Nancy Fraser, "Rethinking the Public Sphere: A Contribution to the Critique of Actually Existing Democracy," in Calhoun, ed., *Habermas and the Public Sphere*, p. 109.

51. Hohendahl, "Critical Theory," p. 92.

52. Nicholas Garnham, "The Media and the Public Sphere," 360, in Calhoun, ed., *Habermas and the Public Sphere*, p. 360.

53. Communication as means of reaching judgment is one alternative; other possibilities are references to foundational values or an appeal to a neutral actor behind a Rawlsian "veil of ignorance." For discussions of these other possibilities, see J. Donald Moon, "Constrained Discourse and Public Life," *Political Theory* 19 (1991): 202–29; and McCarthy, *The Critical Theory of Jürgen Habermas*.

54. Held, *Introduction to Critical Theory*, p. 331.

55. Some feminists have charged that this is a limitation in itself because questions about justice have historically involved the public sphere and ignored the private sphere. See the discussions by Seyla Benhabib, "Models of Public Space: Hannah Arendt, the Liberal Tradition and Jürgen Habermas," in Calhoun, ed., *Habermas and the Public Sphere*, pp. 73–98; Nancy Fraser, "What's Critical About Critical Theory? The Case of Habermas and Gender," pp. 31–56, and Iris Marion Young, "Impartiality and the Civic Public: Some Implications of Feminist Critiques of Moral and Political Philosophy," pp. 56–76, both in Seyla Benhabib and Drucilla Cornell, eds., *Feminism as Critique: On the Politics of Gender* (Minneapolis: University of Minnesota Press, 1987).

56. See Moon, "Constrained Discourse and Public Life"; Bruce Ackerman, "Why Dialogue?" *Journal of Philosophy* 86 (1989): 5–22; and Hannah Arendt, *The Human Condition* (Chicago: University of Chicago Press, 1958), for their defense of distinctions among public, private, and social.

57. Ackerman, "Why Dialogue?" p. 6.

58. Ackerman's call for restricted communication may be interpreted as a pragmatic but normatively charged reaction to Habermas. Ackerman writes, "The world of practical politics does not seem at all close to anybody's idea of an ideal speech situation. Politicians do talk a lot, but it is not unduly cynical to suppose that they mean less of what they say than other folk" ("Why Dialogue?" p. 8). In contrast, Benhabib argues that although Habermas's theory of the ideal speech community is

utopian, its view of the public sphere is better suited to contemporary politics than other such theories are.

59. On free spaces, see Sara Evans and Harry Boyte, *Free Spaces* (New York: Harper & Row, 1986); on narratives, see Richard A. Couto, "Narrative, Free Space, and Political Leadership in Social Movements," *Journal of Politics* 55 (1993): 57–79; and on the co-optation of social movements, see Frances Fox Piven and Richard A. Cloward, *Poor People's Movements: Why They Succeed, How They Fail* (New York: Vintage Books, 1979).

60. See James Scott, *Domination and the Arts of Resistance* (New Haven, CT: Yale University Press, 1990), and *Weapons of the Weak: Everyday Forms of Peasant Resistance* (New Haven, CT: Yale University Press, 1985).

61. See David Ingram, "The Limits and Possibilities of Communicative Ethics for Democratic Theory," *Political Theory* 21 (1993): 294–321. On bureaucracies and communication, see also John Dryzek, *Discursive Democracy: Politics, Policy, and Political Science* (Cambridge: Cambridge University Press, 1990).

62. Moon, "Constrained Discourse and Public Life," p. 202.

63. Habermas, *Toward a Rational Society*, p. 69.

64. Some scholars argue that institutions should be redesigned to prevent instrumental rationality from limiting public discourse. See John Dryzek and John Forester, "Questioning and Organizing Attention: Toward a Critical Theory of Planning and Administrative Practice," *Administration and Society* 13 (1981): 161–205.

65. See Noam Chomsky, *Necessary Illusions: Thought Control in Democratic Societies* (Boston: South End Press, 1989).

66. See W. Lance Bennett, "Toward a Theory of Press–State Relations in the United States," *Journal of Communication* 40 (1990): 124–25; and W. Lance Bennett, "Marginalizing the Majority: Conditioning Public Opinion to Accept Managerial Democracy," in Michael Margolis and Gary A. Mauser, eds., *Manipulating Public Opinion: Essays on Public Opinion as a Dependent Variable*, pp. 231–61 (Pacific Grove, CA: Brooks/Cole, 1989).

67. Ginsberg, *The Captive Public*, p. 83.

68. Herbst, *Numbered Voices*.

Chapter 2, Mapping the Echo Chamber

1. Of course, a good deal of political conversation occurs among citizens as well. This sort of communication has important implications for the information to which citizens are exposed and for the development of a climate of opinion that may silence many with minority opinions. See Robert Huckfeldt and John Sprague, *Citizens, Politics, and Social Communication* (Cambridge: Cambridge University Press, 1995); and Elisabeth Noelle-Neumann, *The Spiral of Silence: Public Opinion—Our Social Skin* (Chicago: University of Chicago Press, 1984).

2. On political symbols, see Murray Edelman, *The Symbolic Uses of Politics* (Urbana: University of Illinois Press, 1964), and *Politics as Symbolic Action* (New

York: Academic Press, 1971). On metaphors, see George Lakoff and Mark Johnson, *Metaphors We Live By* (Chicago: University of Chicago Press, 1980).

3. Bruce Ackerman, "Why Dialogue?" *Journal of Philosophy* 86 (1989): 22.

4. Ibid., p. 16. These are Ackerman's characterizations of the positions of Habermas, Bentham, and Rawls.

5. Donald J. Moon, "Constrained Discourse and Public Life," *Political Theory* 19 (1991): 202–29; Seyla Benhabib, "Models of Public Space: Hannah Arendt, the Liberal Tradition, and Jürgen Habermas," in Craig Calhoun, ed., *Habermas and the Public Sphere*, pp. 73–98 (Cambridge, MA: MIT Press, 1992).

6. Moon, "Constrained Discourse and Public Life," p. 213.

7. Habermas argues that in the political public sphere, status was not a factor deciding whether one could participate or whether one's argument would prevail. Instead, the quality of argument and the capacity to engage with others were most important. This marked a change from the status-centered, aristocratic system that preceded the bourgeois public sphere. As Habermas's critics have pointed out, however, these requirements in fact limited the working class's participation. See Jürgen Habermas, *The Structural Transformation of the Public Sphere* (Cambridge, MA: MIT Press, 1989). For criticisms and commentary, see Calhoun, ed., *Habermas and the Public Sphere.*

8. Sidney Verba and Norman H. Nie, *Participation in America* (New York: Harper & Row, 1978); Steven J. Rosenstone and John Mark Hansen, *Mobilization, Participation, and Democracy in America* (New York: Macmillan, 1993); and Sidney Verba, Kay Lehman Schlozman, and Henry Brady, *Voice and Equality: Civic Voluntarism in American Politics* (Cambridge, MA: Harvard University Press, 1995).

9. Applause, booing, and walking out are components of this model of communication between citizens and elites and bear a family resemblance to Hirschman's concepts of exit, voice, and loyalty. See Albert O. Hirschman, *Exit, Voice, and Loyalty* (Cambridge, MA: Harvard University Press, 1970). Of course, actual audiences attending particular speeches or performances have these options as well. For a review of research on rhetorical strategies used to promote audience reactions and the media's inclusion of audience reactions in news stories, see John C. Heritage, Steven Clayman, and Don H. Zimmermann, "Discourse and Message Analysis: The Micro-Structure of Mass Media Messages," in Robert P. Hawkins, John M. Wiemann, and Suzanne Pingree, eds., *Advancing Communication Science*, pp. 77–109 (Newbury Park, CA: Sage, 1988).

10. See Susan Herbst, *Numbered Voices: How Opinion Polling Has Shaped American Politics* (Chicago: University of Chicago Press, 1993).

11. Jennifer L. Hochschild, *What's Fair? American Beliefs About Redistributive Justice* (Cambridge, MA: Harvard University Press, 1981); and John R. Zaller, *The Nature and Origins of Mass Opinion* (Cambridge: Cambridge University Press, 1992).

12. The major participants also interpret one another's positions and may mischaracterize their opponents' points of view to gain political advantage.

13. Benjamin Ginsberg, *The Captive Public: How Mass Opinion Promotes State Power* (New York: Basic Books, 1986).

14. Shared public discourse among citizens may be more possible in small communities. See Jane Mansbridge, *Beyond Adversary Democracy* (New York: Basic Books, 1980); and Frank Bryan and John McClaughry, *The Vermont Papers: Recreating Democracy on a Human Scale* (Chelsea, VT: Chelsea Green, 1989).

15. Although citizens can communicate with one another directly through the Internet, Internet discussions have not influenced the terms and issues used in the commercial media, the main locale for political discourse. On the democratic possibilities of new technologies, see Michael T. Hayes, "Interest Groups: Pluralism or Mass Society?" in Allan J. Cigler and Burdett A. Loomis, eds., *Interest Group Politics*, pp. 110–25 (Washington, DC: Congressional Quarterly Press, 1983); James S. Fishkin, *Democracy and Deliberation: New Directions for Democratic Reform* (New Haven, CT: Yale University Press, 1991); and James S. Fishkin, *The Dialogue of Justice: Toward a Self-Reflective Society* (New Haven, CT: Yale University Press, 1992).

16. Simone Chambers, *Reasonable Democracy: Jürgen Habermas and the Politics of Discourse* (Ithaca: Cornell University Press, 1996), p. 171.

17. Alexis de Tocqueville, *Democracy in America* (Garden City, NY: Doubleday, 1969), p. 435. For other editions of *Democracy in America*, see vol. 2, part 1, ch. 2.

18. On the applicability of Tocqueville's ideas on public opinion, see Ginsberg, *The Captive Public*. For discussions of Tocquevillean individualism in contemporary America, see Robert Bellah, Richard Madsen, William W. Sullivan, Ann Swidler, and Steven Tipton, *Habits of the Heart: Individualism and Commitment in American Life* (New York: Harper & Row, 1985). See also William Sullivan, *Reconstructing Public Philosophy* (Berkeley and Los Angeles: University of California Press, 1982).

19. Carroll Glynn and Jack M. McLeod, "Implications of the Spiral of Silence Theory for Communication and Public Opinion Research," pp. 43–65, and Charles T. Salmon and Gerald F. Kline, "The Spiral of Silence Ten Years Later: An Examination and Evaluation," pp. 3–30, both in Keith R. Sanders, Lynda Lee Kaid, and Dan Nimmo, eds., *Political Communication Yearbook* (Carbondale: Southern Illinois University Press, 1985).

20. Vincent Price and Scott Allen, "Opinion Spirals, Silent and Otherwise: Applying Small-Group Research to Public Opinion Phenomena," *Communication Research* 17 (1990): 369–92; and Salmon and Kline, "The Spiral of Silence."

21. James M. Fields and Howard Schuman, "Public Beliefs About the Beliefs of the Public," *Public Opinion Quarterly* 40 (1976): 427–48; D. Garth Taylor, "Pluralistic Ignorance and the Spiral of Silence: A Formal Analysis," *Public Opinion Quarterly* 46 (1982): 311–35; and G. Marks and N. Miller, "Ten Years of Research on the False Consensus Effect: An Empirical and Theoretical Review," *Psychological Bulletin* 102 (1987): 72–90.

22. Huckfeldt and Sprague, *Citizens, Politics, and Social Communication*, p. 143.

23. Glynn and McLeod, "Public Opinion About Public Opinion"; and Salmon and Kline, "The Spiral of Silence Ten Years Later."

24. Hernando Gonzalez, "Mass Media and the Spiral of Silence: The Philippines from Marcos to Aquino," *Journal of Communication* 38 (1988): 33–48.

25. As Noelle-Neumann herself points out in *The Spiral of Silence*, different sorts of issues influence whether a spiral of silence occurs and the strength of its effect. However, this issue has not been well developed theoretically.

26. Nina Eliasoph, "Political Culture and the Presentation of a Political Self," *Theory and Society* 19 (1990): 465–94.

27. Dominic L. Lasora, "Political Outspokenness: Factors Working Against the Spiral of Silence," *Journalism Quarterly* 68 (1991): 131–40.

28. Charles T. Salmon and Kurt Neuwirth, "Perceptions of Opinion 'Climates' and Willingness to Discuss the Issue of Abortion," *Journalism Quarterly* 67 (1990): 567–77.

29. For the literature review, see Diana C. Mutz, "The Political Effects of Perceptions of Mass Opinion," in Michael X. Delli Carpini, Leonie Huddy, and Robert Y. Shapiro, eds., *Research in Micropolitics: New Directions in Political Psychology*, vol. 4, pp. 143–67 (Greenwich, CT: JAI Press, 1994). Also see Diana C. Mutz's experimental study, "Impersonal Influence: Effects of Representations of Public Opinion on Political Attitudes," *Political Behavior* 14 (1992): 89–122.

30. See Stanley Feldman, "Answering Survey Questions: The Measurement and Meaning of Public Opinion," in Milton Lodge and Kathleen M. McGraw, eds., *Political Judgment: Structure and Process*, pp. 249–70 (Ann Arbor: University of Michigan Press, 1995); and John R. Zaller and Stanley Feldman, "A Simple Theory of the Survey Response: Answering Questions Versus Revealing Preferences," *American Journal of Political Science* 36 (1992): 579–616.

31. Neither Key nor Habermas wrote on public opinion with the benefit of Noelle-Neumann's work. However, Habermas was influenced by the Frankfurt school and by Adorno's research on authoritarianism and so took heed of psychological effects of social and cultural systems. Key cannot be said to have been a psychologically oriented writer, yet he was quite aware that individual differences in political activity and engagement affected the distributions of public opinion for different issues. In arguing that concern for individual-level dynamics should not dominate investigations of politics, Key insisted, "The theory of the workings of a democratic order must make room for mass opinion, but its role needs to be treated as a part of a complex system of interactions within the circles of influence and leadership, and between them and mass opinion." See V. O. Key, *Public Opinion and American Democracy* (New York: Knopf, 1961), p. 76.

32. See Shanto Iyengar and Donald R. Kinder, *News That Matters* (Chicago: University of Chicago Press, 1987); Shanto Iyengar, *Is Anyone Responsible? How Television Frames Political Issues* (Chicago: University of Chicago Press, 1991); Marc Howard Ross, "Television News and Candidate Fortunes in Presidential Nomination Campaigns: The Case of 1984," *American Politics Quarterly* 20 (1992): 69–98;

Benjamin Page, Robert Shapiro, and Glenn Dempsey, "What Moves Public Opinion?" *American Political Science Review* 81 (1987): 23–43; Jeffery Mondak, "Media Exposure and Political Discussion in U.S. Elections," *Journal of Politics* 57 (1995): 62–85; Diana Mutz, "Contextualizing Personal Experience: The Role of Mass Media," *Journal of Politics* 56 (1994): 689–714; and Stephen Ansolabehere, Roy Behr, and Shanto Iyengar, "Mass Media and Elections," *American Politics Quarterly* 19 (1991): 109–39. Other sorts of media effects may influence communication and the potential for political manipulation. For example, Putnam argues that television usage decreases civic involvement, leading to a decline in "social capital" and in commitments to community. Persons isolated from active engagement with others and who instead devote a good deal of time to watching television may well be more vulnerable to the frames used by elites and the media. See Robert D. Putnam, "The Strange Disappearance of Civic America," *The American Prospect* 24 (1996): 34–48.

33. Aileen Yagade and David M. Dozier, "The Media Agenda-Setting Effect of Concrete Versus Abstract Issues," *Journalism Quarterly* 67 (1990): 3–10.

34. Page, Shapiro, and Dempsey, "What Moves Public Opinion?"

35. Another limitation of media power is that members of the public can frame issues differently from the way the media do. See Russell W. Neuman, Marion R. Just, and Ann N. Crigler, *Common Knowledge: News and the Construction of Political Meaning* (Chicago: University of Chicago Press, 1992).

36. Jon A. Krosnick and Donald R. Kinder, "Altering the Foundations of Support for the President Through Priming," *American Political Science Review* 84 (1990): 497–512.

37. Recent scholarship in communication studies has been concerned with the construction of a socially perceived public opinion and its relationship to the communication system. However, as Elihu Katz points out in the introduction to a collection focusing on this sort of public opinion, this emerging scholarship has not investigated the political meaning of such public opinion. Katz writes, "We need to know much more about how politicians take account of public opinion in day-to-day functioning and in policy-making, as well as the kinds of actions that bring public opinion out of privacy, out of public space, onto the agendas of the powerful." See Elihu Katz, Introduction to Theodore L. Glasser and Charles T. Salmon, eds., *Public Opinion and the Communication of Consent* (New York, Guilford Press, 1995), p. xxxi.

38. Robert M. Entman, *Democracy Without Citizens: Media and the Decay of American Politics* (New York: Oxford University Press, 1989).

39. Doug Underwood, *When MBAs Rule the Newsroom* (New York: Columbia University Press, 1993).

40. Murray Edelman, *Constructing the Political Spectacle* (Chicago: University of Chicago Press, 1988), p. 90.

41. Eric Alterman, *Sound and Fury: The Washington Punditocracy and the Collapse of American Politics* (New York: HarperCollins, 1992); and Dan Nimmo and James E. Combs, *The Political Pundits* (New York: Praeger, 1992).

42. Page, Shapiro, and Dempsey, "What Moves Public Opinion?"

43. Barbara Allen, "The Spiral of Silence & Institutional Design: Tocqueville's Analysis of Public Opinion & Democracy," *Polity* 24 (1991): 243–67.

44. Stephen Engelberg, "A New Breed of Hired Hands Cultivates Grass-Roots Anger," *New York Times*, March 17, 1993, pp. A1+.

45. See W. Lance Bennett, *News: The Politics of Illusion* (New York: Longman, 1983); Edelman, *Constructing the Political Spectacle*; and Kathleen Hall Jamieson, *Dirty Politics: Deception, Distraction, and Democracy* (New York: Oxford University Press, 1992).

46. Key, *Public Opinion and American Democracy*, p. 528.

47. Lawrence R. Jacobs, *The Health of Nations: Public Opinion and the Making of American and British Health Policy* (Ithaca, NY: Cornell University Press, 1993), p. 17.

48. The Reagan White House Communications Office took public opinion into account when designing their press strategy. Pollster Richard Wirthlin was hired and soon began to meet with administrative staff almost daily. During Reagan's second term, Wirthlin began to assess reactions to presidential speeches by using a system to monitor citizens' reactions moment by moment. This method had been used in advertising and "could measure their positive or negative reaction, interest or boredom, understanding or confusion, as well as their view of the speaker's credibility." Wirthlin also found what he called "power phrases" or "resonators," the lines most effective in altering public feeling." See Jane Mayer and Doyle McManus, *Landslide: The Unmaking of the President, 1984–1988* (Boston: Houghton Mifflin, 1988), p. 44.

49. Samuel Kernell, *Going Public: New Strategies of Presidential Leadership* (Washington, DC: Congressional Quarterly Press, 1986).

50. King and Schudson argue that a major reason that President Reagan was believed to be more popular than opinion polls indicated was that he was able to draw from the well-mobilized New Right. See Elliot King and Michael Schudson, "The Press and the Illusion of Public Opinion: The Strange Case of Ronald Reagan's 'Popularity,' " in Theodore L. Glasser and Charles T. Salmon, eds., *Public Opinion and the Communication of Consent*, pp. 132–55 (New York: Guilford Press, 1995).

51. The literature on presidential popularity is immense. For a good study and summary, see Paul Brace and Barbara Hinckely, *Follow the Leader: Opinion Polls and the Modern Presidents* (New York: Basic Books, 1992).

52. Marjorie Randon Hershey, "The Constructed Explanation: Interpreting Election Results in the 1984 Presidential Race," *Journal of Politics* 54 (1992): 943–76.

53. On learning from others and from similar circumstances in political campaigns, see Marjorie Randon Hershey, *Running for Office: The Political Education of Campaigners* (Chatham, NJ: Chatham House, 1984).

54. John W. Kingdon, *Agendas, Alternatives, and Public Policies* (Boston: Little, Brown, 1984), pp. 63–64.

55. Herbst, *Numbered Voices.*

56. Stephen Engelberg, "A New Breed of Hired Hands Cultivates Grass-Roots Anger," *New York Times*, March 17, 1993, p. A1; and William Greider, *Who Will Tell the People?* (New York: Simon & Schuster, 1992).

57. Joe R. Feagin, Anthony M. Orum, and Gideon Sjoberg, eds., *A Case for the Case Study* (Chapel Hill: University of North Carolina Press, 1991).

58. Merrill McLoughlin, *U.S News & World Report*, July 27, 1987, p. 18.

59. Thomas Burger, *Max Weber's Theory of Concept Formation: History, Laws, and Ideal Types* (Durham, NC: Duke University Press, 1976), p. 136.

60. Kai Erickson, "Sociology and Contemporary Events," in Walter W. Powell and Richard Robbins, eds., *Conflict and Consensus: A Festschrift in Honor of Lewis A. Coser*, p. 306 (New York: Free Press, 1984).

61. Theodore Draper, *A Very Thin Line: The Iran–Contra Affairs* (New York: Hill & Wang, 1991); Harold Hongju Koh, *The National Security Constitution: Sharing Power After the Iran–Contra Affair* (New Haven, CT: Yale University Press, 1990); Peter Kornbluh and Malcom Byrne, eds., *The Iran–Contra Scandal: The Declassified History* (New York: New Press, 1993); and Larry N. George, "Tocqueville's Caveat: Centralized Executive Foreign Policy and American Democracy," *Polity* 22 (1990): 419–41.

Chapter 3, Oliver North and the Politics of Hero Creation

1. Theodore Draper, *A Very Thin Line: The Iran–Contra Affairs* (New York: Hill & Wang, 1991), p. vix.

2. On these issues, see Harold Hongju Koh, *The National Security Constitution: Sharing Power After the Iran–Contra Affair* (New Haven, CT: Yale University Press); and Draper, *A Very Thin Line.*

3. Draper, *A Very Thin Line*, p. 4.

4. Peter Kornbluh and Malcolm Byrne, *The Iran–Contra Scandal: The Declassified History* (New York: New Press, 1993), p. 122.

5. Draper, *A Very Thin Line*, p. 120.

6. *Report of the Congressional Committees Investigating the Iran–Contra Affair. With Supplemental, Minority, and Additional Views* (Washington, DC: U.S. Government Printing Office, November 1987), p. 278.

7. Draper, *A Very Thin Line*, pp. 16–17.

8. Kornbluh and Byrne, *The Iran–Contra Scandal*, p. 385.

9. Draper, *A Very Thin Line*, pp. 24–26.

10. Ibid., p. 33.

11. *White propaganda* and *public diplomacy* were the terms used by the Reagan administration and were established under a National Security Decision Directive (NSDD) signed by President Reagan in January 14, 1983. Information about these activities was present in a draft chapter of the congressional investigating committee's report but did not appear in the final report. Kornbluh and Byrne maintain

that this chapter was removed because of Republican members' objections. See Kornbluh and Byrne, *The Iran–Contra Scandal,* p. 4.

12. Years later both Oliver North and some commentators wondered whether the highly public White House revelations of the diversion were themselves a tactic to divert the public from other details of the Iranian and contra operations. See Oliver L. North, with William Novak, *Under Fire* (New York: HarperCollins, 1991); and Kornbluh and Byrne, *The Iran–Contra Scandal.*

13. Draper, *A Very Thin Line,* p. 111. Draper says that a story on June 24, 1985, in the *Miami Herald,* "U.S. Found to Skirt Ban on Aid to Contras," by Alfonso Chardy, was the first media story to mention North by name in this connection.

14. In October 1991, Assistant Secretary of State Elliott Abrams pled guilty to two misdemeanor counts of withholding information from Congress regarding the Hasenfus matter and other contra support. See Lawrence E. Walsh, *Final Report of the Independent Counsel for Iran/Contra Matters* (Washington, DC: U.S. Government Printing Office, 1993).

15. Draper, *A Very Thin Line,* p. 486.

16. Ibid., p. 494.

17. See Kornbluh and Byrne, *The Iran–Contra Scandal,* pp. 319–21, for a facsimile of this memo; the quotation is from p. 323.

18. John Tower, Edmund Muskie, and Brent Scowcroft, *Report of the President's Special Review Board* (Washington, DC: U.S. Government Printing Office, 1987), pp. 72–73.

19. "Television's Blinding Power," *U.S. News & World Report,* July 27, 1987, p. 18.

20. Quoted in Steven Pressman, "Public Sympathy Proves Effective Shield for North Against Committee Critics," *Congressional Quarterly* 18 (July 1987): 1564–65.

21. Because of the deadline, the committee was not able to interview everyone they would have liked or to examine a number of documents they desired. Committee staff were still taking depositions in October, and committee members reported that they were unable to process all the information. See William S. Cohen and George J. Mitchell, *Men of Zeal: A Candid Inside Story of the Iran–Contra Hearings* (New York: Viking, 1988); and Stephen Engelberg and David E. Rosenbaum, "What the Iran Contra Committees Wish They Had Done Differently," *New York Times,* November 20, 1987, p. A1.

22. For example, the majority report criticized dealings with Iran. In addition to grave doubts about the advisability of the policy, the majority found fault with the discrepancy with the public efforts to limit arms availability to Iran (i.e., Operation Staunch), the lack of consultation with Congress, and the probable violation of the Arms Export Control Act. The majority report also agreed with the Tower Commission that it was inappropriate to use NSC staff for operational roles and that private, profit-seeking persons should not play major roles in carrying out American foreign policy initiatives.

23. *Report of the Congressional Committees,* pp. 395, 411, 412.

24. Ibid., p. 411.

25. Ibid., pp. 440, 437.

26. Ibid., pp. 437–38.

27. The independent counsel's decision to drop these two charges against North was part of a January 1989 agreement brokered with Attorney General Richard Thornburgh regarding the disclosure of classified information. See Walsh, *Final Report*; and Jeffrey Toobin, *Opening Arguments-A Young Lawyer's First Case: United States v. Oliver North* (New York: Viking, 1991). The Classified Information Procedures Act (CIPA) was intended to prevent "graymail," or the dropping of charges (particularly against spies), because of the threat of revealing certain information. However, some critics claimed that the Iran–contra cases demonstrated that the CIPA provisions could also be used to block revelations that would be embarrassing or politically damaging to an administration.

28. The conspiracy charge had already been undermined by the June 1988 judicial decision to try North, Poindexter, Secord, and Hakim separately.

29. See Walsh, *Final Report*, vol. 1, pp. xiv–xv, 556–58, on the appeals court ruling; the quotation is from p. 556.

30. Draper, *A Very Thin Line*, ch. 26.

31. Koh, *The National Security Constitution*, p. 13.

32. This notion of political culture is different from the individualistic "orientations toward political objects" perspective of Almond and Verba. See Gabriel Almond and Sidney Verba, *The Civic Culture* (Princeton, NJ: Princeton University Press, 1963). For discussions of alternative views of culture, see S. H. Ortner, "Theory in Anthropology Since the Sixties," *Comparative Studies in Society and History* 26 (1984): 126–66; R. Keesing, "Anthropology as Interpretive Quest," *Current Anthropology* 28 (1987): 161–76; and Michael Schudson, "How Culture Works: Perspectives from Media Studies on the Efficacy of Symbols," *Theory and Society* 18 (1989): 153–80. Ortner demonstrates that anthropologists have developed a view of culture that combines attention to agents and structures. Cultural symbols are contingent, and it is hard to predict how powerful they will be, but they derive their power from broader structures.

33. Clifford Geertz, *The Interpretation of Cultures* (New York: Basic Books, 1973), p. 5.

34. See John E. Bodnar, *Remaking America: Public Memory, Commemoration, and Patriotism in the Twentieth Century* (Princeton, NJ: Princeton University Press, 1992); and John J. Gillis, *Commemorations: The Politics of National Identity* (Princeton, NJ: Princeton University Press, 1994).

35. Ann Swidler, "Culture in Action: Symbols and Strategies," *American Sociological Review* 51 (1986): 273–86.

36. For extensions and discussions of Gallie and essentially contested concepts, see William Connolly, *The Terms of Political Discourse* (Princeton, NJ: Princeton University Press, 1974); and James Farr, "Understanding Conceptual Change Politically," in Terence Ball, James Farr, and Russell Hanson, eds., *Political Innovation and Conceptual Change*, pp. 24–49 (Cambridge, Cambridge University Press, 1988).

37. John L. Sullivan, Amy Fried, and Mary G. Dietz, "Patriotism, Politics, and the Presidential Election of 1988," *American Journal of Political Science* 36 (1992): 200–34.

38. Michael Schudson, "How Culture Works: Perspectives from Media Studies on the Efficacy of Symbols," *Theory and Society* 18 (1989): 163.

39. Differences in reactions to symbolic appeals may well fall along gender, ethnic, age, or racial lines. Strategists and the political elites they advise may take account of these differences, whether during elections or outside the election season.

40. Schudson, "How Culture Works," p. 168.

41. Campaign consultants sometimes refer to convincing voters as "closing the sale." Unlike the marketing of a cultural product, however, election campaigns are based on one day's choice. Although strategists follow polls for indications of how citizens will choose, only their votes matter. Opinion preferences are not analogous to early sales or first viewers, since they are not counted on the only day that matters—election day. Campaigners draw on their extensive experience and feedback from varied sources as they attempt to match election time with candidate popularity. On learning in campaigns, see Marjorie Randon Hershey, *Running for Office* (Chatham, NJ: Chatham House Press, 1984). See Popkin on how voters' cognitive processes pick up on the cues provided in campaigns. Samuel Popkin, *The Reasoning Voter* (Chicago: University of Chicago Press, 1991).

42. Amy Fried, " Is Political Action Heroic? Heroism and American Political Culture," *American Politics Quarterly* 21 (1993): 490–517.

43. Joseph Campbell, *The Hero with a Thousand Faces* (Princeton, NJ: Princeton University Press, 1949).

44. North, *Under Fire*, p. 147.

45. On North's attempts to stay with the NSC, see Draper, *A Very Thin Line*, pp. 32, 337–339. On North's fabrications of stories about his closeness to the president and others, see Rachel Wildavsky, "Does Oliver North Tell the Truth?" *Reader's Digest*, June 1993, pp. 75–80.

46. For several examples, see North, *Under Fire*, pp. 148–49, 351.

47. Robert Timberg, *The Nightingale's Song* (New York: Simon & Schuster, 1995); Bernard E. Trainor, "Marines, Uneasy at First, Now See North as Honor to Corps," *New York Times*, July 12, 1987, p. 12. Trainor discusses differences in how senior and junior marine officers assessed North.

48. R. W. Apple, Jr., "The Colonel Stands His Ground," *New York Times*, July 12, 1987, sec. 4, p. 1.

49. James Gibson, *Warrior Dreams: Paramilitary Culture in Post-Vietnam America* (New York: Hill & Wang, 1994), p. 284.

50. Cohen and Mitchell, *Men of Zeal*, p. 156.

51. Daniel J. Boorstin, *The Image: A Guide to Pseudo-Events in America* (New York: Athenaeum, 1987), p. 48.

52. Nina Eliasoph, "Political Culture and the Presentation of a Political Self," *Theory and Society* 19 (1990): 465, 479.

53. See Kathleen Hall Jamieson, *Dirty Politics: Deception, Distraction, and Democracy* (New York: Oxford University Press, 1992); Also see Thomas E. Patterson, *Out of Order* (New York: Vintage Books, 1994).

54. Richard Sobel, "Public Opinion About United States Intervention in El Salvador and Nicaragua," *Public Opinion Quarterly* 53 (1989): 115.

55. Ibid.

56. Reported in Benjamin I. Page and Robert Y. Shapiro, *The Rational Public: Fifty Years of Trends in Americans' Policy Preferences* (Chicago: University of Chicago Press, 1992).

57. Gordon L. Bowen, "Presidential Action and Public Opinion About U.S. Nicaraguan Policy: Limits of the 'Rally Round the Flag' Syndrome," *PS* (1989): 793–800.

58. *U.S. News & World Report*, July 13, 1987, p. 23.

59. *Time*, July 20, 1987, p. 15.

60. Kornbluh and Byrne, *The Iran–Contra Scandal*, p. 304.

61. John R. Zaller, *The Nature and Origins of Mass Opinion* (Cambridge: Cambridge University Press, 1992), p. 181.

62. *U.S. News & World Report*, July 13, 1987, p. 22.

63. Jon A. Krosnick and Donald R. Kinder, "Altering the Foundations of Support for the President Through Priming," *American Political Science Review* 84 (1990): 497–512.

64. Zaller, *The Nature and Origins of Mass Opinion*, pp. 168–69. Zaller also demonstrates that citizens with a very low awareness of politics were hardly moved by the Iran–contra revelations.

65. Polling information is available in the data base maintained by the Roper Center for Public Opinion Research. For a summary of surveys about favorable and unfavorable views of North, see *Public Opinion*, May–June 1988.

66. *Time*, July 20, 1987, p. 15.

67. Ibid.

68. For results of the Q-study, see Amy Fried, "Is Political Action Heroic?" and "Political Heroism and Political Culture in the United States" (Ph.D. diss., University of Minnesota, 1991). With Q-methodology, the subjects are presented with a set of statements reflecting a broad range of views. Unlike a typical survey, the subjects do not respond to each statement one at a time but instead arrange the statements according to a pattern supplied by the investigator. Small numbers of statements are placed at the ends of the pattern, which represent the views that the subjects most support or reject. Larger numbers of statements are put toward the middle, creating a shape that looks like a normal distribution. Similar patterns are grouped together to identify a smaller, basic set of perspectives. Although the range of possible responses is more limited than possible with intensive interviews, Q-methodology is more sensitive to the respondents' subjective understandings than traditional surveys are. See Steven Brown, *Political Subjectivity* (New Haven, CT: Yale University Press, 1980).

69. Five persons each were involved in the Veterans of Foreign Wars, Women Against Military Madness, the Rotary Club, local unions, an Evangelical Free Church, a Lutheran Church, the Independent–Republican Party, and the Democratic–Farmer Labor Party, and ten of the subjects were students.

70. Philip E. Converse, "The Nature of Belief Systems in Mass Publics," in David E. Apter, ed., *Ideology and Discontent*, pp. 206–61 (New York: Free Press, 1964); and Zaller, *The Nature and Origins of Mass Opinion*.

71. Jennifer L. Hochschild, *What's Fair? American Beliefs About Redistributive Justice* (Cambridge, MA: Harvard University Press, 1981), p. 25.

72. Additional information about citizens' views of Oliver North during the congressional Iran–contra hearings is provided in David Thelen's *Becoming Citizens in the Age of Television: How Americans Challenged the Media and Seized Political Initiative During the Iran–Contra Debate* (Chicago: University of Chicago Press, 1996), which was published as this book went to press. Thelen analyzed letters written to committee members, especially those to Representative Lee Hamilton (Democrat, Indiana), and found a similar set of reactions. As with my interview respondents, many citizens were critical of North, balanced concerns of secrecy and democratic accountability, and believed him to be sincere in his convictions. Unlike the interviews, these letters are the contemporaneous reactions of a self-selected group.

Chapter 4, Telling the Public What It Thinks

1. On legislators' use of the media, see Timothy Cook, *Making Laws and Making News: Media Strategies in the House of Representatives* (Washington, DC: Brookings Institution, 1989).

2. W. Lance Bennett and Murray Edelman, "Toward a New Political Narrative," *Journal of Communication* 35 (Autumn 1985): 158–59.

3. See Bethami A. Dobkin, *Tales of Terror: Television News and the Construction of the Terrorist Threat* (New York: Praeger, 1992); Gaye Tuchman, *Making News: A Study in the Construction of Reality* (New York: Free Press, 1978); Herbert Gans, *Deciding What's News* (New York: Pantheon, 1979); Shanto Iyengar and Donald R. Kinder, *News That Matters* (Chicago: University of Chicago Press, 1987); Shanto Iyengar, *Is Anyone Responsible? How Television Frames Political Issues* (Chicago: University of Chicago Press, 1991); Russell W. Neuman, Marion R. Just, and Ann N. Crigler, *Common Knowledge: News and the Construction of Political Meaning* (Chicago: University of Chicago Press, 1992); and Barbie Zelizer, *Covering the Body: The Kennedy Assassination, the Media, and the Shaping of Collective Memory* (Chicago: University of Chicago Press, 1992). As Iyengar points out, most news coverage is framed around particular events (the episodic frame) rather than broader contexts (the thematic frame).

4. On the development of objectivity as a journalistic value, see Michael Schudson, *Discovering the News: A Social History of American Newspapers* (New York: Basic Books, 1978).

5. In the Persian Gulf War, for example, the U.S. media constructed a shared narrative presenting the conflict as a victory over evil, in which our troops and weapons performed flawlessly and the nation erased any hesitation left over from the Vietnam War about using force. The story told in other nations about the Gulf War was different. People who watched a lot of television knew less about the war than did people who did not. See Michael Morgan, Justin Lewis, and Sut Jhally, "More Viewing, Less Knowledge," in Hamid Mawlana, George Gerber, and Herbert I. Schiller, eds., *Triumph of the Image: The Media's War in the Persian Gulf—A Global Perspective*, pp. 216–35 (Boulder, CO: Westview Press, 1992). On the Gulf War and the media, see Robert E. Denton, ed., *The Media and the Persian Gulf War* (Westport, CT: Praeger, 1993); Susan Jeffords and Lauren Rabinowitz, *Seeing Through the Media: The Persian Gulf War* (New Brunswick, NJ: Rutgers University Press, 1994); and Philip M. Taylor, *War and the Media: Propaganda and Persuasion in the Gulf War* (Manchester: Manchester University Press, 1992). On politicians' perceptions of policy and public opinion, see John R. Zaller, "Strategic Politicians, Public Opinion, and the Gulf Crisis," in W. Lance Bennett and David L. Paletz, eds., *Taken by Storm: The Media, Public Opinion and U.S. Foreign Policy in the Gulf War*, pp. 250–74 (Chicago: University of Chicago Press, 1994). For a cross-national study on perceptions of the war, see David L. Swanson and Larry David Smith, "War in the Global Village: A Seven Country Comparison of Television News Coverage of the Beginning of the Gulf War," in Robert E. Denton, ed., *The Media and the Persian Gulf War*, pp. 165–96 (Westport, CT: Praeger, 1993).

6. Timothy Crouse, *The Boys on the Bus* (New York: Random House, 1973); W. Lance Bennett, "Toward a Theory of Press–State Relations in the United States," *Journal of Communication* 40 (1990): 103–25; Zelizer, *Covering the Body*; Robert M. Entman, *Democracy Without Citizens: Media and the Decay of American Politics* (New York: Oxford University Press, 1989); Kathleen Hall Jamieson, *Dirty Politics: Deception, Distraction, and Democracy* (New York: Oxford University Press, 1992); and Michael Schudson, *Watergate in American Memory: How We Remember, Forget, and Reconstruct the Past* (New York: Basic Books, 1992).

7. Iyengar and Kinder, *News That Matters*.

8. News has become more like entertainment because of commercial pressures, changes in the newspaper industry, and the rise of mixed forms such as docudramas. See Jeffrey Goldfarb, *The Cynical Society: The Culture of Politics and the Politics of Culture in American Life* (Chicago: University of Chicago Press, 1991); Doug Underwood, *When MBAs Rule the Newsroom* (New York: Columbia University Press, 1993); Jamieson, *Dirty Politics*; John Anthony Maltese, *Spin Control: The White House Office of Communications and the Management of Presidential News* (Chapel Hill: University of North Carolina Press, 1992); and Thomas E. Patterson, *Out of Order* (New York: Vintage Books, 1994).

9. Patterson, *Out of Order*.

10. Neuman et al., *Common Knowledge*, p. 77.

11. See James Scott, *Weapons of the Weak: Everyday Forms of Peasant Resistance* (New Haven, CT: Yale University Press, 1985); and James Scott, *Domination and the Arts of Resistance* (New Haven, CT: Yale University Press, 1990).

12. Marjorie Randon Hershey, "The Constructed Explanation: Interpreting Election Results in the 1984 Presidential Race," *Journal of Politics* 54 (1992): 975 (italics in original).

13. Kurt Lang and Gladys Engel Lang, "The Unique Perspective of Television and Its Effect: A Pilot Study," *American Sociological Review* 18 (1953): 7.

14. Gladys Engel Lang and Kurt Lang, *The Battle for Public Opinion: The President, the Press, and the Polls During Watergate* (New York: Columbia University Press, 1983), p. 22.

15. Although there are numerous studies of media polls, little research has been done on the media's presentation of public opinion in general. For an exception, see J. David Kennamer, ed., *Public Opinion, the Press, and Public Policy* (Westport, CT: Praeger, 1992).

16. Andrew Kohut, *The Vocal Minority in American Politics* (Washington, DC: Times Mirror Center for the People and the Press, 1993).

17. See Susan T. Fiske and Shelley E. Taylor, *Social Cognition* (Reading, MA: Addison-Wesley, 1984); also Samuel Popkin, *The Reasoning Voter* (Chicago: University of Chicago Press, 1991); and John E. Newhagen and Byron Reeves, "The Evening's Bad News: Effects of Compelling Negative Television News Images on Memory," *Journal of Communication* 42 (1992): 25–41. Dramatic images are not necessarily remembered better, although they do contribute to less cognitive complexity. See Michael A. Milburn and Anne B. McGrail, "The Dramatic Presentation of News and Its Effects on Cognitive Complexity," *Political Psychology* 13 (1992): 613–32.

18. Mark Hertsgaard, *On Bended Knee: The Press and the Reagan Presidency* (New York: Farrar, Straus & Giroux, 1988), pp. 162–63.

19. John Mueller, *Policy and Opinion in the Gulf War* (Chicago: University of Chicago Press, 1994), pp. 74–75.

20. The quotation is from Deaver's memoirs and is reproduced in Hertsgaard, *On Bended Knee*, p. 4. Hertsgaard also includes remarks from editors and journalists about the kind treatment that Reagan received.

21. Good discussions of the Reagan administration's communications strategies can be found in Hertsgaard, *On Bended Knee*; and Maltese, *Spin Control*.

22. Despite the press's claims that Reagan was an exceptionally popular president, polling data do not bear this out. See Thomas Ferguson and Joel Rogers, *Right Turn* (New York: Hill & Wang, 1984); and Elliot King and Michael Schudson, "The Press and the Illusion of Public Opinion: The Strange Case of Ronald Reagan's 'Popularity,' " in Theodore L. Glasser and Charles T. Salmon, eds., *Public Opinion and the Communication of Consent*, pp. 132–55 (New York: Guilford Press, 1995).

23. William Greider, then assistant managing editor of the *Washington Post*, told Mark Hertsgaard, "They have managed to create the sense, which is known by any-

body at all close to the White House not to be true, that this is a very activist President . . . It's a theme they peddle that is implicit in all those images, because what the public sees of him is an activist President" (quoted in Hertzgaard, *On Bended Knee*, p. 26).

24. Stephen Skowronek, *The Politics Presidents Make: Leadership from John Adams to George Bush* (Cambridge, MA: Belknap Press of Harvard University Press, 1993), p. 425.

25. Michael Kammen, *Mystic Chords of Memory: The Transformation of Tradition in American Culture* (New York: Knopf, 1991), p. 652.

26. See Dobkin, *Tales of Terror*.

27. Iyengar, *Is Anyone Responsible?* pp. 71–73. Iyengar also reports that nearly all coverage was episodic, emphasizing daily events and developments such as political reactions and various investigations rather than policy considerations. Media experiments testing how news frames influenced attributions for the decision to sell arms to Iran found that "the predominant political frame, which focused on the criticism and controversy surrounding the uncertain role of the president in the decision to sell arms to Iran, encouraged viewers to attribute causal responsibility to the president, while coverage that focused on the arms sale as an instrument of U.S. foreign policy tended to produce more contextual, nonpresidential attributions" (pp. 128–29).

28. Theodore Draper, *A Very Thin Line: The Iran–Contra Affairs* (New York: Hill & Wang, 1991), p. 337.

29. On the press's coverage of Iran–contra while it was still covert, see Scott Armstrong, "Iran–Contra: Was the Press Any Match for All the President's Men?" *Columbia Journalism Review*, May–June 1990, pp. 27–35; Dom Bonafede, "Scandal Time," *National Journal*, January 24, 1987, pp. 199–207; Hertzgaard, *On Bended Knee*; Eleanor Randolph, "How the Newshounds Blew the Iran–Contra Story," *Washington Post*, November 15, 1987, pp. C1+.

30. Jane Mayer and Doyle McManus, *Landslide: The Unmaking of the President, 1984–1988* (Boston: Houghton Mifflin, 1988), p. 300.

31. Patrick J. Buchanan, "No One Gave the Order to Abandon Reagan's Ship," *Washington Post*, December 8, 1986, p. A15.

32. Maltese, *Spin Control*, pp. 209, 212.

33. This implicit comparison could be seen in the labels Iran-Gate and Contra-Gate, which were adopted by various observers. The experience and collective memory of Watergate influenced people other than journalists in significant ways. According to Schudson, "Because Watergate was so traumatic, it proved no ordinary frame of reference but a 'preemptive' metaphor that kept the administration from making the kind of errors that could have turned a scandal into a rout, instilled in the Congress a cautiousness about pursuing the president, and inspired in critics an expectation of decisive congressional action and media heroics" (Schudson, *Watergate in American Memory*, p. 182).

34. Some, including Oliver North and a number of congressional staffers, argued that the revelation of the diversion was itself a diversion, designed to divert

press and public attention from other issues. See Oliver L. North with William Novak, *Under Fire* (New York: HarperCollins, 1991), pp. 7–8; Hertsgaard, *On Bended Knee*, pp. 11, 323.

35. Michael Cornfield and David Yalof, "Innocent by Reason of Analogy: How the Watergate Analogy Served Both Reagan and the Press During the Iran Contra Affair," *Corruption and Reform* 3 (1988): 199.

36. Armstrong, "Iran–Contra," p. 30.

37. Cornfield and Yalof, "Innocent by Reason of Analogy," pp. 194, 202.

38. President Reagan gave several seemingly contradictory statements about trying to maintain support for the contras. At some points, he appeared not to know that it had been proved that there was a diversion at all. For example, at Poindexter's 1990 trial, Reagan testified that it was only then that he learned that the diversion had taken place, even though he and Meese had admitted it in November 1986. See Draper, *A Very Thin Line*, p. 571. Whether Reagan knew of the diversion in advance was, of course, a key issue in the numerous investigations. He was clearly informed of the Iranian arms transfers.

39. For example, President Reagan wrote in his autobiography that "I never met with him [North] privately and never had a one-on-one conversation with him until I called him on his last day at the NSC to wish him well." See Ronald Reagan, *An American Life* (New York: Simon & Schuster, 1990), p. 486. Reagan's press secretary, Larry Speakes, said that North often made up stories, including a claim that he had been with Reagan during the invasion of Grenada and that they had watched the grateful reactions of an American medical student on television. See Larry Speakes with Robert Pack, *Speaking Out: The Reagan Presidency from Inside the White House* (New York: Scribner, 1988), pp. 112–13, 282–86.

40. Reagan, *An American Life*, p. 541.

41. *Time*, December 8, 1986, p. 18.

42. According to Larry Speakes, Reagan often read Sidey's work and chatted with him. "Hugh thought he had a press-office-approved interview, while the President thought he was talking to an old friend with whom he could let his hair down, so Reagan made his famous remark to Sidey that "Ollie North is a national hero" (Speakes, *Speaking Out*, p. 112). Mayer and McManus reported that "Sidey was as close to a friend as Reagan had in the press; his daughter had even worked in the White House" (Mayer and McManus, *Landslide*, p. 354).

43. Reagan, *An American Life*, p. 541.

44. North, *Under Fire*, p. 16.

45. Ibid., p. 9 (italics in the original).

46. Buchanan, "No One Gave the Order to Abandon Reagan's Ship."

47. Speakes, *Speaking Out*, p. 112.

48. Draper, *A Very Thin Line*, p. 549.

49. Lou Cannon, *President Reagan: The Role of a Lifetime* (New York: Simon & Schuster, 1991), p. 717.

50. See Frank P. Tomasulo, "Colonel North Goes to Washington: Observations

on the Intertextual Re-presentation of History," *Journal of Popular Film and Television* 17 (1989): 82–88.

51. Hans Mathias Kepplinger, "Visual Biases in Campaign Coverage," *Communication Research* 9 (1982): 432–46; and Doris A. Graber, "Seeing Is Remembering: How Visuals Contribute to Learning from Television News," *Journal of Communication* 40 (1990): 134–55.

52. *Time*, July 20, 1987, p. 14.

53. *Newsweek*, July 20, 1987, p. 12.

54. Neither magazine reported on who organized the demonstrations. According to the *Washington Times*, July 6, 1987, p. A3, demonstrations across the country were planned and organized by one of North's personal friends before the hearings began. The demonstrations in Washington, D.C., were organized by the Legal Affairs Council and the Unification Church (interview with L. Brent Bozell, president of the Media Research Center, October 20, 1993, Alexandria, VA).

55. *Newsweek*, July 13, 1987, p. 60.

56. *Time*, July 20, 1987, pp. 29, 15.

57. Jamieson, *Dirty Politics*, p. 171.

58. Patterson, *Out of Order*.

59. Jonathan Alter with Eleanor Clift, "A TV Viewer's Guide," *Newsweek*, May 11, 1987, p. 23.

60. "Performance Counts in Irangate 'Show,' " *Chicago Tribune*, May 14, 1987, p. C1.

61. Lance Morrow, "Charging up Capitol Hill: How Oliver North Captured the Imagination of America," *Time*, July 20, 1987, p. 12.

62. Jonathan Alter, "Ollie Enters Folklore," *Newsweek*, July 20, 1987, pp. 19+.

63. Daniel Henniger, "The Anchorman Chronicles: Ollie," *Wall Street Journal*, July 15, 1987, p. 26.

64. "The Next Witness," *Newsweek*, July 20, 1987, p. 27.

65. John Corry, "Poindexter Testimony: A Decrease in Drama," *New York Times*, July 16, 1987, p. 21.

66. Alter, "Ollie Enters Folklore," p. 19.

67. David Denby, "Ollie North, the Movie," *New Republic*, August 3, 1987, p. 9.

68. Armstrong, "Iran-Contra," p. 31.

69. Denby, "Ollie North, the Movie," p. 9.

70. Ibid., p. 7.

71. One response to this reading of journalists' coverage of public opinion might be that North was indeed quite popular, but only for a short time. Indeed, Page and Shapiro's data suggest that North's testimony, largely unchallenged, likely moved a segment of the public to support the contras but that this support faded rapidly. See Benjamin I. Page and Robert Y. Shapiro, *The Rational Public: Fifty Years of Trends in Americans' Policy Preferences* (Chicago: University of Chicago Press, 1992). However, this change in opinion does not necessarily mean that people esteemed North, and indeed, many of the poll data show otherwise. The analysis presented

in chapter 3 indicates that poll results were mixed and ambivalent because even though people believed that North was sincere, they also largely thought he acted inappropriately.

72. Susan Herbst, *Numbered Voices: How Opinion Polling Has Shaped American Politics* (Chicago: University of Chicago Press, 1993).

73. E. E. Schattschneider, *The Semisovereign People: A Realist's View of Democracy in America* (New York: Holt, Rinehart and Winston, 1960).

Chapter 5, Taking an Interest in the Public

1. Susan Herbst, Numbered Voices: How *Opinion Polling Has Shaped American Politics* (Chicago: University of Chicago Press, 1993), p. 158.

2. Not all interest-group scholars have appreciated the interest groups' concern with the public. As David Austen-Smith notes, "interest groups are typically seen to influence policy in two ways: through the giving of campaign contributions and through the distribution of specialist information." David Austen-Smith, "Information and Influence: Lobbying for Agendas and Votes," *American Journal of Political Science* 37 (1993): 799.

3. Thomas L. Gais and Jack L. Walker, "Pathways to Influence in American Politics," in Jack L. Walker, *Mobilizing Interest Groups in America: Patrons, Professions, and Social Movements*, p. 105 (Ann Arbor: University of Michigan Press, 1991).

4. Kay Lehman Schlozman and John T. Tierney, *Organized Interests and American Democracy* (New York: Harper & Row, 1986).

5. Leo Bogart, "Public Opinion and Collective Behavior," *Public Opinion Quarterly* 47 (1983): 488.

6. In 1965 Mancur Olson argued that lobbying is a mere "by-product" for groups seeking to provide public goods. See Mancur Olson, *The Logic of Collective Action* (Cambridge, MA: Harvard University Press, 1965). Since then, scholars have investigated groups' attention to policy goals versus organizational requisites. On the role of patrons and policy entrepreneurs, see Jack L. Walker, "The Origins and Maintenance of Interest Groups in America," *American Political Science Review* 77 (1983): 390–406; and Robert H. Salisbury, *Interests and Institutions: Substance and Structure in American Politics* (Pittsburgh: University of Pittsburgh Press, 1992). On group members' policy commitments, see Paul Sabatier and Susan McLaughlin, "Belief Congruence Between Interest Group Leaders and Their Members," *Journal of Politics* 52 (1990): 914–35; and Lawrence S. Rothenberg, *Linking Citizens to Government: Interest Group Politics at Common Cause* (Cambridge: Cambridge University Press, 1992).

7. As Kingdon points out, groups' influence on agenda setting is often indirect. Groups influence the media, and the media influence policy priorities and the acceptability of particular policy options. See John W. Kingdon, *Agendas, Alternatives, and Public Policies* (Boston: Little, Brown, 1984), ch. 3.

8. Cynthia J. Arnson and Philip Brenner, "The Limits of Lobbying: Interest Groups, Congress, and Aid to the Contras," in Richard Sobel, ed., *Public Opinion in U.S. Foreign Policy: The Controversy over Contra Aid*, p. 192 (Lanham, MD: Rowman & Littlefield, 1993). For a good overview of U.S. policy toward Central America from 1976 to 1993, see Cynthia Arnson, *Crossroads: Congress, the President, and Central America, 1976–1993*, 2nd ed. (University Park: Pennsylvania State University Press, 1993).

9. Interview with Charles Orndorff, vice chairman of the Conservative Caucus, Vienna, VA, October 22, 1993.

10. Like the situation in the liberal group Common Cause that Rothenberg described, group leaders were ahead of their members in putting an issue on the organizational agenda.

11. "Groups on Both Sides of Contra Aid Issue Working on the Hill and at the Grass Roots," *National Journal*, April 14, 1985, p. 786.

12. Interviews with L. Brent Bozell, president of the Media Research Center, Alexandria, VA, October 20, 1993, and Charles Orndorff of the Conservative Caucus. See also Arnson and Brenner, "The Limits of Lobbying," p. 206.

13. Concerned Women of America, direct mail item, June 1988, pp. 2–3, from file on Concerned Women of America, People for the American Way, Washington, DC.

14. Ronald Brownstein, "Reagan Reaches out for Public Support for CIA Aid to Nicaraguan Insurgents," *National Journal*, April 14, 1985, pp. 785–86.

15. See Theodore Draper, *A Very Thin Line: The Iran–Contra Affairs* (New York: Hill & Wang, 1991), ch. 3; Robert Parry and Peter Kornbluh, "Iran–Contra's Untold Story," *Foreign Policy* 72 (Fall 1988): 3–30; and Peter Kornbluh, "The Contra Lobby," *Village Voice*, October 13, 1987, pp. 23–28.

16. These efforts were established under National Security Decision Directive 77, signed by President Reagan on January 14, 1983.

17. Daniel "Jake" Jacobowitz, "Public Diplomacy Action Plan: Support for the White House Educational Campaign," in Peter Kornbluh and Malcolm Byrne, eds., *The Iran–Contra Scandal: The Declassified History*, p. 25 (New York: New Press, 1993).

18. Jim Kocklow, "Pro-Contra Groups Uses TV, Truth Squads," *National Journal*, March 22, 1986, p. 722.

19. Other private groups were involved in aiding the contras as well; see Peter Kornbluh and Malcolm Byrne, eds., *The Iran–Contra Scandal: The Declassified History* (New York: New Press, 1993).

20. Ben Bradlee Jr., *Guts and Glory: The Rise and Fall of Oliver North* (New York: Donald I. Fine, 1988), p. 222.

21. Draper, *A Very Thin Line*, p. 67.

22. U.S. House Committee on Foreign Affairs, *State Department and Intelligence Community Involvement in Domestic Activities Related to the Iran–Contra Affair* (Washington, DC: U.S. Government Printing Office, 1992), p. 18.

23. In addition, the media's major interpretation of Reagan's 1984 victory did not involve foreign policy but, rather, Mondale's position on taxes and problems with the Democratic Party coalition. See Marjorie Randon Hershey, "The Constructed Explanation: Interpreting Election Results in the 1984 Presidential Race," *Journal of Politics* 54 (1992): 943–76.

24. Dick Kirschten, "Reagan Looks to Religious Leaders for Continuing Support in 1984," *National Journal,* August 20, 1983, p. 1727.

25. Penn Kemble, director of the Institute on Religion and Democracy, quoted in "Groups on Both Sides of Contra Aid Issue," p. 788.

26. Fenton Communications is unusual among Washington, D.C., public relations firms because it does not accept corporate clients. Interview with Jim McAvoy, president of Burson-Marsteller's Advocacy Communications Team, Washington, DC, September 10, 1993. For an overview of recent activities by Fenton Communications, see David Daley, "David Fenton: Pitchman for the Politically Correct," *National Journal,* October 3, 1992, p. 2266. For a discussion of Fenton's anticontra activities from a conservative perspective, see Don Kowet, "Fenton's Ties to Leftists Aimed at the Contras," *Washington Times,* October 19, 1987, p. A1; and Don Kowet, "It's a Long Climb Through the Left for Sandinista's U.S. Press Agent," *Washington Times,* October 20, 1987, p. A1.

27. Witness for Peace members who returned from Nicaragua devoted much time to presenting their point of view in local, grassroots forums. They often received local news coverage, particularly in small-to-medium media markets. Interview with Leigh Carter, executive director of Witness for Peace, Washington, DC, January 4, 1994.

28. One reader has suggested that congressional reactions to revelations about the CIA's mining of the Managua harbor and Ortega's trip to the Soviet Union are indirect effects of public opinion, in which members of Congress reacted to anticipated public opinion. This may be true, but it also is possible that these events independently influenced some legislators. In the first case, for example, Senator Barry Goldwater, a firm supporter of contra aid, was deeply troubled by news of this and other CIA-sponsored activities.

29. John R. Zaller, *The Nature and Origins of Mass Opinion* (Cambridge: Cambridge University Press, 1992).

30. Arnson and Brenner argue that groups had less impact on the general policy agenda and very little influence on other aspects of the Reagan administration's Nicaragua policy. Within the "opportunities for influence offered to them by the Congress . . . their sustained efforts in the contra aid debate had some impact on the Congress, the public, and the way in which U.S. policy was carried out" (Arnson and Brenner, "The Limits of Lobbying," p. 216).

31. Bozell, interview.

32. Orndorff, interview.

33. Arnson and Brenner, "The Limits of Lobbying," p. 209.

34. Former National Security Adviser Robert McFarlane reported that President Reagan gave him these instructions in 1984. See Draper, *A Very Thin Line*, p. 33.

35. Information about the involvement of the Legal Affairs Council comes from my interviews with Robert G. Grant, president of the American Freedom Coalition, Falls Church, VA, October 21, 1993, and L. Brent Bozell of the Media Research Center. Mr. Bozell told me about the organizing efforts of Young Americans for Freedom and the Unification Church.

36. John McCaslin, "North Classmate Plans Rallies in His Support," *Washington Times*, July 6, 1987, p. A3.

37. Conservative Caucus, direct mail item, "Emergency Mailgram to Stop Liberal Witch-Hunt," July 1, 1987, from the files of the Conservative Caucus, Vienna, VA.

38. Concerned Women of America, June 1988 direct mail item, p. 3, from the file on Concerned Women of America at the Washington, DC, office of People for the American Way.

39. Bozell, interview.

40. David Thelen, *Becoming Citizens in the Age of Television: How Americans Challenged the Media and Seized Political Initiative During the Iran–Contra Hearings* (Chicago: University of Chicago Press, 1996), p. 66.

41. Orndorff, interview.

42. "White House Exuberant over North Success," *Christian Science Monitor*, July 14, 1987, p. 1.

43. Bozell, interview.

44. "Pro-Contra Ad Campaign Targets the President," *Washington Times*, August 21, 1987, p. A6.

45. For example, Paul Weyrich, president of the Free Congress Foundation, argued that "conservatives don't know the difference between power and influence. Conservatives have had influence in the Reagan era. . . . But we have no power. Power presupposes holding 'territory.' We hold no territory. Nowhere are conservative agendas moving through state legislatures. . . . Political power in this country is not just in legislatures, however. It also resides in political groupings and organizations. Here again, conservatives hold no territory. . . . Republicans have done almost nothing to foster local issue-oriented black and Hispanic movements, so the liberals are still in the driver's seat." Paul M. Weyrich, "The Reagan Revolution That Wasn't: Why Conservatives Have Achieved So Little," *Policy Review* 41 (Summer 1987): 51.

46. Richard L. Berke, "Col. North Bolstering Fund Effort," *New York Times*, July 15, 1987, p. A1.

47. See Alessandra Stanley, "Faith in a True Believer: Oliver North Draws Support from Conservatives and Charismatics," *Time*, February 16, 1987, p. 23.

48. North's appearance was marked by some controversy and was met by a small group of protestors. See "North Says Criminal Charges Against Him Are 'an

Honor,' " *New York Times*, May 3, 1988, p. A26; Scott Baradell, "For Some, Ex-Marine's Presence Was Unwelcome," *Lynchburg (VA) News and Daily Advance*, May 3, 1988, p. A1; John H. Buchanan, "North's Typical When Values Go South," *Lynchburg (VA) News and Daily Advance*, May 2, 1988; and Donald P. Baker, "Charges a 'Badge of Honor,' North Says at Liberty U.," *Washington Post*, May 3, 1988, p. A8.

49. See "Religious Right Courts Oliver North," *Christian Century*, August 17–24, 1988, p. 727. This article notes that North left the Catholic Church in anger over the 1983 pastoral letter on nuclear weapons. Mr. North then joined "an evangelical–charismatic Episcopal parish in northern Virginia." See also "Religious Right Drums up Support for North," *Los Angeles Times*, September 3, 1988, p. 6.

50. See the following discussion of North's relationship with the American Freedom Coalition. North addressed the Southern Baptist Convention's Pastors Conference in 1991 and the Christian Coalition in 1993.

51. For several reports of North's fee, see Thomas M. DeFrank, "Ollie North's Road Show," *Newsweek*, August 1, 1988, p. 24; and Philip Weiss, "Oliver North's Next War," *New York Times Magazine*, July 4, 1993, pp. 12+. On the fund-raiser for a Wisconsin candidate, see Mary Belcher, "Oliver North," *Washington Times*, August 30, 1988, p. E1. On various speaking engagements, see Michele P. Fulcher, "North Calls Communist Threat Real," *Denver Post*, December 18, 1988, p. 1B; Fern Shen, "Ollie North's Roadshow," *Washington Post*, September 28, 1989, p. D1; Lee May, "Conservatives Reaffirm Support of 'Hero' North," *Los Angeles Times*, July 6, 1989, p. I18; and David Johnston, "To His Audiences, North Is Still the Inspiring Freedom Fighter," *New York Times*, June 3, 1989, p. A2.

52. Robert W. Stewart, "Oliver North Takes a Little Friendly Skewering at Roast," *Los Angeles Times*, March 23, 1990, p. E2.

53. "The North Lobby," *National Journal*, March 26, 1988, p. 837.

54. Pamela Stallsmith, "Falwell's North Effort Draws Fire," *Lynchburg (VA) News and Daily Advance*, May 7, 1988, p. A4.

55. A transcription of the television advertisement is available in a People for the American Way internal memo, dated May 19, 1988, "Oliver North Pardon Petition," in files on Jerry Falwell and Oliver North at People for the American Way, Washington, DC.

56. "Religious Right Drums up Support for North," p. 6.

57. Pamphlet from the North Defense Trust, January 1989, from file on Oliver North at the offices of the People for the American Way, Washington, DC.

58. In Joe Pichirallo, "North's Secretive 'Defense Trust,' " *Washington Post*, April 18, 1989, p. A27.

59. Mancur Olson introduced the term *selective incentive*; see his *The Logic of Collective Action*. Olson's work sparked a reassessment of pluralist views of group formation and led to a scholarly controversy about why people join groups. See James Q. Wilson, *Political Organizations* (New York: Basic Books, 1973); Terry M. Moe, *The Organization of Interests* (Chicago: University of Chicago Press, 1980); and David C.

King and Jack L. Walker, "The Provision of Benefits by Interest Groups in the United States," *Journal of Politics* 54 (1992): 394–426. For a good discussion of this debate, see Paul M. Sabatier, "Interest Group Membership and Organization," in Mark P. Petracca, ed., *The Politics of Interests*, pp. 99–129 (Boulder, CO: Westview Press, 1992).

60. The information about the Concerned Women of America and the cost of the Legal Affair Council albums is from Jill Abramson, "Campaign to Pardon North Raises Funds, but Not All for Ollie: Little of What Is Collected by Conservative Groups Trickles to Defense Fund," *Wall Street Journal*, December 1, 1988, p. C19. Information about the money given to North by the Legal Affairs Council is from *Legal Briefs* 2 (Winter 1988–89), a publication of the Legal Affairs Council, from the files of People for the American Way, Washington, DC.

61. These connections proved to be somewhat of a political embarrassment when they become public. On links between the American Freedom Coalition and the Unification Church, see "Freedom Group Denies Moonie Control," *National Journal*, November 19, 1988, p. 2942; Andrew Leigh, "Inside Moon's Washington," *Washington Post*, October 29, 1989, p. B1; and Robert Grant, "The American Freedom Coalition and Rev. Moon," *Washington Post*, October 29, 1989, p. 7. In the last of these articles, Robert Grant, president of the AFC, acknowledged that his organization received more than $5 million from business interests of the Unification Church.

62. Grant, interview.

63. Ibid.

64. Ibid.

65. "Religious Right Drums up Support for North," p. 7.

66. Amy Moritz, "The New Right, It's Time We Led: Conservatism's Parched Grass Roots," *Policy Review* 44 (1988): 23. Moritz is identified as the executive director of the National Center for Public Policy Research.

67. B. Drummond Ayres Jr., "North Pursuing Many Missions with One Goal," *New York Times*, April 21, 1990, p. A6.

68. *Washington Times*, November 30, 1989, and March 28, 1990. Copies from the files on Oliver North, People for the American Way, Washington, DC.

69. It is no small irony that in 1991 General Norman Schwarzkopf, then hero of the day, objected to the Freedom Alliance's use of his name in its mailings. See *USA Today*, December 17, 1991.

70. Figures on North's fund-raising and the quotation from Thomas Mann are from Kent Jenkins Jr., "Fundraising Prowess Makes North a Force, High-Priced Senate Bid May Lie Ahead," *Washington Post*, March 22, 1993, p. A1. See also Kent Jenkins Jr., "North Not Looking Back. Iran Contra Figure Pressing on for Senate," *Washington Post*, September 1, 1993, p. A1.

Chapter 6, Trying to Hear the Echoes

1. James M. Lindsay and Randall B. Ripley, "How Congress Influences Foreign and Defense Policy," in Randall B. Ripley and James M. Lindsay, eds., *Congress*

Resurgent: Foreign and Defense Policy on Capitol Hill, p. 34 (Ann Arbor: University of Michigan Press, 1993).

2. For a discussion of representation, see Hanna Pitkin, *The Concept of Representation* (Berkeley and Los Angeles: University of California Press, 1967). For an example of democratic elitism, see Joseph A. Schumpeter, *Capitalism, Socialism and Democracy*, 3rd ed. (New York: Harper & Row, 1950).

3. John W. Kingdon, *Congressmen's Voting Decisions*, 3rd ed. (Ann Arbor: University of Michigan Press, 1989); and R. Douglas Arnold, *The Logic of Congressional Action* (New Haven, CT: Yale University Press, 1990).

4. David Mayhew, *Congress: The Electoral Connection* (New Haven, CT: Yale University Press, 1974).

5. John W. Kingdon, "Politicians, Self-Interest, and Ideas," in George E. Marcus and Russell L. Hanson, eds., *Reconsidering the Democratic Public*, p. 82 (University Park: Pennsylvania State University Press, 1993).

6. Because voting on legislation requires choosing among dichotomous options, legislators are not always able to select their most preferred policy. Compared with the average legislator, coalition leaders in the legislature have a greater ability to craft policy alternatives. See Arnold, *The Logic of Congressional Action*.

7. For discussions of the impact of public opinion on legislative stages before voting, see L. Martin Overby, "Assessing Constituency Influence: Congressional Voting on the Nuclear Freeze, 1992–93," *Legislative Studies Quarterly* 16 (1991): 297–312; and Peter M. VanDoren, "Can We Learn the Causes of Congressional Decisions from Roll-Call Data?" *Legislative Studies Quarterly* 15 (1990): 311–40.

8. On constituent service, see Morris Fiorina, *Congress: Keystone of the Washington Establishment*, 2nd ed. (New Haven, CT: Yale University Press, 1989); and Bruce Cain, John Ferejohn, and Morris Fiorina, *The Personal Vote: Constituency Service and Electoral Independence* (Cambridge, MA: Harvard University Press, 1987).

9. Heinz Eulau and Paul D. Karps, "The Puzzle of Representation: Specifying Components of Responsiveness," *Legislative Studies Quarterly* 2 (1977): 233–54. See also Mayhew, *Congress: The Electoral Connection*.

10. William T. Bianco, *Trust: Representatives and Constituents* (Ann Arbor: University of Michigan Press, 1994). See also Richard F. Fenno, Jr., *Home Style: House Members in Their Districts* (Boston: Little, Brown, 1978). Work that has built on Fenno's includes that by Glenn R. Parker, *Homeward Bound: Explaining Changes in Congressional Behavior* (Pittsburgh: University of Pittsburgh Press, 1986); and Morris P. Fiorina and David W. Rohde, eds., *Home Style and Washington Work* (Ann Arbor: University of Michigan Press, 1989).

11. Catherine R. Shapiro, David W. Brody, and John Ferejohn, "Linking Constituency Opinion and Senate Voting Scores: A Hybrid Explanation," *Legislative Studies Quarterly* 15 (1990): 599–920; Eileen Burgin, "The Influence of Constituents: Congressional Decision Making on Issues of Foreign and Defense Policy," in Randall B. Ripley and James M. Lindsay, eds., *Congress Resurgent:*

Foreign and Defense Policy on Capitol Hill, pp. 67–88 (Ann Arbor: University of Michigan Press, 1993); Fenno, *Home Style.*

12. Kingdon, *Congressmen's Voting Decisions.*

13. Arnold, *The Logic of Congressional Action,* p. 267.

14. Kingdon, "Politicians, Self-Interest, and Ideas," p. 78. For a discussion of why constituency preferences are hard to discern, see Aage R. Clausen, "The Accuracy of Leader Perceptions of Constituency Views," *Legislative Studies Quarterly* 2 (1977): 361–84.

15. Although it is clear that fewer voters now label themselves Democrats or Republicans, some research suggests that many independents retain their attachment to a political party. See Jay A. DeSart, "Information Processing and Partisan Neutrality: A Reexamination of the Party Decline Thesis," *Journal of Politics* 57 (1995): 776–95; and John E. Stanga and James F. Sheffield, "The Myth of Zero Partisanship: Attitudes Toward American Political Parties, 1964–84," *American Journal of Political Science* 31 (1987): 829–55.

16. Timothy Cook, *Making Laws and Making News: Media Strategies in the House of Representatives* (Washington, DC: Brookings Institution, 1989).

17. On increases in party unity, see Barbara Sinclair, "The Emergence of Strong Leadership in the 1980s House of Representatives," *Journal of Politics* 54 (1992): 657–84; and David W. Rohde, *Parties and Leaders in the Postreform House* (Chicago: University of Chicago Press, 1991). Following the 1994 Republican capture of the House of Representatives, Speaker Newt Gingrich took a number of steps to further Republican unity: in an effort to consolidate power and enforce party discipline, he placed committee and subcommittee chairs under his control. Party unity has also increased in the Senate, although not to the same extent as in the House.

18. Bruce Russett, *Controlling the Sword: The Democratic Governance of National Security* (Cambridge, MA: Harvard University Press, 1990), p. 110.

19. The classic article on representation is by Warren E. Miller and Donald E. Stokes, "Constituency Influence in Congress," *American Political Science Review* 57 (1963): 45–56. Others include VanDoren, "Can We Learn Causes of Congressional Decisions from Roll-Call Data?"; Christopher H. Achen, "Measuring Representation," *American Journal of Political Science* 22 (1978): 475–510; Robert S. Erickson, "Constituency Opinion and Congressional Behavior: A Reexamination of the Miller–Stokes Representation Data," *American Journal of Political Science* 22 (1978): 511–35; Malcolm E. Jewell, "Legislature–Constituency Relations and the Representative Process," *Legislative Studies Quarterly* 8 (1983): 303–37; Benjamin I. Page and Robert Y. Shapiro, "Effects of Public Opinion on Policy," *American Political Science Review* 77 (1983): 175–90; and James A. Stimson, Michael B. Mackuen, and Robert S. Erickson, "Dynamic Representation," *American Political Science Review* 89 (1995): 543–65.

20. James Lindsay, "Parochialism, Policy and Constituency Constraints: Congressional Voting on Strategic Weapons Systems," *American Journal of Political Science* 34 (1990): 936–60, 949.

21. See Burgin, "The Influence of Constituents"; Overby, "Assessing Constituency Influence"; John R. Hibbing, "Washington on 75 Dollars a Day: Members of Congress Voting on Their Own Tax Break," *Legislative Studies Quarterly* 8 (1983): 219–30; and John D. Wilkerson, "Reelection and Representation in Conflict: The Case of Agenda Manipulation," *Legislative Studies Quarterly* 15 (1990): 263–82.

22. For an influential statement of this position, see Gabriel A. Almond, *The American People and Foreign Policy* (New York: Praeger, 1950).

23. Ole R. Holsti, "Public Opinion and Foreign Policy: Challenges to the Almond–Lippmann Consensus, Mershon Series: Research Programs and Debates," *International Studies Quarterly* 36 (1992) 439–66; John H. Aldrich, John L. Sullivan, and Eugene Borgida, "Foreign Affairs and Issue Voting: Do Presidential Candidates 'Waltz Before a Blind Audience?' " *American Political Science Review* 83 (1989): 123–42; Eugene R. Wittkopf, *Faces of Internationalism: Public Opinion and American Foreign Policy* (Durham, NC: Duke University Press, 1990); and Thomas Hartley and Bruce Russett, "Public Opinion and the Common Defense: Who Governs Military Spending in the United States?" *American Political Science Review* 86 (1992): 905–15. On normative issues regarding public control over foreign policy, see Russett, *Controlling the Sword*; and Miroslav Nincic, *Democracy and Foreign Policy: The Fallacy of Political Realism* (New York: Columbia University Press, 1992).

24. Jon Hurwitz and Mark Peffley, "How Are Foreign Policy Attitudes Structured? A Hierarchical Model," *American Political Science Review* 81 (1987): 1099–120.

25. Aldrich, Sullivan, and Borgida, "Foreign Affairs and Issue Voting."

26. Hartley and Russett, "Public Opinion and the Common Defense."

27. Thomas Risse-Kappen, "Public Opinion, Domestic Structure, and Foreign Policy in Liberal Democracies," *World Politics* 43 (1991): 479–512.

28. Russett, *Controlling the Sword*, p. 110.

29. On policy moods and Congress, see Mayhew, *Divided We Govern*; and John W. Kingdon, *Agendas, Alternatives, and Public Policies* (Boston: Little, Brown, 1984). For data on the public's moods and swings, see James A. Stimson, *Public Opinion in America: Moods, Cycles, and Swings* (Boulder, CO: Westview Press, 1991).

30. William M. LeoGrande, "Did the Public Matter? The Impact of Opinion on Congressional Support for Ronald Reagan's Nicaragua Policy," in Sobel, ed., *Public Opinion in U.S. Foreign Policy*, p. 181.

31. Eugene R. Wittkopf and James M. McCormick, "The Domestic Politics of Contra Aid: Public Opinion, Congress, and the President," in Sobel, ed., *Public Opinion in U.S. Foreign Policy*, p. 91.

32. Remarks by Elliott Abrams quoted in Sobel, ed., *Public Opinion in U.S. Foreign Policy*, pp. 106, 114.

33. Remarks by Ronald Hinckley, former director of special studies at the NSC, in Sobel, ed., *Public Opinion in U.S. Foreign Policy*, pp. 160, 159.

34. Richard Sobel, "Epilogue: What Have We Learned About Public Opinion in U.S. Foreign Policy?" in Sobel, ed., *Public Opinion in U.S. Foreign Policy*, p. 276.

35. This view is repeated a number of times in Sobel, ed., *Public Opinion in U.S. Foreign Policy*, and I also heard this idea in the interviews I conducted.

36. LeoGrande and Brenner's study does not find an impact of public opinion per se. Instead they attribute changes in the vote to changes in Reagan's popularity and crucial events, such as Ortega's trip to Moscow in 1985. Although their explanation is plausible, it is important to realize that they do not have opinion data from congressional districts and instead use surrogates such as the district vote for Reagan in 1984. See William M. LeoGrande and Philip Brenner, "The House Divided: Ideological Polarization over Aid to the Nicaraguan 'Contras,' " *Legislative Studies Quarterly* 18 (1993): 105–36.

37. Remarks by Bill Richardson, Democratic representative from New Mexico, in Sobel, ed., *Public Opinion in U.S. Foreign Policy*, pp. 247–49.

38. Cynthia J. Arnson, *Crossroads: Congress, the President, and Central America, 1976–1993*, 2nd ed. (University Park: Pennsylvania State University Press, 1993), p. 21.

39. Remarks by William Schneider quoted in Richard Sobel, ed., *Public Opinion in U.S. Foreign Policy: The Controversy over Contra Aid*, p. 242 (Lanham, MD: Rowman & Littlefield, 1993).

40. LeoGrande, "Did the Public Matter?" p. 186. LeoGrande also argues that some Republicans were afraid that protests like those waged against the Vietnam War might develop. He concludes, "What the public actually thought about Nicaragua had vastly less influence over the shape of U.S. policy than the specter of what fury the public might unleash if the contra aid policy went awry"(p. 187).

41. On the organization of committee staff, see William S. Cohen and George J. Mitchell, *Men of Zeal: A Candid Inside Story of the Iran–Contra Hearings* (New York: Viking, 1988).

42. Some legislators and staff told me that they were not particularly surprised by the contra side of Iran–contra. A few said that the efforts with Iran had not surprised them either.

43. Haynes Johnson, *Sleepwalking Through History: America in the Reagan Years* (New York: Norton, 1991), p. 277.

44. On lies to Congress, see Theodore Draper, *A Very Thin Line: The Iran–Contra Affairs* (New York: Hill & Wang, 1991); Johnson, *Sleepwalking Through History*; Peter Kornbluh and Malcolm Byrne, eds., *The Iran–Contra Scandal: The Declassified History* (New York: New Press, 1993). Only about a month before the first presidential news conference on Iran–contra, Assistant Secretary of State Elliott Abrams was called to testify about the shooting down of Eugene Hasenfus in Nicaragua. Abrams misinformed Congress about the administration's involvement in transferring ammunition and equipment to the contras. On October 7, 1992, Abrams pled guilty to two counts of withholding information from Congress.

45. On Iran–contra and Watergate, see Cohen and Mitchell, *Men of Zeal*; and Michael Schudson, *Watergate in American Memory: How We Remember, Forget, and*

Reconstruct the Past (New York: Basic Books, 1992), ch. 9. When the Senate committee chairman, Inouye, offered Arthur Liman the job of counsel to the Senate committee counsel, he told him that he wanted to resolve the impeachment question quickly. According to Haynes Johnson, Inouye believed that "if the evidence demonstrated that the president should be removed, then he should be removed promptly and American would get a new president. If the evidence didn't warrant his removal, Inouye added, then we should end this investigation, report the facts, and let the country continue with its business" (*Sleepwalking Through History*, p. 331) These sentiments also were expressed in some of the interviews I conducted.

46. Interview with Senator Warren Rudman, Washington, DC, January 4, 1994.

47. Schudson, *Watergate in American Memory*, pp. 167–72.

48. Cohen and Mitchell, *Men of Zeal*, p. 17.

49. A great deal happened in a short amount of time. The news conference announcing the diversion was held on November 25, 1986, and the Tower Commission was appointed on November 26. The House and Senate announced plans to hold an investigation on December 4, and the Select Committees were created on January 6 (Senate) and January 7 (House). The independent counsel was appointed on December 19. The Senate Select Committee on Intelligence began a preliminary investigation on December 1, and they reported their findings on January 29, 1987. The Tower Commission released its report on February 26. See Draper, *A Very Thin Line*; and Cohen and Mitchell, *Men of Zeal*.

50. Rudman, interview: "When they made those charges I thought to myself, "Well, I don't understand. . . . They don't want to investigate? They want the pope to appoint a college of cardinals to investigate? Should we go to Gallup and ask twelve coal miners to investigate? Or should we go to Colgate and get the political science department to investigate? And what kind of foolishness is this? The Constitution says we have to do it."

51. For example, when Arthur Liman was interviewed for the post of Senate counsel, he talked to senators about a number of problems he anticipated. Three of the issues Liman discussed involved public opinion: the popularity of President Reagan, the public's lack of interest, and possible reactions to Liman's being Jewish. The other two main problems Liman mentioned were his lack of Washington experience and the difficulty in determining truth when a subordinate is asked about the activities of a superior. See Johnson, *Sleepwalking Through History*, pp. 329–30.

52. Cohen and Mitchell, *Men of Zeal*, p. 315.

53. Johnson, *Sleepwalking Through History*, p. 328; Cohen and Mitchell, *Men of Zeal*, p. 22.

54. Walsh turned out to be correct that this would cause problems for North's prosecution. "Use immunity" and the need to rely on top-secret information "resulted in hundreds of hours of additional legal work, countless pretrial hearings, and months of delay. In the end, they combined to undermine the ability of the independent counsel to prosecute, independently, the criminality of the Iran–Contra scandal." See Kornbluh and Byrne, The *Iran–Contra Scandal*, p. 332.

55. Ben Bradlee Jr., *Guts and Glory: The Rise and Fall of Oliver North* (New York: Donald I. Fine, 1988), p. 494.

56. Ibid., p. 494.

57. Johnson, *Sleepwalking Through History*, p. 340.

58. Draper, *A Very Thin Line*, p. 39.

59. Cohen and Mitchell, *Men of Zeal*, p. 69.

60. Ibid., p. 74.

61. Johnson, *Sleepwalking Through History*, p. 357.

62. Cohen and Mitchell, *Men of Zeal*, p. 70.

63. Confidential interview with committee staff member.

64. Cohen and Mitchell, *Men of Zeal*, p. 77.

65. Johnson, *Sleepwalking Through History*, p. 358.

66. Cohen and Mitchell, *Men of Zeal*, p. 152.

67. Michael Schudson, "How Culture Works: Perspectives from Media Studies on the Efficacy of Symbols," *Theory and Society* 18 (1989): 153–80.

68. Frank P. Tomasulo, "Colonel North Goes to Washington: Observations on the Intertextual Re-presentation of History," *Journal of Popular Film and Television* 17 (1989): 83, 86.

69. I would argue, however, that no one in the 1980s was as good as drawing on cultural frames and vocabularies as Ronald Reagan. His skill as an actor and his White House Communications Office were focused on planning effective images and presentations. North's oft-noted catch in the throat was not unlike the one used by Reagan to signal sincerity. Reagan himself told David Brinkley in a December 1988 interview, "There have been times in this office when I've wondered how you could do the job if you hadn't been an actor." See Lou Cannon, *President Reagan: The Role of a Lifetime* (New York: Simon & Schuster, 1991), p. 51. On the catch in the throat and the story about choking up on cue when telling an apocryphal World War II story about a plane going down, see Johnson, *Sleepwalking Through History*, p. 60.

70. Interview with L. Britt Snyder, Washington, DC, October 19, 1993.

71. David Thelen, *Becoming Citizens in the Age of Television: How Americans Challenged the Media and Seized Political Initiative During the Iran–Contra Hearings* (Chicago: University of Chicago Press, 1996), p. 19.

72. Rudman, interview.

73. Interview with Representative Henry Hyde, Washington, DC, October 25, 1993.

74. Interview with Don Morrisey, Washington, DC, October 23, 1993.

75. Remarks by these members of Congress and staff are consistent with the findings of a study of congressional mail. According to Hansen and Miller, members of Congress reported that they were most influenced by mail that appeared to be spontaneous and demonstrated strongly held views. Organized mail was effective only if there were many individual letters, the issue was salient or emotional, and the organization provided election support to the legislator. See Orval Hansen

and Ellen Miller, *The Role of Mail in Decision-Making in Congress* (Washington, DC: Center for Responsive Politics, 1987).

76. Thelen, *Becoming Citizens in the Age of Television*, pp. 150–51.

77. Hyde, interview.

78. Interview with Jeffrey H. Smith, Washington, DC, October 25, 1993.

79. Snyder, interview.

80. See Tomasulo, "Colonel North Goes to Washington."

81. Morrisey, interview.

82. Rudman, interview.

83. Smith, interview.

84. "Public Sympathy Proves Effective Shield for North Against Committee Critics," *Congressional Quarterly Weekly Report*, July 18, 1987, pp. 1564–65.

85. Maureen Dowd, "The Tables Turned, Iran Panel Bickers as North Is Praised," *New York Times*, July 11, 1987, p. A1.

86. Stephen Engelberg and David E. Rosenbaum, "What the Iran–Contra Committees Wish They Had Done Differently," *New York Times*, November 20, 1987, p. A1.

87. Cohen and Mitchell, *Men of Zeal*, p. 158. This was obviously somewhat of a sore point for McCollum's supporters. In an interview, Representative McCollum's chief of staff, Don Morrisey, brought up this shift before I asked about it. Morrisey defended McCollum's actions to me, saying that McCollum sometimes approached matters as a lawyer and sometimes as a politician. As a politician (and presumably in July but not in June 1987), McCollum was reacting to the poor "motives" of the Democrats, which had led to the Iran–Contra "show trial."

88. Boren's change of heart was brought up by a number of people in confidential interviews. See also *Congressional Quarterly Weekly Report*, July 18, 1987, p. 1565.

89. Johnson, *Sleepwalking Through History*, p. 358.

90. Interview with Representative Ed Jenkins, Washington, DC, October 20, 1993.

91. Cohen and Mitchell, *Men of Zeal*, p. 172.

92. The diversity in legislators' responses points to a limitation of aggregate studies of relationships between opinion and policy. Not only are underlying political dynamics absent from such research, but the emphasis on correlations also makes invisible very different sorts of legislative reactions.

93. Confidential response by staff member.

94. Interview with Richard Arenberg, Washington, DC, October 19, 1993.

95. Snyder, interview.

96. Arenberg, interview.

97. Johnson, *Sleepwalking Through History*, p. 334.

98. See Dennis Teti, "The Coup That Failed: An Insider's Account of the Iran–Contra Hearings," *Policy Review* 42 (1987): 24–31. Teti was Representative Jim Courter's (Republican, New Jersey) Iran–contra staff member. Not only Republicans criticized bipartisanship. One Democratic staffer remarked that the hearings should

have been more partisan. He maintained that the Senate model of bipartisanship and the attendant pressures to keep the committee together prevented an exhaustive inquiry. "The rules of the Senate encourage consensus. But the goal of an investigation is not consensus but determining the facts." Interview with James J. Schweitzer, Washington, DC, October 25, 1993.

99. Morrisey, interview.

100. As an anonymous reviewer pointed out to me, one irony of Trible's 1988 primary loss is that this election was eventually won by Chuck Robb, who defended his seat against North in 1994. In a sense, North's actions led the Republicans to lose the same Senate seat twice.

101. Jenkins, interview.

102. When asked about pressure from his fellow Republicans, Senator Rudman replied, "Pressure. I laughed at it. Those people weren't interested in finding out the truth. They were interested in protecting the President. I have no interest in protecting Ronald Reagan. . . . I have no interest in protecting anybody. You take an oath of office, you're an American first, you're a Republican second." Rudman, interview.

103. Several years after the congressional report was issued, journalist Seymour Hersh charged that the committee had not pursued some leads that could have led to President Reagan's impeachment, in part because they were "intimidated by the public reaction to the immunized testimony of Marine Lieut. Col. Oliver L. North." See Seymour M. Hersh, "The Iran–Contra Committees: Did They Protect Reagan?" *New York Times Magazine*, April 29, 1990, sec. 6, pp. 47+. Senate Committee Counsel Arthur Liman denied these accusations. See Arthur L. Liman's letter to the editor, *New York Times Magazine*, May 20, 1990, pp. 12+.

104. Cohen and Mitchell, *Men of Zeal*, p. 275.

105. One such disagreement was over how much to discuss State Department public diplomacy efforts and how to characterize them. A draft chapter was excluded from the final report (according to confidential interviews), and instead cursory mention was made in the executive summary. Still, Senators Cohen and Boren objected to these references in their supplementary remarks. See *Report of the Congressional Committees Investigating the Iran–Contra Affair. With Supplemental, Minority, and Additional Views* (Washington, DC: U.S. Government Printing Office, November 1987). For Boren's remarks, see p. 657, and for Cohen's remarks, see p. 674.

106. Confidential response.

107. Rudman, interview.

108. Arenberg, interview.

109. For example, the committee never saw one important source of evidence— the computer messages that North sent and received in the White House. These (PROF notes) were not requested until after the hearings ended, in August 1987. See *Report of the Congressional Committees*, p. 638. Later, Independent Counsel Walsh gained access to them.

110. Smith, interview.

III. Arnson, *Crossroads*, pp. 221, 225–26.

II2. Lawrence E. Walsh, *Final Report of the Independent Counsel for Iran/Contra Matters* (Washington, DC: U.S. Government Printing Office, 1993), p. 32.

II3. Committee structure was important to many of the people I interviewed. Also see Cohen and Mitchell, *Men of Zeal*; Engelberg and Rosenbaum, "What the Iran-Contra Committees Wish They Had Done Differently."

II4. Cohen and Mitchell, *Men of Zeal*, p. 149.

II5. Bradlee, *Guts and Glory*, p. 495.

II6. As one staff member said, "He laid it out, but he didn't lay it out like we thought he was going to. In a way, we sort of never recovered from that." Smith, interview.

II7. Cohen and Mitchell, *Men of Zeal*, pp. 53–54.

II8. Arenberg, interview.

II9. Cohen and Mitchell, *Men of Zeal*, pp. 151, 156–57.

I20. Ibid., p. 163.

Chapter 7, Public Opinion in Political Context

1. For two important efforts to explain how different sorts of policies are associated with particular policy processes, see Theodore J. Lowi, "American Business, Public Policy, Case Studies, and Political Theory," *World Politics* 16 (1964): 677–715; and Michael T. Hayes, "The Semi-Sovereign Pressure Groups: A Critique of Current Theory and an Alternative Typology," *Journal of Politics* 40 (1978): 134–62. Lowi argues that policy processes vary depending on whether a public policy involves distribution, regulation, or redistribution. Each has a "characteristic political structure, political process, elites, and group relations" (pp. 689–90). Hayes contends that the effect of interest groups on Congress depends on more than the type of policy, or what he calls the "supply pattern." Instead, the interest group's actions, or "demand pattern," also has an influence.

2. On business group resources, see Kay Lehman Schlozman, "What Accent the Heavenly Chorus? Political Equality and the American Pressure System," *Journal of Politics* 46 (1984) 1006–32; and Kay Lehman Schlozman and John T. Tierney, *Organized Interests and American Democracy* (New York: Harper & Row, 1986). On the media's coverage of interest groups, see Lucig H. Danielian and Benjamin I. Page, "The Heavenly Chorus: Interest Groups on TV News," *American Journal of Political Science* 38 (1994): 1056–78.

3. Mancur Olson, *The Logic of Collective Action* (New York: Schocken Books, 1979).

4. Herbert McClosky and John Zaller, *The American Ethos: Public Attitudes Toward Capitalism and Democracy* (Cambridge, MA: Harvard University Press, 1984).

5. Charles E. Lindblom, "The Market as Prison," *Journal of Politics* 44 (1982): 324–36.

6. Sidney Verba, Kay Lehman Schlozman, Henry Brady, and Norman H. Nie, "Citizen Activity: Who Participates? What Do They Say?" *American Political Science Review* 87 (1993): 303–18. As Lohmann points out, active citizens influence the information environment confronted by other citizens and legislators. However, although Lohmann believes this influences citizens' decisions about whether to participate, she contends that the resulting "lack of representativeness does not bias political decision making. The political leader discounts the aggregate number of political actions to take into account that some individuals have incentives to manipulate the leader's decision." Susanne Lohmann, "A Signaling Model of Informative and Manipulative Political Action," *American Political Science Review* 87 (1993): 321.

7. On historical patterns in institutional life and the capacity for agents to create change, see Rogers M. Smith, "If Politics Matters: Implications for a 'New Institutionalism,' " *Studies in American Political Development* 6 (1992): 1–36.

8. Symbolic issues are sometimes contrasted with material issues involving self-interest. However, even economic questions that are surely linked to self-interest can take on symbolic dimensions. For example, the ethos of capitalism involves material benefits and also a theory of how the world works, with attendant symbols and personae. In addition, conceptions of self-interest vary and can be associated with a concentration on the self or a concern with the community. See Laura Stoker, "Interests and Ethics in Politics," *American Political Science Review* 86 (1992): 369–80.

9. Murray Edelman, *The Symbolic Uses of Politics* (Urbana: University of Illinois Press, 1985), pp. 6–7.

10. As Popkin points out, symbolic cues can contain substantive information, which can help citizens make reasoned assessments. See Samuel Popkin, *The Reasoning Voter* (Chicago: University of Chicago Press, 1991).

11. Celeste Michelle Condit, *Decoding Abortion Rhetoric* (Urbana: University of Illinois Press, 1990).

12. Kristin Luker, *Abortion and the Politics of Motherhood* (Berkeley and Los Angeles: University of California Press, 1984), p. 35.

13. Faye D. Ginsberg, *Contested Lives: The Abortion Debate in an American Community* (Berkeley and Los Angeles: University of California Press, 1989), p. 7.

14. Condit, *Decoding Abortion Rhetoric*, pp. 80, 93–94. Condit argues that accompanying words interpret the picture for the audience, draw in observers, and establish a connection between the fetus and humanity.

15. Elizabeth Adell Cook, Ted G. Jelen, and Clyde Wilcox, *Between Two Absolutes: Public Opinion and the Politics of Abortion* (Boulder, CO: Westview Press, 1992), p. 37.

16. For polling data, see Cook, Jelen, and Wilcox, *Between Two Absolutes*; Barbara Hinkson Craig and David M. O'Brien, *Abortion and American Politics* (Chatham, NJ: Chatham House, 1993); and Roger Rosenblatt, *Life Itself: Abortion in the Public Mind* (New York: Random House, 1992).

17. E. J. Dionne Jr., *Why Americans Hate Politics* (New York: Simon & Schuster, 1991), p. 341 (italics in original).

18. Amy Fried, "Abortion Politics as Symbolic Politics: An Investigation into Belief Systems," *Social Science Quarterly* 69 (1988): 137–54.

19. On question order, see Howard Schuman, Stanley Presser, and Jacob Ludwig, "Context Effects on Survey Responses to Questions About Abortion," *Public Opinion Quarterly* 45 (1991): 216–23.

20. Rosenblatt, *Life Itself,* pp. 185–6. For a case of selective analysis by prolife forces, see Rosenblatt's discussion of how Americans United for Life presented the results of a 1991 Gallup poll (pp. 183–84).

21. Dionne, *Why Americans Hate Politics*, p. 342.

22. The quotation is from John R. Cranford, "Cap for Credit Card Rates Catches Fire," *Congressional Quarterly*, November 16, 1991, p. 3364. For good overviews of the issue, see Kenneth H. Bacon and David Wessel, "Credit-Card Cap Furor Will Have Big Effect, Economic and Political," *Wall Street Journal*, November 18, 1992, pp. A1+; and David E. Rosenbaum, "High Credit Card Rates: A Luxurious Necessity?" *New York Times*, November 24, 1991, sec. 4, p. 2. According to the *Wall Street Journal* article, the line was added by Bush and had not been part of the draft speech or approved by his economic advisers.

23. On Senator D'Amato's political chances and the credit card cap, see Lindsey Gruson, "On Credit Cards, D'Amato Finds Victory and Defeat," *New York Times*, November 19, 1991, p. B7.

24. Editorial, "The Senate's Credit Card Blunder," *New York Times*, November 20, 1991, p. A26.

25. Gruson, "On Credit Cards, D'Amato Finds Victory and Defeat."

26. Cranford, "Cap for Credit Card Rates Catches Fire."

27. Kenneth H. Bacon, "House Democrats May Eschew a Cap, Give Card-Card Issuers Grace Period," *Wall Street Journal*, November 18, 1991, p. A10.

28. Cranford, "Cap for Credit Card Rates Catches Fire."

29. Bacon, "House Democrats May Eschew a Cap."

30. Kenneth H. Bacon, "House Leader Stalls Plan to Cap Credit-Card Rates," *Wall Street Journal*, November 19, 1991, A3+.

31. Peter H. Stone, "Green, Green Grass," *National Journal*, March 27, 1993, p. 754.

32. Interview with Jack Bonner, president, Bonner & Associates, Washington, DC, September 8, 1993.

33. For discussions of grassroots lobbying firms, see Stephen Engelberg, "A New Breed of Hired Hands Cultivates Grass-Roots Anger," *New York Times*, March 17, 1993, p. A1; Robert E. Norton, "Can Business Win in Washington?" *Fortune*, December 3, 1990, pp. 75–84; and Christopher Drew and Michael Tackett, "More and More, Lobbyists Call Shots in D.C.," *Chicago Tribune*, December 6, 1992, p. 1.

34. Stone, "Green, Green Grass," p. 756.

35. Letter from Donald C. Ogilvie, executive vice president, American Bankers Association, to Jack Bonner, president, Bonner & Associates, December 16, 1991; letter from Bonner & Associates publicity materials.

36. Jerry Knight, "A Night to Play 'Let's Make a Deal,' " *Washington Post*, November 28, 1991, pp. A1+.

37. For a discussion of how the credit card interest rate cap was related to Bush's problems in presenting himself as a leader on economic issues, see James Risen and Karen Tumulty, "Credit Card Cap Uproar Accents Bush Dilemma," *Los Angeles Times*, November 19, 1991, pp. A1+.

38. For good overviews of the politics and content of the 1990 Clean Air Act amendments, see Gary C. Bryner, *Blue Skies, Green Politics: The Clean Air Act of 1990* (Washington, DC: Congressional Quarterly Press, 1993), and "Clean Air Act Rewritten, Tightened," in *1990 Congressional Quarterly Almanac* (Washington, DC: Congressional Quarterly, 1990), pp. 229–79.

39. George Hagar, "The 'White House Effect' Opens a Long-Locked Political Door," *Congressional Quarterly Weekly Report*, January 20, 1990, p. 139.

40. These data are from the microfiche collection issued by Opinion Research Service, Tallahassee, Florida.

41. Bryner, *Blue Skies, Green Politics*, p. 97.

42. Margaret E. Kriz, "Turbulence Ahead for Clean Air Act?" *National Journal*, January 27, 1990, p. 223.

43. For a list of the groups in the National Clean Air Coalition, see Bryner, *Blue Skies, Green Politics*, p. 89. The coalition did not include the full range of environmental organizations. On splits among environmentalists regarding clean air legislation, see Margaret E. Kriz, "Shades of Green," *National Journal*, July 28, 1990, pp. 1826–31. For a good overview of the development of and diversity within the American environmental movement, see Philip Shabecoff, *A Fierce Green Fire: The American Environmental Movement* (New York: Hill & Wang, 1993).

44. Margaret E. Kriz, "Industry's Voice in Clean Air Debate," *National Journal*, May 19, 1990, p. 1238.

45. For a summary of moves in Congress, see "Fuel Efficiency Effort Defeated in Senate," in *Congressional Quarterly Almanac 1990*, pp. 279–81.

46. Polls were conducted in 1989 and 1990 by Republican pollster Vincent Breglio and Democratic pollster Celinda Lake for the Union of Concerned Scientists. The results are detailed in the microfiche collection issued by Opinion Research Service, Tallahassee, Florida.

47. Alyson Pytte, "Japanese Drive a Hard Bargain on Emissions Standards," *Congressional Quarterly Weekly Report*, July 20, 1990, p. 165.

48. Robert E. Norton, "Can Business Win in Washington?" *Fortune*, December 3, 1990, pp. 75+.

49. William Greider, *Who Will Tell the People?* (New York: Simon & Schuster, 1992), p. 37.

50. Ibid., p. 38.

51. George Hagar, "Clean Air Deal Survives First Senate Assaults," *Congressional Quarterly Weekly Report*, March 10, 1990, pp. 738–39.

52. For a classic statement, see E. E. Schattschneider, *Party Government* (New York: Farrar and Rinehart, 1942).

53. Susan Herbst, *Numbered Voices: How Opinion Polling Has Shaped American Politics* (Chicago: University of Chicago Press, 1993). Starting in the 1980s, the national political parties worked to reassert themselves, providing funding and support services to candidates and trying to organize policy fights in Congress. For these and other reasons, in more and more cases, members of Congress voted with members of their political parties. See David W. Rohde, *Parties and Leaders in the Postreform House* (Chicago: University of Chicago Press, 1991; and Barbara Sinclair, "The Emergence of Strong Leadership in the 1980s House of Representatives," *Journal of Politics* 54 (1992): 657–84.

54. Greider, *Who Will Tell the People?* p. 38.

55. Walter Dean Burnham, "The Turnout Problem," in A. James Reichley, ed., *Elections American Style*, pp. 97–133 (Washington, DC: Brookings Institution, 1987).

56. Robin Toner, "Wars Wound Candidates and the Process," *New York Times*, March 19, 1990, pp. A1+, B6.

57. In fact, polls are more useful sources of information during campaigns, since it is usually only then that legislators have information about their constituents' views on a range of topics.

58. Both Herbst and Ginsberg argue that polling has rationalized the expression of public opinion. See Herbst, *Numbered Voices*; and Benjamin Ginsberg, *The Captive Public: How Mass Opinion Promotes State Power* (New York: Basic Books, 1986).

59. Dionne, *Why Americans Hate Politics*.

60. See Sidney Verba, Kay Lehman Schlozman, and Henry Brady, *Voice and Equality: Civic Voluntarism in American Politics* (Cambridge, MA: Harvard University Press, 1995).

61. Steven J. Rosenstone and John Mark Hansen, *Mobilization, Participation, and Democracy in America* (New York: Macmillan, 1993).

62. E. E. Schattschneider, *The Semi-Sovereign People* (New York: Holt, Rinehart and Winston, 1960).

63. Without taking a position on whether citizens are rational, my conclusion is consistent with Page and Shapiro's argument that there is often reasonable opinion change on the collective level. They believe that citizens generally respond to events in sensible ways, although their manipulation by elites is a real problem, especially in security and military matters. See Benjamin I. Page and Robert Y. Shapiro, *The Rational Public: Fifty Years of Trends in Americans' Policy Preferences* (Chicago: University of Chicago Press, 1992).

64. Page and Shapiro report that interest groups' messages delivered by the news media have a slightly negative impact on public opinion. Nonetheless, they argue that "it would be a mistake to conclude from this, however, that organized groups are not major factors affecting opinion in the long run. The messages of protests

and demonstrations may sink in over time. Our findings are also quite consistent with the idea that organized groups—especially those with a lot of talent and money, like business corporations—are able to encourage and publicize the work of chosen experts and quite possibly influence news commentators as well, which in turn affect the opinions of the general public. By these indirect methods, and by other means including institutional advertising and influence upon school textbooks and curricula, interest groups may have an extremely important impact on public opinion" (p. 353).

65. Mark E. Warren, "Deliberative Democracy and Authority," *American Political Science Review* 90 (1996): 56.

66. Diana C. Mutz, "The Political Effects of Perceptions of Mass Opinion," in Michael X. Delli Carpini, Leonie Huddy, and Robert Y. Shapiro, eds., *Research in Micropolitics: New Directions in Political Psychology*, vol. 4, pp. 143–67 (Greenwich, CT: JAI Press, 1994).

67. Michael Oreskes, "American Politics Loses Way as Polls Displace Leadership," *New York Times*, March 18, 1990, p. A1+.

68. Ann Reilly Dowd, "How to Get Things Done in Washington," *Fortune*, August 9, 1993, pp. 60–62.

69. Kathleen Hall Jamieson, "When Harry Met Louise," *Washington Post National Weekly Edition*, August 22–29, 1994, p. 29.

70. Republican experiences in 1995 and 1996 show that the politics of public opinion is an assumed element of contemporary political struggle, which can cut against both political parties. House Speaker Newt Gingrich and his allies tried to take potential public opinion into account when drawing up their budget. Republican consultants conducted polls and focus groups and, on this basis, determined that 1995 Republican Medicare proposals should be framed as efforts to preserve and protect the program. Even so, Democrats and labor unions effectively countered this with other framings, which were frequently incorporated into public opinion polls, news coverage, and statements by public figures. Partisans on both sides often cited what "the American people" wanted in pressing their positions. See Haynes Johnson and David S. Broder, *The System: The American Way of Politics at the Breaking Point* (Boston: Little, Brown, 1996); and David Maraniss and Michael Weisskopf, *Tell Newt to Shut Up!: Prizewinning* Washington Post *Journalists Reveal How Reality Gagged the Gingrich Revolution* (New York: Touchstone, 1996).

Bibliography

Abramson, Jeffrey B., F. Christopher Atherton, and Gary R. Orren. *The Electronic Commonwealth: The Impact of New Media Technologies on Democratic Politics.* New York: Basic Books, 1988.

Achen, Christopher H. "Measuring Representation." *American Journal of Political Science* 22 (1978): 475–510.

Ackerman, Bruce. "Why Dialogue?" *Journal of Philosophy* 86 (1989): 5–22.

Adorno, Theodor W. *The Authoritarian Personality.* New York: Harper, 1950.

Aldrich, John H., John L. Sullivan, and Eugene Borgida. "Foreign Affairs and Issue Voting: Do Presidential Candidates 'Waltz Before a Blind Audience?'" *American Political Science Review* 83 (1989): 123–42.

Allen, Barbara. "The Spiral of Silence & Institutional Design: Tocqueville's Analysis of Public Opinion & Democracy." *Polity* 24 (1991): 243–67.

Almond, Gabriel, and Sidney Verba. *The Civic Culture.* Princeton, NJ: Princeton University Press, 1963.

Alterman, Eric. *Sound and Fury: The Washington Punditocracy and the Collapse of American Politics.* New York: HarperCollins, 1992.

Anderson, Paul A. "The Relevance of Social Cognition for the Study of Elites in Political Institutions, or Why It Isn't Enough to Understand What Goes on in Their Heads." In Richard R. Lau and David O. Sears, eds., *Political Cognition,* pp. 341–46. Hillsdale, NJ: Erlbaum, 1986.

Ansolabehere, Stephen, Roy Behr, and Shanto Iyengar. "Mass Media and Elections." *American Politics Quarterly* 19 (1991): 109–39.

Apple, R. W. Jr. "Challenges from a Headstrong Public." *New York Times*, January 29, 1993, p. A1.

Arendt, Hannah. *The Human Condition.* Chicago: University of Chicago Press, 1958.

Armstrong, Scott. "Iran-Contra: Was the Press Any Match for All the President's Men?" *Columbia Journalism Review*, May–June 1990, pp. 27–35.

Arnold, R. Douglas. *The Logic of Congressional Action.* New Haven, CT: Yale University Press, 1990.

Arnson, Cynthia J. *Crossroads: Congress, the President, and Central America, 1976–1993.* 2nd ed. University Park: Pennsylvania State University Press, 1993.

Arnson, Cynthia J., and Philip Brenner. "The Limits of Lobbying: Interest Groups, Congress, and Aid to the Contras." in Richard Sobel, ed., *Public Opinion in U.S. Foreign Policy: The Controversy over Contra Aid,* pp. 191–219. Lanham, MD: Rowman & Littlefield, 1993.

Austen-Smith, David. "Information and Influence: Lobbying for Agendas and Votes." *American Journal of Political Science* 37 (1993): 799–833.

Bartels, Larry M. "Constituency Opinion and Congressional Policy Making: The Reagan Defense Buildup." *American Political Science Review* 85 (1991): 457–74.

Bellah, Robert, Richard Madsen, William W. Sullivan, Ann Swidler, and Steven Tipton. *Habits of the Heart: Individualism and Commitment in American Life.* New York: Harper & Row, 1985.

Benhabib, Seyla. "Models of Public Space: Hannah Arendt, the Liberal Tradition, and Jürgen Habermas." In Craig Calhoun, ed., *Habermas and the Public Sphere,* pp. 73–98. Cambridge, MA: MIT Press, 1990.

Benhabib, Seyla, and Fred Dallmayr, eds. *The Communicative Ethics Controversy.* Cambridge, MA: MIT Press, 1990.

Beniger, James R. "The Popular Symbolic Repertoire and Mass Communication." *Public Opinion Quarterly* 47 (1983): 479–84.

Bennett, W. Lance. "Marginalizing the Majority: Conditioning Public Opinion to Accept Managerial Democracy." In Michael Margolis and Gary A. Mauser, eds., *Manipulating Public Opinion: Essays on Public Opinion as a Dependent Variable,* pp. 231–61. Pacific Grove, CA: Brooks/Cole.

Bennett, W. Lance. *News: The Politics of Illusion.* New York: Longman, 1983.

Bennett, W. Lance. "Toward a Theory of Press–State Relations in the United States." *Journal of Communication* 40 (1990): 103–25.

Bennett, W. Lance, and Murray Edelman. "Toward a New Political Narrative." *Journal of Communication* 35 (1985): 156–71.

Bianco, William T. *Trust: Representatives and Constituents.* Ann Arbor: University of Michigan Press, 1994.

Blumer, Herbert. "Public Opinion and Public Opinion Polling." *American Sociological Review* 13 (1948): 542–49.

Bodnar, John E. *Remaking America: Public Memory, Commemoration, and Patriotism in the Twentieth Century*. Princeton, NJ: Princeton University Press, 1992.

Bogart, Leo. "Public Opinion and Collective Behavior." *Public Opinion Quarterly* 47 (1983): 484–89.

Bogen, David, and Michael Lynch. *The Spectacle of History: Speech, Text, and Memory at the Iran–Contra Hearings*. Durham, NC: Duke University Press, 1996.

Bonafede, Dom. "Scandal Time." *National Journal*, January 24, 1987, pp. 199–207.

Boorstin, Daniel J. *The Image: A Guide to Pseudo-Events in America*. New York: Atheneum, 1987.

Bowen, Gordon L. "Presidential Action and Public Opinion About U.S. Nicaraguan Policy: Limits to the 'Rally 'Round the Flag' Syndrome." *PS* 22 (1989): 793–800.

Brace, Paul, and Barbara Hinckely. *Follow the Leader: Opinion Polls and the Modern Presidents*. New York: Basic Books, 1992.

Bradlee, Benjamin Jr. *Guts and Glory: The Rise and Fall of Oliver North*. New York: Donald I. Fine, 1988.

Broder, David S. *Behind the Front Page*. New York: Simon & Schuster, 1987.

Brody, Richard A. "Candidate Evaluations and the Vote: Some Considerations Affecting the Application of Cognitive Psychology to Voting Behavior." In Richard R. Lau and David O. Sears, eds., *Political Cognition*, pp. 297–30. Hillsdale, NJ: Erlbaum, 1986.

Brown, Steven. *Political Subjectivity*. New Haven, CT: Yale University Press, 1980.

Browning, Graeme. "Hot-Wiring Washington." *National Journal* 25 (1993): 1624–29.

Bryan, Frank, and John McClaughry. *The Vermont Papers: Recreating Democracy on a Human Scale*. Chelsea, VT: Chelsea Green, 1989.

Burger, Thomas. *Max Weber's Theory of Concept Formation: History, Laws, and Ideal Types*. Durham, NC: Duke University Press, 1976.

Burgin, Eileen. "The Influence of Constituents: Congressional Decision Making on Issues of Foreign and Defense Policy." In Randall B. Ripley and James M. Lindsay, eds., *Congress Resurgent: Foreign and Defense Policy on Capitol Hill*, pp. 67–88. Ann Arbor: University of Michigan Press, 1993.

Cain, Bruce, John Ferejohn, and Morris Fiorina. *The Personal Vote: Constituency Service and Electoral Independence*. Cambridge, MA: Harvard University Press, 1987.

Calhoun, Craig, ed. *Habermas and the Public Sphere*. Cambridge, MA: MIT Press, 1992.

Campbell, Angus, Philip E. Converse, Warren E. Miller, and Donald E. Stokes. *The American Voter*. New York: Wiley, 1960.

Campbell, Joseph. *The Hero with a Thousand Faces*. Princeton, NJ: Princeton University Press, 1949.

Cannon, Lou. *President Reagan: The Role of a Lifetime*. New York: Simon & Schuster, 1991.

Canon, David T., and David J. Sousa. "Party System Change and Political Career Structures in the U.S. Congress." *Legislative Studies Quarterly* 17 (1992): 347–63.

Cantril, Albert H. *The Opinion Connection: Polling, Politics, and the Press.* Washington, DC: Congressional Quarterly Press, 1991.

Carmines, Edward G., and James H. Kuklinski. "Incentives, Opportunities, and the Logic of Public Opinion in American Political Representation." In John A. Ferejohn and James H. Kuklinski, eds., *Information and Democratic Processes,* pp. 240–68. Urbana: University of Illinois Press, 1990.

Ceci, Stephen J., and Edward L. Kahn. "Jumping on the Bandwagon with the Underdog: The Impact of Attitude Polls on Polling Behavior." *Public Opinion Quarterly* 46 (1982): 228–42.

Chambers, Simone. *Reasonable Democracy: Jürgen Habermas and the Politics of Discourse.* Ithaca, NY: Cornell University Press, 1996.

Chomsky, Noam. *Necessary Illusions: Thought Control in Democratic Societies.* Boston: South End Press, 1989.

Clausen, Aage R. "The Accuracy of Leader Perceptions of Constituency Views." *Legislative Studies Quarterly* 2 (1977): 361–84.

Cohen, William S., and George J. Mitchell. *Men of Zeal: A Candid Inside Story of the Iran–Contra Hearings.* New York: Viking, 1988.

Condit, Celeste Michelle. *Decoding Abortion Rhetoric.* Urbana: University of Illinois Press, 1990.

Connolly, William. *The Terms of Political Discourse.* Princeton, NJ: Princeton University Press, 1974.

Conover, Pamela Johnston, and Stanley Feldman. "How People Organize the Political World: A Schematic Model." *American Journal of Political Science* 28 (1984): 95–126.

Conover, Pamela Johnston, and Stanley Feldman. "The Role of Inference in the Perception of Political Candidates." In Richard R. Lau and David O. Sears, eds., *Political Cognition,* pp. 127–58. Hillsdale, NJ: Erlbaum, 1986.

Conover, Pamela Johnston, and Donald Searing. "Democratic Discussion in the Liberal State." Paper presented at the Midwest Political Science Association Annual Meeting, Chicago, 1992.

Converse, Philip E. "The Nature of Belief Systems in Mass Publics." In David E. Apter, ed., *Ideology and Discontent,* pp. 206–61. New York: Free Press, 1964.

Cook, Elizabeth Adell, Ted G. Jelen, and Clyde Wilcox. *Between Two Absolutes: Public Opinion and the Politics of Abortion.* Boulder, CO: Westview Press, 1992.

Cook, Fay Lomax, Tom R. Tyler, Edward G. Goetz, Margaret T. Gordon, David Protess, Donna R. Leff, and Harvey L. Molotch. "Media and Agenda Setting: Effects on the Public, Interest Group Leaders, Policy Makers, and Policy." *Public Opinion Quarterly* 47 (1983): 16–35.

Cook, Timothy. *Making Laws and Making News: Media Strategies in the House of Representatives.* Washington, DC: Brookings Institution, 1989.

Couto, Richad A. "Narrative, Free Space, and Political Leadership in Social Movements." *Journal of Politics* 55 (1993): 57–79.

Craig, Barbara Hinkson, and David M. O'Brien. *Abortion and American Politics.* Chatham, NJ: Chatham House, 1993.

Cranford, John R. "Cap for Credit Card Rates Catches Fire." *Congressional Quarterly*, November 1991, pp. 3364.

Crouse, Timothy. *The Boys on the Bus.* New York: Random House, 1973.

Danielian, Lucig H., and Benjamin I. Page. "The Heavenly Chorus: Interest Groups on TV News." *American Journal of Political Science* 38 (1994): 1056–78.

Delli Carpini, Michael. "Scooping the Voters? The Consequences of the Networks' Early Call of the 1980 Presidential Race." *Journal of Politics* 46 (1984): 866–85.

Denton, Robert E., ed. *The Media and the Persian Gulf War.* Westport, CT: Praeger, 1993.

DeSart, Jay A. "Information Processing and Partisan Neutrality: A Reexamination of the Party Decline Thesis." *Journal of Politics* 57 (1995): 776–95.

Dexter, Lewis Anthony. "What Do Congressmen Hear?" In Robert L. Peabody ed., *New Perspectives on the House of Representatives*, pp. 3–22. Baltimore: Johns Hopkins University Press, 1992.

Dionne, E. J. Jr. *Why Americans Hate Politics.* New York: Simon & Schuster, 1991.

Dobkin, Bethami A. *Tales of Terror: Television News and the Construction of the Terrorist Threat.* New York: Praeger, 1992.

Donsbach, Wolfgang. "The Challenge of the Spiral-of-Silence Theory: Theoretical Implications and Empirical Evidences." *Communicare* 8 (1989): 5–16.

Draper, Theodore. *A Very Thin Line: The Iran–Contra Affairs.* New York: Hill & Wang, 1991.

Dryzek, John. *Discursive Democracy: Politics, Policy, and Political Science.* Cambridge: Cambridge University Press, 1990.

Dunn, John. *Rethinking Modern Political Theory.* Cambridge: Cambridge University Press, 1985.

Edelman, Murray. *Constructing the Political Spectacle.* Chicago: University of Chicago Press, 1988.

Edelman, Murray. *Politics as Symbolic Action.* New York: Academic Press, 1971.

Edelman, Murray. *The Symbolic Uses of Politics.* Urbana: University of Illinois Press, 1964.

Eliasoph, Nina. "Political Culture and the Presentation of a Political Self." *Theory and Society* 19 (1990): 465–94.

Engelberg, Stephen. "A New Breed of Hired Hands Cultivates Grass-Roots Anger." *New York Times*, March 17, 1993, p. A1.

Engelberg, Stephen, and David E. Rosenbaum. "What the Iran–Contra Committees Wish They Had Done Differently." *New York Times*, November 20, 1987, p. A1.

Entman, Robert M. *Democracy Without Citizens: Media and the Decay of American Politics.* New York: Oxford University Press, 1989.

Erickson, Kai. "Sociology and Contemporary Events." In Walter W. Powell and Richard Robbins, eds., *Conflict and Consensus: A Festschrift in Honor of Lewis A. Coser*, pp. 303–10. New York: Free Press, 1984.

Erickson, Robert S. "Constituency Opinion and Congressional Behavior: A Reexamination of the Miller–Stokes Representation Data." *American Journal of Political Science* 22 (1978): 511–35.

Erickson, Robert S., Gerald C. Wright, and John P. McIver. *Statehouse Democracy: Public Opinion and Policy in the American States.* Cambridge: Cambridge University Press, 1993.

Eulau, Heinz, and Paul D. Karps. "The Puzzle of Representation: Specifying Components of Responsiveness." *Legislative Studies Quarterly* 2 (1977): 233–54.

Evans, Sara, and Harry Boyte. *Free Spaces.* New York: Harper & Row, 1986.

Farr, James. "Understanding Conceptual Change Politically." In Terence Ball, James Farr, and Russell Hanson, eds., *Political Innovation and Conceptual Change*, pp. 24–49. Cambridge, Cambridge University Press, 1988.

Fay, Brian. *Social Theory and Political Practice.* London: Allen & Unwin, 1975.

Feagin, Joe R., Anthony M. Orum, and Gideon Sjoberg, eds. *A Case for the Case Study.* Chapel Hill: University of North Carolina Press, 1991.

Feldman, Stanley. "Answering Survey Questions: The Measurement and Meaning of Public Opinion." In Milton Lodge and Kathleen M. McGraw, eds., *Political Judgment: Structure and Process*, pp. 249—70. Ann Arbor: University of Michigan Press, 1995.

Fenno, Richard F. Jr. *Home Style: House Members in Their Districts.* Boston: Little, Brown, 1978.

Ferejohn, John A., and James H. Kuklinski, eds. *Information and Democratic Processes.* Urbana: University of Illinois Press, 1990.

Ferguson, Thomas, and Joel Rogers. *Right Turn.* New York: Hill & Wang, 1984.

Fields, James M., and Howard Schuman. "Public Beliefs About the Beliefs of the Public." *Public Opinion Quarterly* 40 (1976): 427–48.

Fiorina, Morris P. *Congress: Keystone of the Washington Establishment.* 2nd ed. New Haven, CT: Yale University Press, 1989.

Fiorina, Morris P., and David W. Rohde, eds. *Home Style and Washington Work.* Ann Arbor: University of Michigan Press, 1989.

Fishkin, James S. *Democracy and Deliberation: New Directions for Democratic Reform.* New Haven, CT: Yale University Press, 1991.

Fishkin, James S. *The Dialogue of Justice: Toward a Self-Reflective Society.* New Haven, CT: Yale University Press, 1992.

Fiske, Susan T., and Shelley E. Taylor. *Social Cognition.* Reading, MA: Addison-Wesley, 1984.

Forester, John. "Questioning and Organizing Attention: Toward a Critical Theory of Planning and Administrative Practice." *Administration and Society* 13 (1981): 161–205.

Fraser, Nancy. "What's Critical About Critical Theory? The Case of Habermas and Gender." In Seyla Benhabib and Drucilla Cornell, eds., *Feminism as Critique: On the Politics of Gender*, pp. 31–56. Minneapolis: University of Minnesota Press, 1987.

Fried, Amy. "Abortion Politics as Symbolic Politics: An Investigation into Belief Systems." *Social Science Quarterly* 69 (1988): 137–54.

Fried, Amy. "Is Political Action Heroic? Heroism and American Political Culture." *American Politics Quarterly* 21 (1993): 490–517.

Gamson, William A. *Talking Politics*. Cambridge: Cambridge University Press, 1992.

Gans, Herbert J. *Deciding What's News*. New York: Pantheon, 1979.

Geertz, Clifford. *The Interpretation of Cultures*. New York: Basic Books, 1973.

George, Larry N. "Tocqueville's Caveat: Centralized Executive Foreign Policy and American Democracy." *Polity* 22 (1990): 419–41.

Gibson, James. *Warrior Dreams: Paramilitary Culture in Post-Vietnam America*. New York: Hill & Wang, 1994.

Gillis, John J. *Commemorations: The Politics of National Identity*. Princeton, NJ: Princeton University Press, 1994.

Ginsberg, Benjamin. *The Captive Public: How Mass Opinion Promotes State Power*. New York: Basic Books, 1986.

Ginsberg, Faye D. *Contested Lives: The Abortion Debate in an American Community*. Berkeley and Los Angeles: University of California Press, 1989.

Glynn, Carroll, and Jack M. McLeod. "Implications of the Spiral of Silence Theory for Communication and Public Opinion Research." In Keith R. Sanders, Lynda Lee Kaid, and Dan Nimmo, eds., *Political Communication Yearbook, 1984*, pp. 43–65. Carbondale: Southern Illinois University Press, 1985.

Glynn, Carroll, and Ronald E. Ostman. "Public Opinion About Public Opinion." *Journalism Quarterly* 65 (1988): 299–306.

Goldfarb, Jeffrey C. *The Cynical Society: The Culture of Politics and the Politics of Culture in American Life*. Chicago: University of Chicago Press, 1991.

Gonzalez, Hernando. "Mass Media and the Spiral of Silence: The Philippines from Marcos to Aquino." *Journal of Communication* 38 (1988): 33–48.

Graber, Doris A. "Seeing Is Remembering: How Visuals Contribute to Learning from Television News." *Journal of Communication* 40 (1990): 134–55.

Greider, William. *Who Will Tell The People?* New York: Simon & Schuster, 1992.

Griffin, Michael. "Looking at TV News: Strategies for Research." *Communication* 13 (1992): 121–41.

Gunther, Albert C. "Biased Press or Biased Public? Attitudes Toward Media Coverage of Social Groups." *Public Opinion Quarterly* 56 (1992): 147–67.

Habermas, Jürgen. "The Public Sphere." *New German Critique* 3 (1974): 49–55.

Habermas, Jürgen. *The Structural Transformation of the Public Sphere*. Cambridge, MA: MIT Press, 1989.

Habermas, Jürgen. *The Theory of Communicative Action*. Boston: Beacon Press, 1984.

Habermas, Jürgen. *Toward a Rational Society; Student Protest, Science, and Politics*. Boston: Beacon Press, 1970.

Hansen, Orval, and Ellen Miller. *The Role of Mail in Decision-Making in Congress*. Washington, DC: Center for Responsive Politics, 1987.

Hartley, Thomas, and Bruce Russett. "Public Opinion and the Common Defense: Who Governs Military Spending in the United States?" *American Political Science Review* 86 (1992): 905–15.

Hastie, Reid. "A Primer of Information-Processing Theory for the Political Scientist." In Richard R. Lau and David O. Sears, eds., *Political Cognition*, pp. 11–30. Hillsdale, NJ: Erlbaum, 1986.

Hayes, Michael T. "Interest Groups: Pluralism or Mass Society?" In Allan J. Cigler and Burdett A. Loomis, eds., *Interest Group Politics*. 1st ed., pp. 110–25. Washington, DC: Congressional Quarterly Press, 1983.

Hayes, Michael T. "The Semi-Sovereign Pressure Groups: A Critique of Current Theory and an Alternative Typology." *Journal of Politics* 40 (1978): 134–62.

Held, David. *Introduction to Critical Theory*. Berkeley and Los Angeles: University of California Press, 1980.

Herbst, Susan. *Numbered Voices: How Opinion Polling Has Shaped American Politics*. Chicago: University of Chicago Press, 1993.

Herbst, Susan. *Politics at the Margin: Historical Studies of Public Expression Outside the Mainstream*. Cambridge: Cambridge University Press, 1994.

Heritage, John C., Steven Clayman, and Don H. Zimmerman. "Discourse and Message Analysis: The Micro-Structure of Mass Media Messages." In Robert P. Hawkins, John M. Wiemann, and Suzanne Pingree, eds., *Advancing Communication Science*, pp. 77–109. Newbury Park, CA: Sage, 1988.

Herrera, Cheryl Lyn, Richard Herrera, and Eric R. A. N. Smith. "Public Opinion and Congressional Representation." *Public Opinion Quarterly* 56 (1992): 185–205.

Hershey, Marjorie Randon. "The Constructed Explanation: Interpreting Election Results in the 1984 Presidential Race." *Journal of Politics* 54 (1992): 943–76.

Hershey, Marjorie Randon. *Running for Office: The Political Education of Campaigners*. Chatham, NJ: Chatham House, 1984.

Hertsgaard, Mark. *On Bended Knee: The Press and the Reagan Presidency*. New York: Farrar, Straus & Giroux, 1988.

Hibbing, John R. "Washington on 75 Dollars a Day: Members of Congress Voting on Their Own Tax Break." *Legislative Studies Quarterly* 8 (1983): 219–30.

Hirschman, Albert O. *Exit, Voice, and Loyalty*. Cambridge, MA: Harvard University Press, 1979.

Hochschild, Jennifer L. *What's Fair? American Beliefs About Redistributive Justice*. Cambridge, MA: Harvard University Press, 1981.

Hohendahl, Peter Uwe. "Critical Theory, Public Sphere and Culture: Jürgen Habermas and His Critics." *New German Critique* 16 (1979): 89–118.

Holsti, Ole R. "Public Opinion and Foreign Policy: Challenges to the Almond–Lippmann Consensus, Mershon Series: Research Programs and Debates." *International Studies Quarterly* 36 (1992): 439–66.

Horkheimer, Max, and Theodor W. Adorno. *Dialectic of Enlightenment*. Trans. John Cummings. New York: Herder and Herder, 1972.

Huckfeldt, Robert, Eric Plutzer, and John Sprague. "Alternative Contexts of Political Behavior: Churches, Neighborhoods, and Individuals." *Journal of Politics* 55 (1993): 365–81.

Huckfeldt, Robert, and John Sprague. *Citizens, Politics, and Social Communication.* Cambridge: Cambridge University Press, 1995.

Hurwitz, Jon, and Mark Peffley. "How Are Foreign Policy Attitudes Structured? A Hierarchical Model." *American Political Science Review* 81 (1987): 1099–1120.

Ingram, David. "The Limits and Possibilities of Communicative Ethics for Democratic Theory." *Political Theory* 21 (1993): 294–321.

Iyengar, Shanto. *Is Anyone Responsible? How Television Frames Political Issues.* Chicago: University of Chicago Press, 1991.

Iyengar, Shanto, and Donald R. Kinder. *News That Matters.* Chicago: University of Chicago Press, 1987.

Jacobs, Lawrence R. *The Health of Nations: Public Opinion and the Making of American and British Health Policy.* Ithaca, NY: Cornell University Press, 1993.

Jacobs, Lawrence R., and Robert Y. Shapiro. "The Rise of Presidential Polling: The Nixon White House in Historical Perspective." *Public Opinion Quarterly* 59 (1995): 163–95.

Jacobs, Lawrence R., and Robert Y. Shapiro. "Studying Substantive Democracy." *PS* 27 (1994): 9–17.

Jamieson, Kathleen Hall. *Dirty Politics: Deception, Distraction, and Democracy.* New York: Oxford University Press, 1992.

Jay, Martin. *The Dialectical Imagination.* Boston: Little, Brown, 1973.

Jeffords, Susan, and Lauren Rabinowitz. *Seeing Through the Media: The Persian Gulf War.* New Brunswick, NJ: Rutgers University Press, 1994.

Jewell, Malcolm E. "Legislator–Constituency Relations and the Representative Process." *Legislative Studies Quarterly* 8 (1983): 303–37.

Johnson, Haynes. *Sleepwalking Through History: America in the Reagan Years.* New York: Norton, 1991.

Johnson, Haynes, and David S. Broder. *The System: The American Way of Politics at the Breaking Point.* Boston: Little, Brown, 1996.

Johnson, James. "Habermas on Strategic and Communicative Action." *Political Theory* 19 (1991): 181–201.

Kammen, Michael. *Mystic Chords of Memory: The Transformation of Tradition in American Culture.* New York: Knopf, 1991.

Kaplan, Stuart Jay. "A Conceptual Analysis of Form and Content in Visual Metaphors." *Communication* 13 (1993): 197–209.

Katz, Cheryl, and Mark Baldassare. "Using the 'L-Word' in Public: A Test of the Spiral of Silence in Conservative Orange County, California." *Public Opinion Quarterly* 56 (1992): 232–35.

Katz, Elihu. Introduction to Theodore L. Glasser and Charles T. Salmon, eds., *Public Opinion and the Communication of Consent,* pp. xxi–xxxiii. New York: Guilford Press, 1995.

Keesing, Roger M. "Anthropology as Interpretive Quest." *Current Anthropology* 28 (1987): 161–76.

Kennamer, J. David. "Self-Serving Biases in Perceiving the Opinions of Others: Implications for the Spiral of Silence." *Communication Research* 17 (1990): 393–404.

Kennamer, J. David, ed. *Public Opinion, the Press, and Public Policy.* Westport, CT: Praeger, 1992.

Kepplinger, Hans Mathias. "Visual Biases in Campaign Coverage." *Communication Research* 9 (1982): 432–46.

Kernell, Samuel. *Going Public: New Strategies of Presidential Leadership.* Washington, DC: Congressional Quarterly Press, 1986.

Key, V. O. "The Politically Relevant in Surveys." *Public Opinion* 24 (1960): 54–61.

Key, V. O. *Public Opinion and American Democracy.* New York: Knopf, 1961.

Key, V. O. *The Responsible Electorate.* Cambridge, MA: Harvard University Press, 1966.

King, Elliot, and Michael Schudson. "The Press and the Illusion of Public Opinion: The Strange Case of Ronald Reagan's 'Popularity.'" In Theodore L. Glasser and Charles T. Salmon, eds., *Public Opinion and the Communication of Consent,* pp. 132–55. New York: Guilford Press, 1995.

Kingdon, John W. *Agendas, Alternatives, and Public Policies.* Boston: Little, Brown, 1984.

Kingdon, John W. *Congressmen's Voting Decisions.* 3rd ed. Ann Arbor: University of Michigan Press, 1989.

Kingdon, John W. "Politicians, Self-Interest, and Ideas." In George E. Marcus and Russell L. Hanson, eds., *Reconsidering the Democratic Public,* pp. 73–90. University Park: Pennsylvania State University Press, 1993.

Koh, Harold Hongju. *The National Security Constitution: Sharing Power After the Iran–Contra Affair.* New Haven, CT: Yale University Press, 1990.

Kohut, Andrew. "Rating the Polls: The Views of Media Elites and the General Public." *Public Opinion Quarterly* 50 (1986): 1–9.

Kohut, Andrew. *The Vocal Minority in American Politics.* Washington, DC: Times Mirror Center for the People and the Press, 1993.

Kolbert, Elizabeth. "The People Are Heard, at Least Those Who Call Talk Radio." *New York Times,* January 29, 1993, p. A12.

Kornbluh, Peter, and Malcolm Byrne, eds. *The Iran–Contra Scandal: The Declassified History.* New York: New Press, 1993.

Krauthammer, Charles. "Ollie North and the Trajectory of Fame." *Time,* July 27, 1987, p. 76.

Krosnick, Jon A., and Donald R. Kinder. "Altering the Foundations of Support for the President Through Priming." *American Political Science Review* 84 (1990): 497–512.

Kuklinski, James H., Robert C. Luskin, and John Bolland. "Where Is the Schema?

Going Beyond the 'S' Word in Political Psychology." *American Political Science Review* 85 (1991): 1341–56.

Lakatos, Imre. "Falsification and the Methodology of Scientific Research Programmes." In Imre Lakatos and Alan Musgrave, eds., *Criticism and the Growth of Knowledge*, pp. 91–196. Cambridge: Cambridge University Press, 1970.

Lakoff, George, and Mark Johnson. *Metaphors We Live By*. Chicago: University of Chicago Press, 1980.

Lane, Robert. "Patterns of Political Belief." In J. Knutson, ed., *Handbook of Political Psychology*, pp. 83–116. San Francisco: Jossey/Bass, 1973.

Lane, Robert E. "What Are People Trying to Do with Their Schemata? The Question of Purpose." In Richard R. Lau and David O. Sears, eds., *Political Cognition*, pp. 303–18. Hillsdale, NJ: Erlbaum, 1986.

Lang, Gladys Engel, and Kurt Lang. *The Battle for Public Opinion: The President, the Press, and the Polls During Watergate*. New York: Columbia University Press, 1983.

Lang, Kurt, and Gladys Engel Lang. "The Unique Perspective of Television and Its Effect: A Pilot Study." *American Sociological Review* 18 (1953): 3–12.

Lasora, Dominic L. "Political Outspokenness: Factors Working Against the Spiral of Silence." *Journalism Quarterly* 68 (1991): 131–40.

Lau, Richard R. "Political Schemata, Candidate Evaluation, and Voting Behavior." In Richard R. Lau and David O. Sears, eds., *Political Cognition*, pp. 95–126. Hillsdale, NJ: Erlbaum, 1986.

Lau, Richard R., and David O. Sears, eds. *Political Cognition*. Hillsdale, NJ: Erlbaum, 1986.

LeoGrande, William M., and Philip Brenner. "The House Divided: Ideological Polarization over Aid to the Nicaraguan 'Contras.'" *Legislative Studies Quarterly* 18 (1993): 105–36.

Leonard, Stephen T. *Critical Theory in Political Practice*. Princeton, NJ: Princeton University Press, 1990.

Lindblom, Charles E. "The Market as Prison." *Journal of Politics* 44 (1982): 324–36.

Lindsay, James M. "Parochialism, Policy and Constituency Constraints: Congressional Voting on Strategic Weapons Systems." *American Journal of Political Science* 34 (1990): 936–60.

Lindsay, James M., and Randall B. Ripley. "How Congress Influences Foreign and Defense Policy." In Randall B. Ripley and James M. Lindsay, eds., *Congress Resurgent: Foreign and Defense Policy on Capitol Hill*, pp. 17–36. Ann Arbor: University of Michigan Press, 1993.

Lodge, Milton, and Ruth Hamill. "A Partisan Schema for Political Information Processing." *American Political Science Review* 82 (1986): 737–61.

Lodge, Milton, and Kathleen M. McGraw, eds. *Political Judgment: Structure and Processes*. Ann Arbor: University of Michigan Press, 1995.

Lodge, Milton, and Kathleen M. McGraw; Pamela Johnston Conover and Stanley Feldman; and Arthur Miller. "Where Is the Schema? Critiques." *American Political Science Review* 85 (1991): 1357–80.

Lohmann, Susanne. "A Signaling Model of Informative and Manipulative Political Action." *American Political Science Review* 87 (1993): 319–33.

Lowi, Theodore J. "American Business, Public Policy, Case Studies, and Political Theory." *World Politics* 16 (1964): 677–715.

Luker, Kristin. *Abortion and the Politics of Motherhood.* Berkeley and Los Angeles: University of California Press, 1984.

Maltese, John Anthony. *Spin Control: The White House Office of Communications and the Management of Presidential News.* Chapel Hill: University of North Carolina Press, 1992.

Mansbridge, Jane. *Beyond Adversary Democracy.* New York: Basic Books, 1980.

Maraniss, David, and Michael Weisskopf. *Tell Newt to Shut Up!: Prizewinning Washington Post Journalists Reveal How Reality Gagged the Gingrich Revolution.* New York: Touchstone, 1996.

Margolis, Michael, and Gary A. Mauser, eds. *Manipulating Public Opinion: Essays on Public Opinion as a Dependent Variable.* Pacific Grove, CA: Brooks/Cole, 1989.

Marks, G., and N. Miller. "Ten Years of Research on the False Consensus Effect: A Empirical and Theoretical Review." *Psychological Bulletin* 102 (1987): 72–90.

Marshall, Jonathan, Peter Dale Scott, and Jane Hunter. *The Iran–Contra Connection: Secret Teams and Covert Operations in the Reagan Era.* Boston: South End Press, 1987.

Mayer, Jane, and Jill Abramson. *Strange Justice: The Selling of Clarence Thomas.* New York: Houghton Mifflin, 1994.

Mayer, Jane, and Doyle McManus. *Landslide: The Unmaking of the President, 1984–1988.* Boston: Houghton Mifflin, 1988.

Mayhew, David R. *Congress: The Electoral Connection.* New Haven, CT: Yale University Press, 1974.

Mayhew, David R. *Divided We Govern: Party Control, Lawmaking, and Investigations, 1946–1990.* New Haven, CT: Yale University Press, 1991.

McAllister, Ian, and Donley T. Studlar. "Bandwagon, Underdog, or Projection? Opinion Polls and Electoral Choice in Britain, 1979–1987." *Journal of Politics* 53 (1991): 720–41.

McCarthy, Thomas. *The Critical Theory of Jürgen Habermas.* Cambridge, MA: MIT Press, 1988.

McClosky, Herbert, and John Zaller. *The American Ethos: Public Attitudes Toward Capitalism and Democracy.* Cambridge, MA: Harvard University Press, 1984.

McGraw, Kathleen M., Milton Lodge, and Patrick Stroh. "On-Line Processing in Candidate Evaluation: The Effects of Issue Order, Issue Salience, and Sophistication." *Political Behavior* 12 (1990): 41–58.

Merelman, Richard, ed. *Language, Symbolism, and Politics.* Boulder, CO: Westview Press, 1992.

Messaris, Paul. "Visual 'Manipulation': Visual Means of Affecting Responses to Images." *Communication* 13 (1992): 181–95.

Milburn, Michael A., and Anne B. McGrail. "The Dramatic Presentation of News and Its Effects on Cognitive Complexity." *Political Psychology* 13 (1992): 613–32.

Miller, Arthur H., Martin P. Wattenberg, and Oksana Malanchuk. "Schematic Assessments of Presidential Candidates." *American Political Science Review* 90 (1986): 505–40.

Miller, Warren E., and Donald E. Stokes. "Constituency Influence in Congress." *American Political Science Review* 57 (1963): 45–56.

Mondak, Jeffery J. "Media Exposure and Political Discussion in U.S. Elections." *Journal of Politics* 57 (1995): 62–85.

Mondak, Jeffery J. "Source Cues and Policy Approval: The Cognitive Dynamics of Public Support for the Reagan Agenda." *American Journal of Political Science* 37 (1993): 186–212.

Montgomery, Kathryn C. *Target: Prime Time, Advocacy Groups and the Struggle over Entertainment Television*. New York: Oxford University Press, 1989.

Moon, J. Donald. "Constrained Discourse and Public Life." *Political Theory* 19 (1991): 202–29.

Moore, David W. *The Superpollsters: How They Measure and Manipulate Public Opinion in America*. New York: Four Walls Eight Windows, 1992.

Morgan, Michael, Justin Lewis, and Sut Jhally. "More Viewing, Less Knowledge." In Hamid Mawlana, George Gerber, and Herbert I. Schiller, eds., *Triumph of the Image: The Media's War in the Persian Gulf—A Global Perspective*, pp. 216–35. Boulder, CO: Westview Press, 1992.

Moritz, Amy. "The New Right, It's Time We Led. Conservatism's Parched Grass Roots." *Policy Review* 44 (1988): 22–25.

Mueller, John. *Policy and Opinion in the Gulf War*. Chicago: University of Chicago Press, 1994.

Mutz, Diana C. "Contextualizing Personal Experience: The Role of Mass Media." *Journal of Politics* 56 (1994): 689–714.

Mutz, Diana C. "Impersonal Influence: Effects of Representations of Public Opinion on Political Attitudes." *Political Behavior* 14 (1992): 89–122.

Mutz, Diana C. "The Political Effects of Perceptions of Mass Opinion." In Michael X. Delli Carpini, Leonie Huddy, and Robert Y. Shapiro, eds., *Research in Micropolitics: New Directions in Political Psychology*, vol. 4, pp. 143–67. Greenwich, CT: JAI Press, 1994.

Natchez, Peter B. *Images of Voting/Visions of Democracy*. New York: Basic Books, 1985.

Neuman, W. Russell, Marion R. Just, and Ann N. Crigler. *Common Knowledge: News and the Construction of Political Meaning*. Chicago: University of Chicago Press, 1992.

Newhagen, John E., and Byron Reeves. "The Evening's Bad News: Effects of Compelling Negative Television News Images on Memory." *Journal of Communication* 42 (1992): 25–41.

Nimmo, Dan, and James E. Combs. *The Political Pundits.* New York: Praeger, 1992.

Nincic, Miroslav. *Democracy and Foreign Policy: The Fallacy of Political Realism.* New York: Columbia University Press, 1992.

Noelle-Neumann, Elisabeth. *The Spiral of Silence: Public Opinion—Our Social Skin.* Chicago: University of Chicago Press, 1984.

Noelle-Neumann, Elisabeth. "The Spiral of Silence: A Response." In Keith R. Sanders, Lynda Lee Kaid, and Dan Nimmo, eds., *Political Communication Yearbook, 1984,* pp. 66–94. Carbondale: Southern Illinois University Press, 1985.

Noelle-Neumann, Elisabeth. "The Spiral of Silence: A Theory of Public Opinion." *Journal of Communication* 24 (1974): 43–51.

North, Oliver L., with William Novak. *Under Fire.* New York: HarperCollins, 1991.

O'Gorman, Hubert J., and Stephen Gary. "Pluralistic Ignorance—A Replication and Extension." *Public Opinion Quarterly* 40 (1976): 449–58.

Olson, Mancur. *The Logic of Collective Action.* New York: Schocken Books, 1979.

Ortner, Sherry. "Theory in Anthropology Since the Sixties." *Comparative Studies in Society and History* 26 (1984): 126–66.

Overby, L. Marvin. "Assessing Constituency Influence: Congressional Voting on the Nuclear Freeze, 1982–83." *Legislative Studies Quarterly* 16 (1991): 297–312.

Page, Benjamin I. "Democratic Responsiveness? Untangling the Links Between Public Opinion and Policy." *PS* 27 (1994): 25–29.

Page, Benjamin I., and Robert Y. Shapiro. "Effects of Public Opinion on Policy." *American Political Science Review* 77 (1983): 175–90.

Page, Benjamin I., and Robert Y. Shapiro. *The Rational Public: Fifty Years of Trends in Americans' Policy Preferences.* Chicago: University of Chicago Press, 1992.

Page, Benjamin I., Robert Y. Shapiro, and Glenn R. Dempsey. "What Moves Public Opinion?" *American Political Science Review* 81 (1987): 23–43.

Paletz, David L., Jonathan Y. Short, Helen Baker, Barbara Cookman Campbell, Richard J. Cooper, and Rochelle M. Oeslander. "Polls in the Media: Content, Credibility, Consequences." *Public Opinion Quarterly* 44 (1980): 495–513.

Parker, Glenn R. *Homeward Bound: Explaining Changes in Congressional Behavior.* Pittsburgh: University of Pittsburgh Press, 1986.

Parker, Glenn R., and Suzanne L. Parker. 1992. "Correlates and Effects of Attention to District by U.S. House Members." In Robert L. Peabody, ed., *New Perspectives on the House of Representatives,* pp. 53–73. Baltimore: Johns Hopkins University Press, 1992.

Parry, Robert, and Peter Kornbluh. "Iran–Contra's Untold Story." *Foreign Policy* 72 (1988): 3–30.

Patterson, Thomas E. *Out of Order.* New York: Vintage Books, 1994.

Petracca, Mark P., ed. *The Politics of Interests: Interest Groups Transformed.* Boulder, CO: Westview Press, 1992.

Pitkin, Hanna. *The Concept of Representation.* Berkeley and Los Angeles: University of California Press, 1967.

Piven, Frances Fox, and Richard A. Cloward. 1979. *Poor People's Movements: Why They Succeed, How They Fail.* New York: Vintage Books, 1979.

Popkin, Samuel. *The Reasoning Voter.* Chicago: University of Chicago Press, 1991.

Price, Vincent, and Scott Allen. "Opinion Spirals, Silent and Otherwise: Applying Small-Group Research to Public Opinion Phenomena." *Communication Research* 17 (1990): 369–92.

Putnam, Robert D. "The Strange Disappearance of Civic America." *The American Prospect* 24 (1996): 34–48.

Rahn, Wendy M. "The Role of Partisan Stereotypes in Information Processing about Political Candidates." *American Journal of Political Science* 37 (1993): 472–96.

Rahn, Wendy M., John H. Aldrich, Eugene Borgida, and John L. Sullivan. "A Social–Cognitive Model of Candidate Appraisal." In John A. Ferejohn and James H. Kuklinski, eds., *Information and Democratic Processes*, pp. 136–59. Urbana: University of Illinois Press, 1990.

Randolph, Eleanor. 1987. "How the Newshounds Blew the Iran–Contra Story." *Washington Post*, November 15, 1987, pp. C1+.

Reagan, Ronald. *An American Life.* New York: Simon & Schuster, 1990.

Risse-Kappen, Thomas. "Public Opinion, Domestic Structure, and Foreign Policy in Liberal Democracies." *World Politics* 43 (1991): 479–512.

Rilke, Rainer Maria. *Sonnets to Orpheus.* Trans. C. F. MacIntyre. Berkeley and Los Angeles: University of California Press, 1960.

Robinson, Michael J., and Andrew Kohut. "Believability and the Press." *Public Opinion Quarterly* 52 (1988): 174–89.

Rohde, David W. *Parties and Leaders in the Postreform House.* Chicago: University of Chicago Press, 1991.

Rosenblatt, Roger. *Life Itself: Abortion in the American Mind.* New York: Random House, 1992.

Rosenstone, Steven J., and John Mark Hansen. *Mobilization, Participation, and Democracy in America.* New York: Macmillan, 1993.

Ross, Marc Howard. "Television News and Candidate Fortunes in Presidential Nomination Campaigns: The Case of 1984." *American Politics Quarterly* 20 (1992): 69–98.

Rothenberg, Lawrence S. *Linking Citizens to Government: Interest Group Politics at Common Cause.* Cambridge: Cambridge University Press, 1992.

Russett, Bruce. *Controlling the Sword: The Democratic Governance of National Security.* Cambridge, MA: Harvard University Press, 1990.

Salisbury, Robert H. *Interests and Institutions: Substance and Structure in American Politics.* Pittsburgh: University of Pittsburgh Press, 1992.

Salmon, Charles T., and F. Gerald Kline. "The Spiral of Silence Ten Years Later: An Examination and Evaluation." In Keith R. Sanders, Lynda Lee Kaid, and Dan Nimmo, eds., *Political Communication Yearbook, 1984*, pp. 3–30. Carbondale: Southern Illinois University Press, 1985.

Salmon, Charles T., and Kurt Neuwith. "Perceptions of Opinion 'Climates' and Willingness to Discuss the Issue of Abortion." *Journalism Quarterly* 67 (1990): 567–77.

Schattschneider, E. E. *Party Government.* New York: Farrar and Rinehart, 1942.

Schattschneider, E. E. *The Semisovereign People: A Realist's View of Democracy in America.* New York: Holt, Rinehart and Winston, 1960.

Schlozman, Kay Lehman. "What Accent the Heavenly Chorus? Political Equality and the American Pressure System." *Journal of Politics* 46 (1984): 1006–32.

Schlozman, Kay Lehman, and John T. Tierney. *Organized Interests and American Democracy.* New York: Harper & Row, 1986.

Schudson, Michael. *Discovering the News: A Social History of American Newspapers.* New York: Basic Books, 1978.

Schudson, Michael. "How Culture Works: Perspectives from Media Studies on the Efficacy of Symbols." *Theory and Society* 18 (1989): 153–80.

Schudson, Michael. *Watergate in American Memory: How We Remember, Forget, and Reconstruct the Past.* New York: Basic Books, 1992.

Schuman, Howard, Stanley Presser, and Jacob Ludwig. "Context Effects on Survey Responses to Questions About Abortion." *Public Opinion Quarterly* 45 (1991): 216–23.

Schumpeter, Joseph A. *Capitalism, Socialism and Democracy.* 3rd ed. New York: Harper & Row, 1950.

Scott, James. *Domination and the Arts of Resistance.* New Haven, CT: Yale University Press, 1990.

Scott, James. *Weapons of the Weak: Everyday Forms of Peasant Resistance.* New Haven, CT: Yale University Press, 1985.

Secord, Richard, with Jay Wurts. *Honored and Betrayed: Irangate, Covert Affairs, and the Secret War in Laos.* New York: Wiley, 1992.

Shabecoff, Philip. *A Fierce Green Fire: The American Environmental Movement.* New York: Hill & Wang, 1993.

Shapiro, Catherine R., David W. Brady, Richard A. Brody, and John A. Ferejohn. "Linking Constituency Opinion and Senate Voting Scores: A Hybrid Explanation." *Legislative Studies Quarterly* 15 (1990): 599–621.

Shaw, Donald L., and Shannon E. Martin. "The Function of Mass Media Agenda Setting." *Journalism Quarterly* 69 (1992): 902–20.

Sinclair, Barbara. "The Emergence of Strong Leadership in the 1980s House of Representatives." *Journal of Politics* 54 (1992): 657–84.

Skelton, Ike, Mickey Edwards, and Bill Richardson. "Public Opinion and Contra Aid: Congressional Commentaries." In Richard Sobel, ed., *Public Opinion in U.S. Foreign Policy: The Controversy over Contra Aid*, pp. 241–65. Lanham, MD: Rowman & Littlefield, 1993.

Skocpol, Theda. *Protecting Soldiers and Mothers; The Political Origins of Social Policy in the United States.* Cambridge, MA: Belknap Press of Harvard University Press, 1992.

Skowronek, Stephen. *The Politics Presidents Make: Leadership from John Adams to George Bush.* Cambridge, MA: Belknap Press of Harvard University Press, 1993.

Smith, Rogers M. "If Politics Matters: Implications for a 'New Institutionalism.'" *Studies in American Political Development* 6 (1992): 1–36.

Sniderman, Paul M., Richard A. Brody, and Philip E. Tetlock. *Reasoning and Choice: Explorations in Political Psychology.* Cambridge: Cambridge University Press, 1991.

Sobel, Richard. "Public Opinion About United States Intervention in El Salvador and Nicaragua." *Public Opinion Quarterly* 53 (1989): 114–28.

Sobel, Richard, ed. *Public Opinion in U.S. Foreign Policy: The Controversy over Contra Aid.* Lanham, MD: Rowman & Littlefield, 1993.

Speakes, Larry, with Robert Pack. *Speaking Out: The Reagan Presidency from Inside the White House.* New York: Scribner, 1988.

Stanga, John E., and James F. Sheffield. "The Myth of Zero Partisanship: Attitudes Toward American Political Parties, 1964–84." *American Journal of Political Science* 31 (1987): 829–55.

Stimson, James A. "Opinion and Representation." *American Political Science Review* 89 (1995): 179–83.

Stimson, James A. *Public Opinion in America: Moods, Cycles, and Swings.* Boulder, CO: Westview Press, 1991.

Stimson, James A., Michael B. Mackuen, and Robert S. Erickson. "Dynamic Representation." *American Political Science Review* 89 (1995): 543–65.

Stoker, Laura. "Interests and Ethics in Politics." *American Political Science Review* 86 (1992): 369–80.

Stone, Peter H. "Green, Green Grass." *National Journal,* March 27, 1993, pp. 754–57.

Sullivan, Denis G., and Roger D. Masters. "'Happy Warriors': Leaders' Facial Displays, Viewers' Emotions, and Political Support." *American Journal of Political Science* 32 (1988): 345–68.

Sullivan, John L., Amy Fried, and Mary G. Dietz. "Patriotism, Politics, and the Presidential Election of 1988." *American Journal of Political Science* 36 (1992): 200–34.

Sullivan, William M. *Reconstructing Public Philosophy.* Berkeley and Los Angeles: University of California Press, 1982.

Swanson, David L., and Larry David Smith. "War in the Global Village: A Seven-Country Comparison of Television News Coverage of the Beginning of the Gulf War." In Robert E. Denton Jr., ed., *The Media and the Gulf War,* pp. 165–96. Westport, CT: Praeger, 1993.

Swidler, Ann. "Culture in Action: Symbols and Strategies." *American Sociological Review* 51 (1986): 273–86.

Taylor, D. Garth. "Pluralistic Ignorance and the Spiral of Silence: A Formal Analysis." *Public Opinion Quarterly* 46 (1982): 311–35.

Taylor, Philip M. *War and the Media: Propaganda and Persuasion in the Gulf War.* Manchester: Manchester University Press, 1992.

Teti, Dennis. "The Coup That Failed. An Insider's Account of the Iran/Contra Hearings." *Policy Review* 42 (1987): 24–31.

Thelen, David. *Becoming Citizens in the Age of Television: How Americans Challenged the Media and Seized Political Initiative During the Iran–Contra Debate.* Chicago: University of Chicago Press, 1996.

Tierney, John T. "Interest Group Involvement in Congressional Foreign and Defense Policy." In Randall B. Ripley and James M. Lindsay, eds., *Congress Resurgent: Foreign and Defense Policy on Capitol Hill*, pp. 89–111. Ann Arbor: University of Michigan Press, 1993.

Tilly, Charles. "Speaking Your Mind Without Elections, Surveys, or Social Movements." *Public Opinion Quarterly* 47 (1983): 461–78.

Timberg, Robert. *The Nightingale's Song.* New York: Simon & Schuster, 1995.

Tocqueville, Alexis de. *Democracy in America.* Garden City, NY: Doubleday, 1969.

Tomasulo, Frank P. "Colonel North Goes to Washington: Observations on the Intertextual Re-presentation of History." *Journal of Popular Film and Television* 17 (1989): 82–88.

Toobin, Jeffrey. *Opening Arguments—A Young Lawyer's First Case: United States v. Oliver North.* New York: Viking, 1991.

Tower, John, Edmund Muskie, and Brent Scowcroft. *Report of the President's Special Review Board.* Washington, DC: U.S. Government Printing Office, 1987.

Tuchman, Gaye. *Making News: A Study in the Construction of Reality.* New York: Free Press, 1978.

Underwood, Doug. *When MBAs Rule the Newsroom.* New York: Columbia University Press, 1993.

U.S. House and U.S. Senate, *Report of the Congressional Committees Investigating the Iran–Contra Affair. With Supplemental, Minority, and Additional Views.* Washington, DC: U.S. Government Printing Office, November 1987.

VanDoren, Peter M. "Can We Learn the Causes of Congressional Decisions from Roll-Call Data?" *Legislative Studies Quarterly* 15 (1990): 311–40.

Verba, Sidney, and Norman H. Nie. *Participation in America.* New York: Harper & Row, 1978.

Verba, Sidney, Kay Lehman Schlozman, and Henry Brady. *Voice and Equality: Civic Voluntarism in American Politics.* Cambridge, MA: Harvard University Press, 1995.

Verba, Sidney, Kay Lehman Schlozman, Henry Brady, and Norman H. Nie. "Citizen Activity: Who Participates? What Do They Say?" *American Political Science Review* 87 (1993): 303–18.

Walker, Jack L. *Mobilizing Interest Groups in America: Patrons, Professions, and Social Movements.* Ann Arbor: University of Michigan Press, 1991.

Walsh, Lawrence E. *Final Report of the Independent Counsel for Iran/Contra Matters.* Washington, DC: U.S. Government Printing Office, 1993.

Warren, Mark E. "Deliberative Democracy and Authority." *American Political Science Review* 90 (1996): 46–60.

Wilkerson, John D. "Reelection and Representation in Conflict: The Case of Agenda Manipulation." *Legislative Studies Quarterly* 15 (1990): 263–82.

Wirls, Daniel. *Buildup: The Politics of Defense in the Reagan Era.* Ithaca, NY: Cornell University Press, 1992.

Wittkopf, Eugene R. *Faces of Internationalism: Public Opinion and American Foreign Policy.* Durham, NC: Duke University Press, 1990.

Wittkopf, Eugene R., and James M. McCormick. "The Domestic Politics of Contra Aid: Public Opinion, Congress, and the President." In Richard Sobel, ed., *Public Opinion in U.S. Foreign Policy: The Controversy over Contra Aid*, pp. 73–103. Lanham, MD: Rowman & Littlefield, 1993.

Yagade, Aileen, and David M. Dozier. "The Media Agenda-Setting Effect of Concrete Versus Abstract Issues." *Journalism Quarterly* 67 (1990): 3–10.

Yin, Robert K. *Case Study Research.* Beverly Hills, CA: Sage, 1984.

Young, Iris Marion. "Impartiality and the Civic Public: Some Implications of Feminist Critiques of Moral and Political Philosophy." In Seyla Benhabib and Drucilla Cornell, eds., *Feminism as Critique: On the Politics of Gender*, pp. 56–76. Minneapolis: University of Minnesota Press, 1987.

Zaller, John R. *The Nature and Origins of Mass Opinion.* Cambridge: Cambridge University Press, 1992.

Zaller, John R. "Strategic Politicians, Public Opinion, and the Gulf Crisis." In W. Lance Bennett and David L. Paletz, eds., *Taken by Storm: The Media, Public Opinion and U.S. Foreign Policy in the Gulf War*, pp. 250–74. Chicago: University of Chicago Press, 1994.

Zaller, John R., and Stanley Feldman. "A Simple Theory of the Survey Response: Answering Questions Versus Revealing Preferences." *American Journal of Political Science* 36 (1992): 579–616.

Zelizer, Barbie. *Covering the Body: The Kennedy Assassination, the Media, and the Shaping of Collective Memory.* Chicago: University of Chicago Press, 1992.

Index